T0332740

Making the Transition to E-Learning:
Strategies and Issues

Mark Bullen
British Columbia Institute of Technology, Canada

Diane P. Janes
University of Saskatchewan, Canada

 **Information Science Publishing**

Hershey • London • Melbourne • Singapore

Acquisitions Editor:	Michelle Potter
Development Editor:	Kristin Roth
Senior Managing Editor:	Jennifer Neidig
Managing Editor:	Sara Reed
Copy Editor:	Larissa Vinci
Typesetter:	Cindy Consonery
Cover Design:	Lisa Tosheff
Printed at:	Integrated Book Technology

Published in the United States of America by
Information Science Publishing (an imprint of Idea Group Inc.)
701 E. Chocolate Avenue
Hershey PA 17033
Tel: 717-533-8845
Fax: 717-533-8661
E-mail: cust@idea-group.com
Web site: http://www.idea-group.com

and in the United Kingdom by
Information Science Publishing (an imprint of Idea Group Inc.)
3 Henrietta Street
Covent Garden
London WC2E 8LU
Tel: 44 20 7240 0856
Fax: 44 20 7379 0609
Web site: http://www.eurospanonline.com

Library of Congress Cataloging-in-Publication Data

Making the transition to e-learning : strategies and issues / Mark Bullen & Diane P. Janes, editors.
    p. cm.
  Summary: "This book provides insights and experiences from e-learning experts from around the
world; it address the institutional, pedagogical, and technological issues that higher education
institutions are grappling with as they move from conventional face-to-face teaching to e-learning in
its diverse forms"--Provided by publisher.
  ISBN 1-59140-950-0 (hardcover) -- ISBN 1-59140-951-9 (softcover) -- ISBN 1-59140-952-7
(ebook)
  1. Education, Higher--Computer-assisted instruction. 2. Education, Higher--Effect of technological
innovations on. I. Bullen, Mark, 1954- II. Janes, Diane P., 1960-
  LB2395.7.M3 2007
  378.1'758--dc22
                        2006018828

British Cataloguing in Publication Data
A Cataloguing in Publication record for this book is available from the British Library.

Making the Transition to E-Learning:
Strategies and Issues

Table of Contents

Section II: Learning and Teaching Issues

Preface

The rapidly changing needs of the current and future workforce are creating an enormous challenge for higher education around the world. As technology and the corresponding knowledge and skill requirements of the workforce change, the whole notion of higher education is evolving. The need for education and training is growing and it is becoming a lifelong activity.

To meet the increasing demand for education and training, higher education institutions are increasingly turning to e-learning, which is seen as a way of providing convenient and flexible access to education and training, while avoiding the cost of building larger physical campus facilities and infrastructure. At the same time, e-learning is seen as a way of improving the quality of teaching and learning.

However, the institutional response to e-learning is far from consistent and, despite the hype, evidence suggests that while it is a growing phenomenon, enrollments in e-learning are still relatively low at most campus-based institutions. In addition, the widely predicted "paradigm shift" in teaching and learning that e-learning was supposed to usher in has, by all accounts, not yet occurred (OECD, 2005).

We believe this should not be seen as a failure of e-learning, but rather viewed as a failure of institutions to respond appropriately. Organizational arrangements, funding, development processes, faculty and learner support, and other policies vary widely from institution to institution. Quality is also variable and often unflattering. Long pages of lecture notes, poorly designed Web sites, lack of interaction, and the inadequate use of the rich resources available on the Internet characterize much of the present world of online e-learning. Significant institutional barriers to the effective implementation of e-learning still exist: infrastructure and funding have been identified as the most important but skepticism about the pedagogical value of e-learning and faculty development are also key (OECD, 2005).

Of course, not all is bleak. Many institutions have coherent, well-developed e-learning strategies, robust and well-funded organizational structures, and high quality e-learning products ranging from individual modules to fully online e-learning programs. But this is not the norm. The lack of consistency and the concerns about quality stem partly from the novelty of this approach to teaching. The modern Internet, after all, is just over 10 years old and it is only since the turn of the 21st Century that most higher education institutions have begun to pay serious attention to e-learning. This novelty, however, means that many people and institutions are using e-learning without a solid understanding of how to plan and develop instruction, of the underlying teaching and learning theories, and of what makes the Internet a unique medium for teaching and learning.

This book aims to address that gap by exposing educators and administrators to some of the key theoretical and practical issues illustrated in real examples from a variety of institutional contexts. Drawing on the experiences of educators from five countries with extensive experience in e-learning as teachers, administrators, researchers, and instructional designers, this book focuses on pedagogy and on planning and integrating technology with face-to-face teaching. The underlying theme is pedagogy before technology. Too often we make technological decisions in education without considering the pedagogical implications. But the book goes beyond the pedagogy and looks at broader institutional and conceptual issues as well as technology and instructional design issues.

The Meaning of E-Learning

The term e-learning is widely used, but it means different things to different people. To minimize confusion and make the chapters in this book more meaningful we have started from a common understanding of e-learning. We base our conception on the work of Zemsky and Massy (2004) who suggest there are three major categories of e-learning:

1. **E-learning as distance education:** This refers to courses that are delivered entirely, or almost entirely, on the Internet. This is the most common understanding of e-learning, but increasingly, e-learning is not seen as distance education but as any teaching that involves technology, which is the second type of e-learning.

2. **E-learning as electronically mediated learning:** This category includes any teaching or learning that is mediated by technology. Thus, products like computerized test preparation courses that prepare students to take the SAT or GRE; complex, integrated learning packages such as Maple or Mathematica that teach elementary calculus; learning objects that simulate and illustrate various concepts such as chemical reactions, mathematical modeling, social interactions, and musical compositions; and tools like Macromedia's Dreamweaver and Flash that students use to build their own Web sites. Interactive CD-ROMs and the Web sites of book publishers would be part of this category. What all these products and resources have in common is that they involve electronically mediated learning in a digital format that can be used as part of regular on-campus teaching. It is not necessarily distance education.

3. **E-learning as facilitated transactions software:** This category includes the software that is used to organize and manage teaching and learning, learning management systems like the commercial products BlackBoard and WebCT, and open source products like Moodle. These learning management systems link teachers with students, students with each other, and students to resources. Course content, schedules, assignments, and other resources are uploaded to these systems for students to access. In addition, these systems allow for online testing.

When we think of the first two categories, e-learning as distance education and e-learning as electronically mediated learning, we think it is helpful to think of e-learning as fitting into a continuum of delivery modalities. The continuum stretches from fully face-to-face at one end to fully online at the other (Figure 1).

Figure 1. The e-learning continuum

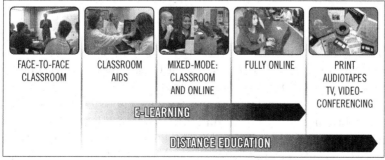

As we move from the full face-to-face end of the continuum, more and more technology is used to replace the face-to-face elements. Initially, this has very little impact on how teaching is organized because the technology is used primarily to enhance the face-to-face teaching. But as we move further along the continuum (from left to right) the nature of teaching and how it is organized is affected by the technology.

Somewhere around the middle of the continuum, we have what is called mixed-mode teaching, where significant amounts of the face-to-face element are replaced by technology-mediated teaching. (Note: The terms blended learning and hybrid courses are often used to describe this part of the e-learning continuum.) Fewer class sessions are held as technology is used increasingly to deliver the teaching and to facilitate the learning. Once we reach the right end of the continuum there is no longer any face-to-face teaching. The second to last box on the right represents fully online e-learning in which all teaching is technology mediated.

According to this framework, e-learning is that part of the continuum that begins when technology is used to replace some of the face-to-face teaching to the point on the continuum where it replaces it all. The framework also helps us to understand the relationship between distance education and e-learning. Distance education overlaps with e-learning. Increasingly, distance education is fully online but historically it has used other technologies, and there is still a considerable amount of distance education that would not be considered e-learning. Accordingly, we can have what we call mixed-mode e-learning in which there is a combination of face-to-face and technology-mediated teaching or distance education e-learning in which all teaching and learning is done without teacher and learners never meeting face-to-face. And there can be distance education that uses print and television that would not be considered e-learning (Bullen, 2006).

With this understanding of e-learning in mind, we like to use the metaphor of home renovations to help understand the importance of making appropriate institutional responses to e-learning. When we decide to renovate part of our homes, we understand that we can only go so far. We can add a new room or a sun deck, we can finish the basement, we can even add a new floor to our house, but at some point, the underlying structure becomes unable to handle all the additions. This is the state we have reached with e-learning. Simply adding e-learning to our existing ways of teaching will put undue stress on the underlying structure of traditional education and ultimately leading to collapse. Overworked instructors will not be able to handle the additional requirements of learning how to use the new technology. They will not have the time to deliver their typical three lectures a week and also develop e-learning resources and moderate online discussions. Students will be left struggling between the traditional educational system and the stresses and potentials of new technologies in their classrooms, whatever the delivery choices. Educational institutions will not be able to afford to continue business as usual and add on the cost of the new technologies. Something has to change.

Organization of This Book

The chapters in this book present a variety of perspectives on how educational institutions can, or are, making the transition to e-learning, but they share a common theme: Moving to e-learning requires us to radically rethink how are institutions are organized, how we teach, and how we support our learners and our faculty. Each chapter deals, in its own way, with how to ensure that e-learning is implemented effectively so that the end product is pedagogically effective and does not put undue stress on the human, financial, and physical infrastructure of our educational institutions. The book is divided into three sections. The chapters in the first section deal with broader institutional and conceptual issues. In the second section we turn to teaching and learning issues and some of the specific approaches and strategies that can be used to teach in an e-learning environment. The focus of the chapters in the third section is on instructional design and technology issues.

Section I: Institutional and Conceptual Issues

Marco Adria and Katy Campbell, of the University of Alberta, start the book off with a fascinating essay that argues that we need to be thinking more broadly about e-learning in ways that take us beyond the instrumental and to higher level considerations such as citizenship and nation building. Adria and Campbell suggest e-learning has the potential to be socially transformative because of its power to support diverse cultures, languages, work contexts, learning needs and styles, prior experiences, generations, economic circumstances, social contexts, and geographic location. They argue that the metaphor of an e-learning nation supports the reflective and progressive development of learning communities in which identity is consciously and critically examined.

Margaret Haughey, also with the University of Alberta, moves us to a more practical level in her chapter in which she examines the different ways in which Canadian universities have organized themselves to respond to the challenge of e-learning. She analyzes the organizational responses to the provision of faculty support for e-learning in six large Canadian universities since 1997. A variety of organizational models are examined including centralized, decentralized, integrated, and parallel units. Their advantages and disadvantages are identified and described and the chapter contains several recommendations for senior administrators involved in e-learning, with a particular focus on issues concerning the goals and culture of the institution, the integration of pedagogical and technological approaches, as well as involvement of faculty and the role of policy.

Next, we move to a different institutional and national context with the first of three chapters that come from the polytechnic sector. Oriel Kelly, from the Manukau Institute of Technology in New Zealand, describes the process that was used to make the transition to e-learning in this large polytechnic. Integral to the process was a matrix that helped faculty to make decisions about the degree of e-learning that was most appropriate. The matrix has guided the transition to e-learning across the entire institute. The chapter discusses the institutional support that was provided for the different levels of e-learning in a way that enabled faculty to retain control over a quality learning experience for their students.

Tony Bates, with Tony Bates Associates, Ltd., brings us back to Canada for the second polytechnic chapter. He provides a timely and interesting examination of how the Southern Alberta Institute of Technology (SAIT) developed a comprehensive strategic plan for e-learning. This is one of the only detailed accounts of how a strategic plan for e-learning has actually been developed and implemented in a particular institution. It is based on his work as the Cisco Chair in E-Learning at SAIT Polytechnic, which ended in 2005. The chapter provides a valuable case study that incorporates planning processes and strategies that could be applied to a wide variety of postsecondary institutions.

In the final chapter dealing with polytechnics, Maggie Beers examines how an institution-wide e-learning initiative was developed and implemented at the British Columbia Institute of Technology. Her chapter focuses on the participatory role faculty played in the first year of the five-year technology-enabled knowledge (TEK) initiative, which is designed to promote educational excellence in learning, teaching, and research through the use of e-learning. She argues that faculty engagement will ultimately determine the success of this e-initiative and, as such, faculty need to be active members in a collaborative process informed by participatory design. This chapter provides a model that can help inform the strategic direction of other institutes implementing similar e-learning initiatives.

The Institutional and Conceptual Issues section concludes with a case study from one of Canada's newest universities, and one of Canada's two laptop universities, the University of Ontario Institute of Technology. Ellen Vogel and Bill Muirhead report on a study that assessed the needs and gaps of nursing faculty in the use of e-learning and attempted to understand the requirements for infusing e-learning into the nursing program.

Section II: Learning and Teaching Issues

Dirk Morrison, of the University of Saskatchewan, begins Section II with a discussion of new theories, models, and environments for online teaching and learning and as well considers the institutional issues associated with the appropriate use of e-learning technologies. This chapter aims to expand the discussion beyond pragmatic questions regarding how to make the transition from face-to-face teaching to e-learning, to include questions regarding how to fundamentally shift the core guiding pedagogical principles of our institutions of higher education.

Gail Wilson, of the University of Western Sydney, focuses her chapter on strategies used to ensure that faculty is sufficiently skilled to work in the online environment and explores the institution's capability to sustain the integration of the new technologies into learning and teaching practices. She adopts the view that faculty development for the e-learning environment is a change process aimed at providing faculty with new sets of skills, knowledge, and capabilities in this innovative and often different context for learning and teaching.

Cathy Gunn and Mandy Harper, with the University of Auckland, New Zealand, explore how learning theories and approaches to teaching can be applied to e-learning in the context of a growing and increasingly diverse student population. They reflect on the scale of the transformation that has taken place over the years, as well as discuss some of the key challenges faced during the process and issues yet to be addressed as development proceeds.

Richard Schwier and Mary Dykes from the University of Saskatchewan, delve into the world of e-learning communities and consider how implementation strategies used can influence the balance of community and content within the course, leaving us with questions on a myriad of topics including assessment. The authors also describe their reflections on the experiences of instructors in the online environment.

Martha Gabriel, from the University of Prince Edward Island, brings us to the question of faculty preparedness, with respect to effective instruction in e-learning, and offers a number of guidelines for new instructors to consider when engaging in the initial stages of course design. Her work will give instructors an opportunity to review their personal teaching styles and to explore teaching methods and pedagogy appropriate to their teaching styles that are effective in e-learning environments. She includes an overview of key categories of effective activities effective in e-learning environments as well as a synthesis of e-learner needs and expectations.

Dianne Conrad, from Athabasca University, continues this discussion of teaching online with her contribution. Her chapter's central argument focuses on Gunawardena's (1992) "letting go"—the movement from teacher-centered to learner-centered pedagogy as the prime focus in moving to online teaching.

The examples and references that illustrate this chapter's premise will resonate most clearly with those who are teaching in formal postsecondary environments. Using Collins and Berge's (1996) designation of four cornerstone functions for teaching online as a starting point, Conrad argues for reconceptualizing online instruction so connection, community, and collaboration are equally valued, along with the traditional cognitive stronghold, content.

Helen Wozniak, with the University of Sydney, Australia, along with the work of Karen Belfer, the British Columbia Institute of Technology, and Tannis Morgan from The University of British Columbia, investigate differing aspects of e-learning communication, with Wozniak exploring effective interaction strategies in asynchronous discussions and Belfer and Morgan proposing a framework for choosing communication activities for e-learning environments.

Wozniak's chapter leads the reader through an action research-based cycle of improvements she made when developing orientation activities that enabled learners to achieve knowledge construction by participating in asynchronous discussions. The improvements in both the design and delivery of the learning program draw heavily on research evidence describing interaction in online discussions. This combined with her research provides practical suggestions to assist readers to develop strategies for learner support in their own context.

Belfer and Morgan present a framework for planning online discussion activities according to the level of structure and potential dialogue. This framework serves as a tool for making decisions about how to give students more or less autonomy, how a series of course activities can be scaffolded, and the amount of structure or instructor facilitation that is needed. The framework they have developed uses transactional distance theory as a construct and the variables as dimensions to represent different instructional strategies.

This section ends with Rick Kenny's work on problem-based learning as a pedagogical approach for e-learning. PBL is a well-established educational strategy in conventional teaching environments in which complex, ill-structured problems serve as the context and the stimulus for learning. It contrasts with more traditional subject-based approaches where students are first taught a body of knowledge and then may have an opportunity to apply what they have learned to sample problems. Kenny provides a case study of how PBL was implemented in an online e-learning course and provides some recommendations for its effective used in e-learning environments.

Section III: Instructional Design and Technology Issues

Luca Botturi, Lorenzo Cantoni, Benedetto Lepori, and Stefano Tardini with the University of Lugano in Switzerland, open this section with their chapter, *Fast Prototyping Development as Communication Catalyst*. They propose a renewed perspective on a known project management model, fast prototyping, which was adapted for the specific issues of e-learning development. Based on extensive experience with large e-learning projects, they argue that this model has a positive impact on e-learning project team communication, and that it provides a good basis for effective management of the design and development process, with specific stress on human-factor management.

From Spain, Albert Sangrà and Lourdes Guàrdia of the Open University of Catalonia and Mercedes González-Sanmamed of the University of Coruña suggest that faculties often try to extend their face-to-face activities to a technological environment without taking into account how the educational context has changed within the environment of a new delivery system. This chapter focuses on the need for redesigning courses and for developing an appropriate educational or instructional model adapted to that new context.

In *Cognitive Tools for Self-Regulated e-Learning*, Tracey Leacock and John Nesbit at Simon Fraser University explore a software application designed to help students take control of their own learning and become better self-regulators. They begin by providing a brief description of self-regulated learning (SRL) and introduce gStudy, a set of cognitive tools developed at Simon Fraser University to support SRL. Their discussion of gStudy includes a case study showing how the application has been used in one undergraduate educational psychology course. Throughout, they look at gStudy both as a practical tool that educators can use in their courses to help students, and as a research tool that researchers can use to learn more about the theories underlying SRL and their practical applications. They conclude by revisiting the importance of SRL and applications such as gStudy in the context of institutional transitions to e-learning.

Elizabeth Murphy of Memorial University of Newfoundland and Thérèse Laferrière of Laval University consider some of the issues related to the adoption of online synchronous communication tools. Their chapter also proposes strategies to help deal with these issues. Two contrasting contexts of the use of online synchronous tools are described.

Adnan Qayyum, with Concordia University, and Brad Eastman, with the University of British Columbia, end the section with their chapter, *Knowledge is PowerPoint: Slideware in E-learning*. They begin by reviewing literature on slideware in e-learning, which includes reviewing research on slideware use and the passionate debate, currently in the Academy, on the cognitive style of PowerPoint. They analyze this debate in the context of educational technology research on media attributes and its influence on learning. They suggest instructional design strategies for using slideware effectively in synchronous and asynchronous e-learning and discuss the uneasy relationship between slideware and learning management systems (LMS). They conclude by advocating that administrators initiate research on slideware use in their institutions to inform decisions about what type of LMS, if any, they really need for e-learning.

The 20 chapters in this manuscript provide readers with diverse perspectives on some of the fundamental organizational, pedagogical, and technological issues facing educators as institutions make the transition to e-learning. These are the perspectives of practitioners and scholars from around the world, in conventional universities, open universities, and polytechnics. They are perspectives that are based on experience, but they are also grounded in theory and research, and we believe each of the chapters provides readers with valuable and practical insights into the key issues facing higher education as it confronts the challenge of making the transition to e-learning.

References

Bullen, M. (2006). When worlds collide: Project management and the collegial culture. In B. L. Pasian & G. A. Woodill (Eds.), *Plan to learn: Case studies in e-learning project management.* Toronto, Canada: CeLEA.

Collins, M. P., & Berge, Z. L. (1996). Facilitating interaction in computer mediated online courses. Retrieved from http://www.emoderators.com/moderators/flcc.html

Gunawardena, C. N. (1992). Changing faculty roles for audiographics and online teaching. *The American Journal of Distance Education, 6*(3), 58-71.

OECD. (2005). *E-Learning and tertiary education: Where do we stand.* Paris: OECD Publishing.

Zemsky, R., & Massy, W. F. (2004). *Thwarted innovation: What happened to e-learning and why.* The Learning Alliance, University of Pennsylvania. Retrieved January 25, 2006, from http://www.irhe.upenn.edu/WeatherStation.html

Acknowledgments

No book of this nature is undertaken alone, and we want take this opportunity to recognize all of those who helped us bring this project to completion. We must of course first acknowledge the incredible talents of our colleague-writers who contributed the chapters you have read that make this such a valuable book. Without their hard work and generosity in sharing their experiences this book would not have been possible. In addition to writing their own chapters, most of the authors also served as reviewers and we want to thank them for the time they took to provide their constructive comments and suggestions. We have also received an enormous amount of support from our colleagues and the staff at each of our institutions, the British Columbia Institute of Technology (BCIT) and the University of Saskatchewan. We must extend special thanks to Sarah Wareing from BCIT for her talented editing of the final manuscript; to Nancy Berke of BCIT for graphic design; to John L. Ruiz of the University of Saskatchewan for her early editing and comments on the manuscript; to Alan Doree of the Distance Education and Technology (DET) Department of the University of British Columbia for developing the book Web site; to the rest of our former DET colleagues who encouraged us when this book was still an idea; to Kristin Roth, Development Editor, and Jan Travers, Managing Director, of Idea Group Inc.; and last but never least, to our family and friends. To each of you, thank you.

Mark Bullen, PhD
Diane P. Janes, PhD
Editors
June 2006

Section I

Institutional and Conceptual Issues

Chapter I

E-Learning as Nation Building

Marco Adria, University of Alberta, Canada

Katy Campbell, University of Alberta, Canada

Abstract

This chapter is concerned with how individuals may examine the potential for social change arising from interactions in an e-learning environment. We explore continuing education as the site for e-learning in the context of developing a civil society. Referring to Anderson's (1991) work on nationalism, and Wenger, McDermott, and Snyder's (2002) discussion of communities of practice, we argue that the transition from face-to-face teaching to e-learning has the potential to appeal to those learners, and their instructors, who are interested in the capacity of a community to contribute to social change. We are particularly interested in the potential of e-learning to be socially transformative in its power to be inclusive, that is, to support diverse cultures, languages, work contexts, learning needs and styles, prior experiences, generations, economic circumstances, social contexts, and geographic location. We have suggested that the metaphor of an e-learning nation supports the reflective and progressive development of learning communities in which identity is consciously and critically examined.

E-Learning in a Social World of Communities

From a sociocultural point of view, we are intrigued by conceptualizing e-learning communities using the metaphor of "the nation." E-learning, defined here as electronically mediated learning (Zemsky & Massy, 2004), offers the higher education community an opportunity to rethink the role of education at many levels and to leverage this opportunity in positive social ways.

We may use e-learning to envision new possibilities for social life and to consider the implications of these possibilities for concrete practice in our teaching. We argue that the transition from face-to-face teaching to e-learning has the potential to appeal to those learners, and their instructors, who are interested in the capacity of a community to contribute to social change. We are particularly interested in the potential of e-learning to be socially transformative in its power to be inclusive, that is, to support diverse cultures, languages, work contexts, learning needs and styles, prior experiences, generations, economic circumstances, social contexts, and geographic location. This chapter is concerned with how individuals may examine the potential for social change arising from interactions in an e-learning environment. We explore continuing education as the site for e-learning in the context of developing a civil society. For purposes of this discussion, we reference Martha Cook Piper's (2002) definition of the civil society:

A vigorous citizenry engaged in the culture and politics of a free society... [in which] the key agent of influence and change is neither the government nor the corporation, but rather the individual, acting alone or with others to strengthen civic life. In turn, how individuals think about themselves and others, the values they espouse and enact, become the essential features of a civil society. (p. 4)

Those of us who teach in and design e-learning courses and environments are challenged to use the advantages and benefits of e-learning technologies while minimizing the disadvantages or risks. By demonstrating to learners, administrators, designers, and prospective instructors that there are many benefits to e-learning, and that disadvantages are recognized and can be addressed, it is more likely that the transition from face-to-face to e-learning can be accomplished.

E-learning can be accomplished in a way that recognizes an important part of learners' day-to-day world, which is the national community in which they live. E-learning itself constitutes another community—a community of learners—which may be regarded as an "emergent nation." Learners may be invited to join this community and encouraged to give attention to its features and attributes as a community with its own identity at various points in their learning journeys. In this way, the nation of e-learning could become part of a distinctive culture of learners and would also extend, and perhaps revise, notions and assumptions of what national culture and identity is and can be. The opportunity exists here for the development of more active and critical citizens who participate in and help shape the tolerant, diverse, and inclusive communities that "stimulate creativity and innovation" (Piper, 2002, p. 5).

If, as we suggest, we all live in a world of nations, we may ask, What are some ways that designers and teachers may use the metaphor of the nation to invite learners into the e-learning environment? And, How might the metaphor of the nation provide a means of transition from the face-to-face teaching context to the e-learning context?

The Imagined Community

Historically, members of the community met and interacted with the entire community. But the development of larger national communities became possible as technologies allowed people to imagine a national group that was larger than the one with which they interacted from day to day. Anderson (1991) points to three important artifacts by which this new kind of imagining took place in the colonial period of the nineteenth century: the census, maps, and museums.

The census provided a measure of how large the imagined community was and at what rate it was increasing or decreasing in size. Members of a nation could use a number to refer to the size of the population, with implications for the potential strength of the nation in terms of economic and cultural production and security, for example, providing a metric of how much force would be needed to establish the security of the nation. In a similar way, the map helped individuals conceptualize the space within which their nation resided, along with adjoining space that they might aspire to control. Dots depicting the emerging national group's cities were contrasted with the size and number of the dots of other cities of the world. The map's borders suggested a national identity within a territory. Sometimes, this sense of boundaries empowered colonized groups to expel the colonizing power. Museums in colonial lands arose in part out of a move towards modern schooling. Archeological discoveries and reconstructions would be a means of instruction in the history and culture for members of the nation. Monuments, including statues, art, and events, were created to celebrate cultural accomplishments within the colony. These discoveries, tools, and accomplishments were then reproduced through lavishly illustrated books and eventually commemorated as well through postage stamps, postcards, and so on. The census, the map, and the museum interlinked with one another to illuminate and represent how the state conceptualized itself: "It was bounded, determinate, and therefore—in principle—countable" (Anderson, 1991, p. 184).

In a similar vein, we propose three artifacts that may contribute to an e-learning nation: lists, networks, and repositories. These artifacts are already used in many e-learning courses and programs of study. Mindful of the power of everyday symbols, instructors and learners may invest these artifacts with new meaning about the relationship between community and learning. The change from face-to-face learning to e-learning may become characterized by continuities and transitions rather than conflicts, disjunctures, and adjustments.

With these ideas in mind, our objectives for this chapter include the following:

- Proposing how e-learning conceptualized as a nation may be used to facilitate the transition from face-to-face learning.

- Describing methods by which the concept of an e-learning nation could be enacted within e-learning courses and programs of study.

- Providing examples from a continuing education faculty at a Canadian university to illustrate the benefits of such an approach.

National Identities and Higher Education

Anderson (1991) argues that nations are made up of people who can imagine a shared community, since the physical and sociocultural scope of the nation is either too large or too abstract to "see" all at once. Technological mediation helps make possible this imaginative aspect of national communities. Historically, for example, by creating a standardized language and venue for discussion of national issues, the printing press enabled the development of imagined national communities. Imagined communities are larger and more diverse than communities that existed before the use the communications technologies—communities that were defined by the face-to-face transmission of narratives and other forms of cultural knowledge. The collective and negotiated memories of those present at a town meeting, for example, limited the scale of the community. However, with the rise of mass audiences corporate memories could be committed to books and other printed artifacts. The number of members, geographical location, and diversity of the community could grow quickly. As we have observed, the census, the map, and the museum provided institutional bases for imagining a nation that was more extensive and more inclusive than what an individual could observe firsthand.

The development of North American universities has been entwined with the development of a national identity (Bendix, 1977; Greene, 1990; Miller, 1995). Systems of higher education have their origins in the social interaction that takes place within a national culture. However, in Canada, as in many other nations, institutions of higher learning are being urged to participate in defining a global society based on "expanding knowledge" and to redefine the sociocultural roles and relationships of institutions, learners, and faculty in order to "play a new and expanded role in the ongoing education of citizens" (Advisory Committee for Online Learning, 2001, p. 24).

A Profound Bond with Machines

The Internet adds to this context of national communities and their educational systems by what Poster (1999) calls a "profound bond with machines." Explanations of how national identity is established, developed, and disseminated must increasingly take account of this change. The Internet is creating a "paranational culture that combines global connectivity with local specificity, a 'glocal' phenomenon that seems to resist national political agendas" (Poster, 1999, p. 236). In this sense, the e-learning community, if conceptualized as an emerging community of national or even transnational scale, can be considered as a means of overcoming parochial and/or local concerns. E-learning has the capacity to span diverse online communities, organized communities, and exclusionary in-groups, because it encourages an exploration of alternatives to such institutional bases. In other words, e-learning provides a model to establish and maintain a new community (in our metaphor, an imagined nation), spanning the boundaries of established territories, such as the physical classroom at the university in which members in a particular course meet at established dates and times. The asynchronicity of e-learning, in particular, breaks down these boundaries.

Portals. The development of learning portals, for example, requires institutions to expand on traditional academic spaces that are defined by physical infrastructures and related resource structures that have shaped the nature of interactions that occur within it (Batson, 2000). This traditional space has had an important socialization function: Members of the community know how to speak and act within these spaces; understand power relationships by the way these spaces organize interactions; and, once acculturated, can subvert the purposes of these spaces. However, this familiar landscape is fundamentally changing and faculty, who have old maps with which to navigate this new landscape, must redefine their relationships with learners with new forms of knowledge representation, with research, and with external communities who are suddenly present in their "classrooms" and who are influencing their planning. The learner in this emerging context is a member of an international community of learners, and it is by addressing this potential that instructors, professors, administrators, instructional designers, project managers, and new media designers can in part enable the transition from face-to-face learning to e-learning. Institutions are responding in many ways; some are seeking new kinds of partnerships.

The media and identity-building. Learners, like other citizens, are constantly reminded of their national identity. This occurs through the routine use of certain symbols and also by patterned language practices. In all nations, national flags are draped and displayed on the walls of commercial, institutional, and domestic buildings, inside and out, and on rooftops, screens, and apparel. This reminder also arrives through common, popular, and high-profile events such as professional sports, newspaper publication, and the circulation of weather reports. National identity is developed not only in special or extraordinary situations but in everyday ones. Billig (1995), for one, argues that national identity is developed in mundane, repetitious, and ubiquitous social situations. The flag of a nation, for example, is implied through the colors and symbols of streetscapes, shopping centers, schools, and workplaces. The most profound of the messages of national identity is that we all live in a world of nations. Canadian hockey provides a widely experienced example of this identity-building, occurring throughout the year at local community ice rinks and in professional arenas, transmitted into our homes by popular media, and underlined by mass marketing of t-shirts and so on. Symbols and practices associated with the hockey season emphasize and repeat the message that we inhabit and participate in a social world of competition and belongingness.

This aspect of nation-building could potentially be acknowledged and leveraged in e-learning courses and programs of study. For example, Campbell teaches an online graduate course in user-centered design that includes several international students, as do most of the courses in the Master of Arts in Communications and Technology (http://www.extension.ualberta.ca/mact/index.aspx). This case-based course explores the social, educational, economic, and ethical dimensions of information design through a critical theory lens. The learning resources and activities, including significant participation in the asynchronous class discussions, require learners to identify and reflect publicly on their own cultural values and beliefs, be critical of the dominant culture approach we typically take in information design in a global community, and apply it to the design of a travel site for an international audience.

E-Learning and the
Metaphor of the Nation

Our social, economic, and cultural life is mediated, organized, and viewed through the lens of the nation. By recognizing the broad reach of the national paradigm, the e-learning environment has the potential to transcend the boundaries of national identity for the purpose of developing an engaged and critical citizenry.

An e-learning community may develop in ways that are parallel to those of the national communities previously discussed. The methods by which instructors and designers choose to structure e-learning environments will help shape the identity of individuals and groups involved in e-learning. We proposed that three artifacts of e-learning that parallel Anderson's census, map, and museum, that is, *lists*, *networks*, and *repositories*, can be utilized creatively as part of the learning environment.

Lists Connect Us Socially Through Time

E-learning lists occur frequently and are similar in function to a census. Some lists are particular to e-learning, while others are part of conventional learning contexts. Lists, whether discipline-specific or in support of a dialogue among professionals in an organization, are a familiar feature in academic life. They connect us socially to our colleagues, near and far, and often encourage us to develop fruitful collaborations for research, teaching, and leadership. Membership in multiple lists, each with its own culture, reminds us that we and our colleagues belong to many interdependent communities. Having a list of other learners for contact via e-mail is a part of many online courses and, if appropriately used, may be used to signify and emphasize the membership of the learner in a learning community within an institution of learners and in fellowship with a community of learners regionally, nationally, and internationally. Lists may encourage interaction with one or more of the other communities. Even if such contact does not actually take place, learners will be reminded through the lists that they are part of not only their own community of learners, but also of a community of communities as well—they now live in a world of learning communities. As with physical communities, these lists operate most effectively if members are part of negotiating and moderating the cultural mores, the "values, ways of doing things, and language of the community" (Campbell & Ben-Zvi, 1999; Rourke, 2005, p. 64). Lists have effectively supported communities engaged in social activism. Winkelman (1997) describes abused women in the community who, through sharing personal narratives online, were able to identify personal and political strategies affecting their situations.

A unifying and enriching aspect of the University of Alberta's Faculty of Extension's continuing education e-learning activities is the history within which they continue to unfold. Lists of e-learning communities that were formed in the recent past within the course are a reminder that there are predecessors and successors to the learning community and signal that e-learning represents a developmental process over time. In some cases, learners may feel that they are "standing on the shoulders of giants." This can assist in moving the e-learning environment away from the concept of information transmission to the concept of meaning creation and identity development. For example, for a recently completed master's project, a student drew on her cohort community for primary data and emotional and editorial support for her final paper (http://www.extension.ualberta.ca/mact/research.aspx). This cohort community was sustained through a list years after the official expectation of participation had ended. Several of the members had, in fact, graduated but stayed connected through the list.

Networks are Technological and Social

The networks of e-learning are the maps of the e-learning nation. E-learning networks are both technological and social. The technological networks of e-learning are increasingly sub networks within the Web. A course or program of study is established as a relatively private network for interaction, from which members of the network may depart to and return from the Web to find information and resources or to communicate with others outside of the course. Yet the e-learning network is only one part of a learner's larger set of social networks. As Wenger et al. (2002) have argued, the meeting of experience and expertise in the learning community is a social act, and learners participate in learning communities as social beings. The social nature of the e-learning activity may be celebrated and encouraged as a means of allowing a transition from face-to-face interactions to e-learning interactions and, through a shared language, enabling us to "create and acknowledge meaning as we engage in discourse and fulfill social obligations …[that] are characterized as moral activities" (Herda, 1999, p. 24) or social action.

By providing signals and symbols of an e-learning course or program of study in relation to networks that are outside of the e-learning environment, learners may become aware of the relationship of their studies to the other parts of their lives. Markus, Manville, and Agres (2000) argue that virtual organizations, and the network structure on which they are built, tend to be successful when certain characteristics exist (for example, when there is something at stake for members of the network, where self-governance skills and practices are developed, and when motivation to accomplish goals is provided) because of the mutual interdependence built into the network. Finally, networks are successful when there are norms and expectations for uses of communications technologies. Effective networks in e-learning design these success factors into the e-learning environment. For example, a network might be established that allows learners to invite experts in the field to visit the e-learning community at a specified time. Such a structure builds mutual indebtedness that is characteristic of networks, in the sense that there are the beginnings of the potentially long-term give-and-take that networks can provide (Woudstra & Adria, 2003). This social capital is the glue that holds a networked community together. It includes the stock of active connections among people, and it involves trust, mutual understanding, respect, and shared values and behaviors within a community. It binds people as members of human networks and communities and makes co-operative action possible (Cohen & Prusak, 2001; Daniel, Schwier, & McCalla, 2003).

Tools that support social networks (social software) are now beginning to emerge. Blogs, and more recently wikis, may exemplify this approach by supporting an interactive community of practitioners and learners who share information, practices, job opportunities, and lively debate. For example, through Rick Schwier's (University of Saskatchewan) course blog, *Rick's Café Canadien* (http://www.omegageek.net/rickscafe/), one of the student participants became aware of an opening in our faculty for an instructional designer and was the successful candidate. This individual has expressed an obligation to continue to participate in the blog in a different role—sharing his experiences as a developing professional. As networked communities, blogs have potential for identity formation; we are exploring this notion in a blog that is a research and professional site in which instructional designers share their stories of practice as "agents of social change" in higher education (http://www.idcop.ca). In this sense, the blog also serves as a repository of cultural knowledge as designers point to instructional resources and objects they have developed or found (Schwier, Campbell, & Kenny, 2004).

Repositories as the Museum of the E-Nation

The use of repositories is the third method by which the metaphor of a nation of e-learning may be developed. Repositories are materials and resources that are made available to learners for their required or discretionary use as part of the e-learning experience. Repositories may include published articles, illustrative diagrams or photos, computer simulations, self-test questions and problems, and so on. Repositories are the museum of the e-learning nation. Like many concrete museums, they may be increasingly interactive, in the sense that they seek to engage the learner in a dialogue about the relevance of the museum's materials to the learner's own context. An example of how a repository may be used to develop the metaphor of the nation of e-learning, one championed by "learning objects economy" advocates, is to encourage and enable learners to develop and contribute their own entries to the repository or to add value to the entries that already exist by extending them with additional resources, media, activities, and so on. If these contributions are archived, dated, and appropriately tagged, the contribution of previous generations of learners would also contribute to the "national life" of the e-learning course or program of study.

The Multimedia Educational Resources for Learning and Online Teaching, or MERLOT (http://www.merlot.org), is an example of such a repository. MERLOT provides a cooperatively developed, free, Web-based resource where faculty can search for discipline-specific learning objects, with evaluations and guidance for use. MERLOT leverages the academic regard for peer review (Hanley & Thomas, 2000) through a board comprised of faculty from the partner postsecondary institutions. Peer review teams are discipline-related and include faculty who are nominated by their colleagues for their disciplinary expertise, excellence in teaching, experience in using technology in teaching and learning, and connections with their discipline's professional organizations. The MERLOT organization provides facilitation and training to peer review teams to plan and conduct reviews, add materials to the collection, and design the collection's categorization scheme, fulfilling a faculty professional development goal. Thus, faculty who have developed learning objects are able to represent their work as scholarship in a manner understood by their cultural community. The peer evaluations of learning objects are equally valuable to faculty who are assured of the quality of the learning objects that they intend to include in their own learning designs (COHERE, 2002).

Conclusion: Implications for the Transition to E-Learning in Higher Education

A cultural community can be a political nation, a social class, a religion, or a race; a language group, an age group, or a gender group; a professional association, a special-interests group, a university, or an online course. E-learning is becoming an everyday event for many people, and it is in this sense that national identity and the ideals of a civil society may be incorporated into the design of e-learning.

For both teachers and learners, the development of citizenship may be part of the transition from face-to-face to e-learning. Both short- and long-term relationships are established through e-learning. Students in a university degree program, for example, may attend a single online course in order to fill in a gap in their programs of study. The relationship with others in the course would be short-term unless friendships were established that might continue after the course ends. The long-term relationship associated with completing a degree program along with other learners in the same program may occur over a period of years rather than months and is more likely to lead to personal or professional relationships extending after the formal e-learning relationship has ended. Both short- and long-term e-learning relationships have the capacity to develop ideal and practical exercises in the civil society.

Future Trends

While emerging research is emphasizing the role of well-designed online discussions in the forms described above in the development of social capital in a learning community, some research is challenging the cognitive benefits of these activities, in terms of increased levels of critical thinking (c.f. Cleveland-Innes & Garrison, 2005; Kanuka & Garrison, 2004; Kanuka, Rourke, & Picard, 2005). A number of emerging learning design heuristics designed to increase the efficacy of these activities include an enhanced and highly structured role for the facilitator, structured response guidelines such as those developed by Scardamalia and Bereiter (1994) in their work with computer-supported collaborative learning, and purposive conversation in which members have a personal stake.

E-Learning and Citizenship

The Faculty of Extension at the University of Alberta has undergone a re-visioning exercise that attempts to answer the questions about the role/value of faculties and units like ours in the modern institution. Our vision, "to be recognized locally and globally for research and scholarship that embrace our community's and our country's values and aspirations" and associated mission, to "contribute responsibly to social and individual betterment through research and scholarship to discover, disseminate and exemplify the ideals of a civil society" provide a context in which we design for access and inclusion through e-learning (McWatter, 2003, p. 14). An example is the Faculty's program in Information Access and Protection of Privacy (http://www.govsource.net/programs/iapp/index.nclk). Through such courses as Privacy in a Liberal Democracy, the program encourages a wider understanding of the social dimensions of information access and protection of privacy, as well as the professional knowledge required to work effectively in this area.

Nationalism is not an unmitigated good in the world and never has been. If we extend Powell's (1997) definition of culture as "the sum total of ways of living, including values, beliefs, aesthetic standards, linguistic expression, patterns of thinking, behavioral norms, and styles of communication, which a group of people has developed to assure its survival in a particular physical and human environment" (p. 15) to include the virtual environment, the argument for the development of the e-learning nation metaphor could contribute to the potential lifting of citizens from the assumption that the world of nations is the only social world that we can inhabit. Instead, there would be many nationalities that individuals hold, including that of their membership in the nation of e-learning, which may encourage a cultural evolution of new ideas.

We have argued that the goals of identity development have historical roots in social, cultural, and political systems, artifacts, language, and behavior, and that these can be used to critically and reflectively manage the transition from face-to-face learning to an e-learning nation that is multicultural, creative, active, and designed for inclusion. With these goals in mind, we may ask the following questions about e-learning courses and programs:

- What are the learning design principles used, and what do they suggest about cultural identity?
- What does the visual appearance suggest about community identity?
- How does language use contribute to a learner's sense of community?
- What assumptions are built into group activities about who the "them" and "us" might be?

We conclude with a consideration of a practical exploration of the relationship between national identity and e-learning design and development. We have presented the metaphor of the nation as a means of imagining e-learning communities that are reflective and active. How might the design of e-learning express and support a reflective and active e-learning community with regard to masculinity and femininity? Dormann and Chisalita (2002) used Hofstede's (1997) model of cultural dimensions (which include the indices of power distance, masculinity, femininity, uncertainty avoidance, and long-term orientation) to explore the extent to which value orientations were expressed through the visual design of Web sites from "masculine" and "feminine" countries. In masculine cultures, social gender roles are clearly distinct, while in feminine cultures social gender roles overlap. Femininity-masculinity is present in several cultural values. For example, masculine cultures promote cultural values such as ambition and competition, while feminine cultures promote values such as good relationships and quality of life. The study examined university Web sites to determine how cultural values are represented in Web design with a view to providing designers with guidelines for culturally relevant Web design.

The researchers found that the most striking difference between masculine and feminine countries resided in the important semantic differences within image types. For example, in the feminine countries representations of people engaged in different activities were more numerous, while in masculine countries different buildings were more numerous. The Italian Web site Study dela Basilicata (http://www.unibas.it), which contained buildings and three columns consisting mostly of links, was typical of a masculine country. The Danish site for the Roskilde University Centre (http://www.ruc.dk) represented a visual site typical for feminine countries. Relationships, conversations, and images of people were at the centre of the site.

We have suggested that the metaphor of an e-learning nation supports the reflective and progressive development of cultural identity. Through attention to conceptual and empirical explorations of the kind initiated by Dormann and Chisalita, those involved in e-learning design and development have the opportunity to create learning communities in which identity is consciously and critically examined. By attending to the images used in e-learning Web sites and course materials, e-learning designers may encourage open and negotiable social gender roles within the e-learning community. Through such design considerations, learners and instructors alike may be encouraged to make the important transition from face-to-face teaching to e-learning.

References

Advisory Committee for Online Learning. (2001, February). *The e-learning e-volution in colleges and universities*. Retrieved July 13, 2005, from http://www.cmec.ca/postsec/evolution.en.pdf

Anderson, B. (1991). *Imagined communities: Reflections on the origin and spread of nationalism* (2nd ed.). London: Verso.

Archer, W., Garrison, D., & Anderson, T. (2000). Adopting disruptive technologies in traditional universities: Continuing education as an incubator for innovation. *Canadian Journal of University Continuing Education, 25*(1), 13-44.

Batson, T. (2000, November). *Campus portals and faculty development.* Paper presented at Syllabus 2000: New Dimensions in Educational Technology Conference, Boston.

Bendix, R. (1977). *Nation-building and citizenship* (new enlarged edition). Berkeley: University of California Press.

Billig, M. (1995). *Banal nationalism.* London: Sage.

Campbell, K., & Ben-Zvi, E. (1999). The teaching of religion: Moral integrity in a technological context. *The Internet and Higher Education, 1*(3), 169-190.

Cleveland-Innes, M., & Garrison, R. (2005, May). *Online learning: Interaction is not enough.* Paper presented at the Annual Meeting of the Canadian Association of Distance Education, Vancouver, BC.

Cohen, D., & Prusak, L. (2001). *In good company. How social capital makes organizations work.* Cambridge, MA: Harvard Business School Press.

Collaboration for Online Higher Education Research (COHERE). (2002). The learning object economy: Implications for developing faculty expertise. *Canadian Journal of Learning and Technology, 28*(3), 121-134.

Daniel, B., Schwier, R. A., & McCalla, G. (2003). Social capital in virtual learning communities and distributed communities of practice. *Canadian Journal of Learning and Technology, 29*(3). Retrieved July 23, 2005, from http://www.cjlt.ca/content/vol29.3/

Dormann, C., & Chisalita, C. (2002, September). *Cultural values in Web site design.* Paper presented for the 11th European Conference on Cognitive Ergonomics ECCEII Catania, Italy.

Duphorne, P., & Gunawardena, C. (2005). The effect of three computer conferencing designs on critical thinking skills of nursing students. *American Journal of Distance Education, 19*(1), 37-50.

Garrison, D. R., Anderson, T., & Archer, W. (2001). Critical thinking, cognitive presence, and computer conferencing in distance education. *American Journal of Distance Education, 15*(1), 7-23.

Greene, A. (1990). *Education and state formation: The rise of education systems in England, France, and the USA.* London: Macmillan.

Hanley, G. L., & Thomas, C. (2000). MERLOT: Peer review of instructional technology. *Syllabus, 14*(3), 16-20.

Herda, E. A. (1999). *Research conversations and narrative: A critical hermeneutic orientation in participatory inquiry.* London: Praeger.

Hofstede, G. (1997). *Cultures and organizations: Software of the mind.* New York: McGraw-Hill.

Kanuka, H., & Garrison, D. R. (2004). Cognitive presence in online learning. *Journal of Computing in Higher Education, 15*(2), 19-30.

Kanuka, H., Rourke, L., & Picard, J. (2005, May). *Moving beyond online discussions.* Paper presented at the Annual Meeting of the Canadian Association of Distance Education. Vancouver, BC.

Markus, M., Manville, B., & Agres, C. (2000). What makes a virtual organization work? *Sloan Management Review, 42*(1), 13-26.

McWatters, C. (2003). *Message from the Dean.* Faculty of Extension, University of Alberta. Retrieved January 29, 2006, from http://www.extension.ualberta.ca/faculty/deansmessage.aspx

Miller, H. (1995). *The management of change in universities: Universities, state, and economy in Australia, Canada, and the United Kingdom.* Buckingham, UK: The Society for Research into Higher Education and Open University Press.

Murphy, E. (2004). Recognizing and promoting collaboration in an online synchronous discussion. *British Journal of Educational Technology, 35*(4), 421-431.

Piper, M. C. (2002, October). *Building a civil society: A new role for the human sciences.* Killam Annual Lecture. Retrieved January 10, 2005, from http://www.president.ubc.ca/president/speeches/24oct02_killam.pdf

Poster, M. (1999). National identities and communications technologies. *The Information Society, 15,* 235-24.

Powell, G. (1997). On being a culturally sensitive instructional designer and educator. *Educational Technology, 37*(2), 6-14.

Rourke, L. (2005). *Learning through online discussion.* Unpublished doctoral dissertation. University of Alberta.

Scardamalia, M., & Bereiter, C. (1994). Computer support for knowledge-building communities. *The Journal of the Learning Sciences, 3*(3), 265-283.

Schwier, R. A., Campbell, K., & Kenny, R. F. (2004). Instructional designers' observations about identity, communities of practice, and change agency. *Australasian Journal of Educational Technology, 20*(1), 69-100.

Sun, H. (2001, October). Building a culturally competent corporate Web site: An exploratory study of cultural makers in multilingual Web design. *Proceedings of SIGDOC'01* (pp. 83-90). Santa Fe, New Mexico.

Wenger, E., McDermott, R., & Snyder, W. (2002). *Cultivating communities of practice: A guide to managing knowledge.* Cambridge, MA: Harvard Business School Press.

Winkelman, C. (1997). Women in the integrated circuit: Morphing the academic/ community divide. *Frontiers: A Journal of Women's Studies, 18*(1), 19-42.

Woudstra, A., & Adria, M. (2003). Issues in organizing for the new network and virtual forms of distance education. In M. Moore & W. Anderson (Eds.), *Handbook of distance education* (pp. 531-548). Mahwah, NJ: Lawrence Erlbaum.

Zemsky, R., & Massy, W. (2004). *Thwarted innovation: What happened to e-learning and why.* A Final Report for The Weatherstation Project of The Learning Alliance at the University of Pennsylvania in cooperation with the Thomson Corporation. University of Pennsylvania.

Chapter II

Organizational Models for Faculty Support:
The Response of Canadian Universities

Margaret Haughey, University of Alberta, Canada

Abstract

This chapter delineates changing organizational responses to the provision of faculty support for teaching and learning in six large Canadian universities since 1997. Various models from centralized to decentralized and from integrated to parallel units are described and their advantages and disadvantages identified. From the analysis, several recommendations pertinent to senior administrators involved in the enhancement of teaching and learning through the integration of digital technologies are provided. In particular, issues concerning the goals and culture of the institution, the integration of pedagogical and technological approaches, as well as involvement of faculty and the role of policy are reviewed.

Organizational Models for Faculty Support: The Response of Canadian Universities

As large Canadian universities moved to deal with the emergence of e-learning and to encourage the integration of digital technologies in teaching and learning, what structures did they put in place to provide support? What was the focus of these organizational units? What was the rationale for their placement? How were they positioned within the institution? How did they link with other units? How have these units changed over time? These questions are the focus of this chapter.

In investigating these questions I have used a time series model, comparing faculty support structures in place in six large universities across Canada in 1997 and then in 2005. From this exploration comes guiding questions for any institution involved in developing faculty support for the use of digital technologies in teaching and learning.

Models for Teaching, Learning, and Technology Support, 2005

Traditionally, universities have had a large service architecture targeted at the provision of support for teaching. These services range from scheduling and timetabling for the allocation of rooms and bookstores principally for the sale of textbooks, to technical services for the maintenance of appropriate instructional equipment and janitorial services for the servicing of classrooms. There was often a media unit where actual production of instructional materials could occur. Depending on the services provided by the institution, there might be a separate unit for the provision of distance education, and most institutions had a small office whose mandate was the enhancement of instructional services (Cuneo et al., 1997). The large-scale introduction of computing technologies in the mid 1990s, coupled with the economic downturn that brought increasing pressure on university budgets, transformed this situation.

Bates (1995) encapsulated these pressures in his exploration of the future of learning, noting government pressure on universities and colleges for greater efficiencies, requiring them to increase enrollments while also reducing funding; government use of earmarked funds for targeted innovations; increases in student fees necessitating many students to be part-time; and the trend toward lifelong learning that was bringing people from the workforce back to university. He concluded that it was not surprising that many postsecondary institutions were turning to technology-based learning as a way to deal with these pressures.

The integration of digital technologies, then, was initially seen as a means to administrative efficiency that businesses had adopted and benefited from. Universities, under pressure to meet escalating costs but with reduced allocations from government, were encouraged to adopt digital technologies as much for the efficiencies they would bring as for any direct benefit to the core mission of the university: research, teaching, and service.

Profiles of six large Canadian universities help provide a description of various universities' responses to the pressures they faced in 1997. They are based on the work of Cuneo et al. (1997) who reviewed the Web sites of 13 major universities across Canada in terms of their technology and teaching support.

University of Toronto (UT)

In 1997, at the central campus of the University of Toronto all technology and teaching support services except computing were organized under a single unit, the Information Commons, and located in the Robarts Library. Operating under this umbrella was the Instructional Technology Support Group, which provided support with computing software, computing labs, and multimedia tools, including sessions on instructional technology. It operated a multimedia lab that faculty and students could use for course and materials development. Other units provided classroom technology support, video production, and adaptive technology resources. The Information Commons also offered a wide range of workshops related to software applications. UT did not have a separate faculty development unit.

Queen's University

In 1997, Queen's University had integrated its computing, media, and instructional support under an umbrella organization, Information Technology Services, located in the Stauffer Library. It included a Learning Technology Unit focused on use of technology in classes; an Instructional Development Centre supporting quality classroom teaching but also providing workshops and advice about technology integration in cooperation with the Learning Technology Unit; Queen's Television, geared to video and multimedia production and video-conferencing, especially in relation to Queen's MBA program; Audio and Multimedia Services; and the SunSite, whose mandate was to develop and promote use of new computing technologies and facilitate development of electronic curricula.

University of Western Ontario (UWO)

UWO had a Technology Leadership Centre that provided courses on topics such as telecommunications, computers, graphics, spreadsheets, and desktop presentations to help foster a learning culture at UWO. Its Information Technology Resources unit supported teaching, research, and administrative computing, and there were separate units for libraries, classroom facilities coordination, and instructional computing labs.

University of British Columbia (UBC)

In 1997, UBC had five organizational units that had some responsibility for the integration of technology, teaching, and learning. The Centre for Educational Technology (CET) supported innovative approaches to teaching using technology. The Centre for Faculty Development and Instructional Services (FDIS) provided instructional skills seminars and peer workshops on a wide range of topics from problem-based learning to group dynamics. It also ran an Instructional Technology electronic mailing list and sponsored a series of instructional technology seminars on topics such as working with WebCT and PowerPoint. Computing and Communications was responsible for the computing, media, and telecommunications infrastructure and services on campus and worked with FDIS. Distance education course development was in a separate unit, Distance Education and Technology (DET). Telestudios provided multimedia production services.

University of Alberta (UA)

University of Alberta had a range of services under the umbrella of the Academic Technologies for Learning (ATL) unit. These were distance education, faculty development, media production, instructional design, and research and evaluation. ATL listed its services as consultation in the development, delivery, and evaluation of innovative teaching/learning multimedia programs; training and professional development focusing on effective application of information and communication technologies in teaching and learning; and consultation and development in distance and distributed (blended) learning. In addition, there was a University Teaching Services unit, which focused on enhancement of classroom teaching and provided a range of services including workshops and orientations, peer consultation and mentoring programs, graduate student teaching awards, access to reference resources, and a newsletter.

McGill University

In 1997, McGill had three main units. The Centre for University Teaching and Learning (CUTL) offered a wide range of services. It provided workshops and seminars on the improvement of teaching, orientation seminars for new faculty, teaching programs for graduate students and teaching assistants, and assistance with course development and evaluation. It conducted funded research on teaching and learning, provided policy advice, and participated in policy development in this area. The Instructional Communications Centre (ICC) provided audio-visual and multimedia services including television and sound production. The Computing Centre provided computer software and hardware applications support. It put on a wide range of workshops on various software programs.

Discussion

By 1997, these Canadian universities had begun to consider the coordination of computing technology and other services and some had moved to integrate units to provide for greater efficiencies and enhance student services. In general, however, instructional development units focused on enhancing classroom teaching, while computing services provided instruction in specific computer applications and libraries helped students develop competencies in database searching and information retrieval. The addition of a unit to assist faculty to integrate digital (usually computer) technologies tended to emphasize using the technology rather than how students learned through the technology. In addition, while there was likely a small group of early adopters, the surge of interest in the wake of the World Wide Web had not yet materialized. Some universities had adopted virtual learning management systems but most had not decided on a proprietary system and instead encouraged the use of Web pages and additional asynchronous discussion software. A large part of universities' concerns in 1997 was provision of sufficient student access to computers. Some universities had anchored their educational technology in student and faculty service centers operating out of the campus library. Other universities saw educational technology units as linking faculty development and computing services, while some still had units operating independently with little coordination of services.

The McMaster group (Cuneo et al., 1997) was particularly interested in computer-based instructional options and argued for the development of a center that focused on alternative learning technologies. They noted that their own university model for faculty support, which was one of separate units providing audio-visual, computing, and instructional services, had resulted in inter-unit competition, protectionism, duplication, and institutional waste. They concluded that this divided approach to supporting learning technologies was not appropriate for the 1990s or the next century and recommended that audio visual, instructional support, library services, and academic computing be integrated.

From their study of staff development structures at 20 Australian universities, Hughes, Hewson, and Nightingale (1997) identified three organizational approaches to supporting the use of information technology—integrated, parallel, and distributed—and the benefits and issues associated with each.

The integrated approach used a single unit to combine units for development of teaching and learning and information technology in teaching, with multimedia and online production facilities. A centralized approach, it emphasized the integration of instructional technology in planning at all levels and the use of plans and objectives for resource allocation decisions. The benefit of this approach is that it has a strong basis in policy, supports coherence in direction, and avoids duplication through rational planning. Its limitations are that much of the work of technology integration happens in individual classrooms and at the department level and the motivation for these innovations can be stifled or renegade units form if direction and approval is solely from the top. Hughes et al. also point out that the focus on technology integration can be too narrow and that much more might be achieved if the focus was on moving from a transmission model of teaching to a facilitation of learning approach.

The parallel approach involved the development of an additional unit or center for technology integration in teaching alongside existing arrangements for the enhancement of teaching and learning. There were some agreements to cross reference, but basically one unit dealt with teaching and learning enhancement and the other focused on enhancement of teaching through technology. The benefits of this approach are that it enlarges the support for teaching development and allows expertise to focus on the issues without reducing capacity for teaching support in general. The issues are that the two units may not cooperate and instead actively compete for clients. Having two centers focused on teaching may confuse faculty members who do not know whether their issues are best resolved, for example, through better curriculum planning or technology integration. This confusion may be exacerbated because the units may well come from competing paradigms, with the technology unit often seen as following a model that privileges teaching while the teaching and learning units are more often linked to learner-centered models. This approach also allows both units to avoid issues they don't want to deal with by labeling them the other unit's problem.

The distributed approach is one where there were units linked to teaching enhancement at various levels throughout the organization. Some were centralized while others were faculty or departmental based. The advantage of this approach is that a variety of units designed to meet the disciplinary concerns of their clientele also provides for local control. Issues can occur if there is too little coordinated planning, if local centers see themselves as autonomous and independent of central units. This can lead to a lack of synergy and fragmentation of effort. It can also result in poor pedagogical practice if the level of services is not consistent across the centers. The approach lacks economies of scale and may result in a wide variability in resources and hence capabilities of individual units. Projects that are not seen to be receiving central support may falter and fail if there is insufficient local support to sustain the innovation over time.

In their study, Cuneo et al. (1997) documented the extent of centralization and cooperation of the various units, but the three Hughes et al. (1997) models highlight more clearly the potential issues associated with the extent of centralization and cooperation. Although the Australians' focus is narrower and doesn't include library or computing services, there was strong evidence of the parallel model in the six Canadian universities, with most having developed a unit that focused on technology; sometimes the parallel units were faculty development and audio-visual services, but more often they were faculty development and computing services or faculty development and online instructional development. In some cases, the two units shared the work, with one doing workshops on teaching enhancement or computer applications and the other more heavily invested in assisting individual faculty on particular projects involving online applications (e.g., UWO, UA, Queen's). The distributed approach was not strongly evident in any of the Canadian universities, although it is likely that all had local audio-visual and multimedia units not identified by Cuneo et al. Also, especially in the large universities, the library was much more likely to be involved in providing online information services.

Models for Teaching, Learning, and Technology Support, 2005

The pressures to integrate digital technologies while enhancing efficiencies and effectiveness in administrative services has remained a major concern for universities. As more students purchased their own computers, the demand for computing lab space gradually eased and was replaced by demand for wireless hotspots. As network access to the Internet became more readily available, universities were able to gain efficiencies by having increasing proportions of their services for students available online (Campbell & Cuneo, 2001). The development of blended or hybrid learning patterns where students combined online and in-class activities became more common, and there was rapid growth in the use of virtual e-learning environments (VLE), usually through a proprietary learning management system supported by the university. More recently, a renewed emphasis on teaching, as evidenced in the strategic plans of the major universities, has accelerated faculty interest in alternative possibilities involving technology and, in many cases, faculty interest has been a deciding factor for renewed interest in technology integration.

The focus on the quality of the undergraduate experience, and its relationship to the knowledge society, to lifelong learning, and to technology integration, are current concerns. This has placed renewed focus on the teaching and learning units as sites to help faculty deal with curriculum redevelopment and learn about active learning or problem-based learning. The emphasis on technology is shifting from a focus on course management systems and presentation software to blended learning and technological assistance in active learning. An analysis of the current Web sites of the six large research universities previously described shows a realignment of services in response to these trends.

University of Toronto

UT has retained the Information Commons, its umbrella organization in the Robarts Library, which links library, media use, academic technology services, and teaching advancement and is a central agency for faculty and students seeking assistance with learning technology issues. UT revised its mandate to stress enabling access to information resources through technology to strengthen teaching, learning, and research and restructured Academic Technology Services and the Adaptive Technology Resource Centre within the Resource Centre for Educational Technology. This unit supports the use of emerging technologies in teaching, learning, and research. It advises the university on trends and best practices in this area, evaluates existing software, and develops new technology-based services to support teaching and learning. The Office of Teaching Advancement, which began in 2002, has a mandate to assist faculty in the development of instructional skills, recognize teaching excellence, and help faculty find an effective balance between research and teaching. These two units cooperate in the offering of seminars related to technology integration. UT also has faculty-based Learning Commons units that provide discipline-specific technology support. In addition, constituent campuses have Teaching Support units that combine enhancement of teaching with technology integration.

Queen's University

Queen's umbrella organization, Information Technology Services, has undergone some realignment. Its new mandate is to develop, promote, and support the application of information technology at Queen's through group and individual initiatives related to teaching, research, scholarship, and administration. This ranges from the provision and maintenance of the computing infrastructure to developing IT expertise throughout the community. The ITS Director reports to the Vice President, Operations and Finance.

Learning Technology and Multimedia Services (LTMS), a division of Information Technology Services, is a partnership of the former Information Technology Services, the Instructional Development Centre (IDC), and the Library. LTMS has three subdivisions, the Learning Technology Unit (LTU), which provides support to faculty; Video and Multimedia Presentations, which provides media production; and Classroom Presentation Technology, which maintains and supports smart classrooms and portable classroom technologies. The Learning Technology Unit focuses on assisting the development of educational computing applications for use in classrooms. The unit funds approximately four part-time, one-year positions for faculty to work with the LTU and the IDC in fostering critical and effective technology use.

IDC's mission is to support instructional development activities in support of quality student learning and to encourage university policy and practices that promote good teaching. IDC has developed partnerships with the Health Sciences department to help provide services in the Clinical Education Centre and has partnered with Engineering in their Integrated Learning Centre to provide discipline-related assistance for faculty development. The IDC Director reports to the Vice President, Academic.

University of Western Ontario

Many of UWO's services have been realigned under an umbrella organization, Information Technology Services (ITS). This unit includes computing infrastructure and network and systems services, and telecom, cabling, and digital infrastructure management. It also provides Web and instructional support for software applications through the Instructional Technology Resource Centre. This resource center, equipped with up-to-date multimedia hardware and software for the development of instructional materials, is for faculty who wish to integrate technology into their courses. It also supports faculty development of some selected multimedia and online projects. It is managed by an Advisory Board involving the Directors of the Libraries, the Educational Development

Office, the Centre for Continuing Studies, and ITS; the Coordinator of Summer and Distance Studies; and 12 faculty members representing each Faculty on campus.

The Teaching Support Centre, formerly the Educational Development Office, provides workshops and resources to assist faculty and support the improvement of teaching and adopts a leadership role in developing new teaching and learning initiatives. It works in partnership with the Library and ITS to provide instructional development to enhance the practice of teaching and learning, to support learning technologies and online course development, and to provide information literacy and research skill development. Its office is in the DB Weldon Library.

The university has recently developed a strategic plan on instructional technology that maintains the faculty-focused nature of ITRC while accepting the need for increased professional staff and financial resources.

University of British Columbia

One of the goals of the university's learning plan, UBC Trek 2000, was to fully integrate information technology with instruction in all areas. In 2001, UBC developed an e-learning strategy. An Executive Steering committee at the vice-presidential level was created to guide the overall direction, and the first of a series of annual town hall meetings was held to create awareness among the community. Specific initiatives included an e-learning infrastructure that was to be wireless by 2003, business processes redesign to increase efficiencies, university networking, and a one-stop portal to be developed by June 2002. People were to be supported through a variety of institution-wide and faculty-based support units. Each Faculty initiated an e-learning support unit to provide a combination of computing, media, and pedagogical support for faculty. In addition, Informational Technology Services (ITS) provided technology support to faculties, especially those without decentralized technology services.

At the institutional level, the Centre for Educational Technology was closed, and five years later (2002) the Office of Learning Technology (OLT) was created with a mandate to facilitate new and improved approaches to teaching and learning through use of technology and to promote UBC's role in this area within the postsecondary system provincially, nationally, and internationally. The Office sought to accomplish this mandate through collaborating on sponsoring workshops and lectures, facilitating discussions among various stakeholders, and coordinating cross-campus learning technology projects. Their partners were the faculty-based and centralized units that focused on enhancement of teaching and learning through technology. The other centralized units were the Centre for Teaching and Academic Growth (TAG) and the Distance Education and Technology unit (DET).

TAG became the central unit for the support of teaching and learning. It offered a wide range of programs from new faculty initiatives to mentoring programs and teaching programs targeted at graduate students. It also provided workshops and seminars for faculty on making appropriate decisions about technology integration in their teaching.

The Distance Education and Technology unit provided design and development support for Faculties offering distance education programs. In 2004, the unit was moved from Continuing Studies to join TAG and OLT in reporting to the Associate Vice President, Academic. A subsequent review (2004) decided to close DET and decentralize most of the distance education development and delivery support to the Faculties. In 2005, this decision was reversed and DET was merged with OLT.

In 2004, the university approved the creation of an Institute for the Scholarship of Teaching and Learning, which reports to the Associate Vice President, Academic. The University's latest strategic plan, Trek 2010 (2004), reconfirms its support for innovations and improvements in teaching through the application of leading-edge technology.

University of Alberta

In 1998 when the UA launched a pilot version of WebCT, faculty immediately expressed interest, and there was substantial grassroots support for the learning management system. The following year WebCT was adopted as the virtual learning environment platform for the university. Over the next two years faculty interest in the use of WebCT mushroomed, and in 2001, a WebCT client support unit was set up within Computing and Network Services to provide technical advice and training to instructors. The unit, called E-Learning Services, provided expertise and support for centrally supported teaching and learning technologies, professional development opportunities and training for faculty and staff, and course design development and support. With the increasing influence of WebCT, more on-campus instructors integrated Web-based elements into their teaching.

Hence by 2001, there were four units on campus associated with the enhancement of teaching through technology: Academic Technologies for Learning (ATL) focused on e-learning development, particularly for specific projects; E-Learning Services provided design and development consultation and technical support to faculty interested in adopting and using WebCT; the Technology Training Centre (under the Libraries Learning Systems umbrella) provided workshops on WebCT and software applications for interested faculty and staff; and University Teaching Services (UTS) focused on classroom instruction, although it too offered some workshops on technology integration.

Based on a series of reports concerned about rationalization of campus computing needs, a number of changes were made in 2005. In March, ATL was closed.
Academic Information and Communications Technology (AICT) replaced the
former Computing Network Services as an integrated service for campus
computing needs. E-Learning Services remained as part of its client support
services. University Teaching Services continued as an independent unit but with
closer ties to E-Learning Services. Also, as part of its preparation for a new
academic plan, the university undertook an e-learning planning exercise to
examine how e-learning technologies might be used to enhance the undergraduate learning experience and to strengthen the teaching-research continuum. The
draft report encouraged the development of local faculty units and proposed a
unit to integrate services and provide policy support and direction for e-learning.

McGill University

In 2004, the McGill University Centre for University Teaching and Learning
(CUTL) was closed and a new unit called Teaching and Learning Services
(TLS) took its place. The TLS mandate was to promote teaching and learning
initiatives, conduct research, and support the development of policies related to
teaching and learning enhancement, whether in classroom or technology-
mediated settings. As part of its work, TLS offered a wide range of professional
development opportunities and its course offerings included workshops on
course design and teaching with technology. It also continued to administer the
Teaching and Learning Improvement Fund, which provided $50,000 annually for
seed grants to encourage teaching and learning enhancement.

Effective October 2004, the Instructional Communications Centre was renamed
Instructional Multimedia Services. The unit continued to provide multimedia
design, development, and production services, including television production
and the loan and maintenance of audio-visual equipment.

Discussion

The integration of digital technologies occurs not only in response to changing
conditions; it is also driven by the vision of the institution. The six vignettes
provide indications of how the particular culture and vision of the various
institutions shaped and were shaped by the impact of the new digital technologies
and what structures were put in place as a result of these changes. These are
discussed in response to the research questions.

What structures were put in place? The most common structure was a central unit that coordinated the work of several service units. This was the case at UWO and Queen's, where the overarching orientation was technology integration in all aspects of the university. At UBC, services were provided through a variety of centralized and decentralized faculty-based units while strategy and policy related to e-learning, e-research, and connectivity were integrated under an Executive Steering Group and e-Strategy Advisory Council. At UA, a centralized unit to include both educational technology and faculty development was planned. At UT, while the Information Commons seemed to include all units, the Office of Learning Enhancement and the Resource Centre for Learning Technology were not listed on the Information Commons Web site but on the Library Web site, although they are located in the same building.

What was the focus of these units? Across the six sites, the range of services seems to indicate that while some universities still focused on technology applications, others offered programs that stressed the integration of technology in teaching. In some, the units with an emphasis on classroom instruction were separated from those focused on technology integration, suggesting that technology was either an add-on or an option. Where these units cooperated, one more often seemed to do introductory workshops to aid awareness while the other specialized in learning designs involving technology, raising the issue of different pedagogical approaches identified by Hughes et al. (1997).

How were they positioned with in the institutions? How did they link with other units? Most universities had a combination of centralized and decentralized units. In some cases, the decentralized units were highly specialized, discipline-specific centers providing student access to computer-mediated environments, while others were more focused on serving faculty (e.g., the Engineering and Clinical Education Centres at Queen's). The relationship of the central units with these centers also varied with some having a high degree of vertical integration (close links to the central unit in policy and practice) while others linked horizontally only (semi-autonomous units with no direct administrative link to the central unit). Yet even with these seeing similarities, the specific combinations of units under the central unit and the particular structural configurations used to link units together varied greatly among universities. While some were loosely coupled, others were more closely aligned within a tight reporting structure. Overall, there was a strong sense of fluidity about these arrangements that perhaps reflects our uncertainty about what technology integration will involve and how best to meet faculty needs.

How have they changed over time? The importance of e-learning in addressing pedagogical and organizational changes surrounding teaching has become clearer. Compared to their structures almost a decade earlier, by 2005 most of these universities had moved to greater coordination and integration of computing technologies with their audio-visual, multimedia, library, and teaching enhancement units. Their differences reflect the universities' changing responses to the following issues: the extent of centralization and the importance of decentralization, the value of coordination and the advantage of competition, the separation of teaching with technology from teaching and learning units and alternatively their integration in a single unit, and the values of top-down mandating and allowing a bottom-up development approach.

These issues are affected by the size, tradition, and culture of the institution; the increasing complexity of the academy; and the interests of the faculty. In any plan, concerns about educational quality, perceived and actual student demands for flexibility, tenure, and promotion criteria concerning teaching, the mix of online and blended learning, and their financial implications need to be addressed. However, the larger question concerns the goals of the institution. Is technology integration an end in itself, or is it part of a larger vision of student learning? How does that involve information resources? How might pedagogical structures be realigned to encourage technology-based initiatives designed to enhance student learning? Advancing these goals involves long-term change processes.

Recommendations

Based on the findings, institutions seeking technology integration in teaching and learning might consider the following points:

1. Universities that adopted digital technologies to bring efficiencies to university systems must now recognize their integral place in research and teaching. The place of digital technologies in the entire mission of the university needs to be clarified. Without such a vision, an organization will find it difficult to achieve such goals through incrementalism alone. Both top-down and bottom-up initiatives are required for sustained change (Newton, 2003).

2. Organizational structures provide a public mark of the relative importance given to technology within the university. Universities have moved to integration of services. However, practical integrated strategies that manage the tensions and disruptive interactions and exploit positive relationships are required (de Freitas & Oliver, 2005; Land, 2004; Newton, 2003). Faculty technology support and faculty development units need to work closely together to ensure that a range of pedagogical models and approaches, whether blended or entirely online, are supported.

3.   The mainstream adoption of digital technology in instruction will require sustained support if the benefits to be gained from digital technologies are to be achieved. Faculty readily recognizes how to use such technologies to obtain efficiencies in their teaching; what they need is to be introduced to the benefits of learner-centered pedagogical designs that are best supported by various technologies (Land, 2004). This aspect seemed to be missing from a number of the sites surveyed.

4.   These large universities seem to be moving to a combination of centralized and decentralized units. The advantages of such a move are that it recognizes the particular pedagogical approaches to disciplinary knowledge and also allows for the development of procedures and materials that are particularly appropriate to that area, while seeking economies and efficiencies through centralization of policies. The disadvantages were highlighted by Hughes et al. (1997).

5.   A panel on the impact of information technology on the future of the research university convened by the U.S. National Research Council (2002) concluded that "The extraordinary pace of information-technology evolution is likely not only to continue for the next several decades but could well accelerate" and that its impact will be "profound, rapid and discontinuous" (p. 2). They recommended that university strategies include "the development of sufficient in-house expertise among faculty and staff to track technological trends and assess various courses of action" (p. 3). Keeping track of technological trends would seem to be prudent in this climate.

6.   In an exploration of the extent to which e-learning policy drives organizational and pedagogic change, de Freitas and Oliver (2005) conclude that e-learning policy does drive change. They suggest the first impact of policy change is on organizational redevelopment, either through formal organizational restructuring or by negotiating changes in existing structures and roles. This organizational change is then followed by changes to teaching practice. This has been the situation at these universities.

7.   Resistance to change is inevitable, and it is essential that ample opportunities for collaboration and discussion are provided to facilitate the change process. Decisions on structures to provide faculty support, then, have to be related to the larger goals of the institution and talked through at multiple levels so that both horizontal and vertical integration may occur, for faculty, staff, students, and administrators have to come to acceptance and understanding of the change themselves through interaction and practice.

References

Bates, T. (1995, November). *The future of learning*. Paper presented at the Minister's Forum on Adult Learning, Edmonton, AB. Retrieved August 29, 2005, from http://bates.cstudies.ubc.ca/paper.html

Campbell, B., & Cuneo, C. (2001). *Technical support in Canadian post-secondary education*. Retrieved August 29, 2005, from http://www.siocom.com/campus-computing//General-Reports/techsupport_report.pdf

Cuneo, C., Archer, N., Baumann, A., Bryant-Lukosius, D., Dwyer, J., Elliott, S., et al. (1997). *Beehive: A proposal to establish a strategic research area in learning technologies at McMaster University*. Retrieved August 29, 2005, from http://socserv2.socsci.mcmaster.ca/soc/beehive/title.htm

de Freitas, S., & Oliver, M. (2005). Does e-learning policy drive change in higher education? A case study relating models of organizational change to e-learning implementation. *Journal of Higher Education Policy and Management, 27*(1), 81-95.

Hughes, C., Hewson, L., & Nightingale, P. (1997). Developing new roles and skills. In P. Yetton (Ed.), *Managing the introduction of technology in the delivery and administration of higher education* (Report 97/3). Canberra: Australian Government Publishing Service. Retrieved August 29, 2005, from http://www.dest.gov.au/archive/highered/eippubs/eip9703/chapter3.htm#head1

Land, R. (2004). *Educational development: Discourse, identity and practice*. New York: Open University Press/McGraw-Hill.

National Research Council Panel. (2002). *Preparing for the revolution. Information technology and the future of the research university*. Washington, DC: National Academies Press.

Newton, J. (2003). Implementing an institution-wide learning and teaching strategy: Lessons in managing change. *Studies in Higher Education, 28*(4), 427-441.

Chapter III

Moving to Blended Delivery in a Polytechnic:
Shifting the Mindset of Faculty and Institutions

Oriel Kelly, Manukau Institute of Technology, New Zealand

Abstract

What strategies and support are effective for shifting the mindset of expert teachers to become expert e-learning teachers? This chapter outlines the process followed in a large polytechnic institution to introduce online and other technologies to begin to replace the traditional with more flexible, blended alternatives, delivered through a commercial course management system (CMS). Integral to the process was a matrix, devised to assist the academic development unit when working with faculty to make decisions about the degree of e-learning appropriate for their purposes. The matrix has guided the incorporation of technologies for teaching across the whole institute. The chapter outlines the institutional support that was provided for the different levels on the matrix, which enabled expert teachers to retain control over a quality learning experience for their students, and briefly explores some of the issues that arose and lessons that were learned.

Introduction

The Manukau Institute of Technology focuses on vocational education and training, offering mainly certificate and diploma qualifications together with an increasing number of degree programs. In 2000, the Blackboard course management system was introduced at the Institute with the main goal of providing students with greater flexibility of time, place, and approach to learning. Unlike the models used by many other postsecondary institutions (Epper & Bates, 2001), the Institute chose to have the e-learning initiative (planning and supporting of learning by technologically supported means) driven from within the Centre for Educational Development (the academic staff development section of the Institute) rather than have it aligned with the Information Technology Services department or in a department of its own.

The Centre for Educational Development (CED) reports to the Executive Director Academic and includes a team who assists with curriculum design and assessment practices, research, and program review. The same section contains the educational resource production unit and is also responsible for delivering academic professional development across the Institute, which includes the compulsory qualification in tertiary teaching, which all academic staff take.

The integration of academic development with e-learning has meant there is one place for academics to go for support, and the use of learning technology is seen as a logical extension of the teaching repertoire. The integrated support model described functions well in a polytechnic environment. As it has proven cost effective, the centralization of e-learning support services in this way may have relevance for the wider tertiary environment, although this case study is limited to working within the governance model used in polytechnics.

Expert Teachers are Planners and Managers of Learning

Expert teachers are excellent managers of their classrooms. They understand the fundamentals of good curriculum design and can translate that into day-to-day learning outcomes for their diverse students. They understand student-centered teaching and learning—*placing learners at the heart of the learning process and meeting their needs (Edwards, 2001)*—and they have a range of strategies they can call upon to facilitate the learning process. They unconsciously alter their behavior in the classroom based on the feedback they are receiving during the teaching and learning process. With reflection, they can eloquently articulate what they are doing to a beginning teacher in the tertiary sector and pass on their good practice.

The philosophy underpinning this case study is that expert teachers are planners and organizers of interactive learning and facilitators of the ongoing process, rather than didactic transmitters of information. The move to some degree of e-learning may alter the way they carry out their role, but should not remove their control of their classroom or change how they manage the learning process and assist students to access, evaluate, and apply information.

If this is the case, why, then, are the reactions of expert teachers to the introduction of technology for teaching very similar to those of a room full of cats to a vacuum cleaner? There are those who high tail it out the cat door, and you never see them again. There are those who do not show such obvious fear, but who walk sedately away, with great dignity, muttering, "That is all very interesting but I really don't have time for that sort of thing." There are those who leap straight to the highest vantage point they can find and criticize loudly from their lofty position about how it is a dreadful thing and would never work for their subject area anyway. There are those who hunker down, shut their eyes, and pretend it isn't happening, because "It, too, shall pass." There are those who initially take refuge behind the nearest piece of furniture, but peer out, mildly interested. They can probably be enticed to play, once it is well established that it's safe to do so and that they will not be in great danger after all. And then there are those who come straight up—who want to play with it, embrace it, and are very willing to go along for the ride, wherever it takes them.

How then does an academic development unit support expert teachers with such diverse reactions to technology to shift their mindset and make the move to e-learning in order to better meet the learning needs of their students? This chapter outlines an approach, based on the use of a matrix illustrating points on the continuum of electronically mediated learning (Zemsky & Massey, 2004). It is aligned with an increasing scale of institutional support that has resulted, after five years, in almost all teachers at the Institute being able to make use of e-learning tools to some degree in their teaching.

The E-Learning Teacher

The qualities that make up an expert e-learning teacher are being established gradually. What seems clear, however, is that expert e-learning teachers are not there to impart knowledge, but to provide guidance and support for the learning process (Lai, 1999). They should organize, plan, establish, and maintain social relationships; provide intellectual stimulation; and encourage participation through the use of e-learning. The integration of technology should result in the redefinition of the teacher's role from that of an instructor to a facilitator or enabler. Other roles that have been suggested for e-learning teachers are process-facilitator, advisor-counselor, assessor, researcher, content facilitator, technologist, designer, manager-administrator, social director, program manager, and technical assistant (Goodyear, Salmon, Spector, Steeples, & Tickner, 2001; Tearle, Dillon, & Davis, 1999). It has been suggested that e-learning teachers move from confident, through constructive, to developmental, facilitating, and eventually to creative in their e-moderating (Salmon, 2000). However, an excellent e-learning teacher is first an excellent teacher who has acquired some technical skills to cope with the challenges of the environment and who is possessed of the resilience, innovativeness, and perseverance of a pioneer (Anderson, 2004).

Underpinning the discussion that follows is the understanding that new approaches to teaching (such as e-learning) must be properly integrated into the existing learning context if they are to be successful (Laurillard, 1993), and that there must be appropriate institutional support if faculty are expected to make the transition to e-learning successfully (Epper & Bates, 2001). The kinds of support that were found to be successful for this initiative were many and varied and encompassed personal as well as infrastructure support. Lai (1999) confirms that professional development for teachers must be aimed at the appropriate stage the teacher is at, so that it scaffolds on and extends their skill base. In this case study, there were many possible starting points, and faculty moved at differing rates toward becoming e-learning teachers at various points on the continuum.

The eMatrix

In 2002, the eMatrix (Figure 1) was designed to assist the Institute's academic development section to work with faculty to make decisions about the degree of e-learning that would suit the delivery of their courses. It considers aspects of communication with students, including lecturer-student and student-student interaction processes; access to materials; methods of handling assessments and assignments; and the type of class contact—all from the lecturer point of view. From an infrastructure and support point of view, it considers the level of access to computers required to meet learning outcomes, the requirements of learning re-design, the degree of faculty support and training necessary, and the departmental administrative support that would be required.

Level One, on the far left of the eMatrix (mainly ones and twos), describes fairly traditional face-to-face delivery scenarios. Level Three, on the far right (mostly fives), describes totally online delivery scenarios. It is possible to be at any point in between the extremes and with varying degrees of blend (Level Two), depending on where faculty members are starting from and how far they want to, or can be supported to, move.

Figure 1.

Degree of blended/distributed course delivery

Least ⟶ Most

	1	2	3	4	5
Announcements for Students	Notices put up in traditional ways.	Moderate CMS announcement and e-mail use.	CMS announcements and e-mail used extensively to communicate with students regularly.		CMS announcements and e-mail are the only way to communicate with students.
Access to Teaching and Learning Materials	No resources on CMS or Web.	Some material available on CMS or Web **and** in class: lecture notes, overheads, copies of handouts etc.	Most teaching materials are available on CMS, Web sites and digital resources are linked for teaching purposes.	Material for teaching is mainly on CMS/Web as course is predominantly taught this way.	Material for teaching is designed and developed for the electronic environment.
Lecturer/Student Interaction	Traditional face to face methods only.	Some use made of e-mail for student/lecturer contact.	Electronic communication is an important aspect of student/lecturer interaction.	Electronic communication is beginning to replace face to face communication, using forums etc.	Almost exclusive use of online communication, e-mail, chat, discussion forums.
Student to Student Interaction	Traditional tutorial, or group work in class.	Students use e-mail to communicate.	Forums are set up for FAQ's, whole class debates, small group work, interacting with online guests in addition to class time.	Online interaction is beginning to replace timetabled face to face interaction.	Planned student interaction for problem solving, completing collaborative assignments is online.
Assignments and Assessment	Assignments are accepted in hard copy only.	Students may e-mail assignments to lecturers and access grades online.	Students are encouraged to submit assignments electronically, online, assessments are available.	Use is made of the online assessments in the CMS for formative and summative purposes.	All assessment and result information is via electronic means.
Contact **Figure shows % of total contact deemed to be eContact** 0%	Contact can be estimated in the traditional way. 0%	Some lecturer time is devoted to using CMS, e-learning. 25%	There is a mix of face to face and "eContact." 50%	Lecturers spend extensive contact time e-moderating online groups and communication. 75%	Lecturers have minimal face to face contact, most contact is via the online medium. 100%
Access to Computers to Meet Learning Outcomes	No access required.	On campus access only required.	Some off and on campus access required.	More off than on campus access required.	Off campus access mandatory.
Learning Design	Traditional learning design.	Little change to learning design required to accommodate CMS features.	Some change to learning design required to integrate CMS /multimedia features effectively.	Extensive redesign needed for integrated and appropriate use of CMS/Web/multimedia features.	Full instructional/learning design required for fully online courses.
Support and Training	No special support and training.	Baseline CMS/Web skill support and training expected for staff and students.	Moderate support and training in CMS features and e-learning teaching needed.	Extensive training and support required for effective e-learning teaching.	Individualised training and support required.
Departmental Administrative Support	No additional admin support required.	Departmental admin support for establishing online filing cabinet courses expected.	Departmental admin support required for setting up courses, supporting student access and learning.	Registry informed that course has substantial e-learning component.	Admin support required to support off campus learning and teaching.
Outcomes:	Level One Mostly 1- 2 Requires Level One CMS/ Web use training to be completed. Departmental strategy specifies look and feel, use of CMS in programme for consistency.		Level Two Mostly 3-4 Requires Level Two CMS/Web training. Signed Departmental approval of level of e-learning in course and programme. Change of delivery mode noted.		Level Three Mostly 5 Signed institute approval in principle for the re/development and mode of delivery change. Further, formal staff development in e-learning teaching required.

The discussion that follows focuses on Level One, where there is still a greater proportion of face-to-face teaching planned, and Level Two, where online teaching is beginning to replace face-to-face in increasing proportions. Level Three developments, where the teaching is conducted completely online, are in the early stages. The only program at the Institute taught completely through the CMS is a qualification about teaching online.

At an overarching departmental level, decision making on the degree of blend (the position on the continuum for Level Two) took into account the subject matter and level of the material, the target market, and the strategic opportunity of moving to a more flexible delivery model. The degree of blend overall had to ensure a consistent experience for students over the whole program. There was also the factor of the extent to which resources were available to teaching departments over and above the centralized assistance that could be allocated to the redevelopment, the staff up-skilling, and to any additional administrative processes that would be necessary. Institutional policies and procedures in relation to delivery through e-learning have subsequently tended to evolve from developing departmental practice rather than from policy directives from management.

Level One

A Level One outcome on the eMatrix describes what has become known at the Institute as the Online Filing Cabinet (OLFC). It can also be thought of as informational (course documents available online), supplemental (some course content provided via the Web) (Harmon and Jones, 2000), or naïve, and attempts should be made as soon as possible to move on through the next three levels of this model—standard, evolutionary, and radical—in order to actively utilize the advantages of the technology to maximize the interaction between students (student-student) and teaching staff (student-lecturer) (Roberts, 2002).

However, the Online Filing Cabinet is at least a starting point for faculty to begin the change process, and it assists them to learn the basics of using a CMS to support their teaching. They also begin to see the possibilities of using the Web in their teaching. The OLFC is extremely popular with students as a base of service and provides more flexible access for both full and part timers who have all the usual pressures on their time and as a result, are not necessarily able to attend every session. In 2002, the in-house research conducted on CMS use found that the majority of students (60%) reported that they mostly used it on campus, 36% in class time, 24% out of class time. The OLFC contributes to improving student retention and success. Students reported they found the approach helped them meet their learning goals and would prefer all courses to provide at least this much.

A typical Level One example would now have the following available on the Web:

- Weekly announcements.

- The course timetable with key events highlighted, maybe linked to the calendar.

- Copies of the assessments/assignments for the course, maybe an exemplar or two, certainly the marking schedules.

- The program handbook in PDF, containing all important information about the processes and regulations.

- Static course materials arranged logically—probably copies of the lecture slides for each session, handouts, links to recommended Web sites, and further readings if available. These are often built up as the course progresses.

- A glossary of common terms.

- FAQ discussion set up for assignments or other issues.

- Maybe access to grades.

- E-mail used for communication.

- Assignment submission and collection via dropbox or e-mail.

OLFCs are now common in all departments across the Institute. Even those faculty members whose initial reaction was to avoid e-learning in any form have been coaxed into participating at least at the naïve level.

Level One is implemented with little disruption to normal teaching and learning. Most of the active or interactive learning still occurs in the face-to-face sessions. OLFCs supplement the teaching but do not replace it. For consistency in student experience, faculty collectively decided on the look and feel for their set of courses across the department. They decided on aspects to be used as standard in all courses in their programs: menu items, consistent navigation, and information. This standardization allowed faculty, like their students, to operate in a structured, familiar environment. Students receive an IT induction from their lecturer that introduces them to the resources being made available and how their lecturer will be using them. Administration staff set up the courses and may load any common documents.

Institutional Support for Level One

Faculty members receive baseline training in operating the CMS so that they can build, maintain, and change the OLFC themselves. The Level One training is organized at scheduled times and on demand through the Centre for Educational Development section. It takes the form of formal classes, informal group sessions, and one-on-one sessions, depending on where the faculty member is at in terms of IT competence. Follow up is in the form of telephone support or individual mentoring—some faculty need relatively little hand holding, others only become comfortable after sustained encouragement. In each department, there were those who lead the charge. Rogers (1995) in his diffusion of innovations theory suggested that innovators and early adopters take up technologies relatively quickly. These folk, fostered by CED, have now become in-house departmental experts and provide advice in addition to the centralized support. Later adopters (Rogers' later majority who make up about 34% of any given group) are put in touch with those in their subject area who are further along the continuum so that they can support each other. The objective is to give faculty the confidence and skills to do it for themselves. They are in control of their face-to-face classroom; they should be able to manage their e-learning classroom just as well.

No special recognition is given to staff for setting up and maintaining an OLFC, although it can be used as an item for consideration for the career progression process. The workload is now regarded as part of normal class preparation and maintenance. The Institute has given all students free e-mail and Internet access and provided computer labs and an Information Commons in the Library so that on-campus access is relatively easy. The Student Learning Centre has also provided extensive generic resources on their own CMS site, which is available 24/7. Introduction to this site forms part of the regular student IT induction, which is run by departments with the assistance of the staff IT trainer as required.

Level Two

More sophisticated skills are required for faculty to embark on Level Two of the matrix. Level 2 describes scenarios where face-to-face sessions are being replaced by e-learning and where true blended or distributed delivery appears. On Harmon and Jones' (2000) model, the developments correspond to essential (the Web must be used to succeed) and communal (both face-to-face and online are in use).

The degree of effort required for a Level Two development has to be justified to faculty members by more than just student convenience. Time has to be spent on the why: Faculty must see credible evidence of how the integration of e-learning can enhance learning outcomes for students, examples of good practice, and models to enable professional judgments to be made on how to best use e-learning for their subject. These discussions are also the time to explore faculty beliefs about teaching and learning.

As far as the CMS features are concerned, an example of Level Two would contain the aspects of Level One, with perhaps the following extras:

- Online assessments for both formative and summative purposes.

- Some grouped resources designed to be accessed in outside class mode with readings, activities, and discussions, compiled with guidance on access and use.

- Extensive use of virtual interactions—discussions, possibly chat sessions, group work.

- Small group tasks to be completed via swapping of files, discussion, chat.

- Quizzes, crosswords, jigsaws, animations, or other constructed learning objects to support and progress the learning process at appropriate points.

Institutional Support for Level Two

The additional CMS skills required for Level Two are minor. Level Two classes and one-on-one sessions are arranged to cover the extra features that the staff member has not used before. Most of the discussion with faculty around the eMatrix at Level Two usually focuses on the two key aspects of learning design and the integration of appropriate and varied interactions with the change to a blended delivery mode.

Learning Design

With the introduction of Level Two development, the learning designer provides support by exploring the course aims with the lecturer and giving advice on the suitability of the range of options available that will still achieve the desired outcomes. The designer also assists with decisions on what needs to be face-to-face and what could be done more effectively in Web-facilitated mode. Some assessments may well need redesigning to ensure continued validity and authenticity in a blended environment. Expert teachers may already be student-centered learning focused or constructivist, but their experience is live classroom based. They need ideas and support to organize collaborative learning for their students that continues outside their classroom and is scheduled at appropriate intervals. They also need to be introduced to the skills required to monitor the learning virtually. The learning designer has the understanding of the likely effects of the various CMS features and e-learning strategies and can show examples and make suggestions, but the teacher has to make the decisions as to which would assist them to teach their subject. Teachers have to feel comfortable (or at least not too uncomfortable) with the degree to which they adopt new strategies, including possibly, the use of sophisticated learning objects that they could design, but which they do not have the skills to actually produce themselves.

Most teaching professionals have mastered the art of creating resources for teaching in the face-to-face mode, but how many IT skills should the e-learning teacher have in order to retain control over the teaching and learning process in a more technology rich environment? Faculty argue that they are not supposed to be experts in software. They don't want or need to know how to create a flash animation—which is true. So where is the line to be drawn? What e-learning teachers do need to be helped to know is how to recognize when technology could be used to get a concept across better than any explanation they could give in person and what that learning object might look. And they need to know how to get the idea out of their head and into a format that the graphic and software experts can use to create it for them. Having to get a group involved in teaching resource production takes more time and organization than the expert teacher is generally aware of if they are used to preparing their own resources. This is an area prone to frustrations on all sides.

Integration of Interaction

At Level Two, student-to-content, student-to-student, and lecturer-to-student interactions will now move more toward CMS-supported features. Interactivity is a multifaceted concept and understanding it is critical to the success of online learning. It can be viewed from the designer's point of view in terms of proactive and reactive inquiry and proactive and mutual elaboration, which are built into the learner-content interactivity. It is also important to consider the kind of scaffolding that can be built in as a guide for learners: conceptual (what to consider), meta-cognitive (how to think about the topic), procedural (how to use the information), and strategic (how to analyze and strategize) (Muirhead & Juwah, 2003).

Student-to-student interactions need to be built in as part of the learning design. The five-step scale devised by Salmon (2000) is another useful scaffold for planning increasingly sophisticated activities (from accessing, to socialization, information exchange, knowledge construction, and development) to the stage dictated by the subject matter and the level of the course.

The art of establishing the appropriate presence in the online environment is something explored by Garrison and Anderson (2003) to support a community of inquiry and not stifle critical reflection and interaction by students. The learning designer can describe the interaction and their effects, but the most successful strategy is to have the beginning e-learning teacher experience them for him or herself.

Informal and Formal Professional Development for Level Two

The principles can be explored in theory, but the practice is best learned by actual participation. Level Two training for the Institute therefore includes an opportunity for faculty to be involved in different kinds of virtual interactions with other staff, both as a student and as a facilitator/moderator, building on what they already know. This strategy of an institution-wide approach was also found effective in the study by Wilson and Stacey (2004), who presented evidence for the need for interaction in online teaching to enable teachers to become confident and competent. Therefore, after viewing examples from archives, faculty at the Institute participate in a series of discussions held over a week or two. These discussions rapidly move through Salmon's (2000) stages to give faculty a feel for the challenges of the virtual environment.

Having faculty initially placed in the position of students is also a method of sharing the Institute's best practice across faculty boundaries. Enrolling them all in a professional development focused CMS course provides a place to showcase examples from every discipline, share expertise, facilitate mentoring, and even advertise appropriate conferences on e-learning.

In addition, the formal baseline lecturer training qualification now has a portion of its courses moved into blended mode, so new-to-teaching faculty are exposed to the different delivery method as part of their learning. This way they are immediately applying their new skills to their own learning, while focusing on teaching and learning issues, rather than on the technology.

Informal professional development also occurs through a series of show-and-tell sessions over lunch, which have proved popular, and through the in-house publication about e-learning initiatives, which includes contributions from across the Institute.

Institutional Issues for Level Two and Beyond

Considerable centralized resources need to be channeled into supporting staff through what is essentially a change process. Providing a "one stop shop" has been effective in this case study. Having teaching and curriculum design advice, assessment design advice, e-learning skill support, and resource production, which could be enhanced as needs got more sophisticated, together in the Centre for Educational Development has proved a sound investment. Rewarding those who do make the shift through career path advancement and teaching excellence awards proves there is something in it for faculty.

The recognition that quality e-learning teaching is as, if not more, contact intensive for the lecturer as managing a face-to-face class needs to be established early. Workload policies are usually based on traditional contact hours. The contact involved in e-learning is less tangible and unless strict office hours are established, often happens outside of normal academic parameters. Interaction and feedback make for a quality learning experience, but take as much if not more time (especially when faculty are still mastering their new skills) than traditional teaching.

Time allowances for re-training of e-learning teachers are also necessary. Expert teachers do not revert to novices with the introduction of student-centered, technology-supported teaching, but they do move back some distance from their established position because of the change in role—a role in which they need to build up expertise. Time given for the establishment of e-learning teaching skills can be recouped later when they become the mentors for other beginning e-learning teachers. This institution has not used the formal, contestable project format, funding the fortunate few, preferring instead to foster Level Two innovation more widely. The result has been a more disseminated development across the whole institute.

Part of providing an environment of support for e-learning is the establishment of an IT infrastructure that makes teaching with the aid of technology a painless and simple extension of normal practice. Only early adopters will put up with major inconvenience; the rest have their confidence shattered by even minor glitches and complicated workarounds. The e-learning classroom has to be comfortable and consistent. The e-learning team has to be involved in high level IT strategy and planning decisions to ensure the teaching and learning environment remains comfortable for the users and integrates associated services—the library, a student management system, the portal development, a content management system—at the same rate as demand for blended delivery advances.

Basic IT skill training that is varied and suited to the diverse needs of both students and faculty needs to be organized and supported at the institute level. This institute employs a staff IT trainer who ensures all new staff have an IT induction on commencement of work. She offers scheduled classes on aspects of commonly used software, phone assistance supported by desktop shadowing capability, and one-on-one sessions when required, as well as producing user friendly documentation that builds up into an IT manual. She is also available to assist staff with student IT inductions. The CED section has promoted a template for blended delivery student handbooks/learning guides that contains up-to-date "getting started" IT information about logging on, accessing mail, CMS basics, and accessing the virtual library, as well as standardized formats to enable departmental and program specific information to be added before distribution to students.

What is being provided for newly experienced e-learning teachers to further extend their skill base and provide a theoretical platform from which to debate the issues? A development that complemented this case study was the recent introduction of a graduate qualification in applied e-learning for tertiary teachers. Taught completely online, it not only provides experiential learning for teaching professionals, it also gives them the opportunity to interact with other early adopters both within and outside the Institute. The formally assessed 600-hour program culminates in an applied project that is designed, implemented, and evaluated.

Conclusion

Although it is difficult, shifting the mindset of academics to adopt sound teaching strategies for e-learning is certainly possible, as long as they are given the resources and support to see the possibilities and are convinced of the benefits for their learners. E-learning teachers need to be given the skills to remain in control of their classrooms. These skills include the ability to plan for and manage quality educational experiences that are as student-centered and interactive for their learners in the online aspects of their classrooms as they are in the face-to-face environment. They include the ability to know when and how to brief other experts to construct the resources they want to use as teachers in the technologically supported environment. And they include the confidence to be a guiding presence in the virtual environment, so that their students achieve the planned goals.

The impact of e-learning on education will go further and deeper than simply providing access to information. It will build on its communicative and interactive features to make learning more interactive, learner-centered, and meaningful (Garrison & Anderson, 2003). One of the Institute's faculty members said recently "Computers are a tool to get closer to our students, not further away." Proof that an e-learning teacher has indeed been created? Shift the mindsets of academics and you shift the mindsets of organizations.

References

Anderson, T. (2004). Teaching in an online learning context. In T. Anderson & F. Elloumi (Eds.), *Theory and practice of online learning* (pp. 273- 294). Canada: Athabasca University.

Edwards, R. (2001). Meeting individual learner needs: Power, subject, subjection. In C. Paechter, M. Preedy, D. Scott, & J. Soler (Eds.), *Knowledge, power, and learning*. London: Sage.

Epper, R. M., & Bates, A. W. (2001). *Teaching faculty how to use technology: Best practices from leading institutions*. Westport, CT: American Council on Education/Oryx Press.

Garrison, D. R., & Anderson, T. (2003). *E-learning in the 21ˢᵗ Century*. London: Routledge.

Goodyear, P., Salmon, G., Spector, J. M., Steeples, C., & Tickner, S. (2001). Competencies for online teaching: A special report. *Educational Technology Research and Development, 49*(1), 65-72.

Harmon, S., & Jones, M. (2000). The five levels of Web use in education: Factors to consider in planning online courses. *Educational Technology, 39*(2), 29-32.

Lai, K. W. (1999). Designing Web-based learning environments. In K. W. Lai (Ed.), *Net-working: Teaching, learning, and professional development* (pp. 123-141). Dunedin: University of Otago Press.

Laurillard, D. (1993). *Rethinking university teaching: A framework for the effective use of educational technology*. London: Routledge.

Muirhead, B., & Juwah, C. (2003). *Interactivity in computer-mediated college and university education: A recent review of the literature.* DEANZ electronic discussion paper. Retrieved July1, 2005, from http://deanz-discuss.massey.ac.nz/muirhead_november2003.html

Roberts, T. M. (2002). *Learner interaction and current practice in asynchronous delivery*. Retrieved July 1, 2005, from http://www.aset.org.au/confs/2002/roberts-t.html

Rogers, E. M. (1995). *Diffusion of innovations* (4ᵗʰ ed.). New York: The Free Press.

Salmon, G. (2000). *E-moderating the key to teaching and learning online*. London: Kogan Page.

Tearle, P., Dillon, P., & Davis, N. (1999). Use of information technology by English university teachers. Developments and trends at the time of the National Inquiry into Higher Education. *Journal of Further and Higher Education, 23*(1), 5-15.

Wilson, G., & Stacey, E. (2004). Online interaction impacts on learning: Teaching the teachers to teach online. *Australasian Journal of Educational Technology, 20*(1) 33-48.

Zemsky, R., & Massy, W. F. (2004). *Thwarted innovation: What happened to e-learning and why*. The Learning Alliance. Retrieved June 2, 2005, from http://www.irhe.upenn.edu/WeatherStation.html

Chapter IV

Strategic Planning for E-Learning in a Polytechnic

Tony Bates, Tony Bates Associates, Ltd., Canada

Abstract

This chapter is a case study of how a polytechnic developed a strategic plan for e-learning. It describes the institution's rationale for moving more strongly into e-learning, the processes followed by the institution to develop a plan and ensure its acceptance through the institutional community, and the factors that facilitated the process. It indicates that attention to objectives, core values and principles, and faculty development and training, are critical for the successful transition from mainly face-to-face teaching to e-learning. The development of key performance indicators will allow the success of the plan to be measured in 2010.

Introduction

In many institutions, the introduction of e-learning follows a fairly standard pattern. Five distinct stages can be observed:

- **Stage 1 – "Lone Rangers" (Bates, 2000):** These are the early adopters. E-learning is introduced through the initiative of individual faculty members or instructors, often with no immediate or direct support from the institution.
- **Stage 2 – Encouragement:** The activities of the early adopters attract the attention of senior administrators, who try to support them with small grants or a slightly reduced teaching load.
- **Stage 3 – Chaos:** After a period of time, a growing number of instructors embrace e-learning, but the administration starts to get worried about quality, duplication of effort, lack of technical standards, such as the need to support different course development platforms, and above all, the costs of scaling up to large numbers of classes and instructors.
- **Stage 4 – Planning:** The senior administration realizes that priorities need to be set, common technical standards established, technical and design support and training for faculty or instructors developed, and cost-effective ways of developing e-learning established so that budget and instructor workload can be controlled.
- **Stage 5 – Sustainability:** The institution has established a stable system of e-learning that is cost effective and scalable. Few institutions to date have reached this stage.

This chapter is about the fourth stage, how one institution developed a compre-hensive, formal strategic plan for e-learning. Stockley (2004) notes that there are many examples of how an institution should develop a strategic plan for integrating educational technology (e.g., Benjamin, Carroll, Jacobi, Krop, & Shires, 1993; Bruce, 1999; Dill, 1996; Ford, 1996) but few of how a strategic plan for e-learning has actually been developed and implemented in a particular institution. This chapter provides a case study of such a process. Although each institution is unique, this case incorporates planning processes and strategies that could be applied to a wide variety of postsecondary institutions.

The Institution and Its Context

The Southern Alberta Institute of Technology (SAIT) Polytechnic is a public two-year, campus-based postsecondary technical institution focused on business, computer technology, health and safety, and trades and vocational training. It is located in Calgary, Alberta. In 2004, SAIT provided courses and programs to approximately 66,000 learners, of which just fewer than 12,000 were full-time, on-campus students. Its total annual budget is in the order of C$200 million.

SAIT first introduced e-learning in 1997 in the form of laptop programs. Laptop programs have been running continuously since. Four of the seven academic departments (Information and Communications Technology, Transportation, Business and Tourism, and Construction) had laptop programs in 2005, representing 26% of the institution's full-time learners.

However, not all programs in these departments required students to have a computer. Students in most other departments at SAIT were not required to use computers in their studies. More recently, a consortium of colleges lead by SAIT and supported by the province of Alberta established a province-wide portal for online learning, called eCampus Alberta, through which all existing online courses from each college could be accessed and taken for credit by any student registered at another college. However, SAIT's laptop programs were not fully online and could not be moved into eCampus Alberta. Lastly, one whole degree program (geographical information systems) was made available fully online. However, the total number of online courses was relatively small, at 42, with just over 1,000 course enrolments, or less than 100 full-time equivalent registrations.

The situation with regard to learning management software was also complex, with departments and programs using different systems. A committee established by the vice president academic recommended that SAIT standardize on WebCT, and the deans' council then requested that all program areas develop at least one fully online course. There was some resistance from instructors to this request.

SAIT's executive management committee's aim is to establish SAIT as Canada's premier polytechnic. They decided that e-learning was one strategy that would move them toward their overall vision for the Institute. SAIT set up an endowed chair in e-learning, partly funded by Cisco Systems Inc., and the chair on appointment was given responsibility for developing a strategic plan for e-learning.

Lastly, the political and economic situation in the province of Alberta was somewhat unusual. Alberta is an oil and gas producing province. The provincial government has eliminated all government debt, and in 2005 it had a budget surplus of almost $7 billion. At the same time, there were (and are) major skills shortages in the province, and the government planned to increase access to advanced education throughout the province by adding another 60,000 seats in the postsecondary sector between 2005 and 2010.

The Planning Process

Detailed work on a strategic plan for e-learning began in September 2004. The vice president academic set up a strategy development committee for e-learning to assist with the planning process. This 10 person committee, chaired by the chair in e-learning, aimed to represent all the key internal stakeholders likely to be affected by e-learning, while keeping the committee to a manageable size. The strategy development committee provided advice and approved the process and recommendations that were developed for the strategic plan.

Between September 2004 and January 2005, the Cisco chair in e-learning assessed the current status of SAIT's e-learning development, delivery, and evaluation strategy. To do this he met individually with all deans; observed laptop classes; held meetings with each academic department involving over 200 instructors; and met with over 60 students, the faculty association executive, and directors of support departments such as the library, IT services, and customer services. He also reviewed all relevant documentation such as the institution's academic and strategic plans.

In particular, the chair in e-learning worked with each of the academic departments to help them develop a concrete vision of how they would like to be teaching in five years time and where e-learning would fit within that vision. These departmental meetings with instructors were crucial for identifying issues that needed to be addressed in the plan.

The full plan contained 82 recommendations, including a strategy for implementation, under the responsibility of a newly appointed associate vice president, academic development. The plan was approved in principle, subject to affordability, by the deans' council and the executive management committee and went to the board for approval in principle in January 2006.

Preparatory Steps in Developing the Plan

Before the plan was developed, five critical steps were taken, all in parallel.

Definition of E-Learning

In 2004, there were at least eight different terms being used to describe teaching with computers at SAIT. Sometimes different terms were used to describe the same activity in different departments; other times the same term was used to describe quite different activities.

The chair in e-learning started with the OECD definitions of e-learning (OECD, 2005):

- None or trivial online presence.
- Web supplemented.
- Web dependent, but without significant reduction in classroom time
- Mixed mode—students' online activities *replace* part of face-to-face teaching/learning, but significant campus attendance remains
- Fully online

Interestingly, the OECD classification did not include laptop programs. To complicate matters, SAIT's Centre for Instructional Technology and Development had a five-category taxonomy related to different types of use of WebCT. These can be summarized as follows:

- **WBT1:** Static administrative site
- **WBT2:** Student tests
- **WBT3A:** Laptop programs and supplementary "static" course resources and testing
- **WBT3B:** Essential use of WebCT—course resources and discussion forums
- **WBT3C:** Virtual course—all materials online (these would include all eCampus Alberta courses)

Figure 1. Revised OECD definition of e-learning

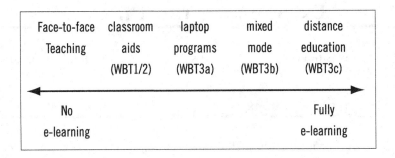

Thus the OECD definition was broadened as shown in Figure 1.

Conceptually, then, e-learning was considered as a continuum, reflecting increased flexibility for learners, from no e-learning to fully online e-learning. This led to the following definition of e-learning at SAIT, which was agreed to by EMC:

All those computer and Internet-based activities that directly or indirectly support teaching and learning at SAIT, both on campus and at a distance.

This broad definition recognizes the dependency of e-learning on other computer-based services, such as information systems, customer services, and the library.

Situational Analysis

The situational analysis looked at strengths/opportunities and weaknesses/threats (a modified SWOT analysis) under the following headings: planning, students, employers, programs, instructors, support services. (Funding is a heading that could have been added, but it was not seen to be an issue at this stage, given that there was an expectation that additional resources would be needed and available.)

The situational analysis identified that there was strong support for e-learning from some employers, from most deans and directors, and from many students. Instructors were more cautious. Although few objected to e-learning in principle, many wanted to be sure that resources and time would be made available to enable good quality e-learning to be developed. A minority believed that for their subject area, e-learning had limited potential. Although the laptop programs were generally judged to be successful by employers, students, and faculty, laptop programs required regular class attendance and therefore did not provide the flexibility of other forms of e-learning. In particular, laptop programs did not provide the flexible access needed by learners in the workforce. Therefore, despite the success of the laptop program, good technology infrastructure, and skilled staff to support e-learning, SAIT was judged to be several years behind the lead institutions in the polytechnic sector with respect to e-learning.

Rationale for E-Learning

The mandate to develop a plan for e-learning came from the executive management committee, but no formal rationale for e-learning had been codified. A detailed rationale for the use of e-learning was developed by the chair; discussed, modified, and approved by the strategy development committee for e-learning; and signed off by EMC.

The following reasons for moving more strongly into e-learning were identified:

- To meet the flexible needs of today's students
- To increase access to SAIT's programming
- To enhance teaching and learning
- To better prepare students for the requirements of business and industry
- To develop independent learning skills through exposure to online programming
- To better accommodate the differing learning styles of SAIT's students

The plan was to provide a means by which SAIT could meet increased market demand, particularly for workplace training, and increase overall student numbers, without the full cost of additional physical facilities. In particular, the plan should enable SAIT to produce graduates with the vocational and trade skills needed in an information-based economy.

Core Values and Principles

Discussion with instructors at the academic department meetings indicated the need for a set of core values and principles for the development of e-learning if any plan was to receive their support. There was understandable concern, for instance, that e-learning would increase instructors' workloads, that it would be used to replace instructors, or that it would be imposed from the top with a one-size-fits-all approach.

The following are examples of the 15 core values and principles taken to EMC and agreed to:

- E-learning will be used only where there are clearly identified benefits (educational, financial, strategic positioning, etc.).

- Decisions about appropriate use of e-learning is an academic decision to be made at departmental level, but based on knowledge and understanding of the strengths and limitations of e-learning.

- E-learning is not being used to replace instructors but to strengthen their role in teaching and learning.

- Increase in workload for instructors and students is to be avoided by following best practices in e-learning, which includes team work, quality assurance processes, new approaches to teaching and learning, organiza-tional change, and project management.

- Instructors will have adequate time and resources for training in the use of e-learning.

- E-learning materials and programs will be developed in a cost-effective manner, although costs will vary depending on the market and the require-ments of the subject matter.

The agreement to these core values and principles was a very important part of the planning process. They enabled points of conflict that had been identified to be addressed before detailed planning began. They provided a context and framework to guide decision making and recommendations and a means of evaluating proposals in the plan. More importantly, they enabled trust to be built with all the key stakeholders.

Vision for E-Learning

A vision statement for e-learning was developed after extensive consultation within the institution and was approved by the EMC.

At the *institutional* level: SAIT will be an international leader in e-learning development and delivery in the post-secondary sector, with a special emphasis on the appropriate and cost-effective use of e-learning for the development of workforce skills in a variety of trades and professions; all SAIT students will graduate with the information technology skills required in their area of specialty.

At the *academic department* level: Each program in each academic department will develop, for approval by the Dean and VP Academic, a vision for teaching and learning, and within this broader vision for teaching and learning, a vision or plan for the role of e-learning within each program. The vision will be reviewed and amended at least every three years.

At the *administrative* level: Students will be able to access all student services through the Web. All departmental information will be Web-based and accessible to the public, as far as privacy and security allow.

Once these preparatory steps were completed, the development of the plan became greatly facilitated.

Academic Issues

The Design of Teaching

E-learning should not be approached as a *technical* solution but as a *learning/business* solution. It is more likely to be successfully implemented if it is seen as part of a broader strategy of institutional renewal and innovation (Bloom, 2004). Although traditional methods of teaching can be transferred to teaching by computer (as in laptop programs), and e-learning can supplement regular face-to-face teaching, the unique strength of e-learning is the flexibility and control it can provide to learners, built around the ability of instructors and students to access the learning materials and processes at any time and any place. However, for flexible learning, designs for teaching are required that are entirely different from the classroom model. E-learning not only requires decisions about the place and time of delivery of programs, but also the type of teaching and learning that should be adopted. Instructors above all need to understand fully the different options available to them and to keep abreast of the changing needs of employers.

Thus e-learning requires a rethinking of the curriculum and how best it can be taught. The plan therefore recommended that *the move to e-learning should be combined with the adoption of new methods of teaching and learning that reflect the needs of a workforce in an information-based society.* This was probably the most important strategic decision that SAIT had to make with regard to e-learning.

Planning for E-Learning in Academic Departments

Apart from laptop programs, most departments had no overall plan for e-learning. E-learning is a tool; therefore, planning for e-learning needs to be integrated within an academic department's overall strategy for teaching and learning. The plan recommended that each department should annually produce a three-year plan for teaching and learning that specifies not only what courses and programs it wishes to offer, but how these programs will be taught and the numbers and types of students it is targeting. This plan would include proposals for e-learning. It would be linked to the budget process and would be the main factor determining allocation of resources to the department for the next fiscal year.

The plan set a target for the development of 450 new courses over five years in either a mixed-mode or fully online format, or roughly 10-15 new courses a year in each department. Laptop programs would continue, but would be modified over time to provide more flexible access. Mixed-mode or fully online programs were to be supported by business plans that identified the rationale for e-learning; the intended market; learning objectives (skills and content); the method of teaching; the costs of developing, delivering and maintaining the course or program; and the likely amount and type of revenue to be generated by the planned course or program. E-learning projects would be developed through a project team involving faculty, instructional designers, Web programmers, and other appropriate support staff.

Academic departments should have a plan to move students from being dependent to independent learners through a gradual increase in e-learning and the deliberate use of teaching strategies to develop independent learning skills. The knowledge of how and when to replace hands-on activity with virtual learning through simulations and other techniques should be seen as a core area of expertise for SAIT. Corporate Training would have a key role to play in developing or brokering e-learning for workforce training and therefore should develop a strategic plan for its activities in e-learning.

Thus, academic departments would have a good degree of autonomy within general directions set by the vice-president academic to determine priorities for e-learning, and e-learning planning would be embedded within overall academic planning within the academic division.

Faculty Development and Other Human Resource Issues

The meetings with academic departments revealed that few of the instructors were adequately prepared to develop quality e-learning. Most instructors came to SAIT with a trades or industry background and, while they are generally very computer literate, they lacked the understanding of educational theory needed to fully exploit e-learning.

E-learning requires substantial up-front planning and development of materials before a course or program is ready for delivery. Extra time would be needed initially to create a large core of e-learning courses. Ongoing training and professional development would need to become an essential and regular part of the work of all instructors. However, instructors at SAIT had a very heavy classroom teaching load (over 20 hours a week in front of a class, on average). Therefore, teaching loads would need to be reduced over several years to free up the necessary time for course development and faculty training. Eventually, a reduction of time spent in class while students are online, a higher proportion of students working independently online, and an increase in support staff should free up at least some of the time needed by instructors for the development of online materials. However, it was recognized that initially e-learning could not become a major part of SAIT's strategy without increasing the number of instructors to reduce current teaching loads. Therefore, it was recommended that a total of 30 additional full-time instructors be hired initially to kick-start mixed-mode and fully online e-learning across the institution.

Furthermore, most professional development was being done in face-to-face small group workshops after the two regular semesters were completed in April. More flexible ways of delivering training and professional development for faculty needed to be explored, such as online courses on how to design e-learning courses and short periods free of teaching during the regular semesters. It was therefore recommended that the Centre for Instructional Technology and Development run Institute-wide workshops where generic needs dealing specifically with the overall design of e-learning could be identified. It was also recommended that each instructor have a training plan in place by June 30, 2006, and that a senior instructor within each department be appointed to organize the department's in-house faculty development program, in collaboration with CITD. Lastly, SAIT needed to examine and upgrade its current personnel policies for e-learning support staff to ensure that terms and conditions of employment were competitive, because SAIT was finding it increasingly difficult to recruit and retain such specialist staff.

Student Computing Policies

The vision statement required all SAIT students to graduate with the information technology skills required in their area of specialty. In discussion with instructors from every department, it was clear that in each program there were topics that would benefit from knowledge in how to use computers and/or the Internet, although the overall importance varied from course to course. Thus, in the near future every student would need computer access at some time in their program. However, programs requiring students to use a computer must have clearly specified added value in terms of the competencies that students would develop through the use of the computer. Every program, therefore, should have a clear policy statement about the need for a computer, the benefits it would provide, how the computer should be supplied, the minimum technical specifications, and the computer skills needed by the student on entry to the program.

It was recommended that programs requiring full attendance on campus continue to operate current laptop policies, where SAIT owned the computers and the cost was included in the student tuition fee. Students would be expected to provide their own computers for fully distance and mixed-mode courses and for campus-based courses where the use of a computer was optional. SAIT should provide a pre-entry course to bring all students up to the minimum computer literacy standards set by SAIT.

E-Learning Support Issues

The Centre for Instructional Technology and Development (CITD)

To ensure the quality of SAIT's e-learning, the plan strongly recommended a team approach to the design and development of e-learning programs, requiring input not only from subject experts (the instructors), but also from instructional designers, Web programmers, and media producers. The Centre for Instructional Technology and Development (CITD) was expected to provide this essential support.

However, as in many institutions, there was an ongoing tension between the academic departments and the central support unit. CITD could not meet all the demands on its services. It was able to provide service to only 22 out of 80 projects in 2004. Furthermore, although CITD had instructional designers and faculty development specialists, some were not trained or experienced in e-learning or project management. Consequently, a number of academic departments had been building a cottage industry in distance education and instructional design based on short-term contracts. However, since it is difficult to find high quality specialists in e-learning, it made sense to provide regular employment, both to recruit good staff and to ensure that experience gained in e-learning remained within the organization. Thus to achieve high standards in e-learning, it was important for e-learning specialists to be funded and staffed with full-time positions, with the ability to move them around the organization as demand among different departments fluctuated.

As a result, it was recommended that CITD increase capacity from 4 to 20 instructional designers, from 11 to 20 multimedia developers, and from two to four faculty development facilitators, over the next five years. At the same time, a matrix model of management of CITD resources was recommended. A committee each year would determine the allocation of CITD resources to different departments through service agreements, but it was strongly recommended that specialist e-learning support staff continue to be funded through and responsible to the director of CITD.

Other Support Departments

The plan also discussed the support requirements in the library, information systems, and customer services. A modest increase in resources was recommended for the Library to strengthen its support for online learners. The IT infrastructure at SAIT was in general of a high level, but there were some weak spots. Some teaching areas had wireless access, but many did not. It was recommended that the whole campus have wireless access by September 2006. An extra technician was needed to provide 24x7 support for WebCT, and additional servers and data centers were required. The main platform would continue to be WebCT, and the strategy development committee would be responsible for recommendations regarding upgrades and developments.

Customer services is a term used at SAIT to cover a range of administrative services to students, including the registrar's office. The more students move to e-learning, the more demand there will be from both instructors and students for online access to administrative services. SAIT had a made a good start by building two portals, mySAIT.ca and myFaculty, through which a number of services could be accessed online. However, new functionality needed to be added. It was recommended that a mySAIT.ca management committee be established, chaired by the Registrar, to determine priorities and to identify and access resources for the up-grading and maintenance of mySAIT.ca. More importantly, SAIT needed a broader, integrated institutional e-strategy that would encompass all uses of the Internet, including e-learning, e-commerce, and e-administration.

Organizational Issues

Intellectual Property and Academic Content Management

E-learning results in the creation of digital content that can be re-used or re-designed for multiple uses. Digital content therefore has potential value that goes beyond its initial use in a specific act of teaching or learning. As Magee (2005) comments, "the considerable investment in [digital] materials requires an organization to receive fair compensation for their use and maintain control over their usage." Despite a great deal of research and development into specific learning objects and standards, little attention has been paid to the issue of the management of digital content from the strategic perspective of an institution.

Some of the strategic issues in academic digital content management are as follows:

*   How best to create digital content so it can be re-used.
*   How to store and make accessible digital content.
*   Who owns the copyright for digital content once created.
*   What uses are permitted of that content and who decides.
*   Quality control or assurance.
*   The business case for digital content management.

It was recommended that SAIT management make a clear statement about its financial goals with respect to the re-use of digital learning materials and online courses, as there are various positions that could be taken, from a free public resource through to charging for everything. It was also recommended that a sub-committee on the management of digital content be established. Its mandate would be to develop a plan for content management, including recommendations on policy and procedures. To assist in developing policies for content management, the business case for the re-use and sale of learning materials should be explored by corporate training. In the meantime, SAIT should establish initially a low-cost central registry of all digital e-learning materials that would enable materials to be quickly and easily identified for third-party use.

Although many IP issues concerning the creation and use of digital materials were covered by current IP policy (which specified that all materials created by employees belonged to SAIT), it was recommended that SAIT develop a generic wording of contracts with third parties to protect moral rights and the integrity of SAIT's digital materials when re-used. Better procedures to ensure both copyright compliance and easier use of copyright materials were needed.

Financial Issues

In the long run, the aim of the plan was to develop a system where e-learning courses and programs could be designed in such a way that there would be no net increase in work for instructors. However, for e-learning to be cost-effective, instructors would need to be skilled and experienced in the design of e-learning and have adequate technical and educational support. Given that this was not the case at the time of the planning, it was recognized that over the first five years following the initial implementation of the plan, substantial investment would be needed to support the design and development of e-learning programs. These costs would be largely offset by additional revenues through increased enrolments of approximately 25%, if the target for new e-learning courses was met. Brokering of online materials and services and contracts with the corporate sector would also generate substantial revenues.

After five years, the costs of e-learning would be an integrated part of the overall academic budget. The main risk would be hiring 30 new instructors to help generate new e-learning programs and to improve the general teaching skills level. However, this risk was offset by the knowledge that student numbers would likely increase and government funding was likely to be available to support such an increase.

Implementation and Monitoring

The new associate vice president of academic development was given the mandate to ensure the plan was implemented. The plan also gave considerable attention to how success in e-learning could be monitored and evaluated. A careful examination of existing evaluation tools and methodologies at SAIT indicated that these on their own were insufficient to assess the success or otherwise of e-learning. Thus the following specific key performance indicators were recommended to monitor and evaluate SAIT's e-learning strategies and activities on an annual basis, using 2005 as the base:

1. Target number of courses using each type of e-learning
2. Target five-year budget projections for e-learning

3.   Cost per enrolled student

4.   Implementation of quality assurance procedures

5.   Student satisfaction

6.   Employer satisfaction

7.   Analysis of student enrolments by type of student

8.   Course completions

9.   Changes in learning outcomes/student performance

10.   More effective use of facilities

11.   Cost per graduate student

12.   Increased revenues or savings due to the introduction of e-learning

SAIT should use its KPIs for e-learning to benchmark its progress against similar institutions, or institutions which SAIT considered to be international leaders in e-learning.

Factors Influencing the Development and Acceptance of the Plan

Strategic planning is a continuous narrative. Although the plan was approved by the EMC in September 2005, it still had to be implemented at the time of writing (December 2005). However, a detailed plan has been approved, and it is possible to review the factors that enabled such a plan to be created.

Institutional Leadership

The plan was driven primarily by the vice-president academic, with full support of the president and her executive team.

The Cisco Chair in E-Learning

The endowment of a chair enabled the VP to hire a specialist in e-learning under flexible conditions of employment to take leadership in developing a plan for e-learning. The chair spent a total of 70 working days over a period of 12 months on developing the plan. There was an advantage in having someone from outside the institute with recognized expertise who could take an independent view on the process of planning, but with a long enough appointment to provide significant input, continuity, and accountability.

Inclusiveness

The process aimed to be as inclusive as possible. Despite limited availability of instructors due to their heavy teaching load, the chair in e-learning met with over 200 instructors and spent several hours in each academic department discussing e-learning, the problems and barriers, and its potential role with instructors and curriculum coordinators. The visioning process, in which departments discussed the future role of e-learning, was both a failure and a success. It was a failure in that few departments were able in the time available to identify innovative or even appropriate roles for e-learning. Nevertheless, it was a valuable exercise in that it indicated the scale of the problem of faculty readiness, the need for more professional development and training in teaching methods, and the difficulties departments faced in finding time for instructors to do anything other than stand in front of a class during the two regular teaching semesters. Students also played an active and important role in the planning process. Students, in fact, were impressively thoughtful and engaged in the process.

There was one important stakeholder group that was not involved at this stage and perhaps should have been. SAIT has close links with employers, and there was a feeling by some instructors and one or two deans that employers or accrediting agencies such as Transport Canada would not understand or support a move to e-learning, especially if it resulted in less time hands-on in skills training. Employers certainly need to be consulted as individual e-learning programs are being planned, and employers would be closely consulted at this stage. However, the college made a decision in principle to increase its e-learning activities, partly as a result of input from some key employers before the plan was developed. Nevertheless, the timing in terms of involving employers in discussions on proposed changes to a public educational institution's teaching strategy is an important consideration.

Political Context

The senior administration was aware of the government's large budget surplus, their intention to dramatically increase enrolments in the post-secondary sector, and their interest in technology investment to improve performance in the colleges and universities. SAIT's senior administration therefore saw increased investment in e-learning as a means by which to meet core government goals for the postsecondary sector in Alberta. Its plan for e-learning would position the institute for the forthcoming government review of postsecondary education, due in December 2005. Thus, the plan for e-learning was aligned as a core element of SAIT's overall strategy.

Conclusion

SAIT's strategy is not to eliminate face-to-face teaching, nor to use e-learning merely as a supplement to classroom teaching. There is no single solution for teaching, and each academic program has to decide the best mix of face-to-face and online teaching, depending on the intended target groups, the nature of the content, and the resources and skills available. At the end of five years, then, the plan envisages that three quarters of all programs would still be largely face-to-face classes. About 50% of all classes would not require computer access or would use e-learning as an optional supplement to classroom teaching. Another 25% of all classes would be laptop programs, requiring regular class attendance. The main change would be to move approximately 15% of all classes into a mixed-mode format, accommodating students who require more flexible access but who do not want to lose face-to-face contact with instructors and other students. The remaining 10% of programs would be fully online aimed at lifelong learners. In addition, there would be a separate but important program linked to corporate training, through re-sale or brokering of online training materials and contracts for the development and/or delivery of corporate specific e-learning programs.

However, it would be a mistake to consider this a modest change in teaching practice. More important than the actual mix of different kinds of e-learning is the shift in teaching methodology, away from an instructor-led classroom model to one where students work more independently and where instructors create learning materials and facilitate and manage learning activities, working with an instructional designer and Web developer in a team. Also, the plan envisages a significant change in the student population. While the high-school leaver wanting full-time, campus-based education will still constitute a majority of students, the plan foresees substantial increases in part-time students and lifelong learners, and a much stronger corporate training market.

Before the Normandy landings, General Eisenhower said "Planning is everything; the plan is nothing." In other words, the process of planning is what provides readiness and flexibility, even if plans have to be changed or abandoned in the light of unpredicted events. Although the plan calls for a change in culture, it follows well substantiated change management processes from the business sector, but adapted to the postsecondary sector (see Bates, 2000).

The real test though still lies in the future. Will the administration be able to support and implement the processes outlined in the plan? Will the key stakeholders—students, instructors, employers—buy into the plan? Will the institution be able to find the financial resources needed to make e-learning a success? And above all, will instructors be able and ready to change their methods of teaching? We will have to wait until 2010 at the earliest for the answers to these questions.

References

Bates, A. W. (2000). *Managing technological change: Strategies for college and university leaders.* San Francisco: Jossey-Bass.

Benjamin, R., Carroll, S., Jacobi, M., Krop, C., & Shires. M. (1993). *The redesign of governance in higher education.* Santa Monica, CA: Rand's Institute on Education and Training.

Bloom, M. (2004). *E-learning in business: The business of e-learning.* Ottawa Conference Board of Canada. Retrieved September 19, 2005, from http://66.102.7.104/search?q=cache:6GuyPh4RhEkJ:www.e-economy.ca/epic/internet/inec2ee-ceace.nsf/vwapj/bloom.pdf/%24FILE/bloom.pdf+Michael+Bloom+Conference+Board+of+Canada+e-Learningandhl=en)

Bruce, R. (1999). *Educational technology planning.* Victoria, BC: Centre for Curriculum, Transfer, and Technology.

Dill, D. D. (1996). Academic planning and organizational design: Lessons from leading American universities. *Higher Education Quarterly, 50*(1), 35-53.

Ford, P. (1996). Information strategies: A UK perspective. *Proceedings of the Institutional Management in Higher Education* (pp. 147-155). Paris.

Magee, M. (2005). *SAIT thin client/career pathways project needs assessment: Intellectual property and digital rights* (Internal Report). Calgary, Alberta: Southern Alberta Institute of Technology.

OECD. (2005). *E-learning and tertiary education: Where do we stand.* Paris: OECD Publishing.

Stockley, D. (2004). Strategic planning for technological innovation in Canadian post secondary education. *Canadian Journal of Learning and Technology, 30*(2), 113-124.

Chapter V

Using E-Learning to Promote Excellence in Polytechnic Education

Maggie Beers, British Columbia Institute of Technology, Canada

Abstract

This chapter describes the participatory role faculty members have played in the first year of a five-year initiative that uses e-learning to promote educational excellence in learning, teaching, and research at a polytechnic institute. It argues that faculty engagement will ultimately determine the success of this e-learning initiative and, as such, faculty need to be active members in a collaborative process informed by participatory design. As this chapter outlines, faculty have used constructivist learning principles to create the educational vision that drives the initiative and provides its focus. They have participated in decision-making processes on the management team and advisory committee, and have piloted tools, learning approaches, and technical and educational support structures to inform the institute-wide implementation of this vision. This chapter aims to provide a model to inform the strategic direction of other institutes implementing similar e-learning initiatives and, therefore, concludes with preliminary lessons learned from year one.

Introduction

In the spring of 2005, the British Columbia Institute of Technology (BCIT) launched its five-year Technology Enabled Knowledge (TEK) Initiative to promote best practices in learning, teaching, and research. This initiative was intended to provide the technical infrastructure, Web-based collaboration tools, educational support structures, and faculty release time to enable its 47,000 learners to engage in exemplary e-learning, as defined by Massy and Zemsky (2004).

TEK has prompted BCIT to rethink how it delivers and supports its core operations at a time when emerging technologies can enable learning approaches that lead to educational excellence. Faculty support and participation will determine the success of this e-learning initiative, so the faculty need to be active members in a collaborative process informed by participatory design. Faculty members have developed the Initiative's educational vision, and they inform the direction of the Initiative through representation on the TEK management team and an established Faculty Advisory committee. In addition, faculty pilot tools, learning approaches, and support systems through funded Grassroots Projects to inform an institute-wide implementation. Through their engagement, faculty members promote a stronger culture of innovative teaching and learning with the use of educational technology.

This chapter describes the central, participatory role faculty members play in first, defining the educational vision that drives the TEK Initiative; second, informing managerial decisions to achieve this vision; and third, piloting tools, learning approaches, and technical and educational support structures to inform an institute-wide implementation of this vision. It concludes with a discussion of preliminary lessons learned from year one.

Context

British Columbia Institute of Technology

As a polytechnic, BCIT maintains close ties with industry and conducts applied research. Its programs are designed in consultation with leading employers in related industries, and students are expected to apply facts and theories to practice. Research conducted at BCIT is focused on activities with industrial or commercial relevance, where partnerships lead to benefits for the Institute, business and industry, and students (BCIT, 2005).

BCIT consists of five campuses, located around the greater Vancouver area, as well as numerous satellite campuses throughout the province of British Columbia, Canada. BCIT offers more than 200 full-time programs, with an additional 190 credentialed programs offered through part-time studies, distance education, or online learning.

In 2005, over 1,600 courses were delivered in business and media, computing and information technology, engineering, applied and natural sciences, health sciences, and trades, vocational, and apprenticeship (BCIT, 2005). These programs lead to one of several credentials: certificate, advanced certificate or post-diploma, diploma of technology, bachelor of technology, bachelor of business administration, or a bachelor of science. Currently, the Institute is developing several applied master's of technology programs and, in the future, intends to offer applied doctoral degrees.

Full-time faculty members are divided between the technologies and the trades, with each group having different teaching loads. Non-teaching faculty members include librarians, applied researchers, and instructional development consultants. Part-time instructors bring valuable industry experience to BCIT and make up a large percentage of the faculty population.

The TEK Initiative is a joint venture between BCIT's Learning and Teaching Centre and its Department of Computer Resources, each of which support faculty in their use of e-learning.

Learning and Teaching Centre

BCIT's Learning and Teaching Centre (LTC) is dedicated to enhancing the quality of education at BCIT and serves the faculty, staff, and students with a wide range of services and resources, including educational research, curriculum development, instructional design and consultation, distributed learning, media production, document production, and audio-visual services. The Centre currently employs over 60 individuals, including instructional development consultants, technical advisors, multimedia developers, video producers, writers and editors, illustrators, media technicians, and support staff. In the TEK Initiative, the LTC provides educational leadership, project management, and front-end technical support for faculty and students.

Computer Resources

Computer Resources (CR), the Institute's information technology department, provides technology services and support programs to address the advanced technology and essential computing and communications needs of learners, faculty, and staff. Within this department, the client support services team provides help for desktop hardware and software issues. The academic computing services team meets the needs of students and faculty in computer labs and works with the schools to provide leading-edge technology to meet the changing learning and teaching requirements of all programs. The application and information services team supports and enhances important information systems including SunGard SCT Banner, Lotus Notes, Lotus Domino applications, Cognos, and WebCT. Technical and infrastructure services staff maintain all hardware and software related to the network, data storage, and backup. Web services enable information access and content publishing through a public Web site and an institute portal that develops and supports Web-based applications, collaboration, and learning tools. In the TEK Initiative, CR provides the technical infrastructure, collaborative Web applications, and back-end technical support.

Participatory Design Process

Lessons learned from technology implementation initiatives at many postsecondary institutions have emphasized the need to involve faculty in the institutional visionary and planning process. These faculty members can be most influential if they are respected by their peers and have already demonstrated innovative, technology-based teaching (Bates, 2000). The primary goal of the TEK Initiative is to improve learning and teaching through the use of educational technology, and it is believed that faculty, along with their students, are in the best position to effect change in this area. Therefore, the Initiative has directly involved faculty in a process informed by participatory design theory (Bannon, 1995; Fischer & Giaccardi, 2005; Gould, 1995), since they are the principle users of any educational or technical systems and tools that TEK will produce.

Participatory design is an approach to computer-based systems planning that advocates active involvement of users throughout the design process. It views user involvement as crucial, since users are experts in the work practice supported by these technologies and will ultimately be the ones creating new practices in response to these technologies. Although there is no single interpretation of participatory design, or agreement on its theoretical foundation, Blomberg and Henderson (1990) provide a few common aspects that guide most practitioners in this approach (pp. 353-354).

First, the goal is to improve the quality of work life of the users. The focus is on the work as a whole and on the technology as a component of that whole. In the context of the TEK Initiative, this corresponds to improving faculty's effectiveness and professional satisfaction. The Initiative aims to provide faculty with the appropriate time, tools, and support structures to enable them to achieve higher standards in teaching and applied research.

Second, the orientation is collaborative. Developers and users work together to design and develop the systems and technology and integrate them into work practice. At BCIT, faculty have helped define TEK's educational vision, to which they aspire, and work with management to actively negotiate the focus and goals for the Initiative.

Finally, the design is iterative, and emerging design ideas are tried out in real work situations. In the TEK Initiative, a program of faculty-led Grassroots Projects pilot innovative learning approaches, emerging tools, and proposed educational and technical support structures in existing courses. These projects are termed Grassroots because they aim to involve faculty in a local, or ground-level, movement to cultivate a culture of innovative teaching with technology through-out BCIT. This Grassroots Program builds on Bates' (2000) concept of "lone rangers" in that it harnesses the collective efforts of a dynamic group of early adopters to inform, test, and modify the proposed solutions to prepare for an institute-wide implementation.

TEK Foundation Goals

In the fall of 2004, the president's executive council set out four broad foundation goals, each intended to support the use of technology in learning, teaching, and research at BCIT:

1. **Collaboration and Connectivity:** Connecting BCIT to the world
2. **Smart Learning Spaces:** Equipping BCIT's learning spaces
3. **Best Teaching Practices:** Supporting effective learning and teaching
4. **Applied Research:** Advancing polytechnic education

In a bottom-up and top-down strategic planning process (Bates, 2000), these goals emerged from focus group studies conducted over the previous two years, involving students, faculty, staff, deans, directors, administrators, program heads from the technologies, and chief instructors from the trades. In the early stage of this initiative, these goals, further articulated with visioning statements below, represented the broad areas for improvement identified by the focus group participants (Golding, 2004).

Collaboration and Connectivity

To increase collaboration and connectivity, TEK links BCIT, its students, its staff, and its services to its local, national, and global communities and industrial partners such that learning, teaching, research, and business practices are optimized. It provides authenticated, robust, and secure anywhere/anytime/anything access to BCIT's intranet, extranet, and the Web. In addition, TEK fully facilitates online information sharing, collaboration, and knowledge building in a global context.

Smart Learning Spaces

To equip its smart learning spaces, TEK ensures that instructors have easy access to the educational technologies that they need to teach on campus or at a distance. It deploys teaching technologies to facilitate best teaching and learning practices across all BCIT campuses and implements new technology support strategies with the aim of achieving complete availability during hours that teaching occurs.

Best Teaching Practices

To encourage and support best teaching practices, TEK provides BCIT educators with the services, resources, and programs to enable them to use educational technologies effectively. It identifies and responds to the barriers as perceived by faculty, monitoring faculty feedback regarding measures implemented. It identifies and communicates student perspectives on effective and creative use of technology in teaching.

Applied Research

To advance its polytechnic applied research agenda and support global research initiatives, TEK provides the infrastructure, security, and capacity to engage its students, and faculty in applied research. TEK delivers the tools to create repositories to capture, store, index, mine, preserve, and redistribute data. It establishes the network capacity to transfer high volumes of data reliably and securely and fully facilitates online information sharing, collaboration, and knowledge-building in a global context.

These foundation goals align with Bates' (2000) recommendations that a model strategic technology plan, which he believes should nest within a wider plan for teaching and learning, cover both technology infrastructure and teaching with technology, and provide a concrete, detailed vision statement.

Educational Vision

From the beginning, the TEK Initiative's primary focus has been on enabling educational excellence, so leadership was placed within the Learning and Teaching Centre. The LTC's first task was to consult with faculty to build an educational vision on sound learning and teaching principles that would dictate the technical design for the Institute's enterprise architecture. The vision required endorsement from the president's executive council, the board of governors, and, ultimately, the BCIT community.

The educational vision is told in two video stories through the eyes of students and instructors from the technologies and trades. The first story takes place in course and clinical placement settings in the medical radiography technology program; the second story takes place in home, shop, and job placement settings in the piping trades program. Faculty members from the LTC led the creation of this educational vision, with consultation from faculty and staff across all campuses, and BCIT students and instructors served as actors. The vision was first presented privately to BCIT's executives, then launched openly to faculty in a public event, and, finally, posted on the TEK Web site for the larger BCIT community.

The educational vision meets the current and near future needs of BCIT and is achievable within three years. It establishes a baseline from which development of innovative methodologies and their enabling technology can be launched for future years of the Initiative. The vision draws from existing teaching practices in exemplary courses across the Institute and ensures the technologies that enable these learning approaches are easy to use, fully supported, and accessible to all BCIT faculty, students, staff, and partners. It represents best practices occurring at other postsecondary institutions and, specifically, LTC's research on the effective use of educational technology in learner-centered, constructivist environments (Beers & Wilson, 2002).

Figure 1. The educational model used in the medical radiography technology and piping trades examples described in the TEK educational vision

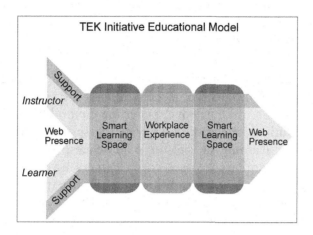

Educational Model

Due to the applied nature of BCIT's programs, professional work experiences, such as clinical practice, work placements, co-ops, and apprenticeships, are integral to the student and instructor polytechnic experience. BCIT students learn, manage their studies, and gain industry experience. Faculty members facilitate learning and conduct applied research. Industry partners provide industry experience and collaborate in applied research. To meet the different, yet overlapping, needs of these distinct groups, the vision presents a flexible educational model that blends highly interactive on-campus, face-to-face learning in smart learning spaces with off-campus work experience (see Figure 1). A Web presence links students, instructors, and industry partners to resources, each other, and technical and educational support systems from any location at any time.

Constructivist Principles

TEK's educational vision is informed by learner-centered, constructivist learning principles that call upon students to solve real-world problems to prepare themselves for the workplace. Constructivism is an educational philosophy that encompasses a variety of views, theories, and instructional models (Beers & Wilson, 2002). In general terms, constructivism defines learning as an active process of constructing, rather than acquiring, knowledge. It sees instruction as a process of supporting that construction, rather than communicating knowledge (Duffy & Cunningham, 1996).

The LTC has identified seven constructivist guiding principles to inform best practices in postsecondary education and the design of e-learning environments (Beers & Wilson, 2002). Constructivist environments facilitate individual and collective construction of knowledge, underline the problem-solving process more than its solutions, incorporate multiple perspectives into the learning experience, anchor learning in real-life experiences, encourage learners to reflect on their own learning processes, coach learners in a cognitive apprentice-ship model, and evaluate learners' abilities to perform expert tasks and defend their decisions. These principles are each discussed below, within the context of the medical radiography technology scenario outlined in TEK's educational vision.

Knowledge Construction

Constructivist learning environments assume that information makes sense only in the context of a problem or application (Jonassen, 1999). In the scenario described in the TEK vision, teams of students construct knowledge in a hybrid e-learning environment, as they interact face-to-face and online to solve a series of problems related to medical radiography. They conduct research by accessing the library's full-text databases and the medical radiography picture archiving database (PACS). They have access to formal and informal knowledge building tools, such as blogs and concept-mapping tools, and they design their own knowledge representations through multimedia presentations.

Problem-Solving Process

Learners need to think in the knowledge domain as an expert user of the domain may think, and so the educational vision encourages students to focus on the problem-solving process, rather than the solutions, or products, of this process. Students learn to think like experts as they perform the tasks of medical radiography technologists in a variety of roles, such as applied researchers, team members, and active members in a community of practice. Students document their learning processes in ePortfolios, which they are able to repurpose, reuse, or revise as they acquire more expert skills. They also have the opportunity to showcase products and solutions through their ePortfolio.

Multiple Perspectives

Learners benefit from constructing multiple perspectives on an issue. This is a dynamic process, since perspectives constantly change as new information becomes available and the views of other perspectives are articulated (Goldman-Segall, 1998). In the vision, students use collaboration tools, virtual Web spaces, and document repositories to share perspectives with peers and experts. As they make the best case possible from each perspective, they explore the domain knowledge from new vantage points, forging a variety of personally meaningful paths into the knowledge they can later transfer to new cases.

Real-Life Experiences

Real-world problems anchored in authentic life experiences, events, or issues are meaningful to the students. Realistic problems allow students to take ownership of their solutions, develop deeper, richer knowledge structures, and require more systematic problem-solving methods (Chan, 2002). In the case of the medical radiography technology students presented in the vision, the students apply theoretical concepts to develop and research case studies on the PACS database in the smart learning space and in their clinical setting. Games and simulations appeal to students' different learning styles and need for just-in-time, self-directed instruction.

Reflective Learning

When students articulate what they have learned, and reflect on the processes and decisions that were made in the process, they understand more and are better able to use the knowledge that they have constructed in new situations (Jonassen, 1999). In applied research teams and other problem-solving activities described in the TEK vision, students use the e-learning tools to articulate what they are doing, the decisions they make, the strategies they use, and the answers they find. Students use inquiry methods to ask questions, investigate a topic, and use a variety of resources to find solutions and answers. As students explore the topic, they draw conclusions and, as exploration continues, they revisit those conclusions. This exploration of questions leads to more questions (Grennon Brooks, n.d.) and the collaborative construction of knowledge.

Cognitive Apprenticeship

In a cognitive apprenticeship model, the instructor models the problem-solving process and coaches students toward expert performance. The e-learning environment provides scaffolding and specific support structures to enable the learners to reach this level of expertise. In the educational model presented in TEK's vision, the instructor and student receive personalized orientation packets at their homes and are invited to enter the Web-based support systems available to them. At any time, learners can access online tutorials to boost their e-learning confidence, improve their library research skills, or develop their technical expertise in the PACS database. Learners are integrated into strong communities of practice (Wenger, 1998) early in their learning experiences to link them to resources and expertise within industry.

Authentic Evaluation

In a constructivist view of knowledge, the goal is to improve the learner's ability to use the content domain in authentic tasks (Brown, Collins, & Duguid, 1989). Evaluation examines the thinking process that has enabled the learner to be successful in completing the task. In TEK's vision, students manage personal ePortfolios—virtual repositories of documents and digital materials that enable them to create, archive, and share their learning accomplishments. They demonstrate their problem-solving processes and defend their decisions with peers, instructors, and industry professionals, all of whom constitute the learner's community of practice in their field.

Realizing the Vision

TEK Direction

Once TEK's educational vision was defined, the LTC and CR collaborated to identify the educational and technical infrastructure and support systems necessary to enable the learning and teaching experiences described in the vision. A management team was struck, for which the activities were divided into four distinct project portfolios: Academic Learning and Teaching, Web and Collaboration, Enterprise Architecture, and User Support and Service Level Projects. TEK remains a faculty-led initiative, driven by educational goals. The Faculty Advisory sits immediately alongside the TEK project manager in the manage-

Figure 2. TEK management hierarchy, indicating the role of the Faculty Advisory in relation to the project manager and the individual project portfolio leads

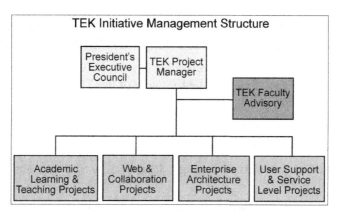

ment hierarchy (see Figure 2). LTC faculty members coordinate and lead all projects in the academic learning and teaching portfolio.

Faculty Advisory

The TEK Faculty Advisory consists of trades and technology faculty representatives from BCIT's six schools, the Library, the applied research facility, and the LTC. As its first task, the Faculty Advisory defined its mandate, which was to provide direction to the TEK Initiative from an instructor's perspective and ensure the focus was on enhancing teaching and learning through the use of new and evolving educational technologies. To achieve this mandate, the advisory makes decisions, provides advice and insight, validates plans, prioritizes actions, and advocates on behalf of the TEK Initiative. It also provides a means for information dissemination and faculty input to the Initiative by representing the interests of all faculty, including those working at satellite campuses throughout the province.

As its second task, the Faculty Advisory selected and assigned funding to faculty-led Grassroots Projects for the first year of TEK. These projects are supported in TEK's Academic Learning and Teaching portfolio.

Grassroots Projects

There are many projects within the four TEK project portfolios, but the faculty-led Grassroots Projects within the Academic Learning and Teaching portfolio are the real motors that drive the TEK Initiative. They serve two functions: first, as pilot studies to test and inform further implementation of emerging technology, and second, as catalysts to foster a stronger culture of innovative teaching and learning with these approaches and tools. From a learning and teaching perspective, nearly all the other activities in TEK work to provide the infrastructure, resources, and support to make these faculty-led Grassroots Projects a success.

The TEK Faculty Advisory, in consultation with LTC faculty, developed six criteria for Grassroots Projects in the first year of the TEK Initiative. Grassroots Projects:

1. Use educational technologies in innovative, creative ways;
2. Encourage collaboration amongst learners, instructors, and community partners;
3. Promote knowledge building through idea sharing;
4. Engage the students in learner-centered teaching strategies;
5. Enable learners to achieve course-learning outcomes; and
6. Support TEK's foundation goals.

In the first year, TEK has funded 50 Grassroots Projects, which span all five campuses and are led by full-time and part-time, teaching and non-teaching, faculty in a broad range of teaching expertise. These projects are examples of creative, leading edge uses of educational technology to improve teaching, learning, and collaboration at BCIT.

The Grassroots Projects are a central focus of success for the TEK Initiative. Examples in year one include online communities of practice where students collaborate with professionals in marketing, forestry, and railway industries; ePortfolios in film, interior design, and aircraft maintenance; blogs in radio, broadcast journalism, and automotive repair; and clicker technologies in large lectures for medical laboratory sciences and mechanical, electrical, and industrial processes.

This Grassroots Program of 50 individual Grassroots Projects improves upon the one-off, lone ranger model Bates cautions against (2000) because it provides a managed, efficient use of resources to support faculty in their innovation. Grassroots Projects have a pre-defined life-cycle, in which faculty receive technical training and support with instructional design, development, and implementation. At the end of this cycle, faculty emerge with a professional, useful educational product, along with the skills and experience to maintain it with limited support. Faculty inform institutional practice when they give feedback to the TEK team to refine the work processes and share their experiences with their colleagues to provide mentorship.

Figure 3. The design team model provides each Grassroots Project with core educational and technical support, along with additional resources as needed

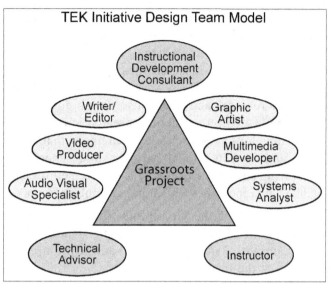

Design Team Approach

TEK uses a collaborative design team model to provide Grassroots faculty with technical and educational support to make each project a success. The core unit of the design team consists of the Grassroots teaching-faculty member (the subject matter expert); an LTC non-teaching faculty member (instructional development consultant), who manages the project, advises on instructional design, and secures additional resources; and the technical advisor, who recommends appropriate technical solutions for the project. As needed, other resources such as writer/editors, video producers, audio-visual specialists, systems analysts, multimedia developers, and graphic artists are called in to contribute their talents (see Figure 3).

The various perspectives each team member contributes to the Grassroots Project prompt important discussions related to the quality of education, ultimately leading to improved practice (Bates, 2000).

Faculty Development

Within the TEK Academic Learning and Teaching portfolio are faculty development programs to support these Grassroots Projects, celebrate their successes, and inform future iterations of activities in the TEK Initiative through lessons learned. These programs include Action Research, eCompetencies, Resources, Showcasing, and Reward and Recognition.

To achieve the reflective practice carried out by the medical radiography technology instructor in TEK's educational vision, BCIT has launched a coordinated Action Research Program as part of the TEK Initiative. Specific Grassroots Projects are identified as action research sites where instructors use their own learning environments to research aspects of their own teaching. Historically, BCIT has focused its research activities on solving industry problems and, as such, does not yet have a culture of action research in education. This Action Research Program develops a research agenda in line with the goals of the TEK Initiative, BCIT, and its educational partners, and supports faculty action researchers in securing approval from BCIT's research ethics board, collecting and analyzing data, and reporting their findings in public forums.

Lessons learned from all of the Grassroots Projects and Action Research Projects contribute to the eCompetencies program within the TEK Initiative, which provides examples of quality teaching and learning to share amongst students and faculty at the Institute.

TEK is consolidating and creating rich banks of technical and educational resources in various media formats to enable faculty and staff to achieve these eCompetencies. Students and faculty are involved in defining needs and creating these resources to share. Topics are divided into technical how-to's, recommendations to achieve exemplary teaching, and case studies of best use at BCIT.

To celebrate the Grassroots Projects, faculty and students are showcasing their projects in a variety of venues, including Webcasts, live observations, workshops, and scholarly articles. One goal of these showcasing activities is to raise the profile of the instructors and students engaged in these innovative activities; the other goal is to provide teaching opportunities to encourage and support other faculty and students in their use of e-learning.

Finally, BCIT recognizes that none of this can happen without the proper support for faculty in terms of time and recognition for the extra efforts they put forth toward improving the quality of education at the Institute. Therefore, ongoing efforts are made to secure funding sources and awards for all eligible faculty members, including full- and part-time, teaching and non-teaching.

Faculty are awarded up to 20 release days per Grassroots Project, above and beyond the time allotted to their normal teaching assignment, to enable them to complete the various stages of the Grassroots Project lifecycle: design, development, implementation, showcasing, TEK feedback, and peer mentoring.

The first year of the TEK Initiative has focused on supporting Grassroots Projects that connect BCIT to the world through collaborative processes, with an emphasis on learning and teaching. Faculty have implemented a wide range of learning approaches to make collaborative experiences happen, enabled by Web-based educational technology. Throughout the Grassroots Projects, faculty members have received educational and technical training and support to help make their projects a success and promote educational excellence in e-learning.

Lessons Learned

BCIT's Technology Enabled Knowledge Initiative is a five-year commitment to innovation and achieving new standards in educational excellence. TEK is a faculty-led initiative, driven by educational goals. To effectively identify and address the needs of faculty, TEK has engaged them early on in a collaborative process informed by participatory design. This section concludes the chapter with a preliminary discussion of lessons learned from year one.

First, the educational vision has provided a clear focus and theme to streamline educational and technical operations within the TEK Initiative. Because of the dynamic nature of this Initiative, ongoing consultations within each school and department can continue to personalize the educational vision to meet specific needs. In year two, and subsequent years, TEK will renew the educational vision to guide the Initiative beyond BCIT's immediate needs.

Second, the Faculty Advisory has been an effective and influential entity within the TEK Initiative. To continue to make informed decisions and provide valuable outreach to the schools and departments they represent, Faculty Advisory representatives need adequate release time from their normal teaching duties and comprehensive education on the learning approaches and enabling technologies the Initiative supports. A permanent chair can provide consistent leadership, communication, and long-term visioning for the committee.

Third, the Grassroots Program has been an effective vehicle to pilot learning approaches and technologies and foster innovation amongst the faculty. Selection criteria has focused on a common theme, connecting BCIT to the world through collaborative processes, which has made it possible to consolidate educational expertise and select and support a manageable, yet complementary, suite of enabling tools. The complexity of simultaneously piloting learning approaches and sometimes unstable technology has made it important for all team members to agree upon success criteria prior to project start-up.

Fourth, the collaborative design team model has provided a well managed, efficient use of resources to support faculty in innovation and provide opportunities for collective dialogue around educational excellence. To be most effective, all design team members require clear definitions of their roles and responsibilities and a base understanding of the learning approaches and educational technology solutions available.

Based on these lessons learned, current preparations for year two include an institute-wide roll-out of these learning approaches and tools, a continuation of the Grassroots Program for emerging approaches and technology, and the development of a second educational vision to advance the Initiative beyond BCIT's immediate needs.

In year one, TEK has fostered a spirit of innovation by engaging 50 faculty members and their students in innovative learning experiences, constituting, by some accounts, a small-scale roll-out, rather than a pilot. The large majority of these Grassroots faculty have emerged with the experience, skills, and customized learning environments to move the TEK Initiative forward and promote excellence in education at BCIT.

References

Bannon, L. (1995). From human factors to human actors: The role of psychology and human-computer interaction studies in systems design. In R. M. Baecker, J. Gruding, W. A. S. Buxton, & S. Greenberg (Eds.), *Readings in human-computer interaction: Toward the year 2000* (pp. 205-214). San Francisco: Morgan Kaufmann Publishers.

Bates, A. W. (2000). *Managing technological change: Strategies for college and university leaders.* San Francisco: Jossey-Bass Publishers.

Beers, M., & Wilson, M. (2002). *Constructivist e-learning methodologies: A module development guide.* Report prepared for the Pan-Canadian Health Informatics Collaboratory: An experimental broadband interactive e-learning environment for health professionals. Burnaby, BC, Canada: British Columbia Institute of Technology, Learning and Teaching Centre.

Blomberg, J., & Henderson, A. (1990). Reflections on participatory design: Lessons from the Trillium experience. *Proceedings of the Human Factors in Computing Systems Conference* (pp. 353-359). Seattle, Washington.

British Columbia Institute of Technology. (2005). *Pathfinder.* Burnaby, BC, Canada: Marketing and Communications Department.

Brown, J. S., Collins, A., & Duguid, P. (1989). Situated cognition and the culture of learning. *Educational Researcher, 18*(1), 32-42.

Chan, D. (2002). *The role of ICT in a constructivist approach to the teaching of thinking skills.* Ngee Ann City, Singapore: Ngee Ann Polytechnic,

Teaching and Learning Centre. Retrieved January 5, 2006, from http://tlcWeb.np.edu.sg/lt/articles/ict.htm

Duffy, T. M., & Cunningham, D. J. (1996). Constructivism: Implications for the design and delivery of instruction. In D. H. Jonassen (Ed.), *Handbook of research for educational communications and technology* (pp. 170-198). New York: Simon Schuster Macmillan.

Fischer, G., & Giaccardi, E. (2005). Meta-design: A framework for the future of end user development. In H. Lieberman, F. Paternò, & V. Wulf (Eds.), *End user development—Empowering people to flexibly employ advanced information and communication technology.* Dordrecht, The Netherlands: Kluwer Academic Publishers. Retrieved December 20, 2005, from http://l3d.cs.colorado.edu/~gerhard/papers/EUD-meta-design-online.pdf

Golding, C. (2004). *BCIT educational technology vision and goals: 2004-2008.* Burnaby, BC, Canada: British Columbia Institute of Technology, Learning and Teaching Centre.

Goldman-Segall, R. (1998). *Points of viewing children's thinking: A digital ethnographer's journey.* Mahwah, NJ: Lawrence Erlbaum Associates.

Gould, J. D. (1995). How to design usable systems. In R. M. Baecker, J. Gruding, W. A. S. Buxton, & S. Greenberg (Eds.), *Readings in human-computer interaction: Toward the year 2000* (pp. 93-122). San Francisco: Morgan Kaufmann Publishers.

Grennon Brooks, J. (n.d.). *Constructivism as a paradigm for teaching and learning.* Retrieved October 31, 2002, from http://www.thirteen.org/edonline/concept2class/constructivism/index.html

Jonassen, D. H. (1999, February). *Designing constructivist learning environments on the Web: Engaging students in meaningful learning.* Keynote paper presented at EdTech99: the Educational Technology Conference and Exhibition, Singapore Exhibition Centre, Suntec City, Singapore. Retrieved October 31, 2002, from http://www.moe.edu.sg/iteducation/edtech/papers/d1.pdf

Massy, W. F., & Zemsky, R. (2004). *Thwarted innovation: What happened to e-learning and why.* A final report for The Weatherstation Project of The Learning Alliance at the University of Pennsylvania in cooperation with the Thomson Corporation. Retrieved November 11, 2005, from http://www.irhe.upenn.edu/Docs/Jun2004/ThwartedInnovation.pdf

Wenger, E. (1998). *Communities of practice: Learning, meaning, and identity.* New York: Cambridge University Press.

Chapter VI

Teaching and Learning in a Laptop Nursing Program:
Institutional and Pedagogical Issues

Ellen Vogel, University of Ontario, Canada

Bill Muirhead, University of Ontario, Canada

Abstract

Increasingly, nurses work in practice settings that employ the latest information and communication technology (ICT) to research, administer, and deliver healthcare to clients. Thus, it is critical that BNSc program graduates be competent with the technology that is embedded in their nursing environments. This chapter explicates the findings of a study designed to assess and prioritize the capacities of nursing faculty in the use of ICT for teaching and learning. Data was gathered over a two-year period through in-depth interviews, questionnaires, learning journals, and document review and synthesis. The authors hope that findings will contribute to the development of core competencies in the use of ICT for teaching and learning. Further, outcomes will inform decision-makers and funding agencies of the needs and gaps related to faculty ICT preparedness in Canadian schools of nursing. Recommendations address key success factors including faculty development and institutional support.

Introduction

In this chapter, the experiences of a nursing faculty are situated within a technology-enhanced teaching and learning environment. In 2003, the University of Ontario Institute of Technology (UOIT) in Oshawa, Ontario formulated a campus-wide strategic vision for the use of information and communication technology (ICT). Concurrently, UOIT constructed a ubiquitous ICT infrastructure while implementing a customized faculty development plan to improve teaching and learning outcomes.

The goal of this study was to provide an overview of the capacities of the UOIT nursing faculty in the use of ICT for teaching and learning. Specifically, the objectives of the two-year study were the following:

- Assess the current needs and gaps of nursing faculty in the use of ICT for teaching and learning.

- Elucidate trends in the early adoption of ICT for teaching and learning to enhance ongoing training and faculty development at UOIT.

- Support the nursing faculty in helping to identify and develop personal research agendas in the application of ICT to nursing education and practice.

UOIT Laptop Program

A unique feature of UOIT is its designation as the second "laptop university" in Canada. The laptop program provides faculty members with a computer free of charge and ubiquitous access to the Internet through the development of a wired and wireless infrastructure. Students are issued a standard IBM laptop computer featuring multimedia capabilities, extensive memory, and the capacity to support complex software required by professional faculties. All software required by both students and faculty is preloaded onto the laptop and refreshed on an annual basis. Computer hardware is refreshed every two years. Students and faculty can access comprehensive IT support during the evenings, weekends, and holidays. Student participation in the laptop program is mandatory. An annual computer leasing fee is determined by each faculty and/or program and averages between $1,680 and $1,750 (Canadian funds) per student.

The decision by founders of UOIT to create a learning environment based on the use of laptop computers, ubiquitous access to the Internet, and the use of course-specific software was premised on a collective belief that campus-wide adoption of ICT would enhance student achievement. Moreover, they maintained that students required ICT skills to prepare for careers in workplaces increasingly defined by technology. A new physical infrastructure facilitated the construction of a learning environment with potential to optimize the use of ICT. A contributing factor of lesser importance was the founders' belief that a state-of-the-art Web-centric campus would differentiate UOIT from other Canadian universities.

The ICT Infrastructure at UOIT

All teaching spaces at UOIT were designed with wired access points for students and faculty. Lecture halls and tutorial rooms were equipped with "smart" podiums to facilitate technologically enhanced teaching strategies. Wireless access points were distributed throughout the university buildings to enable students to use their laptops in a variety of settings including dormitory rooms. The physical infrastructure at UOIT was matched by investments in Web-based services (e.g., a university-wide learning management system and extensive online library resources accessible through the Internet).

The mandatory participation of students in the UOIT Laptop Program was consistent with the recommendations in the literature which suggest e-learning sustainability and the transformation of teaching in ways that fully exploit ICT depend on equitable access to e-learning infrastructures (Arabasz, Priani, & Fawcett, 2003; Atwell, 2004; Zemsky & Massy, 2004).

The Need for Change in Nursing Education

In order to meet students' current and future educational needs, nurse educators must gain knowledge and skills in ICT-enhanced education. In the 1990s, the Canadian Nurses Association facilitated a national working group on Health

Information: Nursing Components (HI:NC), which identified that advances in ICT have created significant opportunities for nurses to increase access to current information for decision-making. The expert group also identified the need for all nurses to become more knowledgeable about health information concepts and technology that are designed to manage and process information (Clarke, 2002).

In 2002, the Canadian Office of Health and Information Highway (OHIH) in collaboration with the Canadian Nurses Association, convened a Vision 2020 Workshop on Information and Communication Technologies in Health Care from the Perspective of the Nursing Profession. The recommended actions were to examine the impact of ICT on the role of the registered nurse and to develop entry-level competencies for nursing informatics (Clarke, 2002).

The enthusiasm for ICT-enhanced education is not shared by all nurse educators. Mallow and Gilje (1999) called for caution in the adoption of ICT in nursing education, suggesting that a technology-based approach may be at odds with the profession's desire and ability to provide humanistic, holistic nursing care.

In contrast to the views of Mallow and Gilje (1999), Simpson (2002) argued that virtual reality is the next innovation in education and the nursing profession needed to immerse students in high-technology education to better prepare them to practice in tomorrow's health care environment and to allow them to bridge the gap between knowledge and application.

Methods

Six nursing faculty members recruited to teach in the collaborative BScN program (a partnership between Durham College and UOIT) were sent a personal letter from the Dean of the Faculty of Health Sciences inviting their participation in the voluntary study. Initially, all six agreed to participate, however, one individual later withdrew when he accepted a new position with the Regional Health Authority. The data pertaining to this individual has not been included in the analysis or reporting of the data. The UOIT research ethics board approved this study.

Nursing deans, in collaboration with UOIT administrators, agreed to offer a needs-based comprehensive faculty development program to the five individuals to support their technological skill acquisition and to assist with course redesign.

Intensive Faculty Development Program

In 2003, prior to the summer break, an intensive four-month training program was offered involving a weekly eight-hour block of classroom instruction. The baseline technical proficiency of participants was assessed through the completion of a self-assessment questionnaire. Topics included basic knowledge and skills related to the Internet, e-mail, file management, and use of network services. A second level of more advanced topics pertained to applications (PowerPoint, Excel, Word), imaging (scanning, Photoshop, digital cameras), Web page design, and use of WebCT (uploading, quizzes, etc.).

Data gleaned through the administration of the questionnaire was used to design the faculty development program. With the exception of one participant, who had previous experience in using laptop computers and WebCT, faculty members indicated that they had a "working knowledge" of the basic topic areas and "minimal" knowledge/skills in the more advanced topic areas. Participants' self reported baseline ICT capacities suggested that they could complete basic tasks but lacked in-depth technical knowledge and skills. More importantly, it was clear that participants were not comfortable with the technology, seeing it as a "burden" rather than an enabling tool.

Description of Sample

The teaching experience of study participants varied from novice to experienced teacher (i.e., 2 to 16 years of postsecondary teaching experience). All participants had obtained a master's degree in nursing or in a related field. At the time the study commenced, two faculty members were enrolled in a doctoral nursing program on a part-time basis.

Data Collection

Data collection strategies included multiple in-depth individual interviews, one focus group interview, electronic faculty learning journals, and an expert review of Web-based teaching materials developed and/or used by study participants.

Data Analysis

Data was analyzed using commonly accepted qualitative data analysis procedures (Miles & Huberman, 1995; Richards, 2005). The use of qualitative data analysis software (NVivo 2.0) allowed for random or specific searches for common words, phrases, or terms that assisted in connecting tentative themes to transcripts, faculty learning journals, and detailed notes kept by the researcher during the interview process. Of further assistance in data analysis was the opportunity to generate graphs of categories, subcategories, themes, and impressions within NVivo. Visual mind maps and charting were used to check for connections and relationships among the observations and experiences of study participants. Researchers maintained an audit trail to document the process that was followed to arrive at their final conclusions.

Findings

Figure 1 (High Tech, High Touch Conceptual Framework) serves to organize the major findings that emerged from the study. The following section discusses the most salient themes from the perspectives of the nursing faculty.

The internal constructs depicted in Figure 1, titled "Pedagogical Decisions and Practices," include faculty experiences pertaining to course development, planning the laptop lecture, classroom management and students' use of MSN (short text messaging), loss of confidence and online interaction, and/or communication with students.

External constructs described in Figure 1 include faculty perceptions and/or experiences of the classroom and ICT infrastructure, institutional and faculty vision, support systems (formal and informal), and the nursing professions' readiness for change. These constructs are addressed in the following section.

Figure 1. High tech, high touch conceptual framework

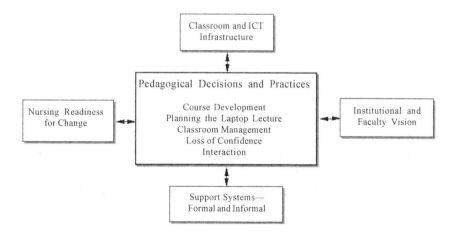

External Constructs

Support Mechanisms: Formal and Informal

When asked to identify success factors pertaining to the use of ICT in teaching, participants identified two specific types of support. First, they emphasized the importance of an accessible faculty support center in providing formal technical and pedagogical training. The Innovation Centre at UOIT assisted faculty to acquire the technical skills necessary to complete hybrid course design and implementation.

When reflecting on the intensive training program, participants highlighted the importance of the "high touch" learning environment in the Innovation Centre. They described the atmosphere as "safe and caring" with personalized instruction and support delivered in a non-judgmental manner. Without exception, participants expressed the importance of asking questions and exploring ideas freely without being made to feel "less capable" or "inferior." One faculty member explained, "I never feel my questions were stupid and [I] feel quite comfortable. I think the learning environment in the class [the training room] is very comforting for me in terms of the teacher's receptiveness."

Second, the faculty emphasized the importance of being able to ask just-in-time questions when attempting new ICT practices for the first time. One faculty member summarized the significance of just-in-time consultation with Innovation Centre staff stating, "I went to the Innovation Center and received help. I know that we had taken it in our courses, and I know I could have gone back to the book, which I tried, but I was getting frustrated, and I thought, No, I can make an appointment, somebody can tell me in five minutes."

Participants reflected on the considerable challenges they faced both personally and professionally in mastering ICT skills and in developing new curricula for the BScN program. Without exception, faculty expressed feelings of anxiety and uncertainty about their own capacity to successfully make the transition from a "traditional" teaching environment to a laptop learning environment. One participant recalled feelings of panic when confronting the challenges associated with the new teaching environment. She described the experience as "a learning curve which was like going up a mountain vertically." The participant acknowledged that the personal and professional support she received from colleagues was a critical success factor. She stated: "We had lots of positive support and getting energy off of other faculty members and supporting emotionally, or encouraging support for one another, was very important."

Another faculty member commented on the significance of having a group of colleagues who could support each other: "I think it's really positive, because I think we're all immersed in it at the same time, we're all hearing the same thing, we're all supporting each other." Repeatedly, findings emphasized that in addition to formal institutional support mechanisms, personal support systems were critical elements for success associated with transformational practice.

Faculty Vision

Initially, in-depth interviews with participants focused on the impact of the laptop program on teaching practice, the clinical knowledge and skills of student nurses, and interaction with students in the classroom and online.

From the onset of the study, participants emphasized the importance of maintaining traditional nursing values, and they cautioned that the use of ICT should not interfere or "get in the way" of the nurse-client relationship. Faculty stated that nursing education was based on the notion of "touching people and communicating with people with your heart." One participant worried that the adoption of ICT into nursing curricula would have negative implications. After reflecting on the "traditional" nursing role, she stated:

I can't do that with this computer. I really find it impinges as to who I am as a person. I don't like that. I'm a touchy-feely person...I'm sure there's ways you can do that with the computer, but I need that human contact; I need that touch.

Other faculty articulated the need to achieve a balance between the "high tech" approach to nursing education and the "high touch" approach embedded in the Caring Curriculum—a philosophy underpinning key pedagogical strategies in the BScN program (University of Ontario Institute of Technology, 2004).

As the study progressed, participants became more aware of the benefits of ICT for teaching and learning. In the process, their vision and understandings of the Laptop Program changed significantly. Faculty began to see the introduction of laptop computers, not as a burden, but as a valued teaching and learning resource. Partially in an effort to justify the cost of the laptop to students, faculty consciously attempted to discover new practices that would enhance learning. One faculty member stated:

I was conscious of the importance of incorporating it [the laptop] to validate that the students had a laptop." Some students at that point were saying, "Why did I spend all this money? I don't really need it." And so at that point I consciously created learning situations that required that they have their laptop there.

By the time the final focus group was conducted with the participants in May 2005, their initial trepidations had faded and they enthusiastically described their personal learning journeys. Over the course of two years, the participants' perceptions of ICT in nursing education had changed significantly. They clearly articulated a role for ICT in bridging the gap between knowledge and application. Furthermore, they saw ICT as supporting and extending traditional methods of nursing instruction consistent with the goals of the Caring Curriculum. A faculty member explained:

I really feel that the laptop program has facilitated and enhanced my role as a teacher. My personal philosophy is that I am a mentor and coach. I refer back to my personal analogy that nursing education be compared to a fragile seedling in a green house. As the teacher, I need to nurture and help each student to grow and bloom. The laptop program has facilitated this.

Institutional Vision

Faculty identified the pressures they felt from both college and university administration to demonstrate the benefits of the laptop program to students and their families. Some participants felt pressured to develop and implement new teaching practices partly to showcase the technology and partly to justify the additional costs. Over time, faculty became increasingly convinced that the adoption of ICT improved both teaching and learning outcomes. However, in some cases, students remained unconvinced of the value-added dimensions. One faculty member summarized the dissonance as follows:

Many students still did not rate the use of the laptop highly. They discuss the cost aspect as the major negative. I see the laptop program as essential. I truly never want to return to the "old" ways. My planning learning now automatically involves integrating the laptop in the classroom experience.

Classroom and ICT Infrastructure

Participants were cognizant of the substantial investment of UOIT in both the physical and technological infrastructure necessary to support a Web-centric learning environment. However, in attempting to design classrooms that would allow all students to use laptops, classrooms were built with fixed seating to accommodate the requisite wiring at each student's seat. This design presented challenges for nursing faculty accustomed to collaborative learning based on small-group activity in the classroom. As one participant explained:

The design is that there are rows, a table, a narrow table...there are probably seven rows. And although it's set up well for computers, I wish they hadn't done it that way. I wish they had done maybe square sections with the cable connections. But I like to circulate in a room.

Another faculty member commenting on the classroom design stated that in addition to teaching skills, she also "required the skills of an acrobat!" She explained:

I like to go from groups of students to groups of students. So when group work was going on, and if it was a group in the centre [of the room], I literally had to be an acrobat to jump over tables and get around people...

In the inaugural fall term (2003), the ICT infrastructure at UOIT presented challenges for faculty and students alike. The accelerated construction schedule associated with the opening of the university resulted in significant technical problems during the first five months of operation. Without exception, participants commented on the resultant challenges:

One week it seemed nothing was working. I went to print and the connection between the laptop and the printer was down. E-mail and WebCT were down and even the photocopier wasn't working. To top it all off, the phone system had also gone down. I had to improvise... I had to be positive with the students and make light of the situation...

Over the course of the study, participants reported fewer challenges associated with technical glitches. By the winter of 2004, participants summed up the situation as follows:

In the winter the technology was pretty consistent for us. We didn't have those momentous download problems or down time problems... I didn't have a lot of problems with my lessons and my using the laptop nor did students.

Nursing Readiness for Change

Over the course of their careers, all participants had experienced on a first-hand basis profound changes in nursing roles and responsibilities as a result of health care reform. Without exception, faculty felt that the "nursing readiness for change" well positioned practitioners to embrace new practices involving information and communication technologies.

As nurse educators, participants saw their central task as preparing future nurses for a lifelong process of personal and professional growth. According to one participant, if nurses are to be successful, "they need to be pretty adaptive people, and used to change." Expanding on this idea, faculty members described themselves as "ready and able" to adopt new teaching and learning strategies. One participant described nursing readiness to change as follows:

I think part of it is that we're used to change, so we're used to change on a daily basis. And so it's about adapting and being flexible, and I think those are important characteristics of a nurse. I think that it's important we embrace change.

Pedagogical Decisions and Practices

Throughout the study, participants spoke at length about pedagogical decisions and practices arising from their experiences teaching in a laptop BScN program. These internal constructs are depicted in Figure 1 (High Tech, High Touch Conceptual Framework). Findings pertained to course development (i.e., how faculty designed new courses and the "evergreening" of these courses), planning the laptop lecture, classroom management and students' use of MSN in the classroom, loss of confidence, and interaction and/or communication with students using new technologies.

Course Development

On completion of the intensive training program offered by the Innovation Center, faculty turned their attention to the development of new nursing courses. When questioned about course redesign, faculty described the task as constructing courses that would look like "distance education and face-to-face meshed together to have the best of both worlds." Participants spoke of the challenges of conceptualizing the classroom environment and an online environment which could work together.

Some faculty saw this "Web-centric" environment as being more akin to a distance education course where students periodically come together for discussion purposes. Others envisioned the use of computers in the classroom in face-to-face environment where students would use computers to access Internet-based materials. This dichotomy was responsible for considerable personal and professional debate among faculty.

The debate was intensified by the nature of the courses that the faculty members were developing. Three of the five participants were developing a first year course that involved extensive discussion in class and small-group activities. The majority of assignments were based on group activities and the sharing of insights about the role of nurses in contemporary healthcare. Without exception, study participants were challenged to balance high-tech teaching practices with high-touch values both in and out of the classroom.

One area where all faculty saw great promise was the use of ICT to develop video clips and for the inclusion of multimedia resources in lecture-based presentations. Many participants saw substantial benefits to using multimedia files for illustrating nursing procedures. One of the most powerful justifications for using multimedia concerned "visualization and desensitization" to help students prepare for medical procedures they might face in clinical settings. One faculty member recalled the following story:

When I first started hospital nursing, I was on an abdominal surgical floor, and I would see students look after a patient with a brand-new colostomy. They would take off the dressing, and they would see this colostomy bag and this colostomy, and their eyes would get big, and they would look shocked. The patient would be embarrassed and think, Oh, that's so ugly...

The participant concluded by saying that realistic images of "fresh, post-op colostomies" would be extremely useful in desensitizing students to situations that they would encounter on the wards.

Planning the Laptop Lecture

To assist in developing laptop lectures, faculty generated a series of key questions to outline next steps in developing course materials:

1.   What instructional design model should faculty use in designing courses that utilized laptop computers to enhance the student learning experience?

2.   How might the faculty role change with the introduction of the laptop program?

3.   How would Internet access impact the culture of the classroom?

4.   How would laptop computers and Internet access enhance group activities, presentations, and contribute to collaborative knowledge development in both classroom and online settings?

5.   Would a laptop learning environment positively or negatively affect management of the classroom?

6.   How could faculty use laptop computers and the Internet to foster greater interaction between themselves and students?

While other questions emerged from the group discussions, the above six issues framed many of the pedagogical decisions facing the faculty. It was clear from the outset, faculty perceptions of the use of ICT for teaching and learning were generally positive. One participant captured the sentiment of the others, saying:

I think information and communication technology will enrich their [students'] learning experiences by making it become a part of their life. Instead of me saying, "You need to look this up," it'll become assimilated and it'll become part of their way of learning.

The faculty identified a number of activities to take advantage of the laptop computer. These involved the use of PowerPoint to organize their lectures, which were then enriched with content from the Internet and multimedia resources. Furthermore, students were directed to the UOIT learning management system to download lecture notes. Faculty requested that students review the lecture notes before class and to augment the notes based on their own reading. Faculty believed that this provided students with a richer set of learning resources than notes taken in class and/or copies of the PowerPoint presentations. Participants also believed that students' access to the Internet during lectures generated a greater range of materials for use in class discussions.

The following example best illustrates the early success of faculty with the laptop lecture. A participant described group presentations completed using laptops and collective editing of the presentation by the whole class. She then went on to describe a "discussion artifact," including the work of all the students:

I have sort of an upfront content discussion with the students; then I usually have some cooperative activities, and the students work in groups on their laptops. We make their collaborative contributions. They contribute their comments, I type them into my piece, and then I download it them to them.

Classroom Management

The process of using networked laptop computers in the classroom was not always easy. When asked to describe the impact of computers in the classroom, participants stated that student attention appeared to have decreased. Faculty observed students dividing their attention between the lecture and activities taking place on their laptops.

Specifically, participants expressed concern over students' use of MSN (short text messaging) during class to communicate with fellow students. One faculty member stated "the use of MSN during class time has certainly been a challenge. At times it makes engagement with the students difficult." A second participant commented on students' use of MSN in the classroom: "I had increasing frustration with students using the laptop during class for other purposes…MSM messaging, playing cards individually or chess between neighbours, etc."

Faculty also observed students surfing the Internet in class. One participant, walking around a lecture hall, witnessed students completing assignments or answering e-mail rather than attending to lecture presentations. The perceived decrease in students' attention was profound, as one faculty member described:

One thing I noticed has been the attention span of the students. While sitting in the third row of the class for student presentations, I noticed a student in the first row on her laptop for the whole length of time her fellow groups were giving their class presentations. She was on numerous screens and typing away for the 20+ minutes of the presentation.

A significant finding emerging from the study was the lack of social protocols among students about the appropriate use of laptop computers in a social setting (e.g., a classroom lecture).

Loss of Confidence

All participants, to varying degrees, articulated a perceived loss of confidence in teaching abilities attributed to the adoption of ICT for teaching and learning.

Some participants described losing confidence when attempting (unsuccessfully) to master specific learning technologies or use particular computer programs. In other cases, participants' loss of confidence appeared most acute when they felt that their ability to make a personal connection with students was compromised because the computer created a communication barrier. One participant, after a particularly frustrating class, described how she began a subsequent class:

I started the class right from the beginning, stating laptops were to be closed once the lecture began. In both cases, some students chose not to comply... I walked up to the student and closed the laptop shut in a firm manner. The message was communicated.

In this situation, she felt that the "lids down" approach was her only option to regain some control over the classroom.

Another participant described her initial challenges in establishing two-way communication in the classroom. She compared her experiences to the type of interaction she was familiar with in the traditional classroom:

I see a huge difference in terms of the interaction component I am having with the students. Eye contact, verbal communication has decreased. I do not sense from the students "they are getting it" in terms of content. Previously I enjoyed interacting with the students in the class. I find the computer has hindered this interaction.

The sense among nursing faculty was that overall interaction in the classroom had *decreased* while interaction online had *increased*. Not surprisingly, in a program where developing and nurturing interpersonal relationships were core values, the adoption of high-tech teaching and learning practices that appeared to reduce high-touch elements initially caused discomfort among faculty.

Interaction

While faculty reported that interaction in the classroom appeared to have decreased, they also reported that online interaction between themselves and students increased and, in some cases, flourished. Faculty reported students preferred to communicate with them through e-mail and that requests for face-to-face meetings had significantly dropped. They also reported that they received few, if any, voicemail messages from students. This latter point was a dramatic change from their experience with former students who preferred to meet with faculty in face-to-face settings. One faculty member embraced this new form of communication:

Since e-mail is their passion, using this medium for communication brings the professor closer with the students. Questions are asked late in the evening and I am able to respond to the students in a timely manner. I try to check the WebCT site each evening from home briefly just before I go to bed.

The participant went on to explain how the use of ICT had fundamentally changed her teaching practices:

My office hours were extended into the evenings as I would log on once during the evening to answer questions. Before in the "old world," I would check my voice mail messages and call a student back. Often they were unavailable and the "phone tag" scenario ensued. With the electronic mail this does not occur.

One interesting finding was that faculty did not feel overwhelmed with the volume of e-mail from students. Several participants speculated that the volume of e-mail was less than expected because many students, rather than asking faculty questions, now turned to fellow students through e-mail to seek information.

Recommendations

In making recommendations, it is important to iterate that there is not a single best practice approach to the introduction of ICT into a learning environment. Rather, each institution working in collaboration with faculty and students must situate the proposed transformation within a local context.

Based on the experiences of UOIT nursing faculty, the following recommendations are offered:

1.   Before embarking on a laptop learning program, institutions must develop and resource a strategic plan that integrates input from across the organization.

2. Classroom design is a vital component of a successful laptop program. Ideally, teaching spaces should accommodate large group ICT-enhanced instruction with flexibility to facilitate small-group collaborative learning activities.

3. A two-prong approach to faculty development is critical. First, it must focus on assisting faculty to become self-sufficient in the use of ICT for teaching and learning. Second, training must expose faculty to additional learning technologies available on campus (e.g., Silicon Chalk or First Class).

4. Faculty requires a learning environment that supports experimentation recognizing that long-term success does not preclude failure in the short term. Supportive mechanisms should be both formal (i.e., programs and services offered through a faculty development center) and informal (peer support, coaching and mentoring).

5. It is critical for faculty to engage in personal and collective reflection concerning instructional design to enhance learning with laptop computers. Faculty must challenge traditional concepts of information transmission and embrace a constructivist environment where students have access to Internet resources, online course content, and library materials.

6. Evaluation is imperative in tracking the teaching and learning outcomes associated with transformational practice. Multiple data collection strategies are necessary to monitor change over time.

7. Practice-based research must be undertaken on new instructional design strategies to inform current and future pedagogical practices in nursing education.

8. The buy-in and ongoing support of senior administration is key in order to fully integrate ICT into the postsecondary environment. Faculty must be provided release time from normal academic responsibilities to acquire the requisite knowledge and skills. Faculty require transition time to transform their practices based on experience rather than seeing the introduction of ICT as an isolated one time activity.

Conclusion

Students of the digital generation have lived in a world increasingly filled with technological advances including the Internet, e-mail, and interactive video games. With the growth of technology, health care is becoming more information intensive and diverse. This creates a challenge for postsecondary educators as they respond to both the needs of students as well as workplace demands for technologically literate employees. Increasingly, nurse educators must build their capacities in ICT to enhance undergraduate education and prepare nurses for the technology that is embedded in their work environments.

Findings from this study confirm that the adoption of ICT in nursing education must meet an instructional need rather than exploiting the "bells and whistles" of technology. Repeatedly, participants cautioned that although there are many advantages in adopting ICT for teaching and learning, the limitations include the need for course development or redesign time, faculty computer competency, and individualized faculty support.

Conclusions emphasize the importance of ongoing institutional supports to build faculty capacities to successfully adopt ICT for teaching and learning. In this study, the provision of initial faculty development opportunities established a solid base for ICT adoption. However, ongoing needs-based faculty support, both formal and informal, was required for successful ICT implementation. Findings indicated that faculty development and training should occur in a safe learning environment conducive to experimentation and personal reflection. Further, academic administrators must ensure that sufficient resources are available for faculty development and that the ICT infrastructure is sufficiently robust to meet present and future demands.

In this study, the pedagogical issues and decisions faced by participants were challenging, requiring new knowledge and skills to successful re-engineer teaching practices both in and out of the classroom. The technologically advanced infrastructure at UOIT offered significant advantages to faculty, including ubiquitous access to the Internet through the development of a wired and wireless infrastructure. However, the use of MSN in the classroom and participants' perceptions that students' attention spans had decreased was of concern. This was further complicated by the lack of protocols regarding the use of the laptop in social learning environments. Further research is necessary to more fully explore these issues and the impact on teaching and learning outcomes.

Postscript to Study

In 2005, the Faculty of Health Sciences received two grants to conduct applied research pertaining to the use of ICT for teaching and learning. These included (1) a grant to examine the use of personal digital assistants for nursing students completing clinical placements, and (2) funding from the provincial Ministry of Health ($700,000 Canadian) to conduct a Nursing Clinical Simulation Initiative to provide students with virtual clinical experiences prior to their clinical placements in local hospitals. The success of these research projects demonstrates the cascading benefits associated with faculty successfully integrating technology into their teaching practices.

Acknowledgments

The authors are deeply indebted to the people from the nursing faculty at UOIT who served as inspiring teachers, learners, mentors, and role models in transformational practice. Their honesty and generosity of spirit in sharing their successes and challenges made this study possible. Special thanks to Eva Sunny for her valued contribution.

References

Atwell, G. (2004). *E-learning and sustainability*. Pontydysgu, University of Breman. Retrieved July 10, 2005, from www.ossite.org/Members/GrahamAttwell/sustainibility/attach/sustainibility4.doc

Clarke, H. F. (2002). *Educating tomorrow's nurses: Where's nursing informatics*. Ottawa, Canada: Canadian Nursing Informatics Association, Health Canada.

Miles, M. B., & Huberman, A. M. (1994). *Qualitative data analysis: An expanded sourcebook* (2nd ed.). Thousand Oaks, CA: Sage Publications.

Richards, L. (2005). *Handling qualitative data: A practical guide*. Thousand Oaks, CA: Sage Publications.

University of Ontario Institute of Technology. (2004). *Collaborative BScN program handbook*. Retrieved March 10, 2004, from http://healthsciences.uoit.ca/assets/Section~specific/Nursing/Student~handbooks/PDF/program_handbook.pdf

Zemsky, R., & Massy, W. (2004). *Thwarted innovation: What happened to e-learning and why*. The Weatherstation Project. University of Pennsylvania. Retrieved January 10, 2004, from www.sloan-c.org/resources/reviews/pdf/review18.pdf

Section II

Learning and Teaching Issues

Chapter VII

E-Learning in Higher Education:
The Need for a New Pedagogy

Dirk Morrison, University of Saskatchewan, Canada

Abstract

This chapter discusses the imperative prerequisite to the effective adoption of e-learning by institutions of higher education, namely, the adoption of new pedagogical perspectives and methods. It examines the purposes and goals of higher education, some grounded in tradition, others born of contemporary demands. By focusing on thinking skills, deep learning, and mature outcomes, the author underscores the need for such pedagogical foci to be integrated into the very fabric of higher education's adoption of e-learning. The hoped for outcome of such a consideration is a transformed institution, enabled to meet the demands of learners and society in the twenty-first century.

Introduction

Increasingly, valid critiques have pointed to the lack of empirical evidence that technology-enhanced learning initiatives actually improve learning outcomes, enhance the teaching enterprise, and are cost-effective for the institution (Clark, 1994; Twigg, 2001; Zemsky & Massy, 2004). Each of these claims, of course, needs careful analysis. One of the conclusions coming out of such criticisms is that technology, in and of itself, cannot be expected to solve the problems of an inefficient, even archaic, approach to pedagogy employed by the vast majority of our institutions of higher education. What, then, does the successful implementation of e-learning in postsecondary education look like? And, what does any evaluation of the success of e-learning need to include?

A critical measure of success for any institution employing e-learning technologies will be the quality of the outcomes (Weigel, 2002). This chapter aims to expand discussion beyond pragmatic questions regarding how to make the transition from face-to-face teaching to e-learning, to include questions regarding how to fundamentally shift the core guiding pedagogical principles of our institutions of higher education. The basic premise of this chapter is that current strategies used to address gaps in performance (e.g., technology-focused faculty development) will fail to realize the hoped-for outcome of an institution shifting to e-learning technologies. A focus on methods and techniques designed to improve the effective implementation of technological products will only be partially useful; what is also needed is a deep and critical discussion regarding the fundamental purposes of designing and employing such products, and a focus on the hoped-for outcomes of such efforts. Throughout this chapter, e-learning is defined as electronically mediated learning, using any variety of media and hardware/software combinations, and usually including the use of facilitated transactions software (e.g., Blackboard, WebCT) (Zemsky & Massy, 2004, p. 5).

To take full advantage of the potential of e-learning, institutions of higher education not only have to radically change how they are organized to support technology-enhanced learning (infrastructures and organizational models), but also face the challenge of creating a more appropriate pedagogical foundation upon which to build revitalized educational systems necessary to meet the demands of current and future knowledge users and creators. Put another way, I argue that the entire system of tertiary education needs revamping from the bottom-up. Current approaches to teaching and learning are an awkward fit with the new information and communications technology (ICT) tools currently used for teaching and learning (May & Short, 2003). In many ways, these new technologies have forced this pedagogical issue and are inherently changing the system from within. Dziuban, Hartman, and Moskal (2004) pointed to a report by the National Research Council Panel on the Impact of Information Technology on the Future of the Research University, which speculated that "information technology will alter the university's usual constraints of space and time, transforming how institutions of higher education are organized and financed, as well as altering their intellectual activities" (p. 8). While it is important to consider the range and variety of factors necessary to ready institutions of higher education for the adoption of e-learning technologies, it is also critical to examine and critique current pedagogical approaches. In addition, not only will instructors and learners be challenged to learn new skills and new ways of working as a result of the adoption of ICT, but they will also be required to change their ways of thinking about the purposes of higher education, the learning process, what it means to be literate, and how knowledge is created. In other words, both faculty and learners will need to re-examine their beliefs, values, perspectives, and resultant approaches to teaching and learning when adopting e-learning technologies.

Higher Education: What's It All About?

Eisner (1997) claimed that knowing how to pursue and capture broad meanings shaped the minds of learners. These minds, in turn, collectively shaped the culture, effected change in democratic societies, and ultimately transformed the global community—no small matter. Bamburg (2002) claimed that the very definition of what it means to be educated has changed. In the past, the educational system concentrated on providing students with the basic skills for working in an industrial economy. Now the system must focus on higher order thinking skills that are needed in our knowledge-based economy.

The implication here is that institutions of higher education have critical responsibilities to provide learning environments conducive to the development of capable and creative minds—minds readied for the challenges of a complex world. They must empower learners to know how to pursue and capture broad and deep meanings and to use holistic thinking as the conduit to deep learning.

Holistic Thinking and Deep Learning

Most educators would willingly promote the idea that, at least within higher education contexts, there is a need to move away from what they would call a surface or "shallow" approach to learning (e.g., emphasis on memorizing, simple recall of facts) to a form of "deep" learning wherein learners construct and integrate complex representations of knowledge into patterns that are personally meaningful (Barell, 1991; Garrison, 1991; Hillfish & Smith, 1961; Paul, 1995; Ruggiero, 1988). The former approach, often characterized as typical of traditional pedagogical methods (e.g., the transmission model of learning), is concomitant with a superficial understanding of the subject matter. Inhibiting the development of thinking skills, this approach prescribes that learners passively accept knowledge as it is presented to them, rather than critically examining and constructing it based on their own experiences and previous knowledge (Burge, 1988; Garrison, 1993; Lauzon, 1992). On the other hand, teaching methods that use active learning participation and interaction are facilitative of deep learning and require both higher-order understanding of content and the active construction of meaning within personal and global contexts (Kember, 1991; Newman, Webb, & Cochran, 1995). Although some course content should be in the form of basic facts to be remembered or skills to be demonstrated (e.g., procedural skills), many would claim that, ideally, most learning opportunities should be presented in ways that encourage and facilitate deep thinking and learning about the subject at hand (Garrison, 1993). Holistic thinking (i.e., critical, creative, and complex thinking) is seen here as a necessary antecedent to deep learning and is implicit in many discussions regarding the transformative, emancipatory, and neo-utilitarian potentials of education (Brookfield, 1987; Gross, 1991; McLaren, 1994; Mezirow, 1990; Paul, 1995; Sternberg, 1996).

Accepting that holistic thinking and deep learning are integrally related and are also important educational outcomes raises two key questions: What does deep learning actually look like? What are the necessary antecedents to realizing such learning?

Holistic Thinking Skills: Necessary Tools for Deep Learning

Morrison (2004) claimed that deep learning is related to the way we see the world, ultimately tied to actions and change, necessarily integrative in nature, and a cumulative process, not a singular event. Many would contend that deep learning generally results in qualitatively changing knowledge constructs; as these constructs grow in complexity, our understanding of the perceived world simultaneously broadens and deepens (Crotty, 1993). According to this view, knowledge gained through deep learning is holistic, and ideas, concepts, principles, perceptions, etc. are not seen as unrelated bits of information to be constructed Lego-set style (Lai & Biggs, 1994), but as a dynamic, fluid, and organic phenomenon in the sense that each knowledge construct generated is related, affects, and is affected by others within the mind of the learner. It is a kind of learning that is integrated, not segmented, and makes a difference in who we are, how we think, and what we do (Draper, 1998). Learning at this level is both personally meaningful and contextually engaging. Further, the learner is, in many ways, inseparable from the learning, and this learning is inseparable from thinking. In other words, deep learning, fuelled by holistic thinking, is learning that does not dissect facts from context, ideas from world-views, and learners from the things to be learned. Deep learning and the holistic thinking associated with it mean being organized around goals of personal knowledge construction rather than simply those of task performance (Bereiter, 1990). Finally, it is important to point out that deep learning and holistic thinking are not just an individual phenomenon. More often than not, these occur within a social context, within a *community* of learners wherein dialogue and exchange of views and thoughts are the norm (Vygotsky, 1978). According to Cust (1996), a deep learning, holistic thinking approach within a social context would have the highest levels of cognitive and affective engagement and would likely be the most meaningful, facilitating, in turn, the production of structurally more complex and affectively satisfying learning outcomes.

So, holistic cognitive processes, among other factors (e.g., context, learning task, individual preferences, and motivations), influence not only the approach to learning but also the end result. Personally meaningful residual knowledge and change, internally or externally manifested as a result of deep learning, are intimately tied not only to *what*, *why*, and *how* we learn but also to the thinking process itself.

Developing Online Environments for Deep Learning

It is critical, then, to move purposefully toward reconfiguring educational goals that include an emphasis on holistic thinking (i.e., critical, creative, complex thinking) for the purposes of facilitating deep learning. However, conceptual frameworks for specifically identifying and evaluating holistic thinking have not been readily available. This latter deficit has been all too often ignored in educational research, although recent efforts have been promising (Garrison, Anderson, & Archer, 2000, 2001). Furthermore, new tools for learning, afforded by the rapid development and expansion of information technologies, have not proven to be a panacea for the development of holistic thinking, let alone deep learning (Weigel, 2002). Many higher education applications of e-learning, for example, have the potential for facilitating holistic thinking and deep learning but may, for a number of reasons, miss the mark (Gibson, 1995; Weigel, 2002). Within the context of educational applications of e-learning there may be nothing inherently facilitative of holistic thinking, despite the best hopes and intuitions otherwise.

Figure 1. Example of an integrated online learning environment

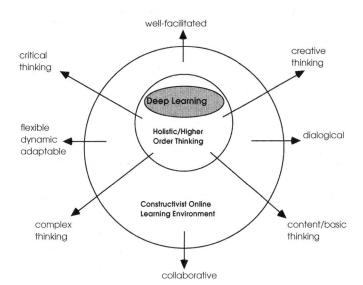

In addition to determining relevant indicators of holistic thinking (Morrison, 2004) and the constellation of factors at play to encourage or discourage thinking (Bullen, 1997), it is equally important to discover, describe, understand, and highlight the critical elements in online learning environments that potentially influence holistic thinking and, by extension, deep learning. The contribution of contextual and process variables, the nature of learning tasks, educational methods utilized, and the "shape" of the technological tools available, among others, are important foci to help illuminate and increase the understanding of the nature of holistic thinking and deep learning in online environments. To support what Weigel (2002) called "depth education" in online learning environments, it would be necessary to include a range of administrative (e.g., faculty training, campus libraries) and technical infrastructures (on/off-campus bandwidth, ICT, educational technologies). Figure 1 provides an example of a conceptual map of interrelated factors important to the construction of an e-learning environment.

While it is useful to focus discussion on the importance of holistic thinking skills as the conduit to the facilitation of deep learning within e-learning environments, it is important to now turn to how this might be translated into a system of learning outcomes for the online classroom.

Maturing Our Outcomes:
A Systems Perspective

In their paper "Maturing Outcomes", Costa and Garmston (1998) presented a model of five nested levels of learning outcomes, each level being broader and more encompassing than the level within. What follows is a contextual adaptation of the conceptual framework described in their work.

Outcomes as Activities

The authors characterized this outcome as reflective of "episodic, teacher-centered thinking" with the goal of the online instructor simply being to keep students engaged with the accomplishment of e-learning activities (Costa & Garmston, 1998, para. 5). Success is often measured in terms of whether students made it through the Web resources, completed the online quizzes, and participated in the online discussions. If learners complete all the activities laid out in the online course, the e-learning application is deemed a success.

Outcomes as Content

As instructors gain familiarity with the online learning environment, they are able to ask, What concepts and principles are students learning by completing the embedded activities? The online activities are now employed as vehicles to learn content. The online instructor's focus is on what concepts students will learn, what understandings they will develop, and how that knowledge will be recognized and assessed.

Outcomes as Processes

As online instructors' skills continue to mature, content begins to be selected for its generative qualities (Costa & Garmston, 1998; Perrone & Kallick, 1997). Content becomes both a source and conduit for experiencing, practicing, and applying the cognitive processes needed to think creatively and critically. These processes are basic to lifelong problem solving and include observing and collecting data, forming and testing hypothesizes, drawing conclusions, and posing questions, to name a few.

This shift from a focus on activities and content to cognitive processes is critical. Process outcomes are of central importance because to deeply understand any content, students must know and practice the processes by which that content came into being (Costa & Garmston, 1998; Paul & Elder, 1991; Tishman & Perkins, 1997). At this level, online instructors need to ask, What specific cognitive processes do I want students to practice and develop? How will this online course and the resources I've supplied help them develop those processes? How will I know if they are practicing and developing them?

Outcomes as Dispositions

The realization of this outcome requires the transcendent qualities of systems thinking found in dispositions or habits of the mind, such as enhancing one's capacities to direct and control persistence; managing impulsivity, creativity, and meta-cognition; striving for precision and accuracy; and listening with empathy, risk-taking, and wonderment (Costa, 1991; Costa & Garmston, 1998; Tishman & Perkins, 1997). These universally desirable qualities, exercised within the context of holistic thinking, are valued across disciplines and are a core goal for higher education. Furthermore, a focus on cognitive dispositions assists in developing lifelong capacities and intellectual foundation for continuous learning. Recall that each level of the model presented subsumes the previous. So within the province of outcome as disposition, activities are designed with purpose; content is selected for its generative nature; and critical processes are identified and practiced. These outcomes now build toward a set of superior, more long-range outcomes.

It is important to note that with the three previous outcome levels a single-talented instructor could likely design and implement an online learning environment conducive to the realization of each. At the level of dispositional outcomes, however, it would be desirable to employ the talents of a variety of faculty and course development support staff (e.g., instructional designers, media specialists, etc.). Each instructional team then decides the following: What dispositions do we collectively want online learners to develop and employ? What will we do to assist their development? How can we determine if online learners are developing such dispositions over time? What will we include as evidence of their growth? When an understanding regarding such meta-level outcomes is shared, the entire development team is able to break out of traditional ways of thinking about online learning. As these common goals are achieved collaboratively, they are more likely to be reinforced, transferred, and revisited across the curriculum, the department, and the university.

Outcomes as Mind States

In their model of maturing outcomes, Costa and Garmston (1998) presented five human capacities, or mind states, namely, efficacy, flexibility, craftsmanship, consciousness, and interdependence. These capacities are not trivial and, according to the authors, "act as catalysts or energy sources fueling human thinking, learning and behaviors at the next level of outcomes" and "are the wellsprings nurturing all high performing individuals, groups and organizations and act as beacons toward increasingly authentic, congruent, and ethical behavior" (Costa & Garmston, 1998, para. 15).

At this level, outcomes are drawn not only from the mind states themselves, but also from the ways they interact with the discipline's, department's, or institution's expressed values, culture, and mission. Again, colleagues and instructional development teams need to consider the following questions: In which mind states do we wish students and colleagues to become more resourceful? What will we do to capacitate their development in an online environment? How will we know when they have been amplified?

Costa and Garmston (1998) stated that as a result of a focus on outcomes at this level:

Staff and students learn to draw upon the five mind states to organize and direct their resources as they resolve complex problems, diagnose human frailty in themselves and others, plan for the most productive interventions in groups, and search out the motivations of their own and other's actions. These mind states become desirable meta-outcomes not only for faculty and students, but also for the wider [learning] community as well (para. 24).

Empowering the
Transition to E-Learning

Attempts to transfer face-to-face courses to an e-learning environment often result in the replication of a limited and inappropriate approach to pedagogy. For example, some authors have pointed out that the adopted outcome expectations fixed at the level of content are reinforced mainly by the ease of measurement afforded by using standard assessment tools (Angelo, 2005; Costa & Garmston, 1998; Cross & Angelo, 1993) and not because of the efficacy of the approach. The focus of most assessment strategies and tools in higher education continues to be on evaluating a learner's demonstration of relatively low levels of knowledge and skills rather than broader, deeper, and more essential outcomes that one would expect. Most of the popular learning management software platforms currently in use in higher education facilitate the continued use of such an approach by building in content-oriented assessment tools. It seems self-evident that transferring such a content-focused approach to learner assessment within an e-learning environment is neither appropriate nor desirable. What needs to be asked is if we are serious about higher order learning outcomes, are we willing to invest the time, energy, and resources to develop appropriate assessment tools?

Often, examples of failures of e-learning innovations are provided as evidence to support the status quo. In fact, these examples need to be carefully analyzed to determine if the failure was in the technology itself or in the inappropriate application of the technology (Weigel, 2002). If the simple transfer to an electronic environment of an ineffective, low-level approach to face-to-face pedagogy occurred, then one should not be surprised if this translated into poor results. Without a re-configuration of the basic pedagogy, no significant difference should be expected when courses are migrated to an e-learning environment (Clark, 1994). In fact, simply porting a poorly designed course to such an environment might even result in an inferior learning experience (e.g., simply posting lecture notes on a Web site).

A Systems Approach to E-Learning in Higher Education

Dilts (1994), extending work done by Bateson (1972), applied systems thinking to education. A major concept of importance here is that any system of activity is a subsystem embedded within another system. The activities associated with an institution's efforts to make a transition to e-learning are likewise situated within the larger context of that institution. For example, political will, budgets, human resources and skills, extent of entrenched ideals, and resistance to change are all elements within the larger institutional system that will retard or advance progress toward a transformed institution fertile for the growth of e-learning.

The larger educational system within which e-learning is taking place will also influence the type of learning that is facilitated. If an institution of higher education is primarily focused on the measurement of content-based learning outcomes (relying on these to market the institution to employers, funding agencies, etc.), then this focus will dictate the type and range of assessment tools and evaluation methods deemed acceptable. Conversely, if an institution is primarily focused on producing high quality minds and high functioning citizens (focus on dispositional and mind state outcomes), then the tools for assessment and concomitant e-learning strategies will be radically different. Dilts (1994, in Costa & Garmston, 1998) proposed that "learning something on an upper level will change things on lower levels but learning something on a lower level may or may not inform and influence levels above it (para. 40)." The implication here is that while efforts can be made to create innovative e-learning environments at the course or program level, these will not likely result in much change at the institutional level. Only when departments and the wider university undertake a re-engineering of the teaching and learning enterprise, will the transition to an innovative e-learning institution prove to be successful.

Building a New Foundation:
Outcomes, Knowledge, and Pedagogy

Expectations are high regarding the potential for e-learning to change the face of tertiary education. To help ensure the transition to e-learning results in an improved institution, it is critical that the expected outcomes of higher education are revamped along the lines of those presented by Costa and Garmston (1998). Proponents must inform the university community about the need for higher level outcomes, connecting them to a clear articulation of the generic cognitive skills required (e.g., holistic thinking, states of mind, etc.). Appropriate instructional tools and methods facilitative of the development of such skills must be developed and applied to e-learning contexts. Faculty development opportunities should be available to enable the necessary shift from a transmittal to a transformative approach to pedagogy. It should be made clear that this emphasis on the development of a wide range and depth of cognitive skills is, in fact, the essential value-addition that higher education can and should offer. I believe, universities should market themselves on the basis of the quality of mental skills acquired and enhanced through their programs—skills that prepare students for a lifetime of work in a knowledge economy—and underscore an increased capacity for critical, creative, and complex thinking, lifelong learning, and citizenry, rather than the many other measures currently used to evaluate the relative quality of one institution against another (e.g., McLean's Guide to Canadian Universities, 2005).

Costa and Liebmann (1997a) point out that our current approach to compartmen-talizing knowledge into static disciplines has had utility as a classification system (writing textbooks, hiring faculty, organizing university departments, etc.) but is fundamentally an archaic conception of the disciplines, conveying an obsolete and myopic view of what constitutes knowledge. While an interdisciplinary curriculum may be a difficult sell at universities, more and more it is becoming obvious that areas of innovation and knowledge breakthroughs are a result of cross-fertilization of ideas across the disciplines (Lattuca, 2004). Therefore, in addition to the emphasis on higher-order outcomes as target goals for our instructional efforts, there should be a constant push for interdisciplinary activities. Breaking down the barriers between knowledge areas, challenging the concept of disciplines, and creating opportunities for scholars and students to understand the points of intersection between their disciplines will take us a long way to an expanded view of knowledge.

Finally, it must be made clear to all involved across the institution that any new technologies need to be used wisely. This means adopting and implementing technology within dynamic and adaptive learning environments specifically designed to address and support higher-order learning outcomes, and not just using them as a glossy, high-tech overlay to an outdated and ineffective pedagogy.

Building Capacity for Institutional Change

Currently there is no consensus as to what really effective online education within the context of tertiary institutions should look like. While some have pointed to the eventual emergence of a "dominant design" (Zemsky & Massy, 2004, p. 7) in e-learning, it is important not to search for an ideal model for e-learning, for there is not one model. Instead, what is required is a dynamic, evolving institution that adapts and re-configures appropriate working models for e-learning. This requires openness to new ideas, especially in the arena of pedagogy (King, 1993); the focus should be on building capacity for transforming institutional norms for teaching and learning from within. Faculty adoption of e-learning needs to draw on the traditional strengths of the academy and nurture collaborative individualism. This process includes building connections and interdependency between people, organizations, and ideas (Smyre, 2000). A focus on synthesis, using living systems as the metaphor (not the factory), is required to support an adaptive, evolving system of e-learning. Open-minded dialogue and not adversarial debate needs to be the communicative environment within which new ideas for e-learning are be explored. Students must encounter choices (curricular and e-course styles), not rigid standardization in order to use what is known, say, about preferred learning styles (Anderson & Adams, 1992) and multiple intelligences (Gardner, 1993, 2000). Institutions must have a forward thinking orientation, drawing on current research and literature to inform decisions regarding the adoption and implementation of e-learning. And these activities must incorporate evaluation mechanisms if institutions of higher education are to make the best use of e-learning.

Conclusion

One of the core premises of this chapter is that simply overlaying poor pedagogy with the veneer of e-learning as innovation is a sham and is sure to produce results as outlined by Zemsky and Massy (2004) and others. This chapter has identified the need to review and reconfigure this pedagogy to be more in line with contemporary research regarding the nature and purposes of learning within the context of higher education. Current findings in brain research and the cognitive sciences hold much promise for providing guideposts as to how to construct effective learning environments. Underscored was the need to create learning environments that require the development of critical, creative, and complex thinking skills. A brief discussion was presented regarding the need to expand our conception of expected terminal outcomes as a result of singular or collective learning experiences within a university education. The consideration of these suggestions would do well to help ensure an institution's smooth transition to and adoption of e-learning.

All of the previous cannot take place, however, unless the larger context itself is altered. Promotion of change and transformation must occur within both the local and global constellations of activity and innovation in higher education. The context within which universities and by extension e-learning are situated is a rapidly evolving and incredibly dynamic environment. Not known for corporate agility and flexibility, universities may be at risk in terms of quickly adjusting fundamental principles and core values (i.e., ways of doing things) in order to take advantage of opportunities (e.g., e-learning). However, universities are not static, inanimate entities, but rather are the sum total of the people involved. So it is people and their ideas about teaching and learning, including e-learning, that need to be changed if a successful transition to e-learning is to occur. Smyre (2000) asked the correct questions:

If context has emerged as a key concept for education, what do we do to help people learn how to understand how to build capacities for transformation? If the underlying assumptions are changing, how do we coach people to think within a futures context? And possibly the most important question... how do we introduce into educational curricula the need to think about the impact of future trends as well as transforming underlying assumptions? How can schools, community colleges, and universities begin to create a learning environment so that issues are considered within an evolving "futures context?" (p. 7)

These are multiple questions with multiple answers. However, if the university is to undertake a successful transition to e-learning, it must simultaneously undertake a transformation of its approach to pedagogy. Cognitive research from the past decade suggests the instructional strategies that we have been using are no longer appropriate (Bamburg, 2002).

Key decision makers within the higher education sector, as well as those responsible for designing and developing the e-learning opportunities, need to use this knowledge to change the way we do things in higher education. A relevant and vital tertiary educational system is at stake.

References

Anderson, J. A., & Adams, M. (1992). Acknowledge the learning styles of diverse student populations: Implications for instructional design. In L. L. B. Chism (Eds.), *Teaching for diversity: New directions in teaching and learning* (No. 42). San Francisco: Jossey Bass.

Angelo, T. (2005). *Doing assessment as if learning matters*. Presentation to the University of Sasktchewan, Saskatoon, SK.

Bamburg, J. D. (2002). Learning, learning organizations, and leadership: Implications for the year 2050. Retrieved May 2005, from http://www.newhorizons.org/trans/bamburg.htm

Barell, J. (1991). *Teaching for thoughtfulness: Classroom strategies to enhance intellectual development.* New York: Longman.

Bateson, G. (1972). *Steps to an ecology of mind.* New York: Chandler.

Bereiter, C. (1990). Aspects of an educational learning theory. *Review of Educational Research, 60*(4), 603-624.

Brookfield, S. (1987). *Developing critical thinkers: Challenging adults to explore alternative ways of thinking and acting.* San Francisco: Jossey-Bass.

Bullen, M. (1997). *A case study of participation and critical thinking in a university-level course delivered by computer conferencing.* Unpublished PhD Thesis: University of British Columbia.

Bullen, M. (1998). Participation and critical thinking in online university distance education. *Journal of Distance Education, 13*(2), 1-32.

Burge, E. J. (1988). Beyond andragogy: Some explorations for distance learning design. *Journal of Distance Education, 3*(1), 5-23.

Clark, R. (1994). Media will never influence learning. *Educational Technology Research and Development, 42*(2), 21-29.

Costa, A. (1991). The search for intelligent life. In A. Costa (Ed.), *The school as a home for the mind*. Palatine, III: Skylight.

Costa, A., & Garmston, J. (1998). *Maturing outcomes*. Retrieved May 2005, from http://www.newhorizons.org/trans/costa_garmston.htm

Costa, A., & Liebmann, R. (1997) Towards renaissance curriculum: An idea whose time has come. In A. Costa & R. Liebmann (Eds.). *Envisioning process as content: Towards renaissance curriculum*. Thousand Oaks, CA: Corwin Press.

Cross, K. P., & Angelo, T. A. (1993). *Classroom assessment techniques* (2nd ed.). San Francisco: Jossey-Bass.

Crotty, T. (1993). *Constructivist theory unites distance education and teacher education*. Ames Teacher Education Center, University of Wisconsin-River Falls, WI. Retrieved November 15, 2003, from http://edie.cprost.sfu.ca/it/constructivist-learning

Cust, J. (1996). A relational view of learning: Implications for nurse education. *Nurse education today, 16*(4), 239-306.

Dilts, R. (1994) Effective presentation skills. In A. Costa & J. Garmston (Eds.), *Maturing outcomes* (p. 3642). Capitola, CA: Meta Publications. Retrieved May 2005, from http://www.newhorizons.org/trans/costa_garmston.htm

Draper, P. (1998). *Understanding student approaches to technology assisted learning*. Queensland Conservatorium Griffith University. Retrieved November 24, 2003, from http://www29.gu.edu.au/staff/draper/tal.html

Eisner, E. (1997). Cognition and representation: A way to pursue the American dream? *Phi Delta Kappan, 78*(5), 348-353.

Gardner, H. (1993). *Multiple intelligences: The theory in practice*. New York: Basic Books.

Gardner, H. (2000). *The disciplined mind: Beyond facts and standardized tests, the K-12 education that every child deserves*. New York: The Penguin Group, Penguin Putnam.

Garrison, D. R. (1991). Critical thinking and adult education: A conceptual model for developing critical thinking in adult learners. *International Journal of Lifelong Education, 10*(4), 287-303.

Garrison, D. R. (1993). A cognitive constructivist view of distance education: An analysis of teaching and learning assumptions. *Distance Education, 14*(2), 199-210.

Garrison, D. R., Anderson, T., & Archer, W. (2000). Critical inquiry in a text-based environment: Computer conferencing in higher education. *The Internet and Higher Education, 2*(2-3), 1-19.

Garrison, D. R., Anderson, T., & Archer, W. (2001). Critical thinking, cognitive presence, and computer conferencing in distance education. *American Journal of Distance Education, 15*(1), 7-23.

Gibson, L. (1995). *Discursive learning spaces: The potential of the Internet as an environment for learning at a distance.* Unpublished MSc Major Research Paper: University of Guelph.

Gross, R. (1991). *Peak learning: A master course in learning how to learn.* Los Angeles, CA: Jeremy P. Tarcher.

Hillfish, G. H., & Smith, P. G. (1961). *Reflective thinking: The method of education.* New York: Dodd, Mead & Company.

Kegan, R. (1994). *In over our heads: The mental demands of modern life.* Cambridge, MA: Harvard University Press.

Kember, D. (1991). Instructional design for meaningful learning. *Instructional Science, 20*(4), 289-310.

King, A. (1993). From sage on the stage to guide on the side. *College Teaching, 31*(1), 30-35.

Kolb, D. A. (1984). *Experiential learning: Experience as the source of learning and development.* NJ: Prentice-Hall.

Lai, P., & Biggs, J. (1994). Who benefits from mastery learning? *Contemporary Educational Psychology, 19*(1), 13-23.

Lattuca, L. (2004). *Creating interdisciplinarity: Interdisciplinary research and teaching among college and university faculty.* Vanderbilt Issues in Higher Education. Nashville, TN: Vanderbilt University Press.

Lauzon, A. C. (1992). Integrating computer-based instruction with computer conferencing: An evaluation of a model for designing online education. *American Journal of Distance Education, 6*(2), 32-46.

MacLean's Guide to Canadian Universities '05. (2005). *MacLean's Magazine.* Toronto, ON: Rogers Media.

May, G. L., & Short, D. (2003). Gardening in cyberspace: A metaphor to enhance online teaching and learning. *Journal of Management Education, 27*(6), 673-693.

McLaren, P. L. (1994). Critical thinking as a political project. In K. S. Walters (Ed.), *Re-thinking reason: New perspectives in critical thinking.* New York: SUNY Press.

Menzies, H. (1996). *Whose brave new world: The information highway and the new economy.* Toronto, ON: Between the Lines.

Mezirow, J. (1990). How critical reflection triggers transformative learning. In J. Mezirow & Associates (Eds.), *Fostering critical reflection in adulthood* (pp. 1-20). San Francisco: Jossey Bass.

Morrison, D. (2004). *A study of holistic thinking in an agricultural leadership development program using asynchronous computer conferencing.* Unpublished doctoral thesis, University of Toronto.

Newman, D. R., Webb, B., & Cochrane, C. (1995). *A content analysis method to measure critical thinking in face-to-face and computer supported groups learning.* Retrieved October, 1998, from listserv@guvm.georgetown.edu

Panel on the Impact of Information Technology on the Future of the Research University. (2002). *Preparing for the revolution: Information technology and the future of the research university.* Washington, DC: The National Academies Press. Retrieved June 2005, from http://www.nap.edu/books/030908640X/html/

Paul, R. (1995). *Critical thinking: How to prepare students for a rapidly changing world.* Sonoma, CA: Foundation for Critical Thinking.

Perrone, V., & Kallick, B. (1997). Generative topics for process curriculum. In A. Costa & R. Liebmann (Eds.), *Supporting the spirit of learning: When process is content.* Thousand Oaks, CA: Corwin Press.

Ruggiero, V. R. (1988). *Teaching thinking across the curriculum.* New York: Harper & Row, Publishers.

Smyre, R. (2000). *Transforming the 20th century mind: The roles of a futures institute.* Retrieved May 2005, from http://www.newhorizons.org/future/smyre.htm

Sternberg, R. J. (1996). *Successful intelligence: How practical and creative intelligence determine success in life.* New York: Simon & Schuster.

Tishman, S., & Perkins, D. (1997, January). The language of thinking. *Phi Delta Kappan, 5*(78), 368-374.

Twigg, C. A. (2001). *Innovations in online learning: Moving beyond no significant difference.* The Pew Symposia in Learning and Technology 2001. Center for Academic Transformation, Rensselaer Polytechnic Institute, Troy, NY.

Vygotsky, L. S. (1978). *Mind in society: The development of higher mental process.* Cambridge, MA: Harvard University Press.

Weigel, V. (2002). *Deep learning for a digital age: Technology's untapped potential to enrich higher education.* San Francisco: Jossey-Bass Publishing.

Zemsky, R., & Massy, W. F. (2004). *Thwarted innovation: What happened to e-learning and why.* A final report for the Weatherstation Project of The Learning Alliance for Higher Education at the University of Pennsylvania.

Chapter VIII

New Skills and Ways of Working:
Faculty Development for E-Learning

Gail Wilson, University of Western Sydney, Australia

Abstract

This chapter analyzes approaches to faculty development for e-learning in post-compulsory institutions. Everett Rogers' (2003) diffusion of innovation theory provides the framework for a review of faculty development strategies adopted by institutions to foster the adoption of information and communication technologies (ICTs) by mainstream faculty into everyday teaching and learning practices. Using examples as illustration, the chapter reviews different approaches to faculty development aimed at achieving a critical mass of staff who are competent working in the e-learning context. These strategies include focusing on the characteristics of innovation; adopting a staged approach to skills acquisition; embedding skills and processes associated with teaching and learning in the e-learning context in formal, accredited courses; fostering peer learning; framing faculty development as project-based learning; and using the online environment to deliver faculty development. The chapter concludes with practical advice concerning faculty development for e-learning practice across institutions.

Introduction

This chapter provides a review and analysis of approaches to faculty development to address the demands faced by teachers in post-compulsory institutions in the adoption and use of e-learning. In my practice as an academic developer, I adopt the view that faculty development for e-learning is a change process aimed at providing faculty with new sets of skills, knowledge, and capabilities in this new and different context for learning and teaching. Thus, the focus in this chapter is on strategies used to ensure that faculty is sufficiently skilled to work in the online environment and to enhance the institution's capability to sustain the integration of the new technologies into learning and teaching practices.

Defining Terms

Throughout the chapter, faculty development is used to mean the provision of opportunities for faculty in higher education to engage in continuous improvement in relation to their role as teachers in the e-learning environment. As a term faculty development is used synonymously with others in use such as academic development, educational development, and staff development. Faculty development is also viewed as workplace learning, defined as "learning from work, at and through work" (Garavan, Morley, Gunnigle, & McGuire, 2002, p. 61).

Faculty development has context, content, and process elements. It contributes to broadening the scope of competence of faculty as learning professionals throughout their careers (Cheetham & Chivers, 2005; Eraut, 2001). It extends the professional knowledge, skills, techniques, attitudes, and understanding of ethical principles that underpin the teaching practices of staff (Beaty, 1998; Brew, 1995). It fosters the growth and development of organizational learning, by leveraging the knowledge assets of the organization at the individual, work group, and organizational levels for the benefit of the learner and to improve institutional performance overall (Boud & Garrick, 1999). Faculty development is also the means by which faculty are afforded the opportunity to challenge their current academic practices and acquire, practice, and adopt new knowledge (Anderson & Kanuka, 1997; Taylor, 1997). The faculty development function is challenged constantly by how best to engage strategically and achieve maximum impact within the institution. It must continually seek to enlist senior management support, assume a "helicopter view" of the organization, and contribute to and help shape institutional goals. Beaty (1995) drew a metaphor of faculty development "working across the hierarchy," balancing organizational and individual priorities and demands, informing policy development, and encouraging innovation between policy-driven faculty development from the top of the institution and innovation-led faculty development from the bottom up. To achieve these aims, the function is structured differently across institutions and faculty developers around the globe have multiple perspectives concerning their roles (Land, 2001a, 2001b).

Other terminology used throughout the chapter requires clarification. E-learning is used to mean "electronically-mediated learning in a digital format that is interactive, but not necessarily remote (Zemsky & Massy, 2004, p. 6). The broad meaning of information and communication technologies (ICTs) or "the new technologies" used in this chapter is provided next:

The range of tools and techniques relating to computer-based hardware and software; to communications including directed and broadcast; to information sources such as CD-ROM and the Internet, and to associated technologies such as robots, video conferencing and digital TV. (Hardy, 2000, p. 3)

Faculty Development as Diffusion of Innovation

The diffusion of innovation perspective, drawn from Everett Rogers' (2003) theory of individual innovativeness, dominates much of the literature that focuses on faculty development in relation to e-learning. Rogers defined diffusion as "the process by which an innovation is communicated through certain channels over time among the members of a social system," emphasizing that the diffusion process always involves some degree of "uncertainty and perceived risk" (p. 35). He theorized that individual adoption rates of innovation are usually distributed along a bell shaped curve and can be grouped under five categories: innovators, early adopters, early majority, late majority, and laggards. In relation to the uptake of information and communication technologies for e-learning, there is a tendency in the literature to speak about *two* groups of staff: the early adopters (innovators and early adopters) and the mainstream majority (early and late majority, and laggards). The innovator is the first to try out new products and processes. The early adopters are confident in their ability to integrate technology into instruction and make the adoption of technology look relatively easy, thereby disguising the knowledge and skills that mainstream staff need in order to adopt it (Jacobsen, 2000). Taylor (1998) argued that these early adopters—

the "lone rangers"—are those that the institutions have traditionally relied upon to take up and pioneer new ways of teaching based on the new technologies. In contrast, the mainstream majority of faculty favor evolutionary change and seek proven applications of the use of technology in teaching.

Embedding the Innovation: Achieving the Critical Mass

What institutions must encourage is *embedding* (Oliver & Dempster, 2003)— the informed adoption of the work of the early adopters by other faculty aimed at achieving a critical mass of staff that are competent working in the e-learning environment. Here the focus of faculty development needs to be on faculty use of ICTs, not just the dissemination of good practices in how to use them. The literature on faculty development for e-learning suggests a broad range of strategies available to institutions to embed innovations associated with the take-up of ICTs (Gosling & D'Andrea, 2002; Hannan & Silver, 2000; Johnston, 1999; Lefoe & Albury, 2002):

- Working across the whole institution within current management structures, developing policies and strategies to encourage and mandate the take-up of innovations.

- Sponsoring of projects within departments and faculties, some with local, others with a wider institutional focus, using project funding to buy out staff time from normal teaching duties.

- Supporting a collaborative approach to change and opportunities for faculty to work together to re-think their teaching, first in disciplines, and later in expanded networks of staff (real or virtual) across disciplines and within and across institutions.

- Seconding teachers to work on particular ICT-based innovations within a central faculty development area, or providing centralized support for faculty working within departmental contexts; recognizing and rewarding these staff who have taken the risks and engaged in faculty development.

- Disseminating institutional-wide communication about the innovation which can include organizing of special events such as showcases and forums.

- Emphasizing the value-added aspects of the innovation, the real improvements to student learning that can be achieved, and that the faculty's other professional priorities will not be undermined.

Specific Strategies for Faculty Development

Specific strategies have been adopted across post-compulsory institutions aimed at embedding the use of ICTs in the e-learning environment. Some of the strategies most commonly in use for engaging faculty are discussed next.

Faculty Development and Characteristics of Innovation

Rogers (2003) held the view that the attributes of an innovation—relative advantage, compatibility, complexity, trialability, and observability—influence an adopter's decision to take-up an innovation. Institutions can use these attributes as a framework for planning faculty development for the new technologies (McLoughlin, 2000). Each of these attributes can be emphasized by faculty developers in the ways suggested next:

- The advantage of the new technologies in terms of the way they can be used to enhance teaching and learning in the e-learning environment. Information sessions or showcases sponsored by faculty development centers, or presentations at faculty or departmental meetings are all opportunities for successful adopters of the technology to talk about their experiences with e-learning and how they took advantage of the best features of the online environment.

- The compatibility of the new technologies with faculty values and current approaches to teaching. Faculty development activities need to gradually extend the repertoire of technical skills and understanding of good pedagogical practices for e-learning through scaffolded activities that build on current practices. It is useful to start with individual faculty's current perceptions about teaching and learning in relation to their current practice, before examining how use of the new technologies can alter these practices and their role as a teacher.

- The complexity or the level of difficulty of the new technologies, including the amount of time and effort required by faculty in learning how to incorporate them successfully into their teaching practices. Workload issues should be acknowledged in discussions with staff concerning the commitment required to use ICTs in their teaching. Using a staged approach to skills development focuses attention on the readiness levels of staff and counters the tendency to push faculty too quickly to adoption of ICTs.

- The trialability of the new technologies, that is, opportunities for faculty to learn about the technical and pedagogical aspects of the innovation. Offering faculty development online engages faculty as learners in the online environment, experiencing first-hand the use of the innovation without having to immediately change their current teaching approach.

- The observability of the new technologies, or how easy it is for faculty to see technology-in-action and observe its features and benefits. Development strategies that demonstrate the technology-in-use are valuable here, by making exemplars available to faculty, and/or encouraging participation in activities where they are using the new technologies themselves.

Faculty Development and Skills Acquisition

Some institutions frame their faculty development for e-learning using an expertise model, based on research (Dreyfus & Dreyfus, 1986) of the skills acquisition processes of airplane pilots, chess players, automobile drivers, and adult learners of a second language. Dreyfus and Dreyfus's research revealed five levels of skills acquisition: novice, advanced beginner, competent, proficient, and expert. Faculty development for e-learning based on this skills acquisition approach draws on the following broad set of principles to frame specific activities for staff:

- A focus on skills in online learning technologies required to construct and deliver e-learning courses and make use of a range of technologies in teaching to enhance the flexibility of learning opportunities. These technologies include Web-based hypermedia and multimedia technologies, asynchronous and synchronous communication tools, Web-based publishing and authoring tools, and presentation and visualization tools (Dabbagh & Bannan-Ritland, 2005).

- A focus on the pedagogy of the online environment and in particular the role of the teacher in supporting learning, with an emphasis on learner-centeredness, and a shift in the role of the teacher from a didactic role to a more supportive, facilitative, and collaborative role.

- A focus on different ways in which faculty can work collaboratively in teams to design, develop, and deliver courses online.

- A focus on changes to faculty work practices that moving to e-learning necessitates. These include supporting students in the e-learning environment, maintaining and updating online content and course Web presence, and managing the workload issues associated with monitoring online discussion activities and responding to student e-mails.

- A focus on the need to continually update the content of faculty development activities to respond to the challenge of faculty who are ready for more advanced skills development and to keep up to date with changes in software and technologies.

Table 1 summarizes current practices in relation to faculty development for e-learning that adopt this skills acquisition approach (Bennett, Priest, & Macpherson, 1999; Collom, Dallas, Jong, & Obexer, 2002; Crock & Andrews, 1997; Ellis & Phelps, 2000; Hadgraft, Prpic, & Ellis, 2001; Haigh, 1998; Hartman & Truman-Davis, 2001). It suggests a staged, four-level approach to development of skills of faculty from "Novice" (Level 1) through to "Expert" (Level 4), with the features of each level highlighted. The lines between each level in this continuum are blurred, and transition to the next level, while planned for, is often difficult to control or direct, in that faculty move at their own pace and are driven by immediate workplace imperatives for skills development and enhancement. As the need for technical expertise declines, there is a corresponding rise in the

Table 1. Faculty development framed as skills acquisition

Level	Faculty at this level	Features of faculty development
Level 1 Novice	Lack familiarity with teaching in the e-learning environment and experience with technology. May wish to seek out information about an ICT innovation that has come to their attention. Have a primary need for opportunities to identify how to use the new technologies effectively. Show varying degrees of interest in e-learning. Some may be reluctant to try out using technology tools in learning and teaching.	Step-by-step approach assisted by resources easy to access and use and that relate to faculty's discipline area. Practice-focused, involving "Show and Tell" activities in form of short seminars and discussion sessions on current use of ICTs in their institution. Use of guest speakers, exemplars and/or work of "early adopters" and enthusiasts aimed at sharing expertise and ideas. Emphasis is on enhancing interest and motivation of faculty to become involved in learning and teaching in the e-learning environment.
Level 2 Developmental	Are required to use technology, with some having limited exposure to use of ICTs. Some may have experience in teaching in flexible learning environments such as print-based distance education. Are "learning the process".	More reflection in faculty development activities is encouraged at this stage to encourage critical evaluation of teaching in the e-learning environment and provide opportunities to discuss with others and share ideas. Resources are provided for faculty to encourage reflection; case studies or problem-solving activities can be utilised for individual and group collaboration, in face-to-face or online settings.

Table 1. continued

Level 3 Proficient	Are using more complex staff-student and student-student interactions in the e-learning environment. Want to become more proficient in the use of innovations in their teaching.	Faculty development at this stage includes project-based learning approaches that feature action-learning processes, peer assessment, reflection, and discussion. Projects can be discipline-based or cross-institutional.
Level 4 Expert	Have integrated ICTs into their teaching. Are seeking out ways of using the innovation beyond what has been achieved by others. Are rewarded by the institution for their efforts.	Faculty at this level are engaged in research and development focused activities relevant to the new technologies. Faculty are role models, mentors, motivators, and resources for other faculty, providing advice, participating in faculty development programs.

emphasis on the pedagogical processes associated with learning and teaching in the e-learning environment.

A popular example of a scaffolded or continuum-based model of faculty development relevant to e-learning is found in the work of Gilly Salmon (2004). Based on research conducted in the Open University in the United Kingdom, Salmon's model offers prospective online teachers a structured, developmental process of five stages spanning a period of several weeks, supported by experienced facilitators at each stage. In Step 1, faculty as "learners" access the online environment and are exposed to the benefits of its use. In Step 2, they are brought together with other learners and exchange communication. Step 3 introduces faculty to the vast information resources available on the World Wide Web. In Step 4, their skills in information exchange are advanced as they engage in debate and begin to formulate views on particular issues and share those views with others in the online environment. In Step 5, both learners and their facilitators are engaged in knowledge construction through challenging each other and engaging in argument that fosters "deeper reflection and learning" (Salmon, 2004, p. 48). A visual representation of Salmon's model can be found at the site "All Things in Moderation" <http://www.atimod.com/e-moderating/5stage.shtml>.

Faculty Development and Accredited Courses

Formal, accredited courses that focus on e-learning and teaching are a way of encouraging the take-up of ICTs and offer different ways of embedding the necessary skills in faculty. These programs combine online and face-to-face learning opportunities. Evaluation processes have revealed the following strategies to be of value when designing such programs (Clegg, Konrad, & Tan, 2000; Edwards, Webb, & Murphy, 2000; Littlejohn, 2002):

- Gaining institutional support for the program by actively marketing the course to organizational leaders.

- Ensuring clearly defined and articulated entry requirements are established for faculty entry into the program.

- Mandating completion of at least one unit, or an entire program, for fulfillment of probationary requirements for new faculty.

- Designing the program so that faculty have opportunities for dialogue and reflection as learners in the program; ensuring that the program is designed to achieve a balance between theoretical and practical components.

- Using a project-based approach to learning in the program and marketing this approach to attract discipline-focused faculty teams with specific departmental and ICT-based outcomes they wish to achieve, supported by appropriate technical skills on a just-in-time (JIT) basis.

One example of a formal, accredited faculty development program that focuses on teaching and learning in e-learning is Keele University's Certificate in Teaching and Learning with Technology. The program combines face-to-face workshops and online discussion and offers virtual attendance alternatives for faculty. Assessment is by a portfolio of evidence to show achievement of a choice of learning outcomes. Details are available from the university Web site at <http://www.keele.ac.uk/depts/aa/landt/lt/talwt/>.

Faculty Development as Peer Learning

There is a strong belief evidenced in the literature that embedding the use of the new technologies within the institution will only succeed when the change being proposed is appropriated by the discipline group concerned. Becher and Trowler (2001) draw attention to discipline-based academic "tribes." As Boud (1999) argued, the discipline group forms the context of academic work. The practice of peer learning—the appointment of faculty to work alongside of and provide support to others engaged in adopting the new technologies for e-learning—is usually associated with discipline-based faculty development. At the heart of peer learning is the building on good practices that already exist within the local context and the development of skills and knowledge based on experiential learning methods or "learning by doing." Faculty involved as peers supporting other faculty are called by different names, for example mentors, support coordinators, or teaching fellows. Despite variations between institutions regarding the appointment of these staff and their roles, peer learning provides the following advantages as a faculty development strategy for e-learning:

- Opportunities to focus on the use of the new technologies in relation to specific disciplines and project teams.

- Opportunities to share expertise, foster collaboration and learning from others, and mentor less-experienced faculty as they move to e-learning.

- Opportunities to disseminate knowledge and understanding of innovative practices for the e-learning.

- Opportunities for faculty to explore and re-think aspects of their teaching.

Peer learning lies at the heart of the Innovative Teaching and Educational Technology (ITET) Fellowship program offered at the University of New South Wales in Australia. ITET Fellows complete a six-month program in skills development in teaching and learning emphasizing e-learning, as well as an e-learning project in their faculty or department. Upon completion of the program, the Fellows offer a symposium for the wider university community and continue to contribute to faculty development within the institution (Russell & Lee, 2005).

Project-Based Faculty Development

Projects are an effective strategy in working with faculty to explore the potential of ICTs. A survey of higher education projects relation to learning technology development in the United Kingdom over a three year period (1998-2002) focused on the adoption or embedding of technology-driven changes in teaching and learning practices through the use of national projects (Dempster & Deepwell, 2003). Lessons learned from this review are valuable guideposts to support project-based faculty development for e-learning:

- Institutional thinking about the use of ICTs can be influenced through the way project knowledge is diffused throughout the institution, from one colleague to another or from one group to another.

- Projects are a way of consolidating skills amongst the faculty working on the project team. If the motivational levels of these staff are high, there is a strong likelihood of project outcomes becoming embedded in institutional practices.

- Embedding of project outcomes is dependent on the need for strong communication channels between centralized and local support for the project team as the project progresses, and on the retention of faculty after the project is completed, so their skills and expertise can be shared with others.

The EFFECTS (Effective Framework for Embedding C&IT using Targeted Support) project was a significant national project that targeted faculty development for e-learning simultaneously across several post-compulsory institutions in the United Kingdom (Beetham & Bailey, 2002). Initially a generic framework for embedding ICTs into subjects was identified, and faculty development programs were used to embed this framework into the five participating institutions. Each of the initial institutional partners in EFFECTS aimed at working with one other institution in the same region in order to broaden the dissemination of project outcomes. Project documentation relating to EFFECTS is found at this Web site : <http://www.elt.ac.uk/AboutEFFECTS.htm>.

Faculty Development Online

What better way to get faculty engaged with e-learning than to use the online environment to deliver development opportunities. Many reasons are provided as rationale for putting faculty development for e-learning online:

- Recognizing the limitations of face-to-face, centralized workshops or one-to-one consultations with their time and place constraints (Hewson &Hughes, 1998; Salter & Hansen, 2001).

- Providing opportunities for faculty separated geographically to work collaboratively across the institution (Kandlbinder, 2001, 2003)

- Creating a "centre of gravity" for innovation in teaching and learning with the new technologies (Donovan & Macklin, 1999)

- Providing faculty with authentic, contextualized tasks to support skills development (Donald, Northover, Koppi, & Matthews, 2002).

- Empowering faculty to make connections with their own experience and knowledge and understanding of teaching (Bennett, Priest, & Macpherson, 1999).

- Putting faculty in the position of the online learner and facilitating their experience in exploring theory and practice of online pedagogy (Devonshire & Philip, 2001; Fitzgibbon & Jones, 2004; Hallas, 2005; O'Reilly & Brown, 2001).

- Creating learning communities among faculty to support peer mentoring and peer learning (Creanor & Littlejohn, 2000).

The four sites described below provide a tiny sample of options in the use of the Web to provide faculty development for e-learning. Each site provides self-paced access to content and online alternatives to face-to-face workshops and/or show and tell sessions:

- The University of Maryland University College Virtual Resource Site for Teaching with Technology <http://www.umuc.edu/virtualteaching/background.html> focuses on appropriate ways for faculty to use ICTs in teaching and learning. Two online modules provide support for teachers in the creation and use of various media to meet specific learning goals and examples of successful practices in online delivery. Each module presents options for users to navigate within the module, with links to additional resources to support the focus of the module.

- The University of Washington Catalyst site <http://catalyst.washington.edu> is designed for faculty access from their desktop on a JIT basis. The site currently features four types of content: Catalyst Web Tools provide Web-based software to help faculty develop online resources, Catalyst Guides provide information for faculty in the form of "how to" guides and profiles of faculty making effective use of ICTs in their teaching, Catalyst Workshops support the use of Web tools or other software, and Catalyst Learning Spaces provide information about the different types of computing facilities available for faculty.

- Deakin University's Contemporary Online Teaching Cases site <http://www.deakin.edu.au/teachlearn/cases/> features the work of over 70 teachers who have planned for and implemented the new technologies in their teaching. Cases can be browsed by discipline, faculty, and individual case participant. Alternative approaches to engagement with the cases are provided. Links take the site user to projects undertaken by Deakin University's Online Teaching and Learning Fellows in 2003.

- The Higher Education Academy (UK) Learning Environments and Pedagogy (LEAP) site <http://www.heacademy.ac.uk/Leap.htm> also provides case studies that focus on how different pedagogies are being used in different virtual learning environments to help faculty choose successful teaching strategies for e-learning. Faculty can access the cases through the key messages from each study, by pedagogy, or by academic subject area.

Conclusion

This chapter has reviewed the varied approaches to faculty development for e-learning. It has emphasized that faculty development is about supporting change in the workplace, and that embedding changes in learning and teaching practices using ICTs is a complex process. Implications for faculty developers drawn from this chapter include the following:

- In focusing on adoption of ICTs, emphasize the innovation, not the technology. Concentrate on the take-up of the technologies, rather than their use. Build on the work of the early adopters, but focus most on the mainstream majority of faculty and the support they require.

- Accept that faculty spend most of their time in their discipline groups and teams. Take into account disciplinary differences and local contexts when planning and implementing faculty development activities.

- Look to the attributes of an innovation as a framework for designing faculty development activities. Consider strategies that address several of these characteristics at the same time. Target development activities to match the institutional presence online. Used a staged approach to development of skills that matches readiness levels of the mainstream faculty. Clearly define entry-level technical skills of faculty.

- Situate faculty development in authentic contexts. Provide opportunities for staff to share ideas, experiences, and reflections with others as they engage as learners with the new technologies. Look to projects and project teams as a context for faculty development. Support campus-wide and even inter-institutional projects that allow for cross-fertilization of ideas and for faculty to learn from each other in supportive environments.

- Draw on different learning frameworks for faculty development such as reflective practice, communities of practice, and action learning, to name a few. Provide peer support for faculty as they tackle the challenges faced in integrating the new technologies into their learning and teaching practices.

- Explore blended learning environments for e-learning faculty development that combine face-to-face and online learning environments and the use of multiple media.

- Use formal, accredited courses to embed faculty development for e-learning by making all or parts of the course a requirement for new faculty. Link completion of these courses to tenure applications and/or performance review. Ensure institutional reward systems support the take-up and appropriation of the new technologies into the curriculum.

- Recognize future trends in technology developments. Be informed about current research in the area of ICTs and learning, and use this research to frame the design of faculty development programs. Look to how your institution can support faculty learning that will increasingly become more user-focused and individualized.

Note

This chapter draws on doctoral research and an article of which the author was principal author, published in 2004 in the Australasian Journal of Educational Technology (AJET) found at http://www.ascilite.org.au/ajet/ajet20/wilson.html.

References

Anderson, T., & Kanuka, H. (1997). On-line forums: New platforms for professional development and group collaboration. *JCMC, 3*(3). Retrieved December 28, 2005, from http://jcmc.indiana.edu/vol3/issue3/anderson.html

Beaty, E. (1995). Working across the hierarchy. In A. Brew (Ed.), *Directions in staff development* (pp. 146-158). Buckingham, UK: The Society for Research into Higher Education & Open University Press.

Beaty, L. (1998). Faculty development of teachers in higher education. *Innovations in Education and Training International, 35*(2), 99-107.

Becher, T., & Trowler, P. (2001). *Academic tribes and territories* (2nd ed.). Buckingham, UK: The Society for Research into Higher Education & Open University Press.

Beetham, H., & Bailey, P. (2002). Faculty development for organizational change. In R. Macdonald & J. Wisdom (Eds.), *Academic and educational development. Research, evaluation, and changing practice in higher education* (pp. 164-176). London: Kogan Page.

Bennett, S., Priest, A. M., & Macpherson, C. (1999). Learning about online learning: An approach to staff development for university teachers. *Australian Journal of Educational Technology, 15*(3), 207-221.

Boud, D. (1999). Situating academic development in professional work: Using peer learning. *International Journal for Academic Development, 4*(1), 3-10.

Boud, D., & Garrick, J. (1999). Understandings of workplace learning. In D. Boud & J. Garrick (Eds.), *Understanding learning at work* (pp. 1-11). London: Routledge.

Brew, A. (1995). *Directions in staff development.* Buckingham, UK: The Society for Research into Higher Education & Open University Press.

Cheetham, G., & Chivers, G. (2005). *Professions, competence and informal learning.* Cheltenham, UK: Edward Elgar.

Clegg, S., Konrad, J., & Tan, J. (2000). Preparing academic staff to use ICTs in support of student learning. *The International Journal for Academic Development, 5*(2), 138-148.

Collom, G., Dallas, A., Jong, R., & Obexer, R. (2002, December 8-11). Six months in a leaky boat: Framing the knowledge and skills needed to teach well online. *Proceedings of the 19th Annual Conference of the Australasian Society for Computers in Learning in Tertiary Education (ASCILITE).* UNITEC, Auckland, New Zealand. Retrieved December 28, 2005, from http://www.ascilite.org.au/conferences/auckland02/proceedings/papers/181.pdf

Creanor, L., & Littlejohn, A. (2000). A cross-institutional approach to staff development in Internet communication. *Journal of Computer Assisted Learning, 16*(3), 271-279.

Crock, M., & Andrews, T. (1997, December). *Providing staff and student support for alternative learning environments.* ultiBASE. Retrieved December 28, 2005, from http://www.ultibase.rmit.edu.au/Articles/dec97/crock1.htm

Dabbagh, N., & Bannan-Ritland, B. (2005). *Online learning. Concepts, strategies, and application.* Upper Saddle River, NJ: Pearson/Merrill Prentice Hall.

Dempster, J., & Deepwell, F. (2003). Experiences of national projects in embedding learning technology into institutional practices in UK higher education. In J. Seale (Ed.), *Learning technology in transition. From individual enthusiasm to institutional implementation* (pp. 45-62). Lisse, The Netherlands: Swets & Zeitlinger.

Devonshire, L., & Philip, R. (2001, September 24-27). *Managing innovation and change in flexible times: Reflecting on the role of the educational developer.* Paper presented at the Open and Distance Learning Association of Australia (ODLAA) 15th Biennial Forum, Sydney, New South Wales, Australia.

Donald, C., Northover, M., Koppi, T., & Matthews, G. (2002). An educational design plan for faculty development about online learning and teaching: SCARIE! *Proceedings of the 19th Annual Conference of The Australasian Society for Computers in Learning in Tertiary Education (ASCILITE),* (December 8-11, 2002). UNITEC, Auckland, New Zealand. Retrieved December 28, 2005, from http://www.ascilite.org.au/conferences/auckland02/proceedings/papers/194.pdf

Donovan, M., & Macklin, S. (1999). The Catalyst project: Supporting faculty uses of the Web...with the Web. *CAUSE/EFFECT, 22*(3). Retrieved December 28, 2005, from http://www.educause.edu/ir/library/html/cem/cem99/cem9934.html

Dreyfus, H., & Dreyfus, S. (1986). *Mind over machine.* New York: The Free Press.

Edwards, H., Webb, G., & Murphy, D. (2000). Modelling practice—Academic development for flexible learning. *The International Journal for Academic Development, 5*(2), 149-155.

Ellis, A., & Phelps, R. (2000). Staff development for online delivery: A collaborative, team based action learning model. *Australian Journal of Educational Technology, 16*(1), 26-44.

Eraut, M. (2001). *Developing professional knowledge and competence.* London: RoutledgeFalmer.

Fitzgibbon, K., & Jones, N. (2004). Jumping the hurdles: Challenges of staff development delivered in a blended learning environment. *Journal of Educational Media, 29*(1), 26-35.

Garavan, T., Morley, M., Gunnigle, P., & McGuire, D. (2002). Human resource development and workplace learning: Emerging theoretical perspectives and organisational practices. *Journal of European Industrial Training, 26*(3/4), 60-71.

Gosling, D., & D'Andrea, V. (2002). How educational development/learning and teaching centres help HEIs manage change. *Educational Developments, 3*(2). Retrieved December 28, 2005, from http://www.seda.ac.uk/ed_devs/vol3/eddevs32.htm

Hadgraft, R., Prpic, K., & Ellis, A. (2001, July 8-11). Resources to aid staff development for flexible learning. *Proceedings of the 24th Annual Conference of the Higher Education Research and Development Society of Australasia (HERDSA).* University of Newcastle, New South Wales, Australia.

Haigh, N. (1998). Staff development. An enabling role. In C. Latcham & F. Lockwood (Eds.), *Staff development in open and flexible learning* (pp. 182-192). London: Routledge.

Hallas, J. (2005, July 3-7). Getting started in flexible learning: Perceptions from an online faculty development workshop. *Proceedings of the 28th Annual Conference of the Higher Education Research and Development Society of Australasia (HERDSA).* University of Sydney, New South Wales, Australia. Retrieved December 28, 2005, from http://www.itl.usyd.edu.au/herdsa2005/pdf/refereed/paper_331.pdf

Hannan, A., & Silver, H. (2000). *Innovating in higher education.* Buckingham, UK: The Society for Research into Higher Education & Open University Press.

Hardy, C. (2000). *Information and communications technology for all.* London: David Fulton.

Hartman, J., & Truman-Davis, B. (2001). Institutionalizing support for faculty use of technology at the University of Central Florida. In R. Epper & A. W.

Bates (Eds.), *Teaching faculty how to use technology. Best practices from leading institutions* (pp. 39-58). Westport, CT: American Council on Education and The Oryz Press.

Hewson, L., & Hughes, C. (1998, April 18-21). *On-line and on-demand: Staff development in the new university.* Paper presented at the Educause in Australasia Conference, Sydney, New South Wales, Australia.

Jacobsen, M. (2000, July 6-9). *Examining technology adoption patterns by faculty in higher education.* Paper presented at the ACEC2000: Learning Technologies, Teaching and the Future of Schools, Melbourne, Victoria, Australia. Retrieved December 28, 2005, from http://www.ucalgary.ca/~dmjacobs/acec/index.html

Johnston, S. (1999). Introducing and supporting change towards more flexible teaching approaches. In A. Tait & R. Mills (Eds.), *The convergence of distance and conventional education: Patterns of flexibility for the individual learner* (pp. 39-50). London: Routledge.

Kandlbinder, P. (2001). *Peeking under the covers: Understanding the foundations of online academic staff development.* In L. Richardson & J. Kidstone (Eds.), *ASET/HERDSA 2000 Flexible learning for a flexible society* (July 2-5, 2000) (pp. 612-617). University of Southern Queensland, Toowoomba, Australia. Retrieved December 28, 2005, from http://www.aset.org.au/confs/aset-herdsa2000/procs/kandlbinder2.html

Kandlbinder, P. (2003). Peeking under the covers: On-line academic staff development in Australia and the United Kingdom. *International Journal for Academic Development, 8*(1/2), 135-148.

Land, R. (2001a). Agency, context, and change in academic development. *The International Journal for Academic Development, 6*(1), 4-20.

Land, R. (2001b). Orientations to educational development. In C. Rust (Ed.), *Improving student learning strategically* (pp. 32-46). Oxford: Oxford University, Centre for Staff and Learning Development.

Lefoe, G., & Albury, R. (2002, December 8-11). Creating new learning environments off campus in the Faculty of Arts: What impact on teaching and learning on campus? *Proceedings of the 19th Annual Conference of the Australasian Society for Computers in Learning in Tertiary Education (ASCILITE)*, UNITEC, Auckland, New Zealand. Retrieved December 28, 2005, from http://www.ascilite.org.au/conferences/auckland02/proceedings/papers/159.pdf

Littlejohn, A. (2002, June). New lessons from past experiences: Recommendations for improving continuing faculty development in the use of ICT. *Journal of Computer Assisted Learning, 18*(2), 166-174.

McLoughlin, C. (2000). Creating partnerships for generative learning and systemic change: redefining academic roles and relationships in support of learning. *The International Journal for Academic Development, 5*(2), 116-128.

Oliver, M., & Dempster, J. (2003). Embedding e-learning practices. In R. Blackwell & P. Blackmore (Eds.), *Towards strategic staff development in higher education* (pp. 142-153). Maidenhead, UK: The Society for Research into Higher Education and Open University Press.

O'Reilly, M., & Brown, J. (2001, April 21-25). *Staff development by immersion in interActive Learning Online.* Paper presented at AusWeb01, the 7th Australian World Wide Web Conference, Coffs Harbour, New South Wales, Australia. Retrieved December 28, 2005, from http://ausweb.scu.edu.au/aw01/papers/refereed/o_reilly/

Rogers, E. M. (2003). *Diffusion of innovations* (5th ed.). New York: The Free Press.

Russell, C., & Lee, A. (2005, September 6-8). *The innovative teaching and educational technology (ITET) fellowship: Cultivating communities of practice in learning and teaching.* Paper presented at ALT-C 2005: Exploring the Frontiers of E-Learning—Borders, Outposts, and Migration, University of Manchester, UK.

Salmon, G. (2004). *E-moderating. The key to teaching and learning online* (2nd ed.). London: Kogan Page.

Salter, G., & Hansen, S. (2001). Facilitating Web-based staff development in higher education. In L. Richardson & J. Kidstone (Eds.), *ASET/HERDSA 2000 Flexible learning for a flexible society,* July 2-5 2000 (pp. 612-617). University of Southern Queensland, Toowoomba, Australia. Retrieved December 28, 2005, from http://www.aset.org.au/confs/aset-herdsa2000/procs/salter1.html

Taylor, P. G. (1997). Creating environments which nurture development: Messages from research into academics' experiences. *International Journal for Academic Development, 2*(2), 42-49.

Taylor, P. G. (1998). Institutional change in uncertain times: Lone ranging is not enough. *Studies in Higher Education, 23*(3), 269-280.

Zemsky, R., & Massy, W. (2004). *Thwarted innovation. What happened to e-learning and why.* PittsburghA: The Learning Alliance at the University of Pennsylvania. Retrieved December 28, 2005, from http://www.thelearningalliance.info/Docs/Jun2004/ThwartedInnovation.pdf

Chapter IX

Using E-Learning to Transform Large Class Teaching

Cathy Gunn, University of Auckland, New Zealand

Mandy Harper, University of Auckland, New Zealand

Abstract

This chapter describes a seven-year, incremental process of e-learning development within science courses at a large research university. The process was driven by common challenges in higher education: increasing class size and diversity, limited resources for teaching, and concern about poor alignment with graduate capability requirements. Following a design-based research approach (The Design Based Research Collective, 2003), each stage of development was grounded in appropriate educational theory and implemented using the best available technology. The impact was monitored through surveys, performance records, system log data, and reflective discussion among teachers and students. The revised educational model increased learner autonomy and choice, integrated classroom teaching and e-learning activities, and put explicit focus on learning strategy development. Implications for faculty development and institutional culture change are identified, as these emerged as significant factors. The chapter concludes with reflections on the scale of the transformation that took place, key challenges faced during the process, and issues yet to be addressed as development continues.

The E-Learning Development Context

First year science courses faced a number of common challenges in the mid-1990s. Student numbers grew rapidly while educational and cultural backgrounds diverged. General first year courses had to serve the needs of different faculties and major subjects, and no formal teaching development strategy supported a shift toward e-learning. Physical teaching spaces were designed for a transmission model of teaching, and any innovation tended to be driven by isolated individuals in low status positions working with limited resources for trials or pilot projects. The traditional lecture-centered model of instruction was struggling to cope with the rate of expansion, while funding and staffing levels were decreasing in relative terms. The quality of student learning and support was compromised by class sizes growing toward 1,000 per semester and the inability of the predominant teaching model to accommodate individual differences. Teaching methods created a culture of dependency, which was at odds with the graduate attributes published by the department and by the university. A crisis point approached as non-completion rates rose and average grades fell. The impact on teachers was equally undesirable. The weight of numbers and institutional pressures limited their ability to apply principles of good teaching practice and offered few incentives for innovation. These factors, coupled with poor student performance, had a negative impact on morale and ran contrary to the emerging international trend of teaching innovation fuelled by the evolving phenomenon of e-learning capability. The simple definition of e-learning used in this context is any learning task or activity that is delivered or mediated through computers and/or the Internet.

Early Trial with E-Learning

Early trials using an online learning management system to streamline administration, communication, and formative assessment functions proved remarkably successful. Evidence produced by the heuristic, design-based research approach showed that reconceptualization of the course delivery model with integrated e-learning at the core, was the only practical way to address the challenges presented by the situation. The design brief then required definition of a model that would cater to individual differences and styles, address the learning requirements of all major subjects being serviced, foster transferable skill development, and promote learner autonomy. For teachers, the goal was to encourage experimentation and empower and reward innovation aimed at supporting continuous improvement.

The educational objectives were that students gain mastery of the basic concepts of the subjects and develop skills to support independence and effective learning at higher levels of study. The discipline of science is dependent on a sound body of knowledge and principles that centuries of scientists have contributed to. Novices working from this solid base of established knowledge benefit from the cognitive activities of many predecessors. This learning culture allows more rapid advancement of ideas by adding to, or further building on, concepts. Existing scientific ideas are the trigger or challenge to explore and investigate new ideas. Hence, mastering the basics is essential preparation that allows students to engage in meaningful ways by building further knowledge and connections. In pursuit of these objectives, the integrated e-learning design brief aimed to address the following specific criteria:

- Provide accessible tools (hardware and networks) and mediate a commitment by students to use these tools;

- Use online testing with explanations and feedback as a catalyst for students to attain mastery;

- Incorporate corrective feedback to exploit the usefulness of errors as a means to address misconceptions and offer the benefits of immediate remedial instruction;

- Build rewards into a formative assessment structure to provide bridging motivation while students become committed to independently defined programs of study;

- Support the accumulation of learning experience and promote a sense of personal achievement;

- Establish a pattern whereby each learner can progress with confidence in cycles from the known to the unknown; and

- Encourage student choice for deep learning by going beyond the information given through traditional activities (lectures and labs) included in the course.

The changing student population and institutional environment was affecting all levels of study. However, the most serious pressure was on large first year classes where students enter an entirely new educational culture. This was identified as the point where reconceptualization should begin.

Theory Driven Learning Design

Existing teaching expertise provided the basis for choice of an appropriate theoretical approach to course design. Despite the prevailing influence of constructivism, mastery learning was chosen as the theoretical basis for entry level courses. With reference to Bloom's (1956) taxonomy, knowledge acquisition with some embedded intellectual ability and skill was the aim. Basic concepts, a complex vocabulary, and scientific principles had to be mastered before students could build confidence to move on to the development of the higher level intellectual abilities that promoted success in later years of study. However, the many dimensions of diversity arising from students' educational backgrounds, major subject choices, and motivation demanded that constructivist principles, such as those described by Jonassen (1998), also be incorporated into the instructional design. The need to build on each individual's prior knowledge and conceptions and to address personal learning styles and goals justified this decision. However, the main focus for the first year was mastery learning. Basic concepts, a complex vocabulary and scientific principles must be mastered before students can build confidence to move on to development of higher level intellectual abilities that promote success in later years of study. The appropriate instructional approach was therefore based on mastery but framed within a constructivist context. Early trials showed this approach to be popular with students, and marked improvement in grades and retention rates won over any initial skeptics among the faculty.

Managing Expectations

Investigation of the variable performance levels revealed that students were confused about the level of learning and autonomy that was required, the depth of understanding necessary, and how to apply their learning to assessment tasks. The basis of this problem seemed to be a widely held perception that rote learning was an appropriate study strategy. Whether this was caused by transmission oriented pedagogies used in university courses or a habit carried over from high school was less important than finding a way to address the problem. Student comments indicated frustration over poor performance and the belief that teachers were responsible. The kind of feedback that indicated progress (or lack of!) came too late for recovery, making achievement of a pass grade impossible in many cases. The result was that many students felt disillusioned early on in their university career. Equally, staff felt frustrated by the disappointing performance. It was common during the course for students to engage in intelligent dialogue about the work and to ask questions that displayed creative thinking around the topics—they simply were not demonstrating their knowledge in the assessments. There appeared to be a barrier that prevented transfer of understanding to the summative assessment activities. A key factor for teachers was the importance of maintaining standards, and concerns about mediocrity were often voiced. A creative solution that addressed all these issues was needed.

Despite obvious challenges, students remained enthusiastic and engaged in dialogue with teachers about their needs. These circumstances prompted the idea of designing a more student-centered course where individual factors such as preferred learning style, educational goals, access to study materials, pace of progress, background, and choice of study approach could be accommodated and transferable skills included to meet graduate capability profiles. The question was how to achieve this with the class roll growing closer to 1,000 each year.

Sowing the Seeds of Change

The concept of an online environment that brought together course management with learning activities and communication tools was the seed for many changes. The Faculty of Business and Economics was, at that time, developing an online learning management system (Cecil™). A number of teachers had used it, and the system architects were keen to try it in other disciplines. With the advent of accessible multimedia development and delivery tools, dynamic visual resources had already been developed for biology courses. An early adopter of technology had achieved promising results with plant reproduction cycle animations (see http://www.sbs.auckland.ac.nz/info/schools/nzplants/) using the dual coding approach described by Mayer and Anderson (1991). Further development of resources and delivery via an online learning management system was an inviting prospect for faculty.

The pilot occurred in the late 1990s when computer literacy was less widespread, so a critical factor was providing access to computers and support for students with limited technology skills. Many did not work intuitively with the technology (reflective of the diversity, including mature students and those from low-socioeconomic backgrounds). A computer facility with on-site help was set up for undergraduate students. This not only ensured fully supported access, but importantly, allowed large files such as animations to be used. Levels of computer literacy among the faculty also varied, and some were acquiring these skills concurrently with their students. Consultations with experts outside the subject area, especially in education technology and interactive multimedia, were important to support teachers' day-to-day progress in online practice and to troubleshoot technical issues.

Integrating E-Learning with Classroom Activities

The e-learning activities were piloted in one module, with the biochemistry component chosen for a number of reasons: faculty were highly motivated to address learning issues, student feedback indicated that this was the most difficult part of the course, and performance in the subject was the poorest in summative testing. The purposely chosen mastery learning design was particularly important for this topic as students needed to acquire a body of knowledge with factual recall and conceptual understanding for the type of assessments used in final exams. Activities that effectively bridged the gap from no knowledge to appropriate selection and application were needed to allow students to construct their own understanding and relate this to prior knowledge, current interests, and educational goals.

All e-learning activities were designed for integration with existing tasks (i.e., lectures and laboratory classes where students carried out experimental investigations). The degree regulations identified these components as compulsory, so deviation from this format was impossible. Nor was it considered desirable, as faculty may have withdrawn support if the development represented radical change. The literature acknowledges the challenge of gaining acceptance from faculty other than the drivers of innovation (Fullan, 2001; Schon, 1967). It was important that changes be seen as realistic and not adding to existing workloads, as departmental managers were unfamiliar with the demands of innovation and did not provide time allowance for development and implementation of e-learning.

The e-learning activities were designed to supplement lectures and also to encourage students to develop a learning strategy. For the first time, students were offered flexibility in their approaches to learning. They were not limited to synchronous activities dictated by the teaching program but could access resources and activities online 24/7. For the growing number of students with family and work commitments, this was revolutionary. The system log data showed that many studied through the night when they could access resources at their own convenience and without delay. This meant they could develop a personally effective deep learning strategy that allowed reinforcement and supported retention beyond summative assessment requirements. It also supported learning in a timely manner to facilitate progress to more complex concepts in subsequent lectures, thus building incrementally on material covered at the beginning of the course. This reinforcement was important to overcome initial barriers to good performance and for bridging any gaps in understanding.

Additional face-to-face sessions were provided through small group workshops at which attendance was voluntary. This offered opportunities for problem solving, but again highlighted the problem of time dependent access, as timetabling did not suit everyone. Students were encouraged to e-mail ahead of sessions with issues and questions. This allowed teachers to monitor frequency and type of questions, give feedback, correct misconceptions, and address gaps in understanding.

Reducing the Administrative Load

Administrative benefits were also anticipated because the course management functions in Cecil were integrated with the university's student records system. This in itself was a powerful feature that allowed authenticated information to be stored and accessed in the course "gradebook" section. Because of the perceived risk factor, trials of the new system had to be conducted in parallel with the existing course delivery and administration procedures. While comparative studies are not always recommended for traditional versus online methods (Ehrmann, 1995), the demands of this situation allowed a direct comparison to be made. Astounding differences in processing times were revealed: two days to process final grade submission versus five minutes using the Cecil gradebook function. This proved the value of Cecil in the administrative arena by saving faculty time.

The gradebook also offered the benefit of flexible access for students wishing to check or discuss their grades. Students had access to full records of their performance on formative and summative assessments. This prompted regular access and queries about marks, thus highlighting students' desire for immediate feedback about grading from all assessments (online and teacher marked). The accessibility of marks created additional opportunities for constructive feedback on individual performance.

Communication features, including class e-mail and discussion boards, were also widely used, becoming a key communication channel for immediate dissemination of important information. Archiving of e-mails and discussion topics ensured they were available for asynchronous access and revision purposes.

Fostering Communication

Asynchronous discussions can be structured into areas that facilitate dialogue between students and different staff from the teaching team and among peers. Discussion postings can be relayed directly to staff e-mail accounts, allowing discussion to continue through the working day and night, depending on the inclination of participating staff and student. Students relish this immediacy. More importantly, the postings are many-to-many, allowing dialogue to reach levels not possible in formal face-to face environments.

Initial concerns were expressed about activating the discussion boards in such a large class. Teachers were already dealing with overload from e-mail, as students used this technology more frequently than traditional office hours for one-to-one communication. As a result of the high volume, responses to e-mails were often too late to fulfill the role of effective feedback, and students may have experienced temporary delays in progress on their learning. The discussion boards, however, offered a workable solution. Monitoring was not always required at the level anticipated because students were highly effective and accurate in commenting on learning issues. Commonly, teachers were able to reinforce student comments with positive feedback (e.g., praising students for the quality of their answers, which were in close proximity to learner understanding at the particular stage of the learning process). The confidence building aspect of this process was significant for students offering the explanations and beneficial to those who required the information to help construct meaning. Exposure to multiple perspectives is a useful approach to learning, as well as a way for teachers to pick up on misunderstanding or misconceptions. Provision of this safe forum for asking questions also allowed students to engage in learning through opportunities to identify gaps and issues through dialogue. These moments were rewarding and exciting for teachers, as for the first time in a large class they were able to observe student dialogue about their learning. Interestingly, the students also engaged in positive feedback about teaching *("btw, the explanation on the lac operon in the lab was superb, I think I speak for most of us on this")*.

Mastery Learning Supported by Formative Assessment

E-learning activities included online quizzes that presented flexible opportunities for formative assessment and immediate feedback. Through the use of these quizzes and by processing the feedback, students were able to gain a clearer idea of the level of knowledge and performance required for postsecondary science. Previous evaluations had identified this as a problem that was resolved too late in the course to allow students to lift their achievement levels. Students were able to access quizzes and receive feedback on their performance as often as they liked, giving them the opportunity to reinforce their learning. O'Reilly's (2001) description of the benefits of well-designed online assessment supports the reasons behind extensive use of this method. Although some of the senior faculty did not initially perceive any value in this exercise, it was tolerated on a trial basis. In contrast, student acceptance of the quizzes resulted in high participation levels, and in subsequent summative assessment, the class performance was lifted with an increase in the mean score by 10 from previous cohorts. This evidence was enough to encourage further development of quizzes for mastery learning. The power of student demand proved to be a strong driver of wider application. In later years, a pre-lecture quiz was introduced as a form of advance organizer that encouraged students to focus their attention during lectures, form questions, and seek clarification.

Another fortuitous aspect of repeated formative assessment is an awareness of the importance of practicing questions repeatedly as preparation for summative assessments. Development of such beneficial study habits demands a high level of self-discipline—a rare trait for students who face multiple demands on a daily basis. It was proposed that quizzes could be used instead of, or in addition to, reading through lecture notes and other study materials. Many students in previous years had not actively engaged in answering questions until they were working under exam conditions. Questions for these quizzes were sourced from a large pool and randomly shuffled to prevent recourse to recall based on order and position of options.

The quizzes were used to encourage students to engage in regular formative assessment as part of a strategy for working toward a high level of achievement. Although participation in this activity was optional, some incentive was provided in the form of a minimal weighting in the final grade. Research has shown that this can act as a real incentive (Rowntree, 1999; Sangster, 2003) and that however small the grade increment is, students respond well to the incentive (Gunn & Barnett, 2001) and quickly come to realize that the value is more than a few additional marks. In this case, the students could make many attempts at each quiz with only the best marks recorded. Although the number of attempts was not shown, overall participation in this activity ranged from 88% to 93% of the student group. Figure 1 relates online quiz scores (0-4) to final grades (A+- D- and DNS) and clearly shows that students with high final grades also achieved high scores on mastery tests over the length of the course. The implicit learning promoted through this activity is self-discipline and frequent self-testing to monitor progress.

Figure 1. Mastery learning quiz scores (0-4) related to final grades (A+-D-)* in 2003

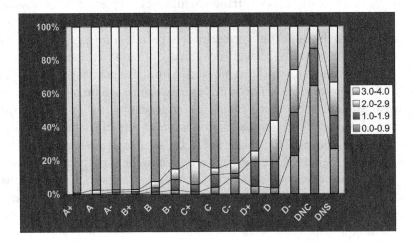

(* A number of students did not complete the course (DNC). Within the DNS band, there are students who did not sit the exam for medical reasons or extenuating circumstances. Many of these students had participated in the mastery test and achieved well. They were later awarded aegrotat passes based on their performance during the semester.)

The variation in preparedness of students entering the course has already been noted. For some, it was expected that these mastery learning activities would serve to confirm their competence in the subject. These students should only need to take each test one or two times for confirmation. For others, regular participation could give critical and timely feedback on their progress. Figure 1 shows that students who went on to achieve high final grades had continued to participate in the formative learning activities until they were achieving a high standard during the semester. Among the lower grade passes, it appears that students did not take advantage of the tests as a way to lift their performance to higher levels.

Teaching Learning Strategies and Skills

In addition to using the quizzes and the later addition of a pre-lecture quiz, students were encouraged to follow a learning process of pre-lecture reading, which included main concepts to be covered with key terminology and learning objectives. This allowed students a level of familiarization, thus making it easier for them to engage more deeply with the lecture. The impact of this strategy on long-term memory was explained so students understood the benefits of applying these strategies.

Lecturers were promoted as experts in their field and regularly incorporated cutting edge research (their own and sourced from current scientific publications) into the lecture context, as a result full attendance at lectures was maintained throughout the e-learning enhancement process. The importance of the lecture as a component of the learning environment has not been threatened, as many learning skeptics expected it might. However, a further challenge for some students arose (and continues to do so) from the need to apply listening skills and engage in simultaneous note taking during lectures. To address this particular learning skills challenge, key resources used during lectures were posted online immediately after the lecture. Students therefore knew that they did not have to rely on their own ability to produce a comprehensive set of notes while attending to the content of the lecture. Other activities were designed to support reinforcement of content knowledge, such as presentation of lecture summaries for integrating and rewriting or condensing notes, a technique for producing notes in summary form for later reference and revision.

Catering to Different Learning Styles

Some of the most powerful and effective resources have been animations that take the static images commonly used in teaching biological concepts and allow the students to experience the dynamic nature of the subject. Much has been written about the appeal to different learning styles of visual and dynamic presentation of subject material over static and descriptive methods (e.g., Emery, 1993; Mayer, 1991). Evidence suggests that this general principle applies equally to the biological and physical sciences (see, e.g., Sarapuu et al., 2005). Activities were designed so that after engaging with dynamic representations, students could check their understanding and retention of conceptual knowledge via feedback from further quizzes.

Obtaining suitable digital resources was challenging. The main source was resources provided with textbooks; therefore, supportive publishing companies prepared to provide copyright permission for restricted online access was essential. Some in-house animation developments occurred where the need was more specific than that catered to by suppliers of generic texts.

Beyond the Pilot Study

E-learning activities for the entire course were implemented during the next iteration of teaching after promising results were recorded from the biochemistry pilot study. Course evaluations and other forms of data collected in the following years showed that students were responding well to the changes. For example, in a 2003 survey, 93% of respondents reported feeling that the use of Cecil to obtain information and resources to help with learning was comfortable and convenient. In the same survey, 73% rated the use of online tests at four or five on a five-point scale for usefulness; 91% reported occasional or no technical problems; and 82% found computer-based learning resources easy to use, with only 13% finding them only difficult at first. The overall level of student performance has also visibly shifted over the years. Figure 2 presents a simplified illustration of this shift, with grades clustered within ranges (i.e., A+, A, and A- clustered under A) shown as a percentage of the total number of students who completed each year. These totals rose from 483 to 980 between 1998 and 2005, when over 1,000 students enrolled at the start of the course.

While the increase in numbers presented challenges of a different nature, it did not continue the earlier trend of poor performance and low completion rates. The proportion of D grades fell from 27% in 1999 to 14% in 2004 in a consistent downward trend that shows a single exception in 2005 when the figure rose again to 17%. At the other end of the scale, the proportion of A grades has risen fairly consistently each year starting at from 22% in 1999 and rising to 44% in 2005. Other teachers were able to see this clear improvement in performance, and

Figure 2. Grade clusters show a significant improvement over the period

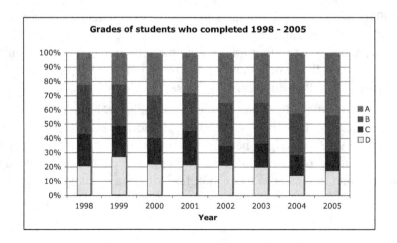

positive student feedback influenced incremental progress toward more courses adopting the e-learning approach. The students in the first year of implementation were working with two styles of delivery (i.e., both flexible and traditional models within one course). There was no question from their perspective that the flexible delivery enhanced their learning experience.

Within two years all stage one biology courses changed to flexible delivery modeled on the style of the initial pilot. This development was facilitated by many factors other than efficacy. Teachers developed a more team/community approach, and the online environment allowed for consistency and high standards to be achieved. There was no longer a sense of working in isolation or frustration from poor results. Perhaps the most critical driver was student expectation. The students who had experienced the online environment normalized the flexible learning aspects with peremptory requests for other courses to adopt the same model. This accelerated further implementation and brought more teaching staff on board with the underlying ideals.

The Challenge of Implementing Educational Change

Teachers involved in the initial phase were highly motivated to implement the shift toward flexible learning and to continuously evaluate, reflect, and incorporate feedback from other teachers and students as part of the ongoing process. As implementation progressed to other courses, flexible learning practices became the norm for most teachers of undergraduate courses. However, as the student-centered model rolled out to a greater number of courses and students, more challenges arose that needed to be resolved. In general, the same design principles that were used in the initial pilot were adopted. However, the learning theory underpinning the pilot was not always appropriate. More advanced courses required deeper learning. Students needed to learn how to apply knowledge gained from the first year courses to appropriate situations. This was challenging on two fronts. First, the students had become confident using the mastery learning strategies and found it difficult to disengage from them when they needed to apply their knowledge and understanding to more problem-based learning. This adjustment required students to use information from previous learning as tools to solve problems rather than to display facts, thus addressing different classes of Bloom's taxonomy (i.e., application, analysis, synthesis, and evaluation) (Bloom, 1956). It also required explicit coaching in learning strategies that would lead to success at this level. When student evaluations and expectations are preponderant in determining perceptions of teaching quality there can be an unfortunate check on further developments and trials, as some teachers are reluctant to receive critical feedback.

This relates to the second aspect of the challenge (i.e., that the use of good practice pedagogy requires access to appropriate professional development opportunities and willingness to take risks with new teaching strategies). Monitoring outcomes of teaching innovations becomes more complex and complicated with the diversity of courses. It is important not to try to make one size fit all, either for e-learning design or evaluation, but to encourage teachers to be creative and become confident enough to explore alternative strategies as technology advances and students' skill levels change. Student involvement in reflection is critical to influencing downstream adjustments. However, this needs to be considered alongside learning skills developed and depth of learning achieved as mapped out in initial course objectives.

Guidelines for E-Learning Innovation

Reflection on seven years experience of e-learning development directed toward the enhancement of classroom teaching and learning in a changing higher education context has revealed a number of principles to guide development of successful student-centered learning environments. We recommend a design-based research approach to e-learning development, as this requires grounding in educational theory, application in authentic contexts, and continuous evaluation and improvement. A successful approach includes the following:

- A theoretically driven solution that supports the development of good practice pedagogy based on the synergy of teaching strategy and technology. This solution must attend to the diverse needs driven by the range of educational backgrounds, abilities, learning styles, interests, and cultural preferences of the target groups of students.

- A staged introduction and an impact evaluation of e-learning innovation that is sensitive enough to identify the influential factors in any given situation.

- Practical ways to address teacher and institutional development issues, including incentives, rewards, and ways to raise awareness about what is involved in e-learning development and implementation.

- Strategies to manage change effectively. Identifying there is a need to make changes in teaching practice, and that this is not just change for the sake of it or because the technology needs to be used. A shared vision and belief in e-learning capability among teachers is a critical factor. Demonstrating successful outcomes from innovative pilot projects and the fact that the institution and its key leaders value these supports this objective.

- Planning for implementation with flexibility to consider downstream reflection and issues.

- Professional development programs that address new skills development areas and that adequately meet the needs of all teachers.

- Reference to and development of an emerging model of integrated face-to-face and e-learning.

Many other issues reflecting the dynamic interplay of teaching and learning have arisen from this e-learning development experience and some are yet to be fully resolved. Given that similar situations may arise in higher education institutions worldwide, these issues are noted as points for further consideration and discussion. We propose the incremental, theory-driven, and experiential approach described in this chapter to be significantly different and more highly sustainable than top-down, external, or professional-development-driven e-learning solutions.

- Avoiding the one size fits all mentality. This applies to software, such as online learning management systems, and to instructional design models for courses in different subjects and at different levels. Limited conceptual models based on the functionality of online learning management systems and perceptions that the same educational design model will suit all levels of study are two challenges addressed by the developers. Learning by experience and example and participative design initiatives are two recommended approaches.

- Overcoming the transmission model encouraged by some online learning management systems. Most of the software suites are actually little more than administrative systems for managing course materials and assignment submission with the addition of communication functions. There is a tendency for stakeholders who are not involved in teaching to assume that these systems are all there is to e-learning. Those with experience know only to well that this is not in fact the case; however, the challenge is to communicate this to others. In this case, student demand, working knowledge, and evidence of the effectiveness of active student-centered learning combined to achieve this aim.

- Defining standards now the bar has been raised. There is a risk that standards might be set unrealistically high once learners are engaged with effective learning environments and generally performing well. The effects of shifting standards on subsequent years of study imply the need for a whole program approach to curriculum revision arising from the transformation at entry level.

• Evaluating the impact on longer term progress. Given what we know about learning being a result of an ongoing process of knowledge acquisition, application, and reflection, it can be hard to measure the true impact of courses within the timeframe normally available, i.e., during a course or immediately after completion. It is also difficult to measure the extent to which generic graduate attributes such as critical thinking, autonomy, sound decision making, and ability to solve problems have been promoted. The task of evaluating the impact on later years of study, future choices, and career paths is a complex one that requires context specific design and data collection methods.

• How to reshape institutional systems and structures to reflect the needs of the integrated face-to-face and e-learning model. Any large institution is likely to take a long time to change to reflect the evolving demands of innovative educational methods. In a situation where many of the innovators are junior faculty, the process is confounded by their lack of power to influence higher-level systems and structures. It was projects at the grassroots of learning such as the one described in this chapter that gave institution leaders the confidence to develop formal e-learning development strategies and support systems.

Final Comment

The challenges involved in meeting the needs of all stakeholders in a rapidly changing higher education system are many. The potential to implement effective learning, teaching, and course management solutions is considerably improved by developments in new technology. The need for a critical and informed perspective is high, as a wide range of interests and agendas come into play. It is clear that the power of prediction about e-learning and educational change is limited with respect to the potential and impact of new technology and that misreading the signs can be expensive (Zemsky & Massy, 2004). From a practitioner's perspective, the best way to proceed is with caution, drawing on established theory, educational design expertise, and heuristic methods such as the design-based research approach described in this chapter.

References

Appleton, K. (1994). *Students' learning in science lessons: Towards under-standing the learning process.* Paper presented at the 25th Annual Conference of the Australasian Science Education Research Association (ASERA), Hobart.

Bloom, B. S. (1956). *Taxonomy of educational objectives: Book 1, cognitive domain.* London: Longman Publishing.

The Design Based Research Collective. (2003). Design-based research: An emerging paradigm for educational Inquiry. *Educational Researcher, 32*(1), 5-8.

Ehrmann, S. (1995). Asking the right questions: What does research tell us about technology and higher learning? *Change Magazine,* (March/April). Retrieved January 31, 2006, from http://www.tltgroup.org/resources/Flashlight/AskingRightQuestion.htm

Emery, D. (1993). Developing effective instructional graphics. *Journal of Interactive Instruction Development, 6*(2), 20-24.

Fullan, M. (2001). *The new meaning of educational change.* New York: Teachers College Press.

Grabinger, S., & Dunlap, J. (2000). Rich environments for active learning: A definition. In D. Squires & G. Conole (Eds.), *The changing face of learning technology* (pp. 8-38). Cardiff, UK: University of Wales Press.

Gunn, C., & Barnett, J. (2001). On-line learning: A quality experience. In P. Roberts & M. Chambers (Eds.), *Digital developments in higher education* (pp. 139-160). Los Angeles, CA: Taylor Graham.

Jonassen, D. (1998). Designing constructivist learning environments. In C. M. Reigeluth (Ed.), *Instructional-design theories and models* (2nd ed.). (pp. 215-239). Mahwah, NJ: Lawrence Erlbaum.

Mayer, R. E., & Anderson, R. B. (1991). Animations need narrations: An experimental test of a dual-coding hypothesis. *Journal of Educational Psychology, 83*(4), 484-490.

O'Reilly, M. (2001). *Improving student learning via online assessment.* Paper presented at the Improving Student Learning Using Learning Technology, Oxford Centre for Staff and Learning Development.

Rowntree, D. (1999). *Designing an assessment system.* Retrieved January 21, 2006, from http://www-iet.open.ac.uk/pp/D.G.F.Rowntree/Assessment.html

Sangster, A. (2003). *The use of computer-based assessment*. Learning Technology. Retrieved January 31, 2006, from http://www.business.heacademy.ac.uk/publications/misc/briefing/cba

Sarapuu, T. (2005). *Designing visualised process through educational technology*. Retrieved July 26, 2005, from http://www.ut.ee/biodida/e/teadust.htm

Schon, D. A. (1967). *Technology and change: The new heraclitus*. London: Pergamon Press.

Zemsky, R., & Massy W. F. (2004). *Thwarted innovation: What happened to e-learning and why?* The Learning Alliance at the University of Pennsylvania in cooperation with the Thomson Corporation. Retrieved October, 2005, from http://www.thelearningalliance.info/WeatherStation.html

Endnote

[1]   A number of students did not complete the course (DNC). Within the DNS band, there are students who did not sit the exam for medical reasons or extenuating circumstances. Many of these students had participated in the mastery test and achieved well. They were later awarded aegrotat passes based on their performance during the semester.

Chapter X

The Continuing Struggle for Community and Content in Blended Technology Courses in Higher Education

Richard A. Schwier, University of Saskatchewan, Canada

Mary E. Dykes, University of Saskatchewan, Canada

Abstract

This chapter reports a three-year case study of communication strategies in online discussions in a graduate seminar and extends preliminary findings from the first two years of the study (Dykes & Schwier, 2003; Schwier & Balbar, 2002). It discusses how different combinations of synchronous and asynchronous communication strategies were implemented in a graduate-level course, and examines how implementation strategies influenced the balance of community, social engagement, and content in online learning environments in higher education.

Introduction

If a course goal is to create an online community, then an instructor must be a participant in online discussions in order to nurture community development and growth. The first and, in our view, most important factor for novice instructors in e-learning environments to consider when using online discussions is that discussions significantly increase their involvement with students compared to a traditional classroom seminar.

Our reflections on online discussions, content, and community in this chapter are intended to provide examples of practical theory within social constructivist pedagogy, and they are consistent with approaches to self-reflection described by Murphy and Loveless (2005). Burge, Laroque, and Boak (2000) encourage instructors and researchers to include reflective descriptions of practice and strategies used in online instruction.

When faced with delivering part or all of a course online, an instructor usually attempts to create an online learning environment based on the familiar classroom setting. The learning environment includes the instructor, content, learners, and learning activities. One can easily transfer content and most learning activities online into a learning management system. But how does the instructor create an atmosphere that nourishes real and deep engagement among the learners, the instructor, and the content? Evidence of learner engagement in the classroom setting is found in dialogue and interaction with the instructor and other learners. The platforms for online chat (or other synchronous communication tools) and discussion boards (or other asynchronous communication tools) available in learning management systems are where many online instructors focus their energies in forming an environment where learners may become an engaged community.

There is no shortage of advocates for virtual communication in traditional and flexible learning in higher education (Burge, 2000; Cohill, 1997; Willis, 1994). There are also voices of dissent (Boehle, 2000; Brook & Boal, 1995; Fabos & Young, 1999), and those who specify the conditions under which online learning is likely to be successful or unsuccessful (Bates, 2000; Kowch & Schwier, 1997; Moller, 1998; Palloff & Pratt, 1999). A growing number of studies describe and examine the contextual experiences and impressions of learners and instructors with collaborative learning online using synchronous and asynchronous communication strategies. This chapter fits into the last category. The experiences documented in this chapter range over a period of three years in a graduate seminar course.

If an online or blended delivery course uses discussions and chat it does not necessarily follow that a learning community will form. It is the learners who determine if they participated in online discussions or if, through online discussions, they became members of a learning community. In formal education settings, virtual learning communities promote the acquisition, transformation, or creation of knowledge by employing online engagement among learners (Schwier, 2001). Learning communities may emerge if the natural flow of communication and the natural development of relationships is supported; where the individual's prior expectations of personal learning needs are not only met, but changed or surpassed through engaged relationships with ideas (content), the instructor, and with other learners. Elements of community may include, in addition to learning and content, participation, integration, identity, historicity, mutuality, plurality, autonomy, technology, future, intensity, and trust.

One central premise of our work is that content and community are both critical to creating effective learning environments, but that community is often given short shrift in the design of online courses. This can be partly attributed to the epistemological assumptions driving course design. Predetermined content is often seen to be what courses are about and that content is defined and bounded externally in formal learning environments. Learning might manifest itself differently depending on the context of the community in which it is created, such as whether communities are bounded or unbounded. Wilson, Ludwig-Hardman, Thornam, and Dunlap (2004) distinguished between bounded and unbounded learning communities and suggested that bounded learning communities are created across courses in higher education or corporate settings. Furthermore, bounded learning communities emerge in direct response to guidance provided by an instructor who is supported by a resource base. Instructional designers, brought up in the traditions of cognitive psychology and models of instructional design, often emphasize bounded environments—their structure, sequence, and control of the learning environment—over the spontaneous, messy, and unpredictable aspects of interpersonal interactions and exploration (Kenny, Zhang, Schwier, & Campbell, 2004) characteristic of unbounded learning communities. Our argument is that in the classroom, especially in the online classroom, instructors and designers must lay a foundation on which bounded community can form around selected content, and they must attempt to accelerate the development of community in order to improve learning outcomes.

Evidence of community is found in interactions that occur between the learner and the instructor, content, and other learners. Anderson (2004), in describing the types of interactions that can take place in online learning environments, gave equal status to learner-content interaction, learner-instructor interaction, learner-learner interaction, and instructor-content interaction. This is a logical and reasonable articulation of engagement in traditional learning environments, and it promotes a way of thinking about online learning environments that emphasizes a balanced view of the importance of content and social engagement. Learner-content interaction, if allowed to dominate a course, naturally emphasizes objectivist principles of learning and correspondence models of instruction.

Learner-learner interaction, by contrast, emphasizes social constructivist models of learning. Moreover, the two, when in balance, offer learners the opportunity to co-create knowledge and the substance to guide their efforts. We do not support the axiom that "content is king" in the design of online courses, but without substantial attention to content, learner engagement runs the risk of becoming a vacuous exercise in sharing folk experiences. Content only comes alive and grows beyond its predetermined boundaries through active, sustained, and legitimate engagement among learners. Our epistemological assumptions about learning are pragmatic. All learning involves construction of understandings that are personal, and learning has a social dimension. Strong, organized content makes important contributions to the quality of construction and co-construction of knowledge that occurs in social constructivist learning environments. Within this epistemology and pedagogical approach, participants seek opportunities for private and open interactions in the learning environment that promote community and learning.

Recent studies from other disciplines describe the connection between community and learning. Downes (2005) argued that the two elements that define community are networks and semantics. Networks are characterized by connections among people, and semantics suggest that the network is about something meaningful—a topic, a value, a cause, or a shared interest. So the webs of relationships that develop are based on the commerce of things that are valued by participants, and within these webs are articulated patterns of relationships, roles played by participants, normative behaviors, and commonly held patterns of language (Paccagnella, 1997). This is particularly resonant with our view that successful virtual learning communities should balance content and community. Content represents the shared "things that are valued," and community represents the networks of relationships that emerge to understand, extend, and co-create the content. Downes' view supports a social capital interpretation of community. The quality of community in the group, indeed the very existence of community, may be determined by the social capital evident in the group. Social capital is a murky social construct, but it is still useful for exploring social networks in online learning environments. Social capital highlights the central importance of networks of strong personal relationships that develop over a period of time. Such relationships provide a basis for trust, cooperation, and collective action. In the context of virtual learning communities, social capital has been defined as "a common social resource that facilitates information exchange, knowledge sharing, and knowledge construction through continuous interaction, built on trust and maintained through shared understanding" (Daniel, Schwier, & McCalla, 2003, p. 114). Over the course of the three years of this study, this emerging research on learning networks and social capital has strengthened our own position on the importance of community in formal learning.

The virtual communities we discuss in this chapter are "bounded" or "formal," and they are fundamentally different structures from informal communities or actual, terrestrial communities. Terrestrial communities are characterized by proximity—I live near you, so we form a community—and a certain randomness of interaction—neighbors bump into each other occasionally and without specific intention. Informal communities abound on the Web, and they are characterized by popularity and shared interests. The meaning and content of informal communities may begin with an imposed structure, but the content is contributed, shaped, and evolved by the participants in the communities. Participants do not just drop in by accident for the most part; they participate voluntarily, intentionally, selectively, and purposefully based on what they find of value in the network. Formal virtual learning communities, on the other hand, feature a high degree of intentional participation, as students must register for courses and pay for them to gain admission to the community. This is typically done in a cohort and on a fixed schedule, although some universities and researchers are investigating ways to employ learner-paced schedules of distance learning (Anderson, Annand, & Wark, 2005). However, regardless of pacing, membership in the community is assigned selectively, either imposed by the requirements of a program or chosen based on reputation or interest. The substance of the community is characterized by organized content and activities; coordinated discussions, sometimes with feedback from the instructor; and external evaluations of individual performance by the instructor. Participation is not voluntary; it is a requirement of membership in the community. Both informal and formal virtual learning communities can be considered semantic networks (networks based on meaning), but a key difference between them is the locus of semantic definition. As we move from informal to formal learning communities, the locus of semantic control moves from being decentralized (meaning provided by participants) to being centralized (meaning provided institutionally). In part, what we are trying to accomplish by employing social constructivist approaches to learning in formal virtual learning communities is to move the locus of semantic control from a centralized to a more decentralized model.

The previous discussion on epistemology and the role of content and community represents our approach at the end of the three years study. In the rest of the chapter we provide data on the communications methods, synchronous and asynchronous communication, that were selected to support instructional goals in the online learning environment of a blended delivery course, and how our approach evolved over the period of the study.

Case Study Design and Context

The case study follows three years of online communication experiences of three groups of students in Educational Communications and Technology as they participated in a blended delivery course on the foundations of educational technology offered over a full academic year (approximately 28 weeks of coursework). Specifically, we wanted to catalog student and instructor experiences and reflect on several lessons learned about how online communication strategies could be manipulated to enhance the learning environment. In addition, we wanted to consider whether a balance between content and community could be achieved with a combination of asynchronous and synchronous online events.

Several sources of data inform the ideas presented in this paper. After each year of the study, instructors reviewed logs for all of the asynchronous and synchronous activities. The instructors and assistants also kept informal reflective journals. In all three years, students provided feedback on online discussion during course delivery. In years two and three some students and their instructors agreed to discuss questions that were used to confirm, challenge, or qualify preliminary data.

In the three years included in this case study, the course, instructor, and basic structure of the course remained constant. In each year, the content was equivalent, and the course included a combination of online instruction and monthly face-to-face meetings of the group. Online events in all three years used WebCT™ course tools for communication, which included text-based synchronous chat sessions or text-based asynchronous threaded discussions. In all deliveries of the course, students took responsibility for moderating the discussions after the instructor and teaching assistant modeled the process in the early part of each year. As stated earlier, complete data for year one were reported by Schwier and Balbar (2002), year two by Dykes and Schwier (2003), and year three by Schwier and Dykes (2004). For details about the research methodologies employed, we direct the reader to the previous works.

Selected Data Analysis and Results

This research was conducted as a thematic analysis of conversations drawn from online transcripts, interviews with students, and focus groups with class cohorts, and with the purpose of extending, refining, and/or altering our understanding of the key factors of the role played by communication, especially online discussion, in the development of virtual communities. Several of the assumptions underlying our interpretation of data included (a) the need to ground our interpretations in data; (b) the belief that learners take an active role in responding to problematic situations; (c) the realization that learners act on the basis of meaning; (d) the understanding that meaning is defined and redefined through interaction; (e) a sensitivity to the evolving and unfolding nature of events (process); and (f) an awareness of the interrelationships among structure, process, and consequences. Data were analyzed using Atlas ti™, a program for analyzing transcripts of information and extracting themes and uncovering relationships among qualitative data.

Having said that communities cannot be created, they can only be nurtured, we describe the interactions and relationships that are present in a community. When using online communication methods for text messaging, it is evident that a real sense of community can be fostered in both synchronous and asynchronous virtual environments, and it is possible to nurture genuine collaboration outside of "real time" engagement. Development of community is not necessarily fast-tracked by the use of synchronous communication, as we initially suspected after the first year of the study, nor is content engagement related only to asynchronous environments, as found in the second year. Rather, the development of community in both environments appears to be related to the meaningful, collaborative engagement of learners with each other and with content. We found that content and communities co-exist in both asynchronous and synchronous environments, and that the instructor can deliberately encourage either or both. We did note that asynchronous discussions promoted a deeper engagement of content. Asynchronous discussion also allows all students to participate equally in discussion. In synchronous discussion, quick thinkers with excellent keying skills can overwhelm other voices.

Content and Community

In all years of our study, we observed periods when student participation in online discussions to be so high and student feedback on the process of online discussions to be so positive that standard terms such as "motivated" and "engaged" seemed tame. Our label for an active, dynamic, focused level of engagement is the "principle of intensity." Content and community are the key ingredients for intensity. When individual learning, group learning, and input from the instructor are present, intensity can form, and it can appear in both synchronous and asynchronous discussions. Furthermore, we regard the principle of intensity as the highest expression of engagement with content and the strongest evidence of community development.

We suspect that exposure to new content challenges students to construct novel arguments and test them internally before making them public—a sort of intellectual quality assurance program. Synchronous communication brings a higher level of urgency to discussions in that less time is allowed for quality assurance tests; synchronous communication promotes sharing ideas that are untested. Despite the challenge this presents to learners, sharing formative thoughts is an important element of synchronous and asynchronous discussions. When a discussion includes formative thinking, subsequent collaborative learning, and high participation from all learners, then we would say the principle of intensity is evident in this discussion. Although it is easier to impart a sense of urgency with synchronous communication, we found that it was also possible to promote it in asynchronous events through the content. The skillful choice of reading material and provocative questions led to strong and intense exchanges, even when they were "out of time."

The development of intensity in the learning process was supported and possibly accelerated by the instructor's online lectures. The instructor's goals for the lectures were to make topics come alive for his student audience and to encourage a critical approach to key questions in the discipline. Before participating in an online discussion for a module, students read the required readings then viewed the online lecture. Many students reported that the instructor's lecture motivated them to write about their own interpretations and ideas in the online discussions.

We put forward our interpretation of some student discussions as learning experiences that fall within the principle of intensity, but novice online instructors might want to concentrate first on building the foundations of content and community that allows learning to take place. Community may form initially either around social interaction or around content. In years one and two of our study, community developed first at a social level and in synchronous communication. In year three, content was identified as one of the most important features of the course, and to our surprise students identified content as very important to the development of a sense of community in the class. Content was also identified as one of the key features students would look for in future online courses. Students expect to receive substance in courses. If a course or set of discussions focus on issues with little substance or importance to the course, students would probably rate it as a less successful learning experience, as the following students comments reveal:

In the future I will be looking for the following things in an E-learning environment: Interesting and challenging material related to my field of practice and interest. The course must also be current and still relevant to me; accessible material and resources using external media, text, or via the Internet (such as WebCT).

I would add that the most important thing for me is that the course is either a requirement or one that interests me. The content is probably number one.

Students regard online discussions as part of the content of courses, particularly when the discussion topic is directly related to its associated module topic. In year three, where instructors controlled discussion topics, some discussion topics were only loosely connected to existing module topics, thus expanding the content of the course, and naturally, its cognitive load. Students revealed that the heavy course load was too much:

I must admit that there are a few people who I have talked with through the use of E-mail and phone to talk about the shear workload of this course. At many times I was feeling very overwhelmed with work and assignments and needed encouragement and help in understanding a module. A kind of support network which was very helpful for me, and them I believe.

Students disclosed useful information about their learning strategies when coping with a content heavy course. When pressed for time, some students focused efforts on content in a public forum (i.e., discussions, neglecting module content). One student wanted discussion topics and module topics to be the same: "When discussion topics are different from the module content, I miss talking about the meat of the course." Some students regarded the extra-module discussion topics as assignments where they did minimum effort, rather than collaborative learning experiences, where they put extra effort. Another student considered any discussion to be the primary content of the course:

I consider the discussions to be the meat of the course. I need to experience ideas and beliefs colliding and reacting. The readings gave us something to talk about, but were they the main reason for talking?

This feedback supports a design strategy for content where discussion topics and module topics are similar.

Social Engagement and Community

Social engagement falls outside the principle of intensity and content but it plays an important role in development of community through a natural flow of communication (i.e., not forced or structured) (Schwier, 2001). There was strong evidence of social community in the three years of this course, which occasionally overlapped or surfaced in the content related community. As a general and casual observation, the synchronous chats in year one exhibited the highest degree of informality and social behavior during discussions, but the mixed approach in year two and the asynchronous approach in year three also generated a significant amount of social behavior. In years two and three, we observed a growing comfort and informality emerge in the asynchronous discussion treatment, with both students and instructors sharing information about cultural issues and other events in their lives in discussion postings. This type of engagement happened much earlier and more spontaneously in the synchronous chat sessions. It appeared that people were using the synchronous medium (online chat) in much the same way that other synchronous media (e.g., telephones, video-conferencing, audio-conferencing) are used. They seemed to first need to engage in "grooming behaviors," such as talking about the weather, work, or family news before engaging the formal content of the discussion. The pattern for asynchronous communication (online discussion) was the opposite. Student postings typically first dealt with the formal content of the discussion, and personal interjections radiated from replies to these initial postings. So, the medium seemed to influence the pattern of communication, but it didn't influence the content of communication. Asynchronous and synchronous media included substantial amounts of content-specific and social commentary. The recommended design for online discussions includes meeting rooms such as the "café," or the "water cooler" to contain social exchanges. We have observed that social communication will not be confined to these areas and that students will get down to business in the academic discussion space without intervention from the instructors.

In a blended delivery course, we suspect that the increased comfort level was also strongly influenced by the infrequent, but regular, face-to-face (f2f) classroom meetings and the social meetings during and immediately after class, such as coffee breaks and lunch. In the third year, participants made several comments about the importance of f2f in forming and maintaining community online. They "met" online much more frequently than f2f, and it was interesting to see how the two approaches reinforced each other in developing an academic as well as a social community. Online discussions were continued in f2f sessions and f2f sessions offered a level of familiarity that supported online discussions. The overall effect was beneficial, regardless of the type of online communication strategy we employed:

f2f sessions allowed the community to grow faster and certainly developed a deeper sense of trust between all members of this community (between students as well as between students and the [instructors]). This sense of community reduced the risk threshold and encouraged all members to jump right into discussions. I believe that within three modules, the risk factor had all but evaporated for most members.

Opportunities for informal conversation and social gatherings outside of formal class time and online discussions played an important part in forming a sense of community in the course. Social aspects of a class, such as having lunch or chatting during coffee breaks, become traditions in classes, and a certain amount of tradition and ceremony seems to be important. In fact, one student suggested that attendance at the lunches should be made compulsory:

I would encourage everyone to join as a group for lunch ... LOL. I know it sounds silly, but I really got to know people who did attend those lunches and it helped me to make them more than a name.

Because face-to-face sessions in the class were critically important to the development of community in the class, there is every reason to suspect that many of the findings for the online environment were mediated by the simple fact that the group met on several occasions. Even the virtual face-to-face sessions (two-way videoconferencing) in year two had a strong influence on developing a sense of community among the students and instructors. While it may be possible to build virtual learning communities in entirely distributed and text-based environments, we suspect it would be much more difficult to accomplish than it was in a mixed-mode class.

As senior scholars in a graduate program, students are expected to lead seminar discussions in many of their courses. The same expectation should be made of students in online discussions. Students were assigned the responsibility of moderating discussions with a team member, in effect, giving them responsibility and authority for co-creating knowledge in the class. From our experience, we extracted several issues, explicit tips and traps for instructors who use student moderated online discussions, and we summarized them in Table 1. Participants volunteered comments about the team moderating activity. They had mixed experiences with team moderating in this course. The team moderating activity was not always positive, mainly because the partner did not participate as fully as expected or share responsibilities equally. But it is significant to note that these factors did not have a negative impact on overall community; students viewed various difficulties as expected features of the experience, or as new examples of experiences they had in earlier class settings:

I haven't had that much experience with group work online, but I would try to avoid it—I've heard too many stories of people not being satisfied with it. But then I'm not really a fan of getting group marks in f2f classes either. Sometimes I think people don't try as hard when it is a group project, and other times I just tend to like my own work better. I enjoyed the case study we did in this course (the constructivist business program), but there were no marks attached, and it was more of a group problem-solving exercise.

One participant commented on the uneven distribution of responses to postings in discussions. A close inspection of the postings by one student who attracted fewer responses revealed that these postings were among the strongest made by the group, and the smaller number of responses could not be attributed to late

Table 1. Issues, tips, and traps associated with student moderated online discussions

Issues for Instructors Using Student Moderated Online Discussions	Tip	Trap
Discussions as content	Emphasize content (i.e., learning) as the purpose for the community	Students may focus efforts in public arena, neglecting other content
New material in content	Encourage student's disclosure of formative thinking	In classes that include both advanced and novice learners, students may elect to discuss content with learners at the same level of understanding
Instructor controlled structure	Allow student in moderator role to focus on learning content	Cognitive overload quickly sets in if selection of discussion topic not clearly seen to be related to module theme
Synchronous communication	Use to explicitly support rapid formation of community at social level	Little evidence of deep learning
Asynchronous communication	Use to explicitly promote deep learning. Social interaction may also surface eventually and is evidence of formation of community	Thoughtful communication takes time to prepare, to read and to comment on thoughtfully. Students must be aware of the amount of time this usually takes.
Face-to-face class and social meetings	Use F2F where feasible to support development and growth of community	Class social events may be uncomfortable for students who are private by nature
Team moderating	Collaboration with team member may promote learning	Team members may not share work equally
Time	Place limits on the amount of writing students do. Keep the total amount at a level that students can consider thoughtfully in the time they have available.	Asynchronous discussions multiply content and can easily grow to unmanageable levels. The instructor's time commitment will also grow, often well beyond the amount of time required to teach a face-to-face class.

posting by the student. Is it possible that other students were impressed with the statements and had little elaboration to offer? Were other students intimidated by the quality of these postings? We can only speculate from the data available, but it is clear that students notice disparate responses in groups, and they are a cause for concern pedagogically. Students in these online discussions, especially asynchronous discussions, prepare their responses carefully and invest a great deal of work in them. When postings fail to attract responses that are equally thoughtful, they may feel a sense of rejection and lose motivation to invest as heavily in their postings:

I had the sense that some people in the course got less replies than others, while others got more than their share of responses. This is hard to control, but the moderators could try to be aware of anyone who is an outsider to the conversation.

There was evidence that the act of moderating a discussion improved learning for the moderators. Participants commented on deeper learning in the moderator role, and that they more carefully read documents being discussed. The positive experiences were also based on the process of moderating. Participants commented positively on the process of moderating and sharing the work of responding to postings. However, previous experiences with academic group work were frequently not positive, partly because of assessment, and some of that experience colored their predispositions to these activities:

When I am moderator I think I learn the content a lot more thoroughly than if I just have to post. When I have to reply to half or more of the postings, I feel like I have to really understand the concepts. And inevitably some people post ideas that I hadn't thought of, so I have to go back to the readings and try to understand things in a different way. Being moderator has definitely helped me in this course.

Conclusion

In this multi-year case study, many of the students, experiencing online learning for the first time, embraced this method of delivery. At the same time, they were aware that the learning environment was the result of much effort on the part of the instructor and their own commitment to participation in a learning community. This level of success as a group, rather than as individual learners, may not be possible to achieve in all online courses. Nevertheless, it raises an interesting question that may have to be addressed more explicitly by academic institutions. If development of community is recognized as one of the factors that promote learning, then should it be explicitly stated as a learning outcome in courses and programs? If community is viewed as a legitimate learning outcome, how should student performance be assessed? There are many well-established methods for evaluating groups and participation in groups, but it strikes us that the very act of evaluating the quality of community and participation in community, may in turn mitigate the development of community.

In blended or mixed-mode delivery of courses, it is possible for students to quickly form a virtual learning community that is firmly anchored in content with the use of asynchronous discussions. The principle of intensity, or strong engagement and motivation, may be promoted in asynchronous discussions with the use of provocative questions and structured interaction between students. When the instructor's role in the delivery of content is not confined to face-to-face sessions, and when the instructor's "voice" is linked with content delivered online, intensity may be increased. But the overall development of community and its effectiveness in promoting learning happens over time and is founded to a significant degree on social engagement and the development of trust. Our review of data from the three offerings of the class described here lead us to conclude that for this course, paying close attention to balancing its content and community features will continue to be a key challenge to the success of the course.

The authors gratefully acknowledge the participation and contributions of graduate students in the courses employed in this study. This research was supported by a grant from the Social Sciences and Humanities Research Council of Canada.

References

Anderson, T. (2004). Toward a theory of online learning. In T. Anderson & F. Elloumi (Eds.), *Theory and practice of online learning* (pp. 33-60). Athabasca, Alberta: Athabasca University Press.

Anderson, T., Annand, D., & Wark, N. (2005). The search for learning community in learner paced distance education: Or, "Having your cake and eating it, too!" *Australasian Journal of Educational Technology, 21*(2), 222-241.

Bates, A. W. (2000). *Managing technological change*. San Francisco: Jossey-Bass.

Boehle, S. (N.D.). *My exasperating life as an online learner*. Retrieved August 15, 2000, from http://www.trainingsupersite.com/publications/magazines/training/006cv3.htm

Brook, J., & Boal, I. A. (1995). *Resisting the virtual life: The culture and politics of information*. San Francisco: City Lights Books.

Burge, E. J. (1994). Learning in computer conferenced contexts: The learners' perspective. *Journal of Distance Education, 9*(1), 19-43.

Burge, E. J., Laroque, D., & Boak, C. (2000). Baring professional souls: Reflections on Web life. *Journal of Distance Education, 15*(1), 81-98.

Burge, L. (2000). *The strategic use of learning technologies*. San Francisco: Jossey-Bass.

Cohill, A. M. (1997). Success factors of the Blacksburg Electronic Village. In A. M. Cohill & A. L. Kavanaugh (Eds.), *Community networks: Lessons from Blacksburg, Virginia* (pp. 297-318). Norwood, MA: Artech House.

Daniel, B., Schwier, R., & McCalla, G. (2003). Social capital in virtual learning communities and distributed communities of practice. *Canadian Journal of Learning and Technology, 29*(3), 113-139.

Downes, S. (2005). *Community blogging*. Presentation to the Northern Voice Conference, Vancouver, BC, February 19, 2005. Retrieved May 15, 2005, from http://www.downes.ca

Dykes, M. E., & Schwier, R. A. (2003). Content and community redux: Instructor and student interpretations of online communication in a graduate seminar. *Canadian Journal of Learning and Technology, 29*(2), 79-99.

Fabos, B., & Young, M. D. (1999). Telecommunication in the classroom: Rhetoric versus reality. *Review of Educational Research, 69*(3), 217-259.

Kenny, R. F., Zhang, Z., Schwier, R. A., & Campbell, K. (2005). A review of what instructional designers do: Questions answered and questions not asked. *Canadian Journal of Learning and Technology, 31*(1), 9-26.

Kowch, E., & Schwier, R. A. (1997). Considerations in the construction of technology-based virtual learning communities. *Canadian Journal of Educational Communication, 26*(1), 1-12.

Moller, L. (1998). Designing communities of learners for asynchronous distance education. *Educational Technology Research and Development, 46*(4), 115-122.

Murphy, E., & Loveless, J. (2005). Students' self analysis of contributions to online asynchronous discussions. *Australasian Journal of Educational Technology, 21*(2), 155-172.

Paccagnella, L. (1997). Getting the seats of your pants dirty: Strategies for ethnographic research on virtual communities. *Journal of Computer-Mediated Communication, 3*(1). Retrieved May 15, 2005, from http://www.ascusc.org/jcmc/vol3/issue1/paccagnella.html

Palloff, R. M., & Pratt, K. (1999). *Building learning communities in cyberspace: Effective strategies for the online classroom.* San Francisco: Jossey-Bass.

Ruberg, L. F., Moore, D. M., & Taylor, C. D. (1996). Student participation, interaction, and regulation in a computer-mediated communication environment: A qualitative study. *Journal of Educational Computing Research, 14*(3), 243-268.

Schwier, R. A. (2001). Catalysts, emphases, and elements of virtual learning communities: Implications for research and practice. *Quarterly Review of Distance Education, 2*(1), 5-18.

Schwier, R., & Dykes, M. (2004). The struggle for community and content in virtual learning communities. *Proceedings of Ed-Media 2004* (pp. 2976-2982). Lugano, Switzerland.

Schwier, R. A., & Balbar, S. (2002). The interplay of content and community in synchronous and asynchronous communication: Virtual communication in a graduate seminar. *Canadian Journal of Learning and Technology, 28*(2), 21-30.

Willis, B. (1994). *Distance education: Opportunities and challenges.* Englewood Cliffs, NJ: Educational Technology Publications.

Wilson, B. G., Ludwig-Hard-Hardman, S., Thorman, C. L., & Dunluap, J. C. (2004). Bounded community: Designing and facilitating learning communities in formal courses. *International Review of Research in Open and Distance Learning, 5*(3). Retrieved April 1, 2005, from http://cade.athabascau.ca/vo5.3/wilson

Zemsky, R., & Massy, W. F. (2004). *Thwarted innovation: What happened to e-learning and why.* Philadelphia: The Learning Alliance at the University of Pennsylvania. Retrieved May 6, 2005, from http://www.irhe.upenn.edu/Docs/Jun2004/ThwartedInnovation.pdf

Chapter XI

Toward Effective Instruction in E-Learning Environments

Martha A. Gabriel, University of Prince Edward Island, Canada

Abstract

This chapter explores the role of instructors and the perspectives they bring to teaching in e-learning environments. It suggests that when instructors are developing e-learning courses, instruction is more effective if individual perspectives on teaching, as well as the principles of good teaching, are taken into consideration. Congruence between principles, perspectives, and practice enhance e-learning pedagogy. The model—reflect on the teaching approach, apply the principles of good teaching throughout the course, choose appropriate learning outcomes and activities, and review choices—is proposed as a guideline for effective teaching in e-learning environments.

Introduction

As postsecondary institutions face the challenges of the learning society, educators and researchers have called for a change in the teaching paradigm of higher education. Thus, the discussion on e-learning in higher education presented in this chapter focuses on a learning paradigm rather than an instruction paradigm. To facilitate the transition to a learning paradigm, instructors must be supported as they experiment with new models of teaching and learning. This chapter presents a synthesis of major issues discussed in the literature on the transition from face-to-face teaching to e-learning with a focus on instructors and their roles in e-learning.

Bates (2000) highlights three main factors driving the need for changes in higher education. The first is the reality that universities are constantly being asked by government to do more with less. The second is the change in what citizens of the twenty-first century must know, given the emphasis on critical thinking, problem solving, and learning how to learn. And finally, Bates underlines the ubiquitous influence of new technologies on learning.

The primary purpose of the chapter, then, is to help instructors adapt more effectively to an e-learning environment. Individuals will have an opportunity to review their personal teaching styles and to explore teaching methods and pedagogy effective in e-learning environments. Key categories of activities in e-learning environments will be discussed, and a synthesis of e-learner needs and expectations will be offered.

The model proposed in this chapter is *reflect, apply, choose, review,* which is depicted in Figure 1.

The initial phase involves reflections by e-instructors on their personal perspectives on teaching. This is addressed in the section "Exploring Instructors' Teaching Styles." The next phase examines how to apply principles of good teaching in the e-learning environment. A third phase involves choosing e-learning activities appropriate to a particular e-learning course. These two stages are explored in the section "Effective Principles and Activities in E-Learning Environments." The final phase of this model involves reviewing choices made from the viewpoint of e-learners. This is addressed in the section on "E-Learners in the Online Environment."

It should be noted that there are a multitude of factors that influence the transition to e-learning, including institutional commitment to the transition; professional development for faculty making the shift to e-learning; an instructional design team to support e-course design; and technical support throughout the design, delivery, and evaluation of e-learning courses. However, this chapter focuses on those factors related to instructor beliefs and behaviors in the shift to e-learning.

Figure 1.

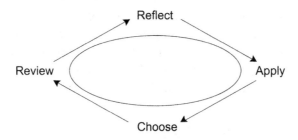

Background

Significant pressures affect today's postsecondary institutions. As premier learning institutions, universities and colleges must respond to social, demographic, and economic changes. Learner demands, combined with changing attitudes toward lifelong learning and work in our society, have required postsecondary institutions to examine and update their traditional approaches. In many ways this is a competitive necessity, for if this re-examination does not occur, other learning organizations are waiting to enter the field left vacant by the universities (Bates, 2000).

Changing previous ways of working and learning is an essential feature of the landscape of a learning society. Those teaching in institutions of higher education must consider how change can be adopted, embraced, and implemented. Duderstadt (1999) has pointed out that:

There is no question that the need for learning institutions such as colleges and universities will become increasingly important in a knowledge-driven future. The real question is not whether higher education will be transformed but rather how *and* by whom. (p. 1)

E-learning has been touted as one means of addressing the challenges posed by the learning society, though the concept itself has not been definitively described. Zemsky and Massy (2004) deconstruct e-learning and identify three perspectives: (a) e-learning as distance education, (b) e-learning as facilitated transactions software, and (c) e-learning as electronically mediated learning (p. 5). The focus herein is mainly on the first perspective identified by Zemsky and Massy, e-learning as distance education. E-learning as education over a distance signals a transactional space between instructor and student that does not exist in a face-to-face learning encounter (Moore & Kearsley, 1996). The result of e-learning is that the transactional distance existing between instructor and students is bridged through information and communication technologies. In this chapter, e-learning is defined as *learning which takes place when Internet technologies are used to facilitate, deliver, and enable learning processes over a distance*.

In their seminal article, Barr and Tagg (1995) propose that the priority in higher education is shifting from instruction to learning, and that the role of students as well as the role of instructor is changing. When the focus is placed squarely on instruction, instructors are perceived as experts who impart knowledge to their students, usually by the lecture method. When instructors focus on learning, however, they assume the roles of facilitator, guide, and coach. Instructors are then responsible for developing the learner-centered environment and experiences that students will encounter. Lectures remain an important teaching method, but become only one method in a larger spectrum of possibilities. E-learning has the potential to facilitate the shift to a learning-centered focus in higher education and to provide an opportunity for instructors to examine seriously their own approaches to teaching and learning.

Teaching and Learning in E-Learning Environments

Exploring Instructors' Teaching Styles

Palmer (1998) suggests that "We teach who we are. Teaching, like any truly human activity, emerges from one's inwardness, for better or worse" (p. 2). If this is so, then reflection should be an integral component of teaching. Instructors could take time to reflect on their own personal beliefs, assumptions, and teaching activities, and consider these in depth. To accomplish this, some instructors keep journals recording student reactions and questions to learning activities. They then use the information as data for making changes in their course(s) and approaches to more effectively accommodate learner needs. In any case, it is only when instructors consider carefully and reflect on their teaching approaches that they fully understand their own teaching perspective and are then enabled to expand consciously their repertoire of teaching strategies.

Pratt and a number of his colleagues have written extensively on the subject of perspectives on teaching (Pratt & Associates, 1998; Pratt & Collins, 2002; Pratt, Arseneau, & Collins, 2001). These researchers define a perspective on teaching as "an inter-related set of beliefs and intentions that gives direction and justification to our actions ... a lens through which we view our work as educators," and instructors are urged to "identify, articulate, and justify their teaching approaches" (Pratt, Arsenault, & Collins, 2001, para. 6). When instructors have discerned their dominant view of teaching, they may be enabled to make instructional choices in tune with their own perspective. The next section draws on the work of Pratt and his colleagues to present the five perspectives on teaching.

Five Perspectives on Teaching

The transmission, developmental, apprenticeship, nurturing, and social reform approaches to teaching all afford the possibility for effective teaching (Pratt & Associates, 1998). Instructors have multiple paths to support student learning and achieve their own educational goals. Pratt and his colleagues suggest that most instructors tend to adopt one perspective, or possibly components of two perspectives, on teaching.

The *transmission perspective* has been the dominant perspective toward teaching in the past. It is based on the philosophical belief that there is an external reality and that learning consists of coming to know that external body of knowledge. A transmission approach emphasizes the importance of the content and suggests that instructors are subject matter experts who transfer their knowledge to their students. The main responsibilities of an instructor teaching from a transmission perspective include offering well-conceptualized lectures, leading thoughtful discussions, and giving students information through answering questions and correcting mistakes. Until recently, this approach has held sway as the dominant traditional approach to teaching in higher education.

A constructivist orientation to teaching proposes that knowledge is subjective. Constructivists believe that learners must construct their own understanding of phenomena through absorbing information, making connections with previously existing knowledge, and working with this new knowledge. Social constructivists believe that this meaning-making works most effectively through interactions with others. Constructivism underpins the *developmental perspective* on teaching. Instructors who teach from this perspective aim to support their students as they develop ever-more complex comprehension of concepts. Instructors use the experiences and interpretations that their students bring to the learning situation as starting points for building understanding. These instructors tend to look for student understanding and ability to reason using new knowledge constructed through active learning.

Instructors who teach from the *apprenticeship perspective* believe that student learning is supported when students work on authentic tasks in real-life environments, such as pre-service teachers in field placements, business students in co-op placements, or medical students on a particular rotation. The notion of mentor is a critical one in this perspective on teaching. Zachary (2002) defines mentoring as "a reciprocal and collaborative learning responsibility between two individuals who share mutual responsibility and accountability for helping a mentee work toward achieving clear and mutually defined learning goals" (p. 28). A rich learning experience occurs when students have opportunities to gain guidance, advice, support, and feedback from their mentor.

Instructors who teach from a *nurturing perspective* believe that it is of critical importance to establish supportive learning environments in which students are able to take risks without fear of failure. The establishment of this atmosphere of confidence and respect is essential for learning to occur. Instructors therefore attempt to enhance learners' perceptions of self-efficacy, offer successful learning opportunities, and challenge students' thinking, in a milieu supporting their growth as learners. Instructors with a nurturing perspective focus on providing encouragement and support and getting to know their students in a deeper, richer way, while striking a balance between challenging and caring in their work with students.

Instructors who teach from a *social reform* perspective believe that the critical examination of all assumptions, concepts, and values is an essential component of learning. The role of the instructor teaching from a social reform perspective is to enable students to see the world around them with new eyes. The instructor expects students to raise critical questions, to challenge the status quo, and to not accept at face value whatever is said or done. There is always an action component to this perspective, because the goal of education is not simply to learn about the world as it is understood today, but to act to change that world for the better.

Further information on the five teaching perspectives suggested by Pratt and his colleagues, and the research-based online inventory, may be found at http://www.teachingperspectives.com.

E-Learning and Teaching Perspectives

As instructors teaching in e-learning environments develop an understanding of their own teaching perspectives, how can they put that knowledge to use in their online courses? What specific strategies might they choose to implement within e-learning environments? These perspectives on teaching can best be understood, perhaps, in terms of how the students are engaged (D. Pratt, personal communication, November 4, 2005). This notion of learner engagement includes engagement with the content, with the instructor, with other learners, as well as with the e-learning context (Kearsley & Shneiderman, 1999).

Transmission perspective. Instructors who approach teaching from a transmission perspective focus on a mastery of the content. Emphasis is on teaching, knowledge reproduction, and independent learning (Pratt & Associates, 1998). Engagement for instructors teaching from this perspective consists of helping students to come to know and understand correctly. Instructors want to ensure that their students clearly understand what they are learning and that the information is accurate. Suggested pedagogical strategies that instructors operating from this perspective might find useful in e-learning environments include the following:

- Posting a course syllabus and calendar online;
- Using e-mail to individual students for communication, submission of assignments, and sending grades;
- Posting lecture notes online on a weekly or module basis;
- Using the quiz or test capabilities of the learning management system (LMS) to test student knowledge and provide feedback;
- Directing students to text and course text Web site (if available); and
- Developing learning materials in conjunction with an instructional design team during course development.

Developmental perspective. Instructors who teach from a developmental perspective place learning, knowledge construction, collaboration, and reflection at the heart of what they do. Their emphasis tends to be learner-centered, and they conceive of their role as a facilitator and coach (Pratt & Associates, 1998). Engagement for instructors teaching from this perspective means that e-learners need to be given time and place to explore the meaning of what they are learning. E-learners need to share their prior knowledge, to enable the instructor to post questions and comments that move the e-learner to a deeper level of understanding. E-learning strategies that instructors teaching from a developmental perspective could use to complement activities include the following:

- Developing learning teams whose members are expected to support one another as they work through projects and assignments;
- Using case studies and real-world examples to help learners move from simpler to more complex understandings of concepts;

- Developing a discussion board thread and posing a problem which students are expected to consider, discuss, and try to resolve;

- Expecting students to share Web-based resources they discover throughout the course; and

- Integrating interactive activities valuable in terms of student learning.

Apprenticeship perspective. Instructors who approach teaching from an apprenticeship perspective help their students work within their "zone of proximal development." Instructors scaffold activities and tasks so that students move from the simple to the complex (Pratt et al., 2001). Instructors who are teaching from an apprenticeship perspective see engagement as a matter of learners working on authentic tasks. The notion of authenticity applies both to the e-learning context, and to the tasks that e-learners are asked to perform. Instructors who have this teaching perspective might use the following e-learning strategies:

- Requiring students to engage in reflection on their learning. The reflections can be a particularly powerful form of learning if students are asked to share these reflections with their peers via the discussion board when they are out in the field.

- Developing activities that allow students to explore real-world contexts, for example, using case studies of actual businesses or critical incidents drawn from actual classroom or hospital occurrences.

- Modeling appropriate responses to a variety of problem-based learning scenarios.

- Designing collaborative activities so that all members of the team must participate for the team to achieve success.

Nurturing perspective. Instructors who approach teaching from a nurturing perspective affirm the efficacy of learning demonstrated by students in their courses. They expect students to learn and provide whatever support and guidance is required for this to occur (Pratt et al., 2001). Engagement for instructors who are teaching from a nurturing perspective focuses on providing high levels of instructor support and ensuring that every e-learner will succeed. E-learning strategies used by instructors who have a nurturing perspective could include the following:

- Developing a strong welcome activity/message to the course for incoming students. Instructors could also share personal experiences with students.
- Recognizing and dealing effectively with problems learners are experiencing. This requires close attention to student engagement with learning materials and with other students.
- Using individual e-mail messages to let students know when they are doing well or when they are not meeting course expectations.
- Providing advice about study skills if this is required for particular students.
- Establishing an active discussion board, and participating in discussions.
- Ensuring that students are aware of support services available to them online.

Social reform perspective. Instructors who work from a social reform perspective expect students to become agents of change. The development of critical perspectives is essential (Pratt et al., 2001). Instructors who are teaching from a social reform perspective view engagement as challenging e-learners to review their ways of thinking, working, and perceiving their world. In order to accomplish this in online environments, instructors could implement these e-learning strategies:

- Developing discussion board threads that address issues of privilege and power.
- Forming teams to develop presentations on the issues addressed in the course. These presentations can be shared online, with other students expected to respond and critique the issues and ideas raised.
- Requiring students to develop critical reflections on discussions and texts.
- Asking students to interrogate their own approach to their work/learning/ social surroundings.

These are suggestions for e-learning strategies that can align closely with the perspectives on teaching adopted by instructors with transmission, developmental, apprenticeship, nurturing, or social reform approaches. However, it is not suggested that these strategies are solely appropriate for instructors with those particular perspectives. A number of the strategies may be used successfully and comfortably by instructors with a variety of perspectives on teaching. As instructors continue to move to a learning paradigm, other pedagogically sound e-learning strategies can be developed and implemented.

Effective Principles and Activities in E-Learning Environments

A significant number of studies exploring the role of online instructors have been conducted (Gabriel, 2004; Hislop & Ellis, 2004; Pawan, 2003; Roberts & Jones, 2000; Rovai, 2004). A multiplicity of roles performed by online instructors have been described, such as researcher, content facilitator, technologist, designer, manager/administrator, process facilitator, advisor/counselor, and assessor (Goodyear, Salmon, Spector, Steeples, & Tickner, 2001). All of these roles require competencies that are addressed within the principles of good teaching developed by Chickering, Gamson, and Ehrman, which will be explored next.

Principles of Good Teaching

Regardless of an instructor's perspective on teaching, there are certain universals of teaching and e-learning. Chickering and Gamson (1987) and Chickering and Ehrman (1997) explored principles of good teaching and then later, the principles of good teaching supported by technology. These principles will be discussed in the context of e-learning, followed by suggestions for effective learning activities in e-learning environments.

Good practice encourages contacts between students and faculty. It is essential that instructors communicate effectively with their students. The technologies of the Internet, including e-mail, Web-based chat, voice over IP, and bulletin board discussions, facilitate improved communication between instructor and students. The instructor must deliberately strive to ensure effective communication by such initiatives as discussion starter questions posted on a discussion board, prompt responses to e-mail queries posted by students, online office hours facilitated by a chat program, and/or voice over IP learner presentation sessions.

Good practice develops reciprocity and cooperation among students. When knowledge is constructed in a collegial atmosphere with the support and interaction of peers, the quality of learning frequently improves. Instructors, then, must build time and space for this collaborative work to occur in their courses. This means ensuring that e-learners in the course know one another, virtual teamwork is clearly explained, and some form of collaborative learning environment is fostered.

Good practice uses active learning techniques. Many technologies available to instructors facilitate active learning. Communication technologies discussed above are one means by which e-learners can become actively engaged in the learning enterprise. Activity-oriented Web sites and technologies are also available for implementation in courses. Inquiry projects based on online simulations or virtual field trips are exemplars.

Good practice gives prompt feedback. E-mail from instructor to e-learners can provide timely feedback on questions or assignments. More instructors are using learner e-portfolios to provide more effective comments and direction to students. Videos of student efforts can afford another effective medium for feedback via e-mail or discussion board.

Good practice emphasizes time on task. Many e-learners and instructors are time-deprived or time-challenged. Using Internet resources, electronic databases, and ebraries can effectively save time. Both students and instructors can respond to assignments at a time best suited to them and their daily schedules.

Good practice communicates high expectations. It seems to be human nature to rise to expectations. If expectations are low, then performance will be lackluster. If, however, expectations are high, then most e-learners strive with great energy to achieve those expectations. The incentive of publishing student projects on the Web or of sharing student assignments online with the class or the team is a strong motivator for e-learners to produce and share their best work.

Good practice respects diverse talents and ways of learning. To accommodate the varying needs of learners, instructors can use technologies to enhance learning through visual, auditory, and kinesthetic channels. E-learners can write journals reflecting on their learning, work in teams to solve real-life problems, and research and respond to case studies. Assignments and learning materials can be developed with a branching structure so that students who require more structure can find it, while those who prefer to experiment are free to learn in that manner. Technology supports the development of a diverse set of learning activities, materials, and assignments that allow instructors to accommodate the needs of e-learners.

These principles of good teaching provide a framework that instructors might use when developing and teaching their courses. The framework can help instructors be more attentive to e-learners' needs and can serve as a lens through which instructors might constructively assess their teaching.

Effective E-Learning Activities

Up to this point, the discussion has focused on perspectives on teaching and the impact that a particular perspective might have on teaching activities implemented in e-learning courses. As well, the seven principles of good teaching that can form a framework for work in e-learning have been examined. Now, categories of activities that might be included in e-learning courses will be proposed. Appropriate activities focus on the learner, allow some self-selection of projects/assignments, and make effective use of interactive tools.

Resource-based learning activities require learners to use resources to search, collect, and synthesize information. WebQuests using Web-based resources are effective and efficient resource-based learning activities that can be focused on the learning outcomes of a wide variety of e-learning courses. WebQuests are predicated on a particular question or problem; e-learners are then divided into teams to use the Internet to research solutions. As a team, e-learners develop a presentation providing their solution to the initial challenge. Examples of WebQuests, articles, rubrics for assessing WebQuests, as well as training materials can be found at http://webquest.sdsu.edu/.

Team-building is a critical component of e-learning courses where team work is required. Team-building activities facilitate the forming, storming, norming, and performing of teams in online environments (Tuckman, 1965). There are a number of traditional team-building activities that can be adapted and expanded in an e-learning environment. Survival scenario exercises present a disaster, such as plane crash or a fire on a ship, and the team is expected to work out how best to deal with the situation. *NASA's Exercise: Survival on the Moon* is available online at http://www.bpccs.com/lcas/Articles/survive.htm. Another type of team-building activity requires each team to develop its own team-building exercise. This activity is very challenging for online teams, but it does result in teams engaging in the critical components of teamwork: developing communication strategies, setting goals, planning together, and working cooperatively/collaboratively.

Critical thinking activities help e-learners identify and challenge commonly held assumptions. Concept mapping and quandary action mazes are e-learning activities that support the development of this essential skill. To complete a concept mapping activity, e-learners develop an initial set of thoughts and ideas about a particular course topic using concept mapping software such as *Inspiration*. E-learners then revise their own concept maps once or twice throughout the course, and at the conclusion of the course, might write a short paper reflecting on their learning. In a quandary action maze e-learners can be presented with a problem or a case. They work through the maze, making decisions about the issues presented at each choice point. These choices encourage e-learners to reflect and bring their prior knowledge and learning to bear on the choices. Examples of quandary mazes are available at the Quandary tutorial site at http://www.halfbakedsoftware.com/quandary_tutorials_examples.php.

Creative thinking activities challenge e-learners to think outside the box and learn to problem solve as they develop non-traditional solutions to issues.

Synectics is a term developed by Gordon (1961) to describe discovering the links that unite seemingly disparate ideas/components. Synectics activities allow e-learners to create new ideas from existing ideas or to see things from new perspectives and link these elements together using metaphorical thinking. Another creative thinking approach is brainstorming and reverse brainstorming. E-learners can conduct these activities in their teams via discussion board, chat room, or e-mail. In both brainstorming and reverse brainstorming, e-learners are asked to list as many ideas as possible, and off-the-wall ideas are particularly useful for eliciting new ideas. Reverse brainstorming focuses on the negative case, for example, list all the ways that our university will *not* be able to integrate technology into our classrooms.

Inquiry approaches allow e-learners to become involved in explorations that lead to understanding. The inquiry approach can be conceptualized as a process of learning that focuses on students asking questions, investigating solutions, and creating new knowledge. Sidebar problems are examples of activities that can lead to deep learning for students. The sidebar problem presents a short scenario related to the course contents. The e-learner reads the sidebar and then answers the question posed at the end of the scenario by clicking on the correct paragraph. The feedback given in the answer allows students to check their own under-standing and then engage in further reflection. Virtual field trips provide e-learners with the opportunity to explore the natural or material world within the context of a particular Web site. These structured explorations can lead to questioning and the search for new understanding.

These are but a few examples of online activities that can provide e-learners with authentic and appropriate learning experiences. Instructors might be inspired to use these ideas as a springboard for their own thinking about innovative ways to integrate technology for effective e-learning.

E-Learners in the Online Environment

E-learning instructors should consider how they might address the varying needs of learners who enroll in their courses. In fact, Brown (2003) suggests that "before teachers attempt to develop more flexible teaching styles, they must be receptive to the idea of change, beginning with a change in their beliefs about the students' role in the learning environment" (p. 2). The traditional notion of education as transmission of knowledge from instructor to student is deeply rooted in our culture. In that conception of education, students were cast in the role of passive listeners and consumers of education who were in the classroom to take notes and learn from the expert. In the new approach—the learning paradigm (Barr & Tagg, 1995)—students are expected to be active in their own learning, to collaborate with others, to monitor their own learning, and to be co-constructors of knowledge.

What are the implications of this shift to a new view of the role of e-learners? Instructors need to support e-learners as they explore implications of their new role in the educational enterprise. The following suggestions are offered as a basic outline of the roles and expectations of e-learners. They are a set of guidelines that instructors working from all five perspectives on teaching might find useful:

- E-learners can acknowledge and accept their roles and responsibilities at the beginning of the course. Instructors may need to support e-learners as they develop an understanding of these new roles and responsibilities. This support might take the form of introductory activities which require e-learners to begin to take responsibility for responding online, using technology appropriately, and learning how to format their work.

- E-learners need to accept that the instructor in a course is one of a number of experts in the learning community and not the sole source of information. This means that students will need to agree to learn from their peers. As well, e-learners must trust their instructor to intervene if incorrect, misleading, or confusing information is posted online.

- The course might be structured to encourage social interaction among participants and to build a community of e-learners. Collaborative learning activities, simulations, case studies, and problem-based learning can support the development of this community.

- E-learners need to recognize that they are responsible for their own learning. They also have a responsibility to contribute to the learning community in the e-learning environment. As a minimum level of participation, e-learners can share ideas, personal news, and comments on the work of their peers.

- There is a tension between the notion of working in a learning community and working independently. Many e-learners are more interested in achieving the goals of the course in their own time and space, rather than coordinating their efforts with a team of colleagues in the online environment. Instructors should find a way to balance the needs of the community with the needs of individual learners. Strategies to help e-learners learn how to work in online teams include effective modeling by the facilitator, allowing time for development and practice, and engaging in online team-building activities before beginning an actual project.

- E-learners should either possess or develop strong organizational, self-regulation, and time management skills in order to learn effectively. If e-learners need to develop these skills, the institution should make workshops and information available for them. The instructor can use e-mail communication to encourage e-learners to develop competencies in these skills.

- E-learners can attempt to connect their learning with their prior knowledge and with their personal life experiences. Therefore, projects or assignments might be applied to real life conditions whenever possible.

- E-learners expect that their instructors will make their presence felt throughout the course. Otherwise, learners feel as if they have been abandoned. Instructors can establish their presence online in a way that fosters the learning community and allows learners to construct their own understanding. Learners should be supported in expressing their views online and exchanging information with others.

- E-learners expect to monitor their progress throughout the course via instructor feedback as well as through online tools for self-assessment. These tools might include rubrics to assess discussion board participation, online journaling, or development of an e-learning portfolio.

- E-learners expect to participate in an effective and functioning learning community online. Clear guidelines and instructor presence should be available to support e-learners as they deal with potential conflicts.

Instructors teaching e-learners could benefit from keeping these considerations in mind while planning, designing, and developing their courses. Being aware of the expectations of e-learners they will teach is one way to build student satisfaction and learning into courses from the ground up.

Conclusion

The thought of beginning to plan, design, and implement a new e-learning course can be intimidating. It seems that there are so many issues to consider as the planning process unfolds. However, though the details are myriad, and must be addressed, the main issues to be considered are limited in number. When moving to e-learning, instructors should first spend time reflecting on their own approach to teaching. Teaching approaches have a direct connection with the learning outcomes chosen for the e-learning course, as well as with the activities chosen to achieve those outcomes. The time spent in reflecting will be time well spent, for it will facilitate the choice of outcomes for e-learners that are in synch with the instructor's personal approach to teaching. Second, e-learning instructors should consider how to implement the principles of good teaching—encouraging contact between students and instructor, building a collaborative learning community, using active learning techniques, providing prompt feedback, emphasizing time on task, communicating high expectations, and respecting diverse talents and ways of learning—throughout the e-learning course. Third, instructors should choose activities for the e-learning course based on their own teaching approach and the principles of good teaching. And finally, instructors should review their course outcomes and activities from the perspective of the e-learner. The question at that point should be, Have I addressed the needs of the e-learners enrolling in this course, so that it will be as fruitful a learning experience as possible?

The realities of e-learning can have a major effect on how institutions of higher education meet the demands of the learning society. As the instruction paradigm shifts to the learning paradigm, all partners in the enterprise of higher education are impacted. This period of change can be a fulfilling time of renewal, as instructors adopt and adapt to the new realities of e-learning environments. Guidelines for instructor engagement in e-learning course development can be encapsulated as *reflect* on the teaching approach, *apply* the principles of good teaching throughout the course, *choose* appropriate learning outcomes and activities, and *review* choices from the e-learner's perspective.

The objectives of this chapter were to facilitate a move toward a learning paradigm by diminishing any unease instructors might feel in navigating such a shift. Clearly there is a growing body of knowledge that is fostering instructional success in the e-learning environment. This chapter has afforded a short but comprehensive overview of this knowledge for instructors intent on improving their role and success in the realm of e-learning.

Acknowledgment

The author would like to acknowledge and express appreciation to Dr. Dan Pratt, University of British Columbia, Canada, for his review of this chapter, and his thoughtful suggestions regarding engagement and perspectives on teaching.

References

Barr, R. B., & Tagg, J. (1995). From teaching to learning: A new paradigm for undergraduate education. *Change, 27*(6), 13-25.

Bates, A. W. (2000). *Managing technological change: Strategies for college and university leaders.* San Francisco: Jossey-Bass.

Brown, B. L. (2003). *Teaching style vs. learning style: Myths and realities.* ERIC Clearinghouse on Adult, Career, and Vocational Education. Washington, DC: Office of Educational Research and Improvement. (ERIC Document Reproduction Service No. 482329)

Chickering, A. W., & Ehrman, S. C. (1996, October 3-6). *Implementing the seven principles: Technology as lever.* AAHE Bulletin. Retrieved January 5, 2006, from http://www.tltgroup.org/programs/seven.html

Chickering, A. W., & Gamson, Z. F. (1987). Seven principles of good practice in undergraduate education. Retrieved January 2, 2006, from http://www.byu.edu/fc/pages/tchlrnpages/7princip.html

Duderstadt, J. (1999). Can colleges and universities survive in the information age? In R. Katz and Associates (Eds.), *Dancing with the devil: Information technology and the new competition* (pp. 1-25). San Francisco: Jossey-Bass.

Gabriel, M. A. (2004). *Better practices in online teaching and learning: Insights from the research.* Unpublished manuscript, University of Prince Edward Island, Charlottetown, Canada.

Goodyear, P., Salmon, G., Spector, J. M., Steeples, C., & Tickner, S. (2001). Competencies for online teaching: A special report. *ETR & D, 49*(1), 65-72.

Gordon, W. J. J. (1961). *Synectics.* New York: Harper & Row.

Hislop, G. W., & Ellis, H. C. (2004). A study of faculty effort in online teaching. *The Internet and Higher Education, 7*(1), 15-31.

Kearsley, G., & Shneiderman, B. (1999). *Engagement theory: A framework for technology-based teaching and learning.* Retrieved January 5, 2006, from http://home.sprynet.com/~gkearsley/engage.htm

Moore, M. G., & Kearsley, G. (1996). *Distance education: A systems view.* New York: Wadsworth Publishing.

Palmer, P. (1998). *The courage to teach.* San Francisco: Jossey-Bass.

Pawan, F. (2003). Reflective teaching online. *TechTrends, 47*(4), 30-34.

Pratt, D. D., Arseneau, R., & Collins, J. (2001). Theoretical foundations: Reconsidering "good teaching" across the continuum of medical education. *Journal of Continuing Education in the Health Professions, 21*(2), 70-81.

Pratt, D. D. & Associates. (1998). *Five perspectives on teaching in adult and higher education.* Malabar, FL: Krieger Publishing.

Pratt, D. D., & Collins, J. (2002). *A summary of five perspectives on "good teaching."* Retrieved January 3, 2006, from http://www.edst.educ.ubc.ca/faculty/pratt/DPtpsum.html

Roberts, T. S., & Jones, D. T. (2000, April). Four models of online teaching. *Proceedings of the Technological Education and National Development Conference*, Abu Dhabi, UAR. (ERIC Document Reproduction Service No. ED 446280)

Rovai, A. P. (2004). A constructivist approach to online college learning. *Internet and Higher Education, 7*(2), 79-93.

Tuckman, B. W. (1965). Developmental sequences in small groups. *Psychological Bulletin, 63*(6), 384-399.

Zachary, L. (2002). The role of teacher as mentor. In J. Ross-Gordon (Ed.), *Contemporary viewpoints on teaching adults effectively.* New Directions for Adult and Continuing Education, No. 93. San Francisco: Jossey-Bass.

Zemsky, R., & Massy, W. F. (2004). *Thwarted innovation: What happened to e-learning and why* (Final Report for the Weatherstation Project). Philadelphia: University of Pennsylvania, Learning Alliance.

Chapter XII

The Plain Hard Work of Teaching Online:
Strategies for Instructors

Dianne Conrad, Athabasca University, Canada

Abstract

Learning to teach online presents new challenges to even seasoned instructors. In an age of technological wizardry, the author of this chapter proposes that there are no secrets to good online teaching. However, the effective application of sound pedagogy online requires time, effort, and planning. Using Collins and Berge's framework for online teaching, this chapter outlines how novice instructors' adaptation to the new medium must include attention to the pedagogical, managerial, technical, and social aspects of teaching. In so doing, online teachers are encouraged to move from a didactic, teacher-centered paradigm to a constructivist-based model where community and collaboration are valued equally with content.

Introduction

Online learning, or e-learning, is no longer new to us. We are familiar with the hyped rhetoric of time-space compression, of technological wizardry, and of globalization. Even those of us who are too old to become digital natives are comfortable with myriad computer-type gadgets that allow us to instantly access or send information visually or verbally to destinations around the world.

As educators, we are learning to handle technologies so that we can feel somewhat technically competent. However, in such a technology-rich world, it remains a challenge to convince novice online instructors that there is no magic bullet and no magic platform to guarantee online teaching success. If there *is* a secret to good online teaching, it is simply hard work—layered, of course, on sound pedagogy. In this chapter, using recent research and my own teaching experience, I will discuss techniques to facilitate the transition of novice instructors to online teaching situations in formal postsecondary environments. The chapter's central argument focuses on Gunawardena's (1992) "letting go"—the moving from teacher-centered to learner-centered pedagogy as the prime focus in making the transition to online teaching (Hase & Ellis, 2002)—and situates such a shift in a socially oriented context of community, collaboration, communication, collegiality, and commitment. The discussion rests on two related sets of assumptions. The first set of assumptions extols the merits and possibilities of experiential learning, as outlined by Alexander and Boud (2002): experience is the foundation of learning, learners actively construct their own experience, learning is holistic and not merely cognitive, learning does not occur in isolation but is socially and culturally constructed, and learning is contextual. The second set of assumptions are those that recognize online learning's potential for deep learning through activities that encourage collaborative learning and critical thinking (Garrison & Archer, 2000; Kanuka, 2002; Oliver, 2002).

The examples and references that illustrate this chapter's premise will resonate most clearly with those who are teaching in formal postsecondary environments. Using as a starting point Collins and Berge's (1996) designation of four cornerstone functions for teaching online, I will advocate for reframing online instruction to equally value connection, community, collaboration, along with the traditional cognitive stronghold, content.

The Eclectic World of Online Teaching: Definitions, Overview, and the Instructional Role

The relative ease of Internet access in western cultures has allowed this medium to become the platform for one of the dominant forms of current distance education practice. Its expansion, however, has also "democratized" its use through the creation of an easily accessible e-language that promises something for everyone in every realm of activity—education, government, business, leisure, and recreation. For purposes of clarity, therefore, some definitions follow. By *online*, I mean:

*The process of **delivering, supporting** and **assessing** teaching and learning through the use of computers and communication networks.... The term online learning is used, at times interchangeably with and at times in place of, many other terms: technology-mediated learning, computer-mediated conferencing, online collaborative learning (OCL), computer-supported collaborative learning (CSCL), telelearning, e-learning, virtual learning, Net-based learning, Web-based learning.* (Conrad, 2005a, p. 442)

When I refer to *distance educators*, I mean those who conduct their "classes" using computer-mediated technology; those who are separated, according to the classic definition of distance education, from their learners by distance (Keegan, 1980) and who will likely not ever see their learners' faces. Because delivery models involving computer-mediated technologies are so varied and so critical to shaping the learning environments of which they are a fundamental part, this chapter addresses issues relevant to distance educators who teach courses *entirely* virtually.

Although I use the terms *teachers* and *instructors* interchangeably, I do not use the term *facilitator* to describe the activity of teaching, keeping in mind Brookfield's (1990) caution that the art of teaching requires a moral stance and comprises more than simply "gate-keeping."

Within the burgeoning electronic world, the art of teaching and learning differs substantially in purpose and nature from other less formal Internet pursuits. Research shows the existence of a different psychology between interactive and collaborative learning commitments and other non-educational pursuits (Wallace, 1999). Although many private and public organizations would have us believe that becoming an online facilitator is only a Web site and a learning module away, almost a decade of research now exists to track the development of complex, higher-order learning that is often more demanding, time-intensive, and academically rewarding than traditional classroom learning (Garrison, Anderson, & Archer, 2000; Kanuka, 2002).

Learning how to adapt to teaching online is complicated by conceptual and definitional confusion in the field, by institutional politics, and by the simple fact of being a field in its infancy. As Salmon (2004) noted, however, recent thinking has moved away from its early emphasis on technology and toward the importance of teaching teachers to teach online.

There are many approaches to training online instructors. Private providers' offers of one-step online facilitation prowess are countered by calls for institution-wide systems of training that promise consistent and standardized approaches to online teaching (Chacon, 2001). While perhaps offering the solution for better pedagogy, implementing such systems rests on complex networks of variables that lessen the probability of their implementation in traditional institutions (Bates, 2000). Between these two extremes, however, the reality of online instruction in most postsecondary institutions remains vague, serendipitous, and largely determined by local policy and favor (Palloff & Pratt, 2001). In many instances, teaching online is an informal, unsanctioned activity that is practiced largely by early adopters and often goes unrewarded on merit scales. Not only are faculty who teach online often self-taught, but the range and types of integration of their teaching activities into more traditional teaching formats is virtually unlimited (Palloff & Pratt, 2001). While this openness can create many exciting approaches to blended learning, it also leaves the term *online teaching* with many meanings and blurs the field with a lack of clarity. To some, the term *online* may denote only the addition of a Web site to an established face-to-face classroom format; to others, it may describe a course conducted entirely online with no physical contact among learners or between learners and instructor. Supplementing face-to-face classes with a Web presence or adding a discussion board for keen learners does not constitute teaching online in the way that I will discuss it here.

This short chapter will not teach you how to teach online. No one *can* teach you how to teach: Teaching is an expertise that you will develop or have already developed by marrying sound theory to real practice. Teaching involves not just your head and all your cognitive knowledge but also your *heart* (Palmer, 1998). In online teaching more so, the contribution of your "self"—*your* heart—is critical to the success of the venture. Because the variables are fewer, the stakes are higher. Parking accessibility, classroom temperature, wardrobe—none of these things will affect the quality of your teaching experience as might be the case in face-to-face environments; online, your level of success is much more dependent on *you.*

That said, a lot of literature offers empirical research on other teachers' experiences, and there is a growing body of material that will help you to plan activities and assist you with instructional design. A vitally important fact to keep in mind when reading such material is that any variation in format or delivery model between what you are doing and what other online teachers have done will change the nature of your online experience. That is, if your class is 13 weeks long and a research study reports results on a class of seven weeks' duration, the outcomes will differ. If you are teaching an undergraduate online course but have been studying data from a graduate online course, the outcomes will differ. The sensitivity of online courses to each contributing design factor is very high due to the absence of external and potentially mitigating factors.

A Theoretical Framework for Thinking about Online Teaching

A number of models explain the nature of online teaching and learning. Most promote constructivism as the underpinning approach to online learning; using a constructivist epistemology allows online participants to contribute to activities that foster knowledge-building through the dialogic exchange of ideas (Jonassen, Davidson, Collins, Campbell, & Haag, 1995; Kanuka & Anderson, 1998; Salmon, 2004). The role of instructors, using this approach, has shifted considerably from more traditional didactic models of instruction.

Salmon (2002, 2004) outlined practical and detailed strategies for moderating and facilitating online teaching. However, because Collins and Berge's framework (1996), wherein they conceptualize online teaching by breaking the teaching role into four areas of responsibility (pedagogy, management, technology, and social issues) resonates so strongly with my own experience, I join with others in using it here as the central theoretical framework for contemplating the transition to online teaching (Bonk, Kirkley, Hara, & Paz Dennen, 2002).

As you think about Collins and Berge's four "tasks" within the teaching role, however, keep in mind that the teaching role itself constitutes only a part of the total teaching-learning exchange that occurs online. Of the many models that explain the fit of teaching into the large picture, one of the most comprehensive and easiest to understand features three types of "presence" (Garrison et al., 2000). In this model, instructional, or teaching, presence combines with social presence and cognitive presence to constitute the total learning picture. Another more fragmented way of understanding the various components of the teaching-learning exchange is to consider the number of interactions that occur. Moore (1989) first presented a breakdown of interactions by naming three major types of interactions: learner-learner, learner-content, and teacher-learner. Other theorists added more interactions over the years (Anderson & Garrison, 2002), demonstrating the many different ways in which online interactions can be understood.

The Online Instructional Role

Using Collins and Berge's model of instructional responsibility as a good starting place for thinking about the transition to online teaching, I will look at the instructional responsibilities through the eyes of Tom, a seasoned philosophy instructor, who is now learning to teach online.

Pedagogy. Pedagogical concerns relate to the learning that occurs as a result of learners' engagement with each other, the instructor, and the content at hand. Depending on the models used, instructors may be responsible for the entire development of the course and the choice of readings, materials, activities, and assessment, or for only the presentation and management of content and learning activities and the resultant assessment. Whatever the model, instructors usually take on, to some degree, the role of content expert, even within a constructivist, learner-centered, model. Novice online instructors feel safest in this role because it is the most familiar one. Tom has spent a lot of time adapting his philosophy course to the online format. His course provides constant opportunities for learners to engage in discussion on philosophical topics with each other and with him, one-on-one. His course manual is *very* thick.

How is knowledge exchanged or constructed online in the absence of a "class," where the teacher shares his or her knowledge with learners, observes and gauges their reactions, interacts with them physically and verbally, and conducts assessments of their learning? The foundational premise that is presented here centers on constructivist and adult education principles. At its heart, it includes the same principles that underscore good pedagogical practice in all learning environments: allow learners to bring their own experience to the fore to facilitate the construction of knowledge; encourage a collaborative community of learners; foster learners' independence, self-direction, and responsibility; provide opportunities for learners to engage in critical thinking; and recognize learners' varying learning styles (Candy, 1991; Garrison & Archer, 2000). In order to make this adaptation, Tom has minimized his lecture time, represented online as mini-bursts of content in text form, and created opportunities for dialogue so that learners can bring their own experiences and ideas forward in discussion. As he works through the design process, in consultation with a design team, Tom is coming to realize that successful online pedagogy also includes attending to the three other areas of instructional responsibility.

Management. When debriefing his first online teaching experience, Tom reported with some chagrin: "I am not a learning manager; I am a teacher." Indeed, Tom had clearly identified one of the adaptations required of online teachers. Managing the presentation of your pedagogy, because it must occur in a planned and deliberate fashion and generally in text format, is time consuming. It often seems awkward and pedantic. "Flying by the seat of your pants," a strategy that often works in face-to-face situations, does not work well online. Learners become frustrated, confused, and even angry when they experience poorly planned courses. Instructors will quickly come to realize how much *extra* work is required—phone calls, private emails, and frantic postings—to correct planning mistakes.

By management, Collins and Berge (1996) mean the many processes that online instructors can use to organize and facilitate the presentation of their content. Effective online management requires the careful synchronization of dates and topics, the detailed explanation of instructions for assignments and activities, the coordination of group work and discussions, the return of assignments and accompanying feedback, and commentaries on and summaries of learners' contributions to course activities.

The fact of asynchronicity, the time-delay factor that is so attractive to online learners' flexibility, also complicates online management. Consider a scenario in which Tom asked his face-to-face class for feedback or response at the end of a difficult lesson. Two or three learners asked questions, and other learners joined in with relevant comments. Tom addressed their concerns, and they moved on to other issues. Online, however, three learners may post responses to Tom's question over a 24-hour period. If he does not get back to those inquiries before other learners have trebled the input to nine messages, five of those messages may lead off on a tangent, away from the central discussion. To effectively manage the discussion, Tom must be either very "present," or he must spend extra time reframing the argument while constructively inviting comments for further interaction. Tom was amazed at the amount of time he spent "digging out" from these kinds of situations.

The time-independence aspect of online learning is also a double-edged sword for learners: "It facilitated their participation and critical thinking but exacerbated their difficulty in managing their time effectively" (Bullen, 1998, p. 7).

Technology. It is a myth that teaching online requires technological expertise. As Tom quickly discovered, his ability to navigate the Internet transferred easily to online software. The most popularly used e-learning systems all feature user-friendly point-and-click interfaces.

Of the four areas for which online teachers must assume responsibility, technology demands the least instructional effort. In spite of that, *any* level of technical involvement may seem overly demanding to those coming to online teaching for the first time because they may not have measured any of their traditional teaching time in terms of technology issues: time spent fidgeting with a temperamental overhead projector, time spend struggling with flipchart paper, or time spent preparing a PowerPoint presentation. In most of these cases, the institution supplies technical help. Similarly, most institutions now provide helpdesk support by e-mail and telephone. Inexperienced online learners, however, tend to approach their instructor first for answers to all questions, as the teacher represents the "face" of the university to them. Ultimately, instructors are required to solve or remedy only very basic technology issues such as, Can I get a transcript from the chat session?

Since the presence of new technology still figures into learners' comfort levels, online teachers must expend a certain amount of energy not so much familiarizing learners with the tool, as assuring them that they *are* already familiar with the tool. As with management issues, Tom discovered that a learner's Thursday night panic caused by a technology glitch escalated dramatically by Friday, especially if an assignment had a weekend deadline. He found that timing and immediacy were key. Tom realized that he must be *more* accessible at the beginning of a course than later on when learners' comfort levels had increased.

Social. Of Collins and Berge's (1996) four areas of instructional responsibility, the social function is the least understood by teachers who are adapting to the online medium. Cranton (1992) outlined 12 specific roles that instructors play for their learners: role model, content expert, advisor, mentor, collaborator, researcher, to name a few. Traditionally, teachers' roles have revolved around learners' engagement with content; that is, teachers' roles have been largely defined cognitively. Tom, the philosopher, feared that he was sacrificing "teaching" for "social convening," as he struggled to find the time and energy to respond genially to learners' casual comments. Adult education literature helped familiarize him with social learning theories that have nudged the understanding of teachers' roles into terms of mentorship, collaboration, and collegiality. Studies in teacher authenticity (Cranton & Carusetta, 2004; Palmer, 1998) emphasize the importance of bringing humanity and even spirituality to the craft of teaching.

These concepts map well onto online theories that hold up social presence as a critical dimension of the learning environment (Gunawardena & Zittle, 1997; Richardson & Swan, 2003). Social presence, defined as "the degree to which participants in computer-mediated communication feel affectively connected one to another ... has been shown to be an important factor in student satisfaction and success in online courses" (Swan & Shih, 2005). Because social presence contributes to the more tangible concept of online community, responsible instructors should stand in the middle of this activity. They are aware of both its existence and the *need* for its existence. They are sensitive to their part in the creation of a social learning community; they nurture and guide group development when necessary and discreetly step back to let that community flourish as its own entity when the time is right. While learners feel that they are co-responsible with instructors for the well-being of their own community, they also feel strongly that the instructor's presence, especially at the start-up of online courses, is important to establishing a sound sense of group community (Conrad, 2005b). In this way, instructors play a key role in this equivalent of Tuckman's (1965) "forming" stage of group dynamics. Salmon's (2004) online teaching and learning model also addresses and updates the notions of group development and level of interactivity of instructors with learners, finding, in short, that the scaffolding process builds from a "directed approach to a constructivist approach ... and from immediate to more holistic learning" (p. 30).

Toward Community: Learning to Let Go

Collins and Berge's (1996) areas of responsibility for online teachers constitute a framework for shifting the understanding of the instructional role toward a learner-centered, constructivist-based approach. In sum, these activities hall-mark instructors' moving away from being "oracles" and didactic presenters-of-information to being consultants and resource providers, from being providers of answers to being askers of expert questions, from being designers of content to designers of learning. As a part of this migration to learner-centeredness, Berge (1995) suggested that instructors should also move toward the following constructivist principles:

- Providing only initial structures and then encouraging learners' self-direction.
- Presenting multiple perspectives and emphasizing salient points.
- Being members of a learning team.
- Introducing broader systems of assessment.
- Co-creating, with learners, the learning space.
- Redefining the teacher-learner power structure.

In time, Tom came to realize that adopting these facilitative strategies required a "letting go" of the teacher-centered paradigms (Gunawardena, 1992) by which he had previously taught. Online instructors who assume center-stage roles not only deny the existence and importance of community among learners—a key factor in social learning theory—but also deny their learners the opportunity to demonstrate self-direction, intrinsic motivation, and the maturity to take owner-ship of their own learning.

Instructors working toward letting go of didactic control in their teaching should be cognizant of learners' struggling to not only assume responsibility for their own learning but also to establish a clear sense of who they are when interacting online with peers. Online learners work through stages similar to Tuckman's (1965) (forming, storming, norming, performing, and adjourning) as they form community in their learning groups. These stages represent the external, social manifestations of group process. Individually, however, learners are also developing their own sense of online identity.

The Plain Hard Work of Teaching Online: Practicing Community, Collaboration, Communication, Collegiality, and Commitment

Eager instructors come to their online teaching assignments with energy, goodwill, and a clear understanding that they are about to undertake an exciting new challenge. But what does it look like? How will success best be achieved? Palmer (1998) cautions that there are no formulas and that relying on the advice of experts is at best only marginally useful. He follows this caveat with the suggestion to "go to the inner ground from which good teaching comes" (p. 141).

Online teaching presents ample opportunity for reflection and self-learning. Novice instructors must leave the safety of the known to embark on a very different adventure that demands re-examination of both assumptions and practices. As outlined in Festinger's (1957) theory of cognitive dissonance, the act of being off-balance offers new vision. Online teachers must re-think not only their curriculum and their pedagogy but also their presentation, their sense of instructional "self," and their personalities. What will entice online learners to show up? What will it take to engage them in critical thought? How much of their time will they give you when their attendance is not mandated once a week?

Building Community, Collaboration, Communication, Collegiality, and Commitment in Online Teaching

The remainder of this chapter suggests this target for instructors learning to teach online: The ideals of community, collaboration, communication, collegiality, and commitment. These five aspects of online teaching are interdependent, non-hierarchical, and non-linear. They share boundaries, strategies, and outcomes.

Taken together, they describe the essence of online learning's affective domain. The importance of the five Cs should be considered along with instructors' attention to content or curriculum. The learning activities that support the five Cs—group work and other manifestations of sustained interaction among learners—should not be sacrificed to curriculum in the interests of time. Learners who complain that managing group work online is often frustrating and time-intensive will also admit, at the end of a course, that working together in small groups provided the most beneficial learning. The energy required to sustain this ambience must arise from both instructors' and learners' commitment to community. Another benefit from this blend of connection and community within online courses is learners' resultant sense of satisfaction and success: Those perceiving the highest level of social presence feel that online interactions and discussions have positively contributed to their success (Swan & Shih, 2005).

A number of strategies follow. Reflecting Palmer's philosophy of teaching, the first strategy involves thinking hard about individual teaching styles and the philosophical foundation beneath them.

Know who you are as teacher. "You teach who you are" (Palmer, 1998), and in order to know who you are as a teacher, you should know your teaching philosophy. Professional and philosophical self-knowledge is essential for the presentation of authentic self, and online teaching demands authenticity because there are very few buffers between teacher and learners: A successful exchange must be authentic (Brookfield, 1990; Cranton & Carusetta, 2004). In addition to influencing learning's affective domain, issues of authenticity also affect the cognitive domain on two fronts: motivation and empowerment. Five characteristics shared by motivating teachers—expertise, empathy, enthusiasm, clarity, and cultural responsiveness—(Wlodkowski, 1999) all contribute to a teacher's authenticity; the latter four traits, especially, also contribute to learners' levels of motivation.

Teachers' self-knowledge and sense of authenticity also helps them to promote their learners' sense of self. Knowing who you are as a teacher empowers you to empower others; Cranton (1994) pointed out that "powerless individuals cannot engage in critical self-reflection" (p. 165). The ability of instructors to "shape" their learners through listening to and appreciating their contributions to online discourse is a result of steady and studied teaching commitment (Lentall, 2003).

Be prepared to commit more time than you thought you would. Be present. Ideally, online teachers should visit their course site every day. An absence of longer than two days is sorely felt by learners. There are three different levels and types of presence:

1. **Housekeeping chores should be tended daily:** Sometimes housekeeping chores involve only answering factual questions ("Where is the Haythornthwaite reading?") or posting a brief message to remind learners of an approaching deadline. Learners' unanswered information-seeking questions can delay their progress, causing them anxiety and often giving rise to several subsequent emails or telephone calls.

2. **Conversational, reinforcing commentary on discussions:** Instructors should *"monitor the discussion and respond selectively to students' comments with encouragement, clarification, [and] redirection"* (Bullen, 1998, p. 7). These types of routine insertions serve as guideposts, benchmarks, and motivators. Learners use them cognitively, to confirm their thoughts and ideas on topics, and affectively, as rewards.

3. **Comprehensive, in-depth critical analysis and summary:** While housekeeping strategies maintain organization and frequent conversational interventions maintain activity levels and motivation, comprehensive and critical commentary makes up the knowledge-building heart of online teaching. Both learners and teachers may generate these thoughtful invitations to knowledge construction. They may appear as questions, as musings, as suppositions, as challenges, or as confirmations. For the teacher—the person who in most cases both assumes or is given supra-responsibility for the learning environment—these types of entries are equivalent to mini-lectures or teachable moments. Opportunities for this type of "deep learning" (Garrison & Archer, 2000) do not occur as predictably as in traditional classrooms; being ready to respond appropriately to whatever prompts sustained investigation into a topic further supports the need for frequent instructional online presence.

Be more organized than you have ever been (probably). All forms of distance education require more front-end preparation than do traditional classroom presentations. The presence of well-organized online teachers serves as reassurance for anxious learners (Conrad, 2002). In a practical sense, 24 online learners might write emails to their instructor seeking clarification on a single overlooked detail. Teaching online creates a very real need for instructors to think clearly and logically through all aspects of their curriculum plan, pacing, and assignment structure.

Use "push and pull" communication strategies. In marketing, consumers receive information in two different ways. It is "pushed" out to them in the form of advertisements and through other direct marketing tools. And in other ways they are "pulled" in to places, such as Web sites, where marketing information resides. Push-and-pull marketing strategies are analogous to techniques that online instructors must make use of in order to ensure functional and comprehensive communication with learners.

Two complementary actions occur at the outset of an online course. The course itself begins to unfold as learners engage in knowledge-building activities through exposure to content. But in addition to that, and perhaps more importantly, given the typically messy starts to online courses, learners are learning once again how to learn. This time, however, they are without familiar comforts—without a classroom and without faces. For at least the first few weeks of an online course, learners are tacitly asked to suspend everything they have come to know about postsecondary learning and try something new. The instructor represents their lifeline to this uncertain future. The importance of building a solid connection among learners and teacher cannot be overstated.

Push-and-pull techniques ensure, as much as possible, that necessary information reaches each learner. Hoping to pull learners into an area in the course where information has been posted is often fruitless as novice learners scramble to familiarize themselves with site navigation. While information should be posted as a precursor to eventual routine, at the beginning of a course it should also be pushed to learners in the form of e-mail, ideally *both* within the course's system and also to learners' regular e-mail addresses. This level of management takes time and imposes on online instructors in ways that they are often unprepared for.

Practice respect. That instructors should exercise respect for learners is both common sense and commonplace. Demonstrating respect for learners online requires more sensitivity and more care. Both learning and personal exchanges exist usually only in words; there are no mitigating body gestures, voice intonations, or other social signals that we have learned to use to soften or hide verbal messages. The expression of ideas and especially criticism must be managed with extreme care. Additionally, posted messages within a course provide an archival record of that course, a fact that often causes learners some discomfort just thinking about such permanence. (In some software, instructors can exercise a delete function if an extreme case warrants. Instructors should be wary, however, of establishing themselves as editors or censors.)

Establish inclusion. "Inclusion is the awareness of learners that they are part of an environment in which they and their instructor are respected by and connected to one another" (Wlodkowski, 1999, p. 69). As with demonstrating respect, establishing a sense of inclusion takes more time, effort, and sensitivity than might otherwise be required in more sensory-rich environments. Using push-pull communication strategy helps learners feel that their presence is desired. Learners who are faltering or unsure of their footing at the beginning of an online experience also benefit from direct contact from the instructor; many such learners report that a telephone call provided them with welcome reassurance.

Conclusion

Educators learning to teach online may encounter challenges that stretch across theory and practice. Varying interpretations of what should be categorized as online learning and which theories should explain it precede the discussion of what represents best practice (Anderson, 2003). As a result, both learners and instructors often suffer poor teaching-learning experiences as they engage in online learning for the first time.

Many of these potential pitfalls are beyond the purview of online instructors and rest in the hands of administrators, designers, or other planners. Ironically—or happily—it is teachers themselves who constitute the most important element of the online teaching-learning dynamic. With that knowledge and with an appreciation of the value of community, connection, and collaboration to support content, online teachers can simply commit to the plain hard work of teaching online.

References

Alexander, S., & Boud, D. (2002). Learners still learn from experience when online. In J. Stephenson (Ed.), *Teaching and learning online: Pedagogies for new technologies* (pp. 3-15). London: Kogan Page.

Anderson, T. (2003). *Getting the mix right again: An updated and theoretical rationale for interaction*. International Review of Research in Open and Distance Learning. Retrieved January 3, 2006, from http://www.irrodl.org/content/v4.2/anderson.html

Anderson, T., & Garrison, D. R. (2002). Learning in a networked world: New roles and responsibilities. In C. C. Gibson (Ed.), *Distance learners in higher education* (pp. 97-112). Madison, WI: Atwood.

Bates, A. W. (2000). *Managing technological change: Strategies for college and university leaders*. San Francisco: Jossey-Bass.

Berge, Z. L. (1995). Facilitating computer conferencing: Recommendations from the field. *Educational Technology, 35*(1), 22-30.

Bishop, A. (2002). Come into my parlour said the spider to the fly: Critical reflections on Web-based education from a student's perspective. *Distance Education, 23*(2), 231-236.

Bonk, C. J., Kirkley, J., Hara, N., & Paz Dennen, V. (2002). Finding the instructor in post-secondary online learning: Pedagogical, social, managerial, and technological locations. In J. Stephenson (Ed.), *Teaching and learning online: Pedagogies for new technologies* (pp. 76-97). London: Kogan Page.

Brookfield, S. D. (1990). *The skillful teacher.* San Francisco: Jossey-Bass.

Bullen, M. (1998). Participation and critical thinking in online university distance education. *Journal of Distance Education, 13*(2), 1-32.

Candy, P. C. (1991). *Self-direction for lifelong learning.* San Francisco: Jossey-Bass.

Chacon, F. (2001). Transforming classroom professors into virtual class mentors. Retrieved January 30, 2006, from http://www.unesco.org/iau/tfit_denmark-chacon.html

Collins, M. P., & Berge, Z. L. (1995). Introduction to volume two. In Z. L. Berge & M. P. Collins (Eds.), *Computer mediated communication and the online* classroom (Vol. 2, pp. 1-10). Cresskill, NJ: Hampton Press.

Collins, M. P., & Berge, Z. L. (1996). Facilitating interaction in computer mediated online courses. Retrieved January 30, 2006, from http://www.emoderators.com/moderators/flcc.html

Conrad, D. (2002). Engagement, excitement, anxiety, and fear: Learners' experiences of starting an online course. *American Journal of Distance Education, 16*(4), 205-226.

Conrad, D. (2004). University instructors' reflections on their first online teaching experiences. *Journal of Asynchronous Learning Networks.* Retrieved January 30, 2006, from http://www.aln.org/publications/jaln/v8n2/v8n2_conrad.asp

Conrad, D. (2005a). Online learning. In L. English (Ed.), *The encyclopedia of adult education.* London: Palgrave McMillan.

Conrad, D. (2005b). Building and maintaining community in cohort-based online learning. *Journal of Distance Education, 20*(1), 1-21.

Cranton, P. (2004). *Finding our way.* Toronto: Wall & Emerson.

Cranton, P., & Carusetta, E. (2004). Perspectives on authenticity in teaching. *Adult Education Quarterly, 55*(1), 5-22.

Festinger, L. (1957). *A theory of cognitive dissonance.* Stanford, CA: Stanford University Press.

Garrison, D. R., Anderson, T., & Archer, W. (2000). Critical inquiry in a text-based environment: Computer conferencing in higher education. *The Internet and Higher Education, 2*(2-3), 87-105.

Garrison, D. R., & Archer, W. (2000). *A transactional perspective on teaching and learning: A framework for adult and higher education.* Amsterdam: Pergamon.

Gunawardena, C. N. (1992). Changing faculty roles for audiographics and online teaching. *The American Journal of Distance Education, 6*(3), 58-71.

Gunawardena, C. N. (1995). Social presence theory and implications for interaction and collaborative learning in computer conferences. *International Journal of Educational Telecommunications, 1*(2/3), 147-166.

Gunawardena, C. N., & Zittle, F. (1997). Social presence as a predictor of satisfaction within a computer mediated conferencing environment. *American Journal of Distance Education, 11*(3), 8-26.

Hase, S., & Ellis, A. (2002). Problems with online learning are systemic, not technical. In J. Stephenson (Ed.), *Teaching and learning online: Pedagogies for new technologies* (pp. 27-34). London: Kogan Page.

Jonassen, D., Davidson, M., Collins, M., Campbell, J., & Haag, B. (1995). Constructivism and computer mediated communication in distance education. *American Journal of Distance Education, 9*(2), 7-25.

Kanuka, H. (2002). Guiding principles for facilitating higher levels of Web-based distance learning in post-secondary settings. *Distance Education, 23*(2), 163-182.

Kanuka, H., & Anderson, T. (1998). Online social interchange, discord, and knowledge construction. *Journal of Distance Education, 13*(1), 57-74.

Keegan, D. J. (1980). On defining distance education. *Distance Education, 1*(1), 13-36.

Lentall, H. (2003). The importance of the tutor in open and distance learning. In A. Tait & R. Mills (Eds.), *Rethinking learner support in distance education: Change and continuity in an international context* (pp. 77-89). London: RoutledgeFalmer.

Moore, M. G. (1989). Three modes of interaction. A presentation of the NUCEA forum: Issues in instructional interactivity. *NUCEA Conference*, Salt Lake City.

Oliver, R. (2002). Exploring the development of critical thinking skills through a Web-supported, problem-based learning environment. In J. Stephenson (Ed.), *Teaching and learning online: Pedagogies for new technologies* (pp. 98-111). London: Kogan Page.

Palloff, R. M., & Pratt, K. (2001). *Lessons from the cyberspace classroom: The realities of online teaching.* San Francisco: Jossey-Bass.

Palmer, P. J. (1998). *The courage to teach: Exploring the inner landscape of a teacher's life.* San Francisco: Jossey-Bass.

Richardson, J. C., & Swan, K. (2003). Examining social presence in online courses in relation to students' perceived learning and satisfaction. *Journal of Asynchronous Learning Networks, 7*(1), 68-88. Retrieved January 30, 2006, from http://www.aln.org/publications/jaln/v7n1/v7n1_richardson.asp

Rourke, L., Anderson, T., Garrison, D. R., & Archer, W. (1999). Assessing social presence in asynchronous text-based computer conferencing. *Journal of Distance Education, 14*(2), 50-71.

Salmon, G. (2002). *E-tivities: The key to active online learning.* London: Kogan Page.

Salmon, G. (2004). *E-moderating: The key to teaching and learning online.* London: RoutledgeFarmer.

Shale, D. (2003). Does "distance education" really say it all—or does it say enough? A commentary on the article by Kanuka and Conrad. *Distance Education, 4*(4), 395-399.

Swan, K., & Shih, L. F. (2005). On the nature and development of social presence in online course discussions. *Journal of Asynchronous Learning, 9*(3). Retrieved from http://www.sloan-c.org/publications/jaln/v9n3/index.asp

Tuckman, B. W. (1965). Developmental sequences in small groups. *Psychological Bulletin*, 63, 384-399.

Wallace, P. (1999). *The psychology of the Internet.* Cambridge: Cambridge University Press.

Wlodkowski, R. (1999). *Enhancing adult motivation to learn: A comprehensive guide for teaching all adults* (2nd ed.). San Francisco: Jossey-Bass.

Chapter XIII

Empowering Learners to Interact Effectively in Asynchronous Discussion Activities

Helen Wozniak, University of Sydney, Australia

Abstract

The encouragement of learner-to-learner interaction in asynchronous discussions can be achieved by providing learner support in the early stages of course delivery. This not only smoothes the transition to e-learning but also contributes to knowledge construction and enhancement of learning outcomes. In this chapter, the author describes improvements to orientation activities that enabled learners to work collaboratively in online groups. The activities are closely aligned with Salmon's five-stage model and illustrate the dynamics of online learning in groups. Research conducted by the author examining the effectiveness of the orientation activities has lead to identification of key issues and practical suggestions that will assist the readers of the chapter to develop approaches to learner support in their own context.

Introduction

In an increasingly resource-stretched higher education environment, the cornerstone for successful e-learning is promoting learner-to-learner interaction. Effective interaction requires not only the careful design of e-learning activities, but more importantly, the empowerment of the learner to engage collaboratively with others.

Making the transition to e-learning requires a clear understanding of the notion of interaction in learning programs, which Moore (1989) described as occurring in three ways: learner-to-content, learner-to-instructor, and learner-to-learner. It is this last type of interaction between one learner and another, individually or in groups, and with or without the presence of an instructor that has become an important dimension in e-learning because it facilitates collaboration and deeper learning (Anderson, 2003).

Learner-to-learner interaction may occur both synchronously (in real time) and asynchronously (over time). Asynchronous discussion is more commonly used as it allows flexibility for learners who are able to control when and where they post and reply to messages in a discussion forum. A collaborative learning environment is created when learners interact by negotiating, debating, reviewing, and reflecting upon existing knowledge and are able to build a deeper understanding of the course content (Garrison & Anderson, 2003; Geer, 2003; Palloff & Pratt, 1999). This differs from face-to-face discussions because the learner is able to consider their responses more carefully and make more in-depth contributions; consequentially, the learner feels freer and less intimidated.

This chapter will lead the reader through an action research based cycle of improvements I have made when developing orientation activities that enable learners to achieve knowledge construction by participation in asynchronous discussions. The improvements in both the design and delivery of the learning program draw heavily on research evidence describing interaction in online discussions. This combined with my research provides practical suggestions to assist the reader to develop strategies for learner support in their own context.

Key aspects identified are:

- Designing tasks that encourage learner interaction.
- Clarifying instructor and learner expectations related to time, interaction, and feedback.
- Encouraging learner participation and the learner's relationship to assessment and learning outcomes.
- Facilitating online group dynamics and development of collaborative groups.

- Scaffolding the learner's online experiences with an adaptation of Gilly Salmon's five-stage model (2000).

Background

From 2000 to 2005, a small health science school at the University of Sydney in Australia adopted the use of asynchronous discussion to facilitate the translation of academic knowledge into clinical practice for up to 50 third and fourth year undergraduate orthoptic students. Students attended some face-to-face sessions, primarily at the beginning of the semester for delivery of academic content materials. For the remainder of the semester, students were off campus undertaking professional practice placements in eye clinics of major hospitals and private ophthalmology practices, at a variety of locations around Australia. At these placements they were isolated from other students and were not able to offer each other regular face-to-face support. Asynchronous discussions were used to

- Keep in regular contact with students while off campus.
- Encourage students to review academic material while having real world clinical experiences.
- Assist in the transfer of knowledge to and from the applied clinical situations.
- Develop the professional skills of case analysis and management.
- Assist students to learn from each other.
- Encourage reflective practice, critical thinking, and self evaluation.

Clinical case-based scenarios addressing key content areas and dilemmas in clinical decision making were debated in private asynchronous discussion groups of up to 10 students. Students interacted with each other by sharing their ideas and opinions about the different approaches to solving clinical problems. Each group formulated a consensus decision for each case, which was posted online after a period of approximately two to four weeks. The instructor then provided feedback online to each group as well as model answers. As part of an assignment, students developed their own case consisting of background to the case, questions to stimulate discussion of key issues related to the case, and model answers that were all checked and graded by the instructor. In the final four weeks of the semester, the students posted their cases in their discussion group and moderated the ensuing discussion by providing feedback to their peers.

Moore's theory of transactional distance assists in highlighting an important interplay of three dimensions that guide such learning processes: structure, dialogue, and autonomy (Gunawardena, 2004; Moore, 1993). In this context, dialogue in the form of asynchronous discussion was used to reduce the transactional distance and support the structured learning activities. At the same time, the students were given the freedom to interact with their peers without excessive intervention by the instructor.

The e-learning framework described in this chapter is centered on the use of "electronically mediated learning" (Zemsky & Massy, 2004, p. 5), which is embedded in the social constructivist paradigm, where knowledge is socially constructed among knowledgeable peers through consensus (Barkley, Cross, & Major, 2005, p. 8). Learners work collaboratively in groups, sharing and reflecting on their experiences, engaging in dialogue, negotiating meanings, and extending their current knowledge. Constructivist learning is often the prevailing learning approach used in online contexts, as it highlights the social and collaborative nature of constructing knowledge, focusing attention on the role of the learner.

Garrison and Anderson (2003) asserted that the dominant educational features of e-learning are communication and interaction, which are best served by building a community of inquiry to enable greater learner autonomy and improved collaboration. A central focus of their e-learning conceptual framework is a consideration of social presence, cognitive presence, and teaching presence in the design of e-learning activities using communication tools. Since, in this context, the students were already known to each other, the focal point of this chapter is to describe how learner orientation to the e-learning environment is enhanced by the design of discussion tasks and by encouraging a climate of inquiry in the ensuing discourse. This most closely relates to Garrison and Anderson's dimensions of cognitive and teaching presence in the asynchronous communication medium.

When the asynchronous discussion activities were first introduced in 2000, there was limited learner dialogue and interaction, which is a common finding in the literature (Hara, Bonk, & Angeli, 2000; Ellis, 2001; Vonderwell, 2002). Consequently, after review, research and redesign improvements were made to enhance learner support in the early stages of their online learning process. A series of orientation sessions that specifically targeted the dynamics of online learning in groups was developed for this program (Appendix I). Although the lessons learnt in this case study relate to the use of asynchronous discussions, it is suggested that these lessons are relevant to supporting learners in any e-learning activity. The next two sections and Table 1 describe the action research based cycle of improvements made to the asynchronous discussion activities and

Table 1. Outline of the changes made to the design of the discussion activities and orientation sessions

Goal of the discussion and orientation activities	Early developments 2000 to 2003	Later developments from 2004
Share ideas and opinions	• Careful design of the discussion task. • Learners practice posting messages with clear subject headings.	• Learners practice threading messages.
Promote learner-to-learner participation	• Provide clear instructions. • Clarify expectations of the instructor and the learner. • Assess participation.	• Assess quality of participation.
Encourage formation of collaborative online groups		• Framework used to scaffold development of online learners. • Learners practice responding to each other's postings. • Learners critically analyze cognitive level of their postings.

orientation sessions. Its initial focus is on the design of the discussion tasks with later emphasis on raising the cognitive level of learner-to-learner discourse.

Early Developments for Supporting Learners in Asynchronous Discussions

Researchers have suggested that learners need guidance to interact effectively in online learning environments, knowledge of how to work online and, more specifically, help with collaborative learning and reflecting thinking (Benfield, 2002; Bozarth, Chapman, & LaMonica, 2004; Maor, 2003; McLoughlin, 2002; Webb, Jones, Barker, & van Schaik, 2004). However, little practical advice has been given to learners beyond simple "getting to know your activities" and technical advice on how to use communication tools

The original orientation activities until 2003 consisted of one or two computer laboratory sessions of two hours duration designed to provide students with an overview of WebCT; to generate rules and guidelines for "netiquette"; to assist students to access, compose, and post messages; and to clarify the role of the student and the instructor in the discussions. The activities used were similar to those described in Activities 1 and 5 in Appendix I. Before 2003, I had emphasized the following three elements in the design of the discussion activities: (a) designing tasks that encourage learner-to-learner interaction, (b) clarifying instructor expectations, and (c) encouraging participation and its relationship to assessment. Each one addresses Garrison and Anderson's (2003) notion of teaching presence and relates to the design and facilitation of online learning experiences.

Designing Tasks that Encourage Learner-to-Learner Interaction

Key determinants of whether learners will participate in discussion tasks are the design of the activity, the perceived value to the learner, and the relationship between the activity and the desired learning outcomes. Suggestions from Benfield (2002) and Klemm (1998), described below, were used to design the asynchronous discussion activities.

- Learners must see the value in participating in the discussion. The activities must have a clear purpose or specific task and involve content resource materials that foster controversies or the consideration of a range of opinions. In this context, clinical case-based scenarios necessitating debate about clinical practice were ideal materials.

- The discussion tasks should require learners to produce a product so that they will devote their time to discussions. The orthoptic students were required to post a group response online to the case being discussed every two to four weeks. The cases (up to a total of five in a 14-week semester) were used to provide formative feedback to the learners regarding their understanding of course content materials.

- If asynchronous discussion is to be used in a blended course, the task needs to have aspects that can be best achieved by learners actually working online and not by other methods, such as over the telephone. More recently, students have started also using a synchronous chat room to solve any disagreements or misconceptions about the case.

- Make sure to reduce the face-to-face activities or other course require-ments to allow time for learners to participate in the discussion activities. In this situation face-to-face tutorials were replaced by asynchronous discussions.

Although the students described in this context had studied together for the previous two years, they commented that this was the first time they had discussed their opinions in a constructive way. Simply designing good discussion tasks does not mean that learners will actually participate in asynchronous discussions. Research shows undergraduate learners, in particular, fail to take full advantage of the opportunities provided by online discussion activities (Hara et al., 2000; Ellis, 2003; Laurillard, 2002; Vondervell, 2002).

Clarifying Instructor Expectations

The discussion activity needs to be carefully planned with clear instructions to avoid unnecessary monitoring by the instructor. VandeVusse and Hanson (2000) found that instructors can get bogged down attending to learners' questions regarding assistance with navigation, explanation of expectations, clarification of the instructor's role, and provision of encouragement to the learners. Salmon (2000, 2002) offers a range of suggestions for clearly articulating what is required in what she terms "e-tivities," including an illustrative title, a spark or stimulus for online action, a participative element, timing, and method of feedback from the instructor or e-moderator. The orientation activities described in Appendix I model these suggestions.

Mazzolini and Maddison (2003) researched the effect of instructor intervention on learner participation in online discussion forums and found that learners produce lengthier discussion threads if instructors intervene in a minimal way. The role of the e-moderator can be viewed on a continuum shown in Figure 1.

In my context, with limited resources and only one e-moderator for up to 50 students averaging 30 postings each per semester, it was necessary to adopt the invisible style. To reduce the time drain from managing so many messages, students were given clear guidance that it was their responsibility to monitor their own contributions and participation.

Figure 1. A continuum of e-moderation

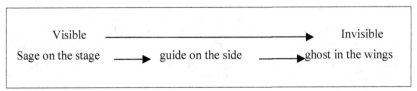

Encouraging Participation and its Relationship to Assessment

Instructors can become discouraged by the lack of learner participation and the time drain associated with the management of online discussions, so the issue of whether online participation should be assessed requires consideration.

When asynchronous discussion was first introduced in the course, a minimum number of postings were used as a prerequisite for participation in a clinical case-based summative assessment. A shortcoming was that the quality of the postings was not guaranteed. Instructors should use criteria for assessing the quality of the postings that reflect the objectives of the discussion activity. For example, rubrics can be used to evaluate learners' postings according to the insight shown by their comments, their understanding of the underlying theory, and their ability to apply knowledge (Knowlton, 2003; Webb et al., 2004; Whipp, 2003).

Assessment of the quality of the posting was not introduced until 2004 and is described in section "Redesign of the Orientation Sessions 2004 to 2005" next.

Reflections of Student Interaction and Participation in Online Discussions over the Period 2000 to 2003

Although students enthusiastically embraced the online learning opportunities, it was noticed that students tended to post their individual ideas, rarely commenting or building on the ideas of others in their group. The discussion board had the appearance of long lists of individual contributions with little threading of messages, making it difficult to follow the flow of content (see Figure 2 for items related to the "Aaron case" described in Appendix I).

The students were not taking full advantage of the collaborative environment. The assumptions that the students would automatically practice cooperative group dynamics online, as they had in face-to-face sessions, and also interact well to reach group consensus on answers were proven to be incorrect by the research undertaken in 2003. When the content of the students' postings was analyzed by two raters according to Salmon's conference analysis categories (2000), it was found that over 93% of the 756 postings demonstrated "individual thinking" where ideas were offered, explanations and examples provided, and personal opinions re-evaluated. Only 7% of postings were considered to show "interactive thinking," described by Salmon as occurring when students critique other student's ideas, challenge opinions with further questions, negotiate new meanings, and summarize contributions (see Wozniak & Silveira, 2004, for a full

Figure 2. Discussion board appearance in 2003

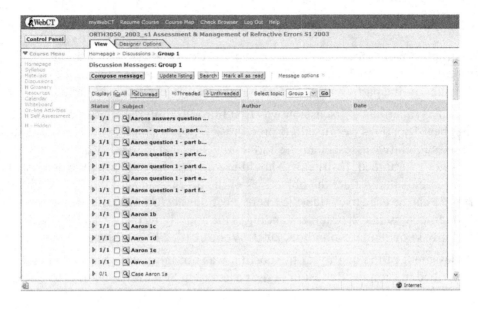

description of the categories used in this analysis). The following section describes modifications that were made to the student orientation activities in 2004 directed at improving the cognitive level of postings.

Redesign of the Orientation Sessions 2004 to 2005

The orientation sessions were subsequently modified to include greater emphasis on the development of collaborative group processes by scaffolding students' early online experiences. The suggestions described below relate to Garrison and Anderson's (2003) notion of cognitive presence where learners are more likely to achieve higher-order learning.

Online Group Dynamics

Much has been written about the positive effects of collaborating in small groups, including the development of team problem-solving skills, stimulation of critical thinking, and improved motivation and social skills (Barkley et al., 2005; Johnson & Johnson, 2000). How to translate this to the online learning environment has been a recent focus of research (Palloff & Pratt, 1999; Roberts, 2004).

From 2004, the orientation sessions included activities for learners to practice sharing ideas and responding to each other (see Activity 3 and 4, Appendix I) as well as offering suggestions regarding how the cognitive level of the postings could encourage greater interaction with peers (Activity 6).

The need for greater scaffolding of group processes has been identified as a key element in fully online courses. Some suggestions include the allocation of different roles to learners, for example, using a "starter and wrapper" model (Hara et al., 2000), "weaving and summarizing" (Salmon, 2002), and labeling postings to signify the type of group processes occurring in the discussion (McLoughlin, 2002).

Using a Framework to Scaffold the Learners' Online Experiences

The role of the instructor in facilitating productive online conferencing has received much attention in the literature. It has been greatly assisted with the development of Salmon's five-stage model of teaching and learning online with communication tools (2000, 2002). This model describes a series of steps to enable e-moderators to assist learners to progress through accessing online communication tools, socializing online, exchanging information, conferencing to construct knowledge, and finally, thinking critically and adopting responsibility for their own learning. Techniques described in the model are directed largely at examining the role of the instructor in the management of online discussions, noted by other researchers as impacting on already stretched resources (Maor, 2003; VandeVusse & Hanson, 2000).

In 2004, this model was adapted for use by learners with orientation activities aligned to Salmon's stages (Figure 3 & Appendix I). By structuring the learner's early online experiences, learners would be able to move quickly to Stage 3 and 4 and attain deeper levels of learning "based on reflection and on the interpretation of experience," which is considered an important element of the online learning experience (Palloff & Pratt, 1999, p. 129).

Figure 3. Orientation activities aligned to Salmon's five-stage model (Adapted to highlight the role of the learner)

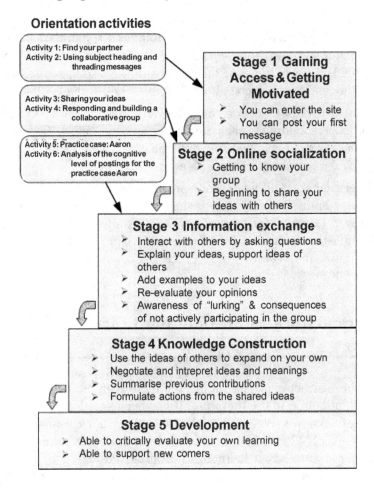

Analysis of Modifications to the Orientation Sessions

The impact of the redesigned orientation activities was investigated by asking students to engage in an analysis of their experiences by completing a reflection report at the end of the orientation sessions and again after their online learning experiences. This was combined with a change in the assessment of the quality of their participation (now 10% of course marks). Guidance was provided to enable them to search their postings, nominate, and justify those that demonstrated the following characteristics:

- Timely posting that allows adequate group conferencing before deadlines.

- Posting that helps to promote further interactions with other group members.

- Posting that demonstrates their role in providing feedback to group members.

In addition, they were required to comment on their level of interactivity based on Salmon's five-stage model and note how the experience would influence their future e-learning participation. This reduced the instructor's time required to assess each student's participation.

As reported by Wozniak and Silveira (2004), when the results of content analysis of the postings in 2004 were compared with the results in 2003 described earlier, there was a significant increase in the number of postings demonstrating interactive thinking (7% to 47%), which supports the notion of higher order learning by a collaborative community of inquiry (Garrison & Anderson, 2003). The use of extended threads with involvement of a large number of students is clearly evident in Figure 4.

The influence of online participation on all students' marks in final assessments was also investigated in 2003 and 2004. Students who achieved a higher number of postings at the interactive levels achieved higher marks for the online cases (rs=0.76, rs=0.69, Silveira, Wozniak, & Heard, 2004). There was also a positive correlation noted between the online assessment mark and overall course mark:

Figure 4. Discussion board appearance in 2004

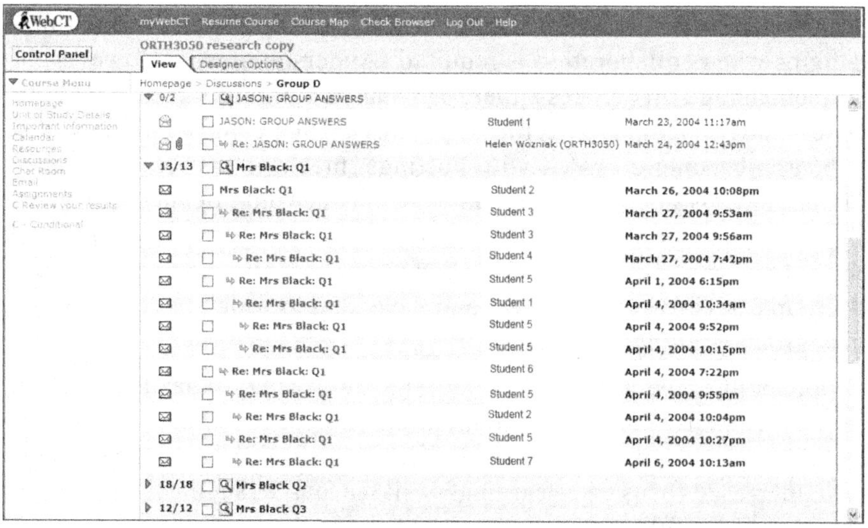

high in one course (rs=0.735, p 0.00) and moderate in another course (rs=0.474, p 0.035). These results suggest that approaches to learning in the online environment were transferred to similar activities in the face-to-face environment (Wozniak & Silveira, 2004).

To examine the impact of the use of Salmon's model, qualitative data gathered from student reflections received in 2004 and 2005 were coded and compared to the student ratings of their stage of development as online learners and participation marks. There was a significant change in the learner's stage of development (z=-4.076 p<0.001) and degree of reflection (z=-4.243 p<0.001) before and after participation, which was positively correlated with online participation assessment results (rs=0.411, p0.005) (Wozniak, 2006).

The relationship between the learning that occurs in the online learning environment and the face-to-face setting in blended courses has been given little attention in the literature. However, it was seen to be a significant motivator for participation when the assessment results previously described were revealed to the learners in the orientation sessions. Wu and Hiltz (2004), who reviewed the available work in this area, concluded that there are many variables that may contribute to the predictability of learning that results from asynchronous online discussions. These include the instructor's role, degree of guidance given, structure of the discussion topics, and learners' learning styles. Establishing a causal relationship between these many factors is an area requiring considerable further research.

Future Trends

Learner-to-learner interaction is critical for learning based on constructivist paradigms when collaboration is required (Anderson, 2003). However, in the rush to encourage this process, there are many emerging issues from both the technical and pedagogical spectra that require further consideration. As discussion boards become crowded with postings, mechanisms for organizing the messages, threads, and content contained within them may demand more flexible designs than are currently available in learning management systems such as WebCT. Greater understanding is needed regarding how groups develop online, how group roles are best managed, and the extent to which instructor presence affects group learning processes.

Questions still to be answered include the following: What is the effect of enhancing learner-to-learner interaction in terms of time and cost savings for resource-stretched higher education environments? Will learners become jaded with an increased focus on e-learning? Will the learner supports described here be transferable to fully online contexts?

Conclusion

The use of e-learning is growing in higher education as is the use of asynchronous discussions. Making the transition to e-learning requires an understanding of the interplay of factors most relevant to this new learning mode, especially the design of the discussion activity, the role the instructor plays in influencing the learner's participation, and the learning outcomes. A key factor in promoting learner-to-learner interaction is the careful management of the demands on the instructors and the shrinking resources available. If learners are carefully prepared and guided through their early online learning experiences, asynchronous discussion activities can achieve group collaboration and higher quality learning.

Acknowledgments

I wish to acknowledge the support of my colleague, Sue Silveira, as we journeyed along the road of discovery making the transition from face-to-face to e-learning, Dr. Rob Heard for the statistical analyses, and Dr. Mary Jane Mahony and Dr. Joy Higgs for their advice in the preparation of this manuscript.

References

Anderson, T. (2003). Getting the mix right: An updated and theoretical rationale for interaction. *International Review of Research in Open and Distance Learning, 4*(2). Retrieved November 2, 2005, from http://www.irrodl.org/content/v4.2/anderson.html

Barkley, E. F., Cross, K. P., & Major, C. H. (2005). *Collaborative learning techniques: A handbook for college faculty.* San Francisco: Jossey-Bass.

Benfield, G. (2002). *Designing and managing effective online discussions* (Learning and Teaching Briefing Papers Series). UK: Oxford Brookes University, Oxford Centre for Staff and Learning Development (OCSLD). Retrieved November 2, 2005, from http://www.brookes.ac.uk/services/ocsd/2_learntch/briefing_papers/online_discussions.pdf

Bozarth, J., Chapman, D. D., & LaMonica, L. (2004). Preparing for distance learning: designing an online student orientation course. *Educational Technology & Society, 7*(1), 87-106.

Ellis, A. (2001). Student-centred collaborative learning via face-to-face and asynchronous online communication: What's the difference? In G. Kennedy, M. Keppell, C. McNaught, & T. Petrovic (Eds.), *Meeting at the crossroads: Proceedings of the 18th Annual Conference of the Australian Society for Computers in Learning in Tertiary Education* (pp. 169-177). Biomedical Multimedia Unit, The University of Melbourne. Retrieved November 2, 2005, from http://www.ascilite.org.au/conferences/melbourne01/pdf/papers/ellisa.pdf

Garrison, D. R., & Anderson, T. (2003). *E-learning in the 21st century: A framework for research and practice.* London: RoutledgeFalmer.

Geer, R. (2003). Initial communicating styles and their impact on further interactions in computer conferences. In G. Crisp, D. Thiele, I. Scholten, S. Barkder, & J. Baron, (Eds.), *Interact, integrate, impact: Proceedings of the 20th Annual Conference of the Australasian Society for Computers in Learning in Tertiary Education* (pp. 194-202). University of Adelaide. Retrieved November 2, 2005, from http://www.ascilite.org.au/conferences/adelaide03/program/conf_prog_index.htm

Gunawardena, C. N. (2004). The challenge of designing inquiry-based online learning environments: Theory into practice. In T. M. Duffy & J. R. Kirkley (Eds.), *Learner-centred theory and practice in distance education: Cases from higher education* (pp. 143-158). Mahwah, NJ: Lawrence Erlbaum Associates.

Hara, N., Bonk, C., & Angeli, C. (2000). Content analysis of online discussion in an applied educational psychology course. *Instructional Science, 28*(2), 115-152.

Klemm, W. R. (1998). Eight ways to get students more engaged in online conferences. *T.H.E. Journal, 26*(1), 62-64.

Knowlton, D. S. (2003). Evaluating college students' effort in asynchronous discussion: A systematic process. *The Quarterly Review of Distance Education, 41*(1), 31-41.

Johnson, D. W., & Johnson, F. P. (2000). *Joining together.* Boston: Allyn & Bacon.

Laurillard, D. (2002). *Rethinking university teaching: A conversational framework for the effective use of learning technologies.* London: RoutledgeFalmer.

Maor, D. (2003). The teacher's role in developing interaction and reflection in an online learning community. *Education Media International, 40*(1-2), 127-137.

Mazzolini, M., & Maddison, S. (2003). Sage, guide, or ghost? The effect of instructor intervention on student participation in online discussion forums. *Computers and Education, 40*, 237-253.

McLoughlin, C. (2002). Computer supported teamwork: An integrative approach to evaluating cooperative learning in an online environment. *Australasian Journal of Educational Technology, 18*(2), 227-254.

Moore, M. (1989). Three types of interaction. *American Journal of Distance Education, 3*(2), 1-6.

Moore, M. (1993). Theory of transactional distance. In D. Keegan (Ed.), *Theoretical principles of distance education* (pp. 22-38). London: Routledge.

Palloff, R. M., & Pratt, K. (1999). *Building learning communities in cyberspace: Effective strategies for the online classroom.* San Francisco: Jossey-Bass.

Roberts, T. S. (2004). *Online collaborative learning: Theory and practice.* Hershey, PA: Idea Group Publishing.

Salmon, G. (2000). *E-moderating: The key to teaching and learning online.* London: Kogan Page.

Salmon, G. (2002). *E-tivities: The key to active online learning.* London: Kogan Page.

Silveira, S., Wozniak, H., & Heard, R. (2004, November 14-17). Using online discussion groups to enhance the learning outcomes of undergraduate orthoptic students. What have we learnt? In D. Verlohr, A. Rydberg, & Z. Georgievski (Eds.), *Global perspectives converge downunder: Transactions of the 10th International Orthoptic Congress* (pp. 359-362).

VandeVusse, L., & Hanson, L. (2000). Evaluation of online course discussions: Faculty facilitation of active student learning. *Computers in Nursing, 18*(4), 181-188.

Vonderwell, S. (2002). An examination of asynchronous communication experiences and perspectives of students in an online course: A case study. *Internet and Higher Education, 6*(1), 77-90.

Webb, E., Jones, A., Barker, P., & van Schaik, P. (2004). Using e-learning dialogues in higher education. *Innovations in Education and Teaching International, 41*(1), 94-103.

Whipp, J. L. (2003). Scaffolding critical reflection in online discussions. *Journal of Teacher Education, 54*(4), 321-333.

Wozniak, H. (2006). Online discussions: Improving the quality of the student experience. In M. Tulloch, S. Relf, & P. Uys (Eds.), *Breaking down boundaries: International experience in open, distance and flexible education — Selected papers* (pp. 170-179). Charles Sturt University, Bathurst: Open and Distance Learning Association of Australia.

Wozniak, H., & Silveira, S. (2004). Online discussions: Promoting effective student-to-student interaction. In R. Atkinson, C. McBeath, D. Jonas-Dwyer, & R. Phillips (Eds.), *Beyond the comfort zone: Proceedings of the 21ˢᵗ ASCILITE Conference* (pp. 956-960). Retrieved November 2, 2005, from http://www.ascilite.org.au/conferences/perth04/procs/wozniak.html

Wu, D., & Hiltz, S. (2004). Predicting learning from asynchronous online discussions. *Journal of Asynchronous Online Learning, 8*(2), 139-152.

Zemsky, R., & Massy, W. F. (2004). *Thwarted innovation: What happened to e-learning and why.* The Learning Alliance, University of Pennsylvania. Retrieved November 2, 2005, from http://www.irhe.upenn.edu/WeatherStation.html

Appendix I: Outline of the Orientation Sessions

Desired learning outcomes:

1. Able to use the discussion tool in WebCT—post and reply to messages, thread messages use clear subject headings.

2. Recognize important elements of group work in the online environment— time management (giving enough time for others in the group to respond), the difference between lurking and active participation, need for encouragement of group members.

3. Able to analyze the cognitive level of messages posted by the group and how to build group ideas through interaction rather than posting individual ideas in isolation.

4. Relate Salmon's five-stage model to your own development as an online learner.

5. Reflect on your online learning experience and plan future online learning participation.

Plan of orientation sessions for blended learning environment

Face-to-face session held in a computer lab		Private study (online)

Session	Before	During	After
1 Week 1	• Learners check access to WebCT site. • Review resource describing technical features of the discussion tool.	• E-moderators outline their rationale for use of discussion tool including roles and responsibilities of students and e-moderators • Introduction to Salmon's five-stage model. • Activity 1.	Activity 2
2 Week 1 or 2	• Activity 3.	• Activity 4.	Learners placed in small private discussion groups of up to 10 Activity 5
3 Week 2		• Activity 6.	Commence next e-tivity for course

Activity 1: Find Your Partner

Purpose	To practice posting messages, reading messages and replying to messages (see Stage 1 of model: Gaining Access & Getting Motivated)
Task	• Go to your mailbox. • Read the message titled: "Find your partner."
Action	• Go to discussion topic "Find your partner." • Post a message which describes or cryptically refers to the word that you were sent in the mailbox without using the word. • Read messages from others and reply to their messages, if you feel that they may be your partner. • In your replies you could ask further questions about their word. • The activity finishes when you can identify the related word- you have found your partner! You should post a message that confirms that you have found your partner.
Complete by	During session 1

Activity 2: Using Subject Headings and Threading Messages

Purpose	Recognize the importance of using clear subject headings and the need to thread messages (see Stage 1 of model: Gaining Access & Getting Motivated)
Task	• Look at the messages posted in the "Find your partner" activity. • Note how important it is to use a subject heading that will enable the reader to decide whether they wish to open the message and read it. • It is also important to make sure that you use the reply function to ensure that messages that are related to the subject appear in the one "thread," otherwise the discussion board will become a long list of single messages. • You should now be aware of how much you are passively "lurking" in the background (by simply reading messages and not replying) or "actively" participating in the discussion.
Action	Nil
Complete by	In your own time after session 1

Activity 3: Sharing Your Ideas

Purpose	To begin to share information about a topic and respond to each other's postings (see Stage 2 of model: Online socialization) This activity is described in Salmon, G. (2002) E-tivities: the key to active online learning, p54.
Task	• Send a "postcard" which says something interesting about what is happening around you. • Keep your message brief, as if you were writing a postcard. • It could be something about the environment you are currently in, what you can see from your window, your favorite food or something you have recently experienced. • Post your postcard in a message in the discussion topic "Postcards."
Action	• Look through the postings made by others, and note who has something in common with you and who has differences to you. • Reply with a comment to at least three other people.
Complete by	Make sure you have posted your postcard within one day of session 1 and that you have given comments on three postcards 1 day before session 2. You may find that you have to visit the topic area several times to complete this task.

Activity 4: Responding and Building a Collaborative Group

Purpose	To review the importance of timely participation and to consider how to promote a collaborative group (see Stage 2 of model: Online socialization)

Task	• Look at the messages posted in the "Postcards" topic.
	• Ask yourself the following questions.
	   1. Did you allow enough time for others to read and respond to your initial posting?
	   2. Did you respond to the postings of three others?
	   3. Did your response acknowledge the contribution of the poster and indicate that you appreciated their posting?
	   4. If you disagreed with the ideas of another person did you restate their point of view to acknowledge their idea and then explain your view point?
	   5. Did you encourage further participation by ending your message with a question?

Action	Reflect on your answers to these questions and discuss any issues that arise with other learners and your e-moderator.
Complete by	During session 2

Activity 5: Practice Case Aaron

Purpose	To interact with the course content and your private group members (see Stage 3 of model: Information exchange)
Task	• Read the scenario below.
Scenario	Aaron aged 2 years is attending for an orthoptic assessment. The ophthalmologist would like your help regarding the correction of his refractive error. The dry ret showed +5.00DS RE, +4.00DS LE, cyclo ret +10.00 RE, +9.00 LE. Question 1: What refractive error is present? What is the likely cause? Question 2: Without any glasses, how much accommodation does he need to exert to have clear vision at near and at 6 metres? Question 3: What is likely to happen if Aaron overcomes his refractive error? Question 4: What strength of glasses would fully correct his refractive error?
Action	• Go to your private group discussion area. • Post your ideas for each question. You should use a new message thread for each of the questions 1-4. Give the message a subject "Question 1" etc. • You should review messages that have already been posted about each question. Rather than starting a new thread for that question, reply to that message so that your ideas appear under the same thread.
Complete by	Make sure you have participated by posting your ideas for each question or responding to the ideas of other participants before session 3.

Activity 6: Analysis of the Cognitive Level of Postings Made in Activity 5

Purpose	To evaluate the content of the postings that were made by your private group to the practice case: Aaron To encourage you to consider the cognitive level of the postings and determine how the content of the posting assists you to achieve Stage 3 Information exchange & Stage 4 Knowledge Construction of the model.

Task	• Review the messages posted in the practice case: Aaron
	• Ask yourself the following questions:
	  ✓ Did the posting give an idea?
	  ✓ Did the poster explain their answer?
	  ✓ Did the poster ask others to respond or critique their answer or opinion or ask further challenging questions?
	  ✓ Does the poster expand on the ideas of others in the group?
	  ✓ Does the poster summarize the thoughts of others?

Action	Discuss your answers to these questions. Go to the discussion topic "Tips for making online discussions work" Post a message that offers what you consider is a key to making online discussion work. Respond to the ideas of others with your comments.
Complete by	During session 3

Chapter XIV

A Framework for Choosing Communication Activities in E-Learning

Tannis Morgan, University of British Columbia, Canada

Karen Belfer, British Columbia Institute of Technology, Canada

Abstract

In this chapter, we present a framework for planning communication activities according to the level of structure and potential dialogue desired in a given course. This framework serves as a tool for making decisions about how to give students more or less autonomy, how a series of course activities can be scaffolded, and the amount of structure or instructor facilitation that is needed. The framework we have developed uses each variable of the transactional distance theory as a dimension, which displayed as a quadrant allows us to represent instructional strategies and various communication activities for e-learning. This framework is beneficial as a tool for planning the instructional design process, informing pedagogy, and conducting research.

Introduction

Over the past 10 years, the use of discussion forums or bulletin boards to support asynchronous learning communications has become a common practice within mixed-mode and online courses. Both pedagogy and context serve to drive and influence the use of this technology. The interest in constructivist approaches in the design of learning contexts has resulted in the creation of communication spaces where interaction, participation and negotiation of meaning can take place. At the same time distance education has increasingly moved online, the choice to use an asynchronous tool for communication seems to be well suited to this mode of delivery where teacher-student (TS), student-student (SS), and student-content (SC) interaction is influenced by geography, time zones, and personal scheduling conflicts.

In distance education, course development can be an individual or collaborative effort involving instructors, course authors, and instructional designers. For the purpose of this chapter, we will refer to the role of the instructional designer, since that is the perspective that we occupy in our own institution. However, regardless of whether development adopts a solo or team approach, there are a myriad of decisions to make when constructing online communication activities that support the TS/SS/SC interactions. These include decisions around how the activity will be organized, the kind of facilitation that is needed, and the type of assessment and feedback that will be provided. Furthermore, the use of technology enables the implementation of collaborative practices, and with a greater emphasis on learner-centered approaches, online learning technologies have evolved considerably in the last ten years. In 1998, Bonk and King recognized the challenge that the new educational landscape presented and noted that "with all these new learning channels, educators are faced with unprecedented educational opportunities and challenges. Without question, the formats for electronic collaboration are proliferating" (Bonk & King, 1998, p. 5). Almost ten years later, while text-based discussion forums still dominate as a means of class communication, these communication spaces now might include voice or video. Although there are many innovators exploring new technologies and approaches, it is still a challenge for instructors to find ways to enable the best potential of the technologies and strategies available.

As instructional designers, in developing courses for online learning we know that learning activities should not be used indistinctively, since each one of them has the potential of being pedagogically effective and enhance the quality of the learning experience for a particular set of course objectives and needs of the students. When instructional designers work with subject matter experts they often offer a choice of different delivery models in an effort to find an approach that will address the needs of the course objectives and content while taking into account the teaching style of the instructor (Belfer, Chu, & Nesbit, 2000). Therefore, how do developers choose between all the options? How can instructional designers ensure that their decisions are pedagogically grounded?

Background

For the purpose of this chapter, we adopt the framework developed by Zemsky and Massy (2004) and define e-learning as distance education. Our planning framework has been developed through the course of our work as instructional designers in the Centre for Distance Education and Technology (DE&T) at the University of British Columbia (UBC). Initially we began compiling asynchronous communication activities into a matrix format, identifying the type of activity, the structure that was needed, the role of the students and the instructors in that activity, and strategies for assessment. The matrix grew to a size that became unmanageable and suffered from two major flaws—although it was useful as an activity selection tool for an instructional designer, (1) it didn't leave much room for consideration of an instructor perspective or their teaching style, and (2) was not able to visually show how activities could potentially evolve during the delivery of the course.

For example, we were able to give recommendations around the components of an instructor-lead class discussion activity, but this said little about the level of control that the instructor might exercise in the facilitation of that discussion activity—an instructor who preferred controlled discussions might take more control of the discussion than an instructor who over time preferred students to take the lead role in the facilitation. We also recognized that the same activity (such as class discussion) could look very different depending on how it was structured, the role the instructor would take, and the role the students might take in that discussion. We also observed that an activity that adopted the same structure and roles for instructors and students could play out very differently depending on who the instructor was, or if students came from different programs. In our personal experience as instructors we know that this is hardly surprising, since instructors recognize that with every group of students the same activity is rarely predictable, even if the instructor remains the same. But it challenged us to attempt to identify the variables that need to be considered in designing communication activities.

This current work has been influenced by dominant ideas in the areas of teaching perspectives and distance education, by Moore (1973), Pratt (1998, 2002), and Saba (2003), as well as current research on student perceptions of asynchronous discussions.

Transactional Distance Theory

Transactional distance theory was introduced by Michael Moore to the field of distance education. This theory dates from 1973 and was developed at a time when distance education was characterized by correspondence courses (usually paper based), where a geographic separation between the student and instructor allowed few opportunities for interaction. However, rather than focusing on the geographic characteristic that defines distance. Moore attempted to identify the psychological distance in distance education.

In his theory, Moore focuses on the interplay of three variables that define the learning transaction between teacher and students—structure, dialogue, and autonomy. Structure refers to the design of the course and the level of control that the instructor or students have within that structure. Dialogue refers to the positive or constructive interactions between the student and the instructor and/or the internal dialogue of the student with him or herself. Autonomy refers to the ability of the student to take responsibility for his or her own learning. Therefore, a learning context that has a high level of structure and little dialogue would have a large transactional distance. A context that had a low level of structure and low level of dialogue would also have a large transactional distance and would additionally require a higher level of autonomy on the part of the learner. However, the same context with a high level of dialogue would potentially be less distant.

There are potentially many secondary variables that have an influence on the transactional distance. These include the mode of communication or communication tools, the characteristics of the learners, the instructor characteristics, and the institutional context. In the context of the student, the mode of communication is particularly relevant since it directly relates to the language of instruction. For example, research indicates that students who are interacting in a second language will benefit more from asynchronous communication (typically text discussion forums) since it allows them more time to process the message, the option to reread or replay, and to construct responses on their own time (Carey, 1999, Carey & Guo, 2003).

It is not difficult to see how asynchronous communications provide a potentially important role in facilitating dialogue and thus reducing distance. Yet, we often see courses that have not adequately considered the relationship between dialogue, autonomy, and structure. In an online context where students are at a distance, we know that some structure needs to be provided in order for students to be able to locate themselves within the environment. When students are left fumbling to understand what is expected of them and how to go about doing it, more autonomy is needed on the part of the student. This is not to say that encouraging students to be more autonomous is detrimental to learning; rather we are suggesting that the push to be more autonomous also needs to be properly planned.

Research has shown asynchronous online discussions do improve students' perceptions of learning, motivation, enjoyability (Wu & Hiltz, 2003), and content mastery (Alavi, 1994). Riddle, Pearce, and Nott (1997) suggest that the reasons behind increased involvement and learning relies on the connectivity between students and teachers. If that is the case, one would expect that any of the implementations that have been documented in the literature regardless of whether they are teacher-lead (Maor, 2003), student-lead (Hara, Bonk, & Angeli, 2001), case-based (Benbunan & Hiltz, 1999), discourse-based (Pincas, 1998), and/or brainstorming-based (Belfer, 2001) would offer the same positive results.

We believe that good implementation relies in part on the course design, since it speaks to how activities should be constructed and facilitated, but that the instructor's facilitation strategies for course activities are an important factor in influencing student perception of the learning experience.

Teaching Perspectives

As instructional designers, we work with course authors who are also instructors in the courses they are developing with us. We are aware that course design should also include some discussion of the instructor/course author's own teaching styles or preferences. In our role it is very important that we are able to communicate with instructors about who they are as teachers and all the options available, both in terms of educational strategies and the available technologies that can enhance and inform the teaching and learning practices. Dan Pratt has written extensively on teaching and his research suggests that teaching styles (actions) are the observable piece of a very complex framework based on a set of beliefs and intentions, that are rarely directly observed by people when we teach. His research suggests that it is useful to think about teaching in five fundamentally different ways, what he calls five perspectives on teaching. These perspectives include transmission, developmental, apprenticeship, nurturing, and social reform.

The transmission oriented teacher focuses on accurately delivering content to the learners and the relationship is largely uni-directional—the teacher delivers content and the student passively receives it. With a developmental approach, the teacher facilitates the learner's cognitive structure and their understanding of the content. In this way, the developmental perspective is more concerned with cultivating ways of thinking. The apprenticeship perspective is concerned with revealing the inner workings of skilled performance in which the teaching event is situated in an authentic learning environment. The nurturers promote a positive climate and use encouragement and support to help students' achieve the learning goals. Finally, as the name suggests, the social reform perspective is characterized by a need to seek a better society. In the social reform model good teachers challenge the status quo and encourage students to reconsider their position in the construction of discourse and practice: their social, political or cultural ideals are an essential focal point of their teaching perspectives (Pratt & Associates, 1998).

In his article, Pratt (2002) emphasizes the fact that no one perspective is better than another, since they only represent an individual's view of teaching. Successful instructors reflect on their experience and evaluate what they do, why they do it, and on what grounds their actions and intentions are justified. In reflecting on this statement, we are reminded that increasingly instructional designers are encouraged to design courses with more constructivist approaches, since this is what is currently valued in our institutions. Yet, how do you create a course with a collaborative approach if the instructor does not want to monitor or facilitate discussions, and prefers a more direct or transmission approach to instruction?

The Framework

The framework we have developed seeks to integrate the dimensions of Transactional Distance theory. In conceptualizing this framework, we began with Saba's (2003) interpretation of the structure component of this construct (see Figure 1). Structure describes the course design, teaching strategies (activities), learning objectives, and evaluation methods (scoring criteria). Structure is a continuous variable for which the instructor holds direct or indirect control. Students normally perceive it as more or less flexible or more or less rigid.

We then incorporated Saba's interpretation of the dialogue construct (see Figure 2). Dialogue describes the level of interaction between the learner and the teacher, the learner and his/her peers, and the learner and the content. Some

Figure 1. Saba's (2003) interpretation of the structure variable of Moore's theory

Figure 2. Saba's (2003) interpretation of the dialogue variable of Moore's theory

elements that influence the students' perception and ability to interact are the language of interaction, the size of the group, and the medium used to mediate the communication. Dialogue is a continuous variable for which the instructor designs activities that require that the student be more active or passive in his/her interactions. Students normally perceive it as more or less interactive.

The third component, autonomy, describes the learner's capacity to self manage, self-regulate and be intrinsically motivated to engage with the content to the level of depth needed. Autonomy is a continuous variable over which the instructor has little control. This component is not visually reflected in our framework, since instructional designers and teachers can only work with those variables over which they have some control (e.g., structure and dialogue). Nonetheless, there are some processes that can be put in place to help and support students that are more or less autonomous, by providing more structure or more opportunities for dialogue.

The quadrant (see Figure 3) is our representation of the structure and dialogue dimensions. As we started working with it we realized that the left lower side of the quadrant represents the teacher-centered approaches with which the instructor has direct control of the structure and students are passively receiving

Figure 3. Our adaptation of Moore's model for ID purposes

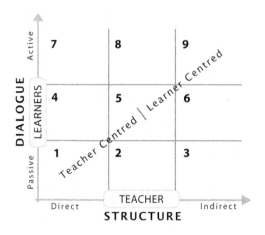

information. In contrast, the top right represents the learner-centered approaches for which the instructor has indirect control of the structure. Students exercise their autonomy and follow their interests, actively participating in the learning process while interacting with the content, peers, and/or the instructor).

The quadrant representation allowed us to begin mapping the different types of communication activities in a given e-learning course onto the quadrant, while considering the teaching perspectives of the instructor. For example, one of the most common learning activities that is present in many online courses is a forum for announcements, which an instructor can use to remind students of deadlines, important events, or to clarify concepts or points that are not clear. This type of activity logically fits into quadrant 1 because it has a particular function of presenting information to students; the structure is very direct, and little or no dialogue is expected of students.

Another common learning activity is an asynchronous class discussion, where a question is discussed over a certain period of time and involves the instructor and the students. Depending on the structure of the activity, this activity would find itself in any of the quadrants. For this activity to be in quadrant 1 or 2 we would expect:

1.   The instructor begins the discussion with a pre-established question.
2.   Students respond once to the discussion according to very specific guidelines.
3.   The instructor closes the discussion after a specified period of time.

For this activity to be in quadrant 8 or 9 we would expect:

1.   A student or group of students presents a question to the forum.
2.   The question is discussed for a period of time or indefinitely.
3.   Students can participate in the discussion and shape the path of the discussion with relative freedom.

As instructional designers, the decision to structure the activities in any of the previous examples is influenced by the instructor's own teaching perspective or style. We would anticipate that different instructors would have a preference for more or less direct control. We might also see a class discussion look more like the first example at the beginning of a course, and then once trust has been established and the community has been built, later class discussions might look more like the second example.

Of course, the location of the activities in the quadrants is also dependent on how the learner approaches the activities. An activity can aim to accomplish and achieve a certain level of activity, but the student can be more active or passive based on his own learning style and willingness to follow the activity as planned, or not as planned. For example, a seemingly passive reading activity can be active if the student is taking notes, chatting with their classmates about the reading, or blogging their thoughts to a wider community of practice. As instructional designers, we often try to activate these types of passive activities by including pre-reading questions, reflective questions, or other cognitive strategies. However, ultimately it is the student's own level of autonomy that determines how the student activates their learning within or outside of the course structure. This is why autonomy and self-direction are important characteristics of learners.

Benefits of Using This Framework

In our recent work as instructional designers for distance education, we have tested the framework as a conceptual tool for course design, as well as a diagnostic tool for understanding why certain activities are not successful in some of our courses. We have found this framework to be beneficial as a tool for planning the instructional design process, informing pedagogy, and conducting research, as discussed next:

A Planning Tool for the ID Process

Although we have stated that there is no correct or incorrect way of recording activities into the quadrants, it provides a visual way of mapping ideas during course planning. It allows multiple types of e-learning communication activities to be presented using one visual aid, making it easier to understand what each of them mean, how they are situated within an entire course, and how, based on the consideration of the different variables and desired learning outcomes, they should be best structured and implemented. For example, when different activities are mapped onto the quadrants, it can help us explain how very structured learning activities can be scaled up to become more learner centered, indirectly structured, or active by increasing dialogue and reducing direct control over the structure (see Figure 4).

When designing and choosing activities for an online course, we are constantly considering the following components: learning outcomes, content, media, teach-

Figure 4. Recording different e-learning communication activities into the framework for ID purposes

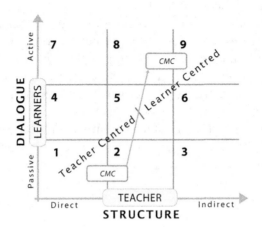

ing perspectives, and learner characteristics. However, we have found in our own work that we often under-emphasize the importance of teaching perspectives and learner characteristics and focus too much on the learning outcomes, content and the media. The framework forces the consideration of these components and adds an additional dimension to transactional distance—instead of trying to find ways to reduce distance, the framework attempts to show how the manipulation of some of these variables can shift an activity to be more or less learner centred. Instructional designers can then decide what variables to work with to increase (or decrease) learner centeredness. For example, if an instructor preferred a transmission approach, online exam activities, and little dialogue with students, the addition of student study groups would be one way of providing more student centered learning within the structure of the course.

The framework is also a tool for facilitating the conversation between instructional designers and instructors when developing or revising online courses and activities. In our own work, we have used this framework as a way to describe the characteristics of a target group of learners whose prior educational experiences were largely transmission oriented and instructor-centred (see Figure 5). We were then able to understand why some of the very constructivist, learner-centred activities that we had introduced failed to produce good results, while the more structured, direct activities were well received.

Figure 5. Prior educational experiences of a group of learners

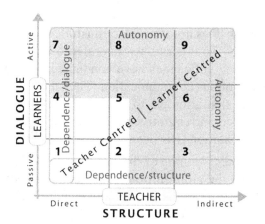

Pedagogical Tool

In some cases, we have found that the framework helps to remind instructors what the key elements of the learning process are and helps them focus on the elements that are most important. Most instructors are willing to try new pedagogical strategies in their courses provided that they will allow their learners to be successful. But many are confounded by a lack of time and a need for specific and clear step-by-step guidelines that they can use or adapt to their own practice without a significant investment of time. The framework could be a tool for assisting the instructor in developing and delivering a successful and engaging learning experience by encouraging them to reflect on their own teaching practices as key design elements, which are often left out of the design process or simply taken for granted.

Research Tool

As a research tool, the framework can allow both instructors and instructional designers to track how the learning activities evolve and gain insight into how instructors and students cope with changing and evolving systems. In our own research, we are looking at the role of teaching presence in the shift from more teacher centred activities to highly learner-centred activities. The framework provides a way of comparing different activities and identifying important variables that shape these activities (Belfer, Morgan, & Underhill, 2005).

As with all course planning tools, the success of any plan is only as good as the learning community that implements it and makes it work. We argue that careful planning provides a foundation on which to build a successful learning community, but our framework does not attempt to illustrate the action components of the learning community. To this end, we can refer to the considerable research that Terry Anderson and colleagues have conducted around the dynamics of course-related asynchronous communication. They have developed a community of inquiry model that attempts to identify some of the factors (teacher presence, social presence, and cognitive presence) that facilitate these dynamics during course implementation (Garrison, Anderson, & Archer, 2000).

Our framework facilitates planning of single course activities but at this point in time does not consider the more informal (and largely unstructured) learning spaces that students engage in parallel to course activities, such as their own communities of practice (Lave & Wenger, 1991) or affinity spaces (Gee, 2004). We believe that these informal spaces are important to the development of learning, identity construction, and learner autonomy, and should perhaps be given more consideration in course or program planning.

Future Trends and Conclusion

It is difficult to ignore how communication technologies have influenced teaching and learning environments by providing greater and more varied TS, SS, and SC communication. Until recently, these technologies have been mainly asynchronous text tools such as email and discussion forums, but in the last couple of years we have witnessed the arrival of various additional asynchronous and synchronous tools. Voice tools such as Wimba and Skype and text tools that allow synchronous and asynchronous collaboration (wikis, blogs, synchronous text editing tools such as Writely) offer functionality and collaboration in ways that the early tools couldn't provide. These tools challenge us to rethink course activities and serve to redefine our teaching and learning spaces in positive ways.

It is our belief that the merging of technologies with teaching and learning will become more and more seamless, where a distinction between e-learning and learning will no longer be necessary. Therefore, course design will become increasingly more complex by virtue of the fact that there will be more technological options for the teaching and learning transactions. With this comes the need for a strong awareness of pedagogy and the complexities of learning in different types of learning environments. Instructional designers have a role in ensuring that instructors understand their teaching perspectives, and have an awareness of how activities can be designed to support more learner-centered approaches (flexible structure, active dialogue, and room for learner autonomy) while considering all the components necessary to the development of an engaging learning environment.

References

Alavi, M. (1994, June). Computer-mediated collaborative learning: An empirical evaluation. *MIS Quarterly, 18*(2), 150-174.

Belfer, K. (2001, June). *De Bono's six thinking hats technique: A metaphorical model of communication in computer mediated classrooms.* Paper presented at Ed-Media World Conference in Multimedia Hypermedia and Telecommunications, Tampere, Finland.

Belfer, K., Chu, S., & Nesbit, J. (2000). *Delivery model specifications.* Unpublished technical report, Technical University of British Columbia, Canada. Retrieved May 30, 2006, from http://www3.telus.net/public/kbelfer/doc/DMSpecs.pdf

Belfer, K., Morgan, T., & Underhill, C. (2005, May). CARNet/UBC: Three approaches to a case study in an international collaboration. *CADE 2005 Conference: Learning Virtually...Anywhere.* UBC, Vancouver, Canada.

Benbunan, R. F., & Hiltz, R. S. (1999). Educational applications of CMCS: Solving case studies through asynchronous learning networks. *Journal of Computer-Mediated Communication, 4*(3). Retrieved January 27, 2006, from http://jcmc.indiana.edu/vol4/issue3/benbunan-fich.html

Bonk, C. J., & King, K. S. (1998). Computer conferencing and collaborative writing tools: Starting a dialogue about student dialogue. In C. J. Bonk & K. S. King (Eds.), *Electronic collaborators: Learner-centered technologies for literacy, apprenticeship, and discourse* (pp. 3-23). Mahwah, NJ: Lawrence Erlbaum.

Carey, S. (1999). The use of WebCT for a highly interactive virtual graduate seminar. *Computer Assisted Language Learning, 12*(1), 85-98.

Carey, S., & Guo, XG. R. (2003). Conditions for ESL acquisition on WebCT. *The International Journal of Learning, 9*, 491-498.

Garrison, D. R., Anderson, T., & Archer, W. (2000). Critical inquiry in a text-based environment: Computer conferencing in higher education. *The Internet and Higher Education, 2*(2-3), 87-105.

Gee, J. P. (2004). *Situated language and learning: A critique of traditional schooling.* New York: Routledge.

Hara, N., Bonk, C. J., & Angeli, C. (2000). Content analysis of online discussion in an applied educational psychology course. *Instructional Science*, *28*(2), 115-152.

Lave, J., & Wenger, E. (1991). *Situated learning. Legitimate peripheral participation*. Cambridge: University of Cambridge Press.

Maor, D. (2003). The teacher's role in developing interaction and reflection in an online learning community. *Educational Media International*, *40*(1-2), 127-138.

Moore, M. G. (1973). Towards a theory of independent learning and teaching. *Journal of Higher Education*, *44*(9), 661-79.

Pincas, A. (1998). Successful online course design: Virtual frameworks for discourse construction. *Educational Technology & Society*, *1*(1). Retrieved January 26, 2005, from http://ifets.ieee.org/periodical/vol_1_98/pincas.html

Pratt, D. D. (2002). Good teaching: One size fits all. In J. Ross-Gordon (Ed.), *An up-date on teaching theory*. San Francisco: Jossey-Bass.

Pratt, D. D. & Associates (1998). *Five perspectives on teaching in adult and higher education*. Malabar, FL: Krieger.

Riddle, M. D., Pearce, J. M., & Nott, M. W. (1997). *Re-examining "interactive multimedia" in tertiary science teaching*. Paper presented in ASCILITE.

Saba, F. (2003). Distance education theory, methodology, and epistemology: A pragmatic paradigm. In M. G. Moore & W. G. Anderson (Eds.), *Handbook of distance education* (pp. 3-20). Mahwah, NJ: Lawrence Erlbaum Associates.

Wu, D., & Hiltz, S. R. (2003, August 4-6). Online discussions and perceived learning. *Proceedings of the 9th Americas Conference on Information Systems* (pp. 687-696). Tampa, Florida. Retrieved January 5, 2005, from http://www.alnresearch.org/Data_Files/articles/full_text/wu_Hiltz(2003).pdf

Zemsky, R., & Massy, W. (2004). *Thwarted innovation. What happened to e-learning and why*. The Learning Alliance at the University of Pennsylvania. Retrieved January 5, 2005, from http://www.irhe.upenn.edu/WeatherStation.html

Chapter XV

Using Problem-Based Learning in Online Courses: A New Hope?[1]

Richard F. Kenny, Athabasca University, Canada

Abstract

In this chapter, I argue that instructional designers must use research and theory to guide them to new and justified instructional practices when designing e-learning. I introduce a well-established pedagogy, problem-based learning (PBL), in which complex, ill-structured problems serve as the context and stimulus for learning, and students work collaboratively to understand the problem and learn about the broader related concepts. I describe the structure of PBL and discuss Barrow's (1998) concept of "authentic" PBL. I then review the support for PBL in the research literature and describe its relationship to cognitive and constructivist learning theory. I conclude the chapter by demonstrating how authentic PBL can be applied to e-learning using supporting examples from an undergraduate online course in agriculture.

Introduction

Nichols and Anderson (2005, para. 12) make two important points about instructional design for e-learning:

1. E-learning pedagogies must be defensible, used with reference to proven educational practice and theory.
2. E-learning pedagogies are evolving. E-learning practice must make the most of new opportunities.

In designing e-learning, instructional designers must use research and theory to guide them to new and justified instructional practices. In this chapter, I examine the use in e-learning of a well-researched pedagogy, problem-based learning (PBL), in which complex, ill-structured problems serve as the context and stimulus for learning. PBL contrasts with traditional subject-based approaches where students are taught a body of knowledge and then asked to apply what they have learned to sample problems. Students work collaboratively to identify what they need to learn to understand the problem and learn about the broader concepts related to the problem. PBL, therefore, encourages active participation by immersing students in a situation, requiring them to define their own learning needs within broad goals set by faculty and search for the knowledge needed to approach the problem.

PBL was developed the 1960s and used most widely in medical education. However, it has also been employed in such fields, as nursing, dentistry, and agriculture (Barrows, 1996, 1998; Boud & Faletti, 1991; Savory & Duffy, 2001). Research on PBL has focused on comparing PBL methods to more traditional instruction (Albanese, 2000; Albanese & Mitchell, 1993; Colliver, 2000; Smits, Verbeek, & Buisonjé, 2002; Vernon & Blake, 1993), rather than on the specific learning processes occurring in students engaged in PBL (Norman & Schmidt, 1992) or on the applicability to an online, distance education context, although there has been some recent work on what has been termed distributed problem-based learning (dPBL) (e.g., Barrows, 2002; Björck, 2002; Lehtinen, 2002; Lopez-Ortiz & Lin, L., 2005; Lou, 2004; Oliver & Omari, 2001; Orrill, 2002; Ronteltap & Eurelings, 2002).

Before we can consider PBL as viable for use in e-learning, we need to understand what it is. Therefore, I will begin with criteria for "authentic" PBL developed by Howard Barrows (1986, 1998), originator of the method, and present an example of how PBL is typically structured in face-to-face instruction.

Second, we should consider whether PBL is defensible. Is there evidence to indicate that PBL can facilitate learning in face-to-face settings? I will next examine the extensive literature on the effectiveness of PBL and review what light current learning theory sheds on the question.

Finally, even if PBL is effective in face-to-face instruction, does that mean that it can be applied in e-learning? In the remainder of the chapter, I will consider how PBL might be structured in online learning, arguably the most widely used form of e-learning. How would an online PBL course be structured? I will conclude the chapter by describing an online course developed for the Faculty of Land and Food Systems at the University of British Columbia and discuss how the critical features of face-to-face PBL were achieved in this context.

Online Learning and E-Learning

Massy and Zemsky (2004) suggest that there are three ways to view e-learning:

1. E-learning as distance education;
2. E-learning as course management systems; and
3. E-learning as electronically mediated learning, providing interactive, but not necessarily remote, learning in a digital format.

If we accept Keegan's (1996) definition of distance education as the "quasi-permanent separation of the teacher and learner" (p. 50), then the third view subsumes the first two and includes distributed learning[2] and will, therefore, be accepted here. Moreover, since Kearsley (2005, p. xi) defines online education as the "use of networked computers to learn or teach," it can be seen as a subset of e-learning. This chapter, then, will focus specifically on online PBL as an exemplar of e-learning.

Is Your Instruction PBL?

Perhaps the most well known proponent of PBL is Howard Barrows, who pioneered its use at McMaster University in the 1960s in response to "the impoverished knowledge base that medical students accrued during their neurology clinical clerkships [residencies]" (Maudsley, 1999, p. 178). In response to an ever-evolving number of variations on PBL, Barrows (1998) defined "authentic" PBL to address several educational objectives:

1. Acquisition of deeply understood knowledge *integrated* from a variety of disciplines;
2. Development of effective clinical problem solving;
3. Development of self-directed learning;
4. Development of team and interpersonal skills; and
5. Development of a desire to continually learn.

To accomplish these goals, authentic PBL should meet several important criteria.

Problem-Based

PBL begins with the presentation of a real-life (authentic) problem as might be encountered by practitioners. These problems consist of descriptions of events that need explanation and provide limited information (Norman & Schmidt, 1992). In medical education, they describe patients presenting complaints supplemented with some critical symptoms. In such areas as nursing and agriculture, learners are presented with problematic situations relevant to those fields. In all cases, learners then generate hypotheses about the cause of the problem to determine the important facts in the case and develop a solution. Norman and Schmidt (1992) provide the following example of a medical PBL problem:

A 55-year-old woman lies crawling on the floor in obvious pain. The pain emerges in waves and extends from the right lumbar region to the right side of the groin and to the right leg. (p. 2)

In this case, students need to find an explanation of the source of the pain described, describe what physiological processes are occurring, and determine how it is extending to other areas of the body.

Problem-Solving

Authentic PBL supports the application of problem-solving skills required in clinical practice. The tutor facilitates the application and development of an effective problem-solving process.

Student-Centered

Students assume responsibility for their own learning and faculty act as facilitators. Teachers must avoid making students dependent on them for what they should learn and know (Barrows, 1998).

Self-Directed Learning

Authentic PBL develops research skills. Students need to learn how to get information when it is needed and will be current, as this is an essential skill for professional performance.

Reflection

Reflection takes place on completion of problem work and enhances transfer of learning to new problems. This is best accomplished through group discussions about what was learned with the problem, its essential elements, and how it relates to previously encountered problems (Barrows, 1998).

Is PBL an Effective Instructional Strategy?

A review of the literature on PBL in face-to-face instructional settings leads to mixed conclusions. Several meta-analyses have been conducted over the last 12 years examining the use of PBL in medical education. While comparison research on media effectiveness has led to decades of no significance difference results (Clark, 1983, 1994; Russell, 1999), these reviews have promise because they compare entire curricula using PBL or "traditional methods" over a period of several years.

Two early meta-analyses conducted are the most frequently cited as demonstrating that PBL is more effective than traditional methods of medical education (specifically lecture courses). Vernon and Blake (1993) found that PBL was superior with respect to students' clinical performance, but determined that PBL and traditional methods did not differ substantially on tests of factual knowledge. However, students taught using traditional methods did outperform their PBL counterparts on the US National Board of Medical Examiners (NMBE) Part 1 (basic science concepts) license exam. Albanese and Blake (1993) produced similar findings. Students of conventional curricula outperformed PBL students on measures of basic science (NMBE Pt. 1), but PBL students scored higher on clinical examinations (e.g., NMBE Pt. 2).

Two recent studies (Dochy, Segers, Van den Bossche, & Gijbels, 2003; Gijbels, Dochy, Van den Bossche, & Segers, 2005) produced similar overall results. Dochy et al. (2003) found a mild negative effect favoring traditional approaches for the assessment of student knowledge. However, these differences were encountered in first and second year of medical school and evened out in the last two years. PBL students gained slightly less knowledge but remembered more of it over time (retention); however, the results for skills development consistently favored the PBL curriculum.

Gijbels et al. (2005) examined the depth of student knowledge acquisition by applying Sugrue's (1995, as cited in Gijbels et al., 2005) integrated model of the cognitive components of problem solving. This model proposes that learners' knowledge structures consist of three levels: (a) understanding of concepts, (b) understanding of the principles linking concepts, and (c) understanding the links from concepts and principles to conditions and procedures for application. Results supported PBL at all three levels but showed that it had the most positive effects when the constructs were being assessed at the level of understanding principles that link concepts.

So, is PBL effective? There appears to be some evidence for its effect over time when used in whole curricula, but, given the mixed results, it is uncertain that it would make any difference in instruction of shorter duration.

Is PBL Supported by Learning Theory?

Experimental research studies and quantitative review methods may permit relatively strong statements of certainty about effectiveness, but these statements are typically quite broad, e.g., PBL facilitates the learning of clinical reasoning skills. Such conclusions tell little about the cognitive processes underlying learning in such contexts and how specific instructional strategies affect such processes. For instance, Barrows and other proponents of PBL have argued strongly that this instructional approach sets the conditions for effective and deep learning of both disciplinary knowledge and problem solving (e.g., Albanese, 2000; Barrows, 1998; Norman & Schmidt, 1992, 2000). Moreover, Barrows (1998) claimed that only authentic PBL could foster both the acquisition of a deeply understood knowledge *integrated* from a variety of disciplines and the development of effective clinical problem solving. Does theory and research on human learning provide support for these claims?

Problem-Based Learning and Cognitive Theory

Albanese (2000) contended that information processing theory provided the most robust theoretical support for PBL. Broadly, this theory has three main elements, all commonly stressed in PBL: (a) activation of prior knowledge, (b) encoding specificity, and (c) elaboration of knowledge.

- **Activation of prior knowledge:** Learners recall and use knowledge they already possess to understand and structure new material to be learned. PBL brainstorming, for example, can be used to trigger recall and prepare learners' cognitive structure for encoding the new material.

- **Encoding specificity:** The closer the situation where something is learned resembles that in which it will be applied, the more likely transfer of learning will occur. PBL problems focus on real-life situations and present situations commonly seen in practice.

- **Elaboration of knowledge:** Information is better understood and remembered if learners actively work with the material to be learned. Elaboration includes strategies like discussion, spatial mapping, teaching peers, and critiquing, all used in the PBL process.

Problem-Based Learning and Constructivist Theory

While cognitive theory supports PBL, theorists have found stronger connections with constructivist theory, which is currently in the ascendancy. Savory and Duffy (2001) consider PBL one of the best exemplars of a constructivist learning environment. In their view, constructivism can be captured with three primary propositions:

Table 1. A comparison of the characteristics of authentic PBL to constructivist instructional principles

Characteristics of Authentic PBL	Constructivist Instructional Principles
Problem-based	• Anchor all learning activities to a larger task or problem. • Design the task and learning environment to reflect the complexity of the practice environment. • Design an authentic task.
Problem-solving	• Encourage testing ideas against alternative views and alternative contexts. • Design the learning environment to support and challenge the learner's thinking.
Student-centered	• Support the learner in developing ownership for the overall problem or task
Self-directed learning	• Give the learner ownership of the process used to develop a solution.
Reflection	• Provide opportunity for reflection on both the content learned and the learning process.

1. Understanding is constructed individually through our interactions with the environment, and we can only test how much our individual understandings are compatible.

2. Cognitive conflict is the stimulus for learning and determines the organization and nature of what is learned.

3. Knowledge evolves through social negotiation and through the evaluation of individual understandings.

Savory and Duffy (2001) identified eight principles for design of a constructivist learning environment and argued that PBL exemplifies all eight. Table 1 compares Duffy and Savory's principles to Barrow's characteristics of authentic PBL.

What is PBL Like in an Online Learning Context?

Can the transition be made from the use of PBL in a face-to-face context to its application in online learning? What are the critical factors for the design of authentic online PBL? In the following section, I will overview the structure for an online course, Agro 260, AgroEcology, a PBL course taught in the Faculty of Land and Food Systems at the University of British Columbia, and assess each

Figure 1. Agro 260 Splash Page (Used with permission of the University of British Columbia Faculty of Land and Food Sciences)

online design feature in terms of both Barrows' characteristics for authentic PBL and Savory and Duffy's (2001) constructivist principles. This course was delivered using WebCT™ Campus Edition 3.8. The course homepage is shown in Figure 1.

Incomplete Case Studies

Barrows (1998) states that PBL must be *problem-based*, i.e., begin with the presentation of a real-life (authentic) problem stated as it might be encountered by practitioners. These problems describe sets of events that need explanation and provide only limited information. The course material in Agro 260 is introduced through four cases concerning the practice of agroecology: (a) grazing ecosystems, (b) organic vegetable production, (c) tree fruit agroecosystems, and (d) genetically modified organisms and rural communities. Students are asked to play the role of consultants to "clients" presented in the case, and the course assignments are structured as consulting reports. All case activities flow directly from these cases and meet Savory and Duffy's (2001) constructivist principle of anchoring all learning activities to a larger task or problem.

Each case consists of multiple rounds, each including several disclosures. These introduce the problem that students are asked to address (Figure 2) or else

Figure 2. Agro 260 Case 1 problem statement (Used with permission of the University of British Columbia Faculty of Land and Food Sciences)

provide more information (supplementary disclosures). In most cases, disclosures are made available as learners discuss the scenario and identify further information required. These case problems were carefully crafted to engage the students in the significant issues of the field and to ensure that they cover required content and, therefore, address Savory and Duffy's principles of authenticity and accurate reflection of the complexity of the practice environment.

Asynchronous Discussion Forums for Process

*A*uthentic PBL must be *student-centered* (Barrows, 1998). Students assume responsibility for their own learning and faculty act as facilitators. In Agro 260, each PBL group uses an asynchronous process and evaluation forum to review and discuss ground rules for collaboration as well as the overall process for conducting work within each working round. It provides an opportunity to define and critique the group process and to give individual feedback separate from the

Figure 3. Agro 260 discussion groups (Used with permission of the University of British Columbia Faculty of Land and Food Sciences)

content discussions in the working rounds discussion forum. Figure 3 shows the organization of the discussion groups. Each group member must make at least one contribution to this forum in the first two days of the case, when the ground rules are established. The forum remains open for the length of the case to allow group members and the tutor to raise concerns about how the group is working and how the case is proceeding. The use of process forums addresses Savory and Duffy's (2001) constructivist principle that PBL should support the learner in developing ownership for the overall problem or task.

Asynchronous Discussion Forums for Problem-Solving

Barrows (1998) stresses that authentic PBL problems support the application of *problem-solving* skills required in practice. The tutor facilitates the development of an effective problem-solving process. In Agro 260, each scenario is accompanied by general guidance and discussion questions (Figure 4) to help the group identify the problem, what the learners already know to help solve the problem, and what further information they will need. Discussion questions help

Figure 4. Agro 260 Case 1 discussion questions (Used with permission of the University of British Columbia Faculty of Land and Food Sciences)

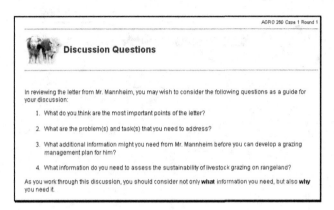

the group to identify *learning issues,* i.e., specific questions that group members will research.

The discussion of these questions, identification of learning issues, and reporting all take place in a separate (working) asynchronous forum. The working forum replaces face-to-face meetings where learners engage in such group processes as definition of the problem, development of working hypotheses, organization of the elements of the problem, agreement on research tasks, and reporting back on research completed. The tutor monitors the discussions and makes timely postings to encourage student participation, guides the discussion of controversial points, ensures that concepts are mastered, encourages depth of thinking, and verifies the quality of resources used. The working forum, then, is the application of Savory and Duffy's (2001) constructivist principles that the learning environment supports and challenges learners' thinking and encourages testing ideas against alternative views and contexts.

Provision of Print-Based and Online Resources

To use authentic PBL, a course must provide for *self-directed learning* (Barrows, 1998). By this, he means that students must learn to locate current information when needed, as this is essential for professional performance. In this course, most of the resources needed are provided on the course Web site or via links to other Web sites, especially governmental sites (Figure 5). Students are also required to complete readings for each case from a purchased course

Figure 5. Agro 260 Case 1 supplementary disclosure providing online resources (Used with permission of the University of British Columbia Faculty of Land and Food Sciences)

textbook. In this regard, Agro 260 falls short of authentic PBL, since students are neither required to do much independent research nor taught how to do it. The course does not, therefore, adhere to Savory and Duffy's (2001) constructivist principles, since the students are not given ownership of the research aspect of the process used to develop a solution.

However, in considering the transition to e-learning, we should be clear that this explicit provision of information was a choice of the course authors and not a restriction of the online learning context. Rather than supply resources directly, it is certainly feasible to require learners to seek their own as would an individual engaged in practice. In fact, online learning using a learning management system affords learners easy access to many electronic resources through research in libraries and other sources on the Internet, and while learners are not required to do the research themselves, Agro 260 makes abundant use of these sources of information.

Figure 6. Agro 260 Assignment 1 (Case 1) instructions (Used with permission of the University of British Columbia Faculty of Land and Food Sciences)

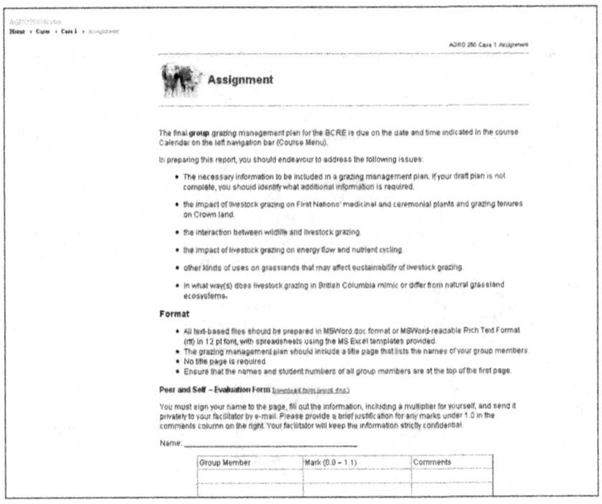

Assignments, Learning Objectives, and Evaluation Forums

Barrows' (1998) final characteristic of PBL is *reflection*, which should take place following completion of problem work to enhance transfer of learning to new problems. Barrows claims this is best accomplished through group discussions about what was learned with the problem, its essential elements, and how it relates to previously encountered problems.

Assignments. While the learning process in PBL is designed as a cooperative effort, student assessments in Agro 260 consist mainly of individual assignments and examinations. There is one group assignment in Case 1 (see Figure 6) requiring the collaborative effort of the group to develop a single submission. Otherwise, group members complete an individual assignments designed to address the problem(s) raised in the case after the PBL process has been completed. While the assignments are not based on group discussion, they do allow for reflection on the content in the case as per Savory and Duffy's (2001) constructivist principle that PBL provides opportunity for and supports reflection on both the content learned and the learning process.

Learning objectives. On the final day of each case, the learning objectives for the case are made available via a time-released case icon and inform the students what they were expected to learn from the case. The final and mid-term exams are based on the learning objectives from all four cases. As is the case for the assignments, the provision of learning outcomes affords an opportunity to reflect

Figure 7. Agro 260 Case 1 learning outcomes (Used with permission of the University of British Columbia Faculty of Land and Food Sciences)

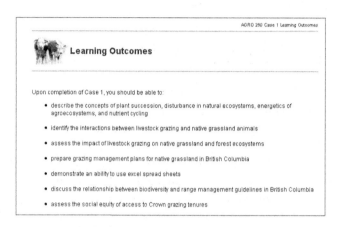

back on the content, but also on the PBL process itself in terms of what learning did or did not occur.

Process and evaluation forum. This forum remains open for the length of the case. In Agro 260, there is also an evaluation component of this forum that assesses both group process and individual participation. It involves self-evaluation, peer-evaluation, and facilitator-evaluation, as well as an assessment of how well each student thinks his or her group is working. Participation is rated on a pass-fail basis. No marks are assigned for participation per se, but if a student's involvement is not rated as satisfactory, he or she fails the course regardless of the other marks assigned. These processes provide ample opportunity for reflection at the end of the case and, again, address Savory and Duffy's (2001) principle to support reflection on the learning process.

What Should You Consider When Implementing Online PBL?

The preceding description of Agro 260 and discussion of how research and theory applies to its instructional design provides one clear example of how the transition can be made from the use of PBL in face-to-face contexts to its application in e-learning. Not only is it possible to make the transition, but online PBL can provide opportunities that are more difficult to provide or unavailable in face-to-face contexts. However, online PBL can lead to some distinct challenges as well. I conclude this chapter with a brief discussion of some of the opportunities and challenges one faces in taking PBL online.

Opportunities Provided by Online PBL

Enriched authentic problem situations. In certain respects, the affordances of online and other computer-based environments are ideally suited to enhance the perception of authenticity of the problem situations. Video, audio, and photographs can be easily and efficiently delivered online and used to add realism to the presentation. For instance, in Agro 260, Case 1, learners develop a grazing plan for a novice rancher with property in the British Columbia interior. The client could have been introduced to the students in a video presentation to make the scenario seem less contrived and to foster interest in the problem. In terms of Keller's (1987a, as cited in Driscoll, 2005) ARCS model of motivational design, this can serve to gain attention to the problem and to enhance the relevance of the situation. In addition, video and photographs could have been provided to show the property in question in order to clarify the extent of the problem situation and to make the situation more concrete for learners, that is, in cognitive theory terms, to enhance activation of prior knowledge and encoding specificity.

However, when striving for increased realism, designers must avoid adding too much detail in the presentation of the problem statement since, in authentic PBL, self-directed learning is critical. Students need to learn to retrieve information when needed, as this is an essential skill for professional performance. Designers should also remember that the increased use of media in online settings may restrict access to learning. The use of streaming audio and video can increase computer technology and connectivity requirements (e.g., cable or DSL Internet access rather than modem connection), which can make the instruction more costly or even inaccessible for those in remote locations.

Efficient, flexible control over the PBL process. Online learning environments also afford immediacy and flexible control over the timing of instructional delivery. In face-to-face PBL, engagement in the PBL process is restricted to scheduled classes or to times when group members can arrange additional meetings. Subject to some of the challenges considered below, an online PBL process can be structured to proceed more continuously over the days and weeks of the course and to be available at times most convenient to the group members. Further, online learning affords the automatic time release of additional information in the form of controlled disclosures. In Agro 260, each case guides learners through multiple rounds or stages of the problem. Each round provides supplementary information when learners are prepared to (or advised to) identify further information that they require. Again, a caveat is that the PBL process not be so rigidly structured that it is totally instructor-centered and students are not engaged in a self-directed learning process.

Efficient provision of learning resources. Online learning environments can provide convenient and timely access to unlimited electronic resources in various formats. Learners can be supplied with materials in the environment itself or can be provided facilities for online searches. Such resources can greatly enhance learners' abilities to effectively and efficiently search for and locate information required to help solve the problem at hand. In Agro 260, most of the resources students need are provided in the course textbook, on the course Web site, or via links to other Web sites. The advantage for learners is that the needed resources are readily available and they are, therefore, not required to expend much time searching for needed information.

Again, the trade-off is that the course authors may have done too much of the research for the learners and undermined the development of the self-directed learning skills that PBL is supposed to foster. In providing learners with such a convenient and rich set of resources, Agro 260 may be too instructor-centered, since students are neither required to do much independent research nor taught how to do it.

Challenges Inherent in Online PBL

Engaging in PBL process using asynchronous tools. The PBL process in an asynchronous environment is much slower and less efficient than face-to-face discussion. While discussion in live classes is more or less instantaneous, in online PBL, learners have to access and read forum postings, compose and type in their reply, and then wait for an undetermined period of time for a reply. While asynchronous responses can be nearly immediate if learners log on to the course Web site at the same time, at other times, fellow students may take days to reply, and such time delays can negatively affect motivation to engage in the task at hand as well as delay the group's progress.

However, asynchronous conferencing, as used in Agro 260, has some potential advantages over face-to-face discussion. First, it is flexible. Within limits, learners can engage in the process on their own schedule. Second, it may afford more time for learners to consider and support their contributions than they would have in live discussion and, therefore, enable them to engage in more thoughtful, in-depth interactions. Third, in asynchronous (network-based) environments, all interactions are retained and visible to the group members and can serve as a joint point of reference to facilitate understanding during follow-up discussion (Lehtinen, 2002). In addition, such a record makes visible milestones in the group process when pivotal decisions occur.

Interestingly, Ronteltap and Eurelings (2002), in a study of dPBL (combined live and online study), noted that PBL students in face-to-face contexts expressed the need for more time for communication, as the opportunity to explain or discuss their work provided them with renewed motivation. The addition of asynchronous tools, available permanently and for unlimited use, helped to remove restrictions to the communication process.

Engaging in PBL process using synchronous tools. Online PBL, however, is not limited to asynchronous tools. Audio-conferencing software and chat tools allow for synchronous (real time) audio conversation and document-sharing and share many of the advantages of face-to-face PBL sessions. They afford the speed of interaction and efficiency of real time verbal discussions and more readily permit efficient participation in such learning processes as brainstorming and group development of hypotheses. They even provide one advantage over live discussions in providing for the automatic recording of those discussions for later review.

Nevertheless, synchronous online interactions also have disadvantages. Participants lack the visual cues of face-to-face encounters and may find the interactions more stilted and impersonal. Such tools also depend on the quality of the technology available and technical difficulties can easily impact such sessions. In addition, their use with the use of audio and visual materials may affect learner access to learning by increasing technology requirements. Finally, synchronous sessions require participants to be online at the same time. This may lead to difficulties arranging sessions when learners reside in different countries and time zones.

One part of the online PBL process in which synchronous tools may be especially effective is fostering group reflection. Barrows (1998) advocates reflection following the completion of problem work to enhance transfer of learning to new problems and claims this is best accomplished through group discussions. In Agro 260, this process is accomplished using asynchronous conferencing and is the one part of the PBL process in which there is generally the lowest participation. Students are required to contribute to the PBL discussions and research to pass the course and are assigned marks on the basis of assignments and exams. The reflection process, on the other hand, mainly consists of the tutor's feedback at the end of the case on how well the group (and individuals) engaged in the PBL process, and there is no requirement that students reply. This is one activity that might be enhanced by a synchronous audio post conference in which learners are required to participate and where the efficiency of verbal communication might afford more thorough reflection as stipulated by authentic PBL.

Should You Take the Plunge?

While various learning tools can support the productivity of PBL in an online setting, technical capability is not the critical issue in making the transition from its use in face-to-face learning contexts. Most important is how such tools are used. The learning behavior of the students involved in the process is influenced by much more than the functionality of the technology (Ronteltap & Eurelings, 2002). Many other factors come into play in small group tutorial learning such as PBL and apply equally to live and online instructional situations. These factors include careful selection and design of the problems presented to students (Barrows, 1998), fostering of strong teacher presence via active influence of the tutor on group process (Anderson, Rourke, Garrison, & Archer, 2001), consideration of the cognitive processes elicited by small-group discussion (Schmidt & Moust, 2002), and level of cognitive activity engendered in the learners (Ronteltap & Eurelings, 2002). To effect a full transition of PBL to e-learning, you need to look beyond the lure of the technology and keep in mind that however it is delivered, PBL is first and foremost a specific pedagogy, and you must be sure that you take into account the influence of these factors in the process.

Acknowledgment

I wish to thank Katie Nolan, instructor for Agro 260, and the Faculty of Land and Food Systems at the University of British Columbia for permission to use their course as an example in this chapter.

References

Albanese, M. A. (2000). Problem-based learning: Why curricula are likely to show little effect on knowledge and clinical skills. *Medical Education, 34,* 729-738.

Albanese, M. A., & Mitchell, S. (1993). Problem-based learning: A review of the literature on its outcomes and implementation issues. *Academic Medicine, 68*(1), 68-81.

Anderson, T., Rourke, L., Garrison, D. R., Archer, W. (2000). Assessing teaching presence in a computer conference environment. *Journal of Asynchronous Learning Networks, 5*(2). Retrieved November 16, 2005, from http://www.aln.org/publications/jaln/v5n2/v5n2_anderson.asp

Barrows, H. S. (1986). A taxonomy of problem-based learning methods. *Medical Education, 20,* 481-186.

Barrows, H. S. (1996). Problem-based learning in medicine and beyond: A brief overview. *New Directions for Teaching and Learning, 68,* 3-12.

Barrows, H. S. (1998). The essentials of problem-based learning. *Journal of Dental Education, 62*(9), 630-633.

Barrows, H. S. (2002). Is it truly possible to have such a thing as dPBL? *Distance Education, 23*(1), 119-122.

Björck, U. (2002). Distributed problem-based learning in social economy: Key issues in students' mastery of a structured method for education. *Distance Education, 23*(1), 85-103.

Boud, D., & Faletti, G. (1991). *The challenge of problem-based learning.* London: Kogan Page.

Clark, R. E. (1983). Reconsidering research on learning from media. *Review of Educational Research, 53*(4), 445-459.

Clark, R. E. (1994). Media will never influence learning. *Educational Technology, Research and Development, 42*(2), 21-29.

Colliver, J. A. (2000). Effectiveness of problem-based learning curricula: Research and theory. *Academic Medicine, 75*(3), 259-266.

Dede, C. (1996). Emerging technologies and distributed learning. *American Journal of Distance Education 10*(2), 4-36.

Dochy, F., Segers, M., Van den Bossche, P., & Gijbels, D. (2003). Effects of problem-based learning: A meta-analysis. *Learning and Instruction, 13,* 533-568.

Driscoll, M. P. (2005). *Psychology of learning for instruction* (3rd ed.). Boston: Pearson Education.

Gijbels, D., Dochy, F., Van den Bossche, P., & Segers, M. (2005). Effects of problem-based learning: A meta-analysis from the angle of assessment. *Review of Educational Research, 75*(1), 27-61.

Kearsley, G. (2005). *Online learning: Personal reflections on the transformation of education.* Englewood Cliffs, NJ: Educational Technology Publications.

Keegan, D. (1996). *Foundations of distance education* (3rd ed.). London: Routledge.

Lehtinen, E. (2002.). Developing models for distributed problem-based learning: Theoretical and methodological reflection. *Distance Education, 23*(1), 109-117.

Lopez-Ortiz, B. I., & Lin, L. (2005). What makes an online group project work? Students' perceptions before and after an online collaborative problem/project-based learning (PBL) experience. *International Journal of Instructional Technology and Distance Learning, 2*(2). Retrieved July 7, 2005, from http://www.itdl.org/Journal/Feb_05/article04.htm

Lou, Y. (2004). Learning to solve complex problems through between-group collaboration in project-based online courses. *Distance Education, 25*(1), 49-66.

Massy, R., & Zemsky, W. F. (2004). *Thwarted innovation: What happened to e-learning and why?* West Chester: The University of Pennsylvania, Report of the Learning Alliance for Higher Education.

Maudsley, G. (1999). Do we all mean the same thing by "problem-based learning?" A review of the concepts and a formulation of the ground rules. *Academic Medicine, 74*, 178-185.

Nichols, M., & Anderson, B. (2005). *Strategic e-learning implementation.* Discussion paper of the International Forum of Educational Technology & Society. Retrieved July 7, 2005, from http://ifets.ieee.org/discussions/discuss_july2005.html

Norman, G. R., & Schmidt, H. G. (1992). The psychological basis of problem-based learning: A review of the evidence. *Academic Medicine, 67*, 557-565.

Norman, G. R., & Schmidt, H. G. (2000). The effectiveness of problem-based learning curricula: Theory, practice and paper darts. *Medical Education, 34*, 721-728.

Oliver, R., & Omari, A. (2001). Student responses to collaborating and learning in a Web-based environment. *Journal of Computer-Assisted Learning, 17*, 34-47.

Orrill, C. H. (2002.). Supporting online PBL: Design considerations for supporting distributed problem-solving. *Distance Education, 23*(1), 43-57.

Ronteltap, F., & Eurelings, A. (2002). Activity and interaction of students in an electronic learning environment for problem-based learning. *Distance Education, 23*(1), 11-22.

Russell, T. (1999). *The no significant difference phenomenon: A comparative research annotated bibliography on technology for distance education.* Montgomery, AL: The International Distance Education Certification Center.

Savory, J. R., & Duffy, T. M. (2001). *Problem based learning: An instructional model and its constructivist framework* (Tech. Rep. No. 16-01). Indiana University, Center for Research on Learning and Technology.

Schmidt, H. G., & Moust, J. O. S. (2002). Factors affecting small-group tutorial learning: A review of the research. In D. Evensen & C. F. Hmelo (Eds.), *Problem-based learning* (pp. 19-51). Mahwah, NJ: Lawrence Erlbaum Associates.

Smits, P. B. A., Verbeek, J. H. A. M., & de Buisonjé, C. D. (2002). Problem-based learning in continuing medical education: A review of controlled evaluation studies. *British Medical Journal, 324*, 153-156.

Vernon, D. A., & Blake, R. L. (1993). Does problem-based learning work? A meta-analysis of evaluative research. *Academic Medicine, 68*(7), 550-563.

Endnotes

[1] With apologies to Star Wars fans everywhere! I considered the title, "Online Problem-based Learning: a New Hope or the Empire Strikes Back?"—but that was too tacky...

[2] Dede (1996, p. 6) defines distributed learning as "educational activities orchestrated via information technology across classrooms, workplaces, homes, and community settings and based on a mixture of presentational and 'constructivist' pedagogies."

Section III

Instructional Design and Technology Issues

Chapter XVI

Fast Prototyping as a Communication Catalyst for E-Learning Design

Luca Botturi, University of Lugano, Switzerland

Lorenzo Cantoni, University of Lugano, Switzerland

Benedetto Lepori, University of Lugano, Switzerland

Stefano Tardini, University of Lugano, Switzerland

Abstract

This chapter proposes a renewed perspective on a known project management model, fast prototyping, which was adapted for the specific issues of e-learning development. Based on extensive experience with large e-learning projects, we argue that this model has a positive impact on e-learning project team communication, and that it provides a good basis for effective management of the design and development process, with specific stress on human-factor management. The chapter stems from the experience gained at the eLab (eLearning laboratory—www.elearninglab.org), a lab *run jointly by the Università della Svizzera italiana (USI—University of Lugano) and the Scuola Universitaria Professionale della Svizzera Italiana (SUPSI—University of Applied Sciences of Southern Switzerland) in Switzerland. It contains three case studies of different applications of the fast prototyping model and has a strongly practical focus.*

Introduction: Some Issues in Large E-Learning Projects

The transition to e-learning in higher education institutions, at course, program, or institutional level, always requires a radical change in the organization. This means that instructors, teaching assistants, and subject matter experts are faced with a new situation in which many of the assumptions on which they previously relied are brought into discussion. Moreover, they need to work in teams with other professionals—graphic designers, Web programmers, instructional designers, etc.—who might not share their professional language and understanding of the topic and of teaching and learning as such (Botturi, 2006). In many cases, the team members are novices in the field of e-learning and do not have sound design practices or established routines for their tasks; consequently, the team cannot rely on common ground for mutual understanding (Clark, 1996).

From the point of view of the teaching staff, we should consider at least two main layers: (a) knowledge/skills and (b) the attitudes required to implement effective and efficient e-learning experiences. In the first layer, the main issues are concerned with a radical change in the teaching development context, moving from a craftsmanship model—the teacher looking after the whole teaching process, from conception to delivery, from materials development to evaluation—to an industrial model, where many different people, with different professional backgrounds, are to collaborate in order to design and implement the e-learning experience (Bates & Poole, 2003). In the second layer, an instance of the well-known process of diffusion of innovation is found: People fear innovation and resist it unless positive conditions occur (Rogers, 1995).

The design model, which embodies the overall approach to e-learning, plays a key role in tackling these issues. This chapter addresses them in the context of large e-learning projects where a fast prototyping model has been adopted, stressing two areas of intervention in the two layers.

1. The first area is collaboration in working groups, where people with different backgrounds and expectations are to collaborate, in order to

develop e-learning applications. In fact, the design, development, and delivery of an e-learning course or program is a team activity that requires a high level of coordination and cooperation, as well as integration in the organization's culture (Engwall, 2003). The people who take part in the process should feel at ease if they are to express real commitment to the project and establish trust in each other. This is particularly true for teachers and instructors who play the key role in an online course, as they are mainly responsible for content production and course delivery.

2. In the second layer, fast prototyping provides e-learning projects with the attribute of *trialability*, so important in fostering the adoption of innovations. Trainers not accustomed to the e-learning field are offered a concrete experience of what courseware could be; this, in turn, helps them leave aside prejudices and negative attitudes.

The following section will provide some background about the management of e-learning projects and the institutional context of the Swiss Virtual Campus (SVC), from which our case studies are drawn. We will then introduce some reference to the design models from instructional design (ID) research and then move on to present the eLab fast prototyping model, which will be described and discussed through three case studies.

Background

Institutional Context

This chapter mainly focuses on the introduction of information and communication technologies in traditional campus-based universities; namely, we will deal with the projects promoted by the Swiss Virtual Campus (SVC, www.virtualcampus.ch) program to introduce e-learning in Swiss higher education institutions (Lepori & Succi, 2003). The SVC program understands *e-learning* as defined by the Commission of the European Community: "the use of new multimedia technologies and the Internet to improve the quality of learning by facilitating access to resources and services as well as remote exchanges and collaboration" (CEC, 2001). This definition includes all e-learning models that could be situated on the continuum between fully face-to-face teaching and fully distance education through the Internet (Bates, 1999).

SVC projects bring together a network of higher education institutions for the development of shared e-learning resources. Project team members usually speak different languages and have a different background and education; moreover, for most of them, it is their first experience in e-learning. These situations are characterized by the lack of established routines and of common ground, so that developing a shared understanding and setting clear goals is often an issue.

There is a growing body of literature concerning the adoption of e-learning in European universities showing a consistent pattern (e.g., Collis & Van der Wende, 2002; Lepori & Succi, 2004; Van der Wende & van der Ven, 2003). In most cases e-learning is introduced in a very decentralized way and as an instrument to improve existing face-to-face activities rather than to radically transform them (Collis & Van der Wende, 2002); moreover, only in some cases does the introduction of technologies lead to the creation of new educational offerings and of specialized subunits—e-learning is generally embedded into the existing curricula and departments (Lepori, Cantoni, & Succi, 2003).

There are some features here that are not easily compatible with conventional ID models and practice, especially in e-learning (Lepori & Perret, 2004):

1. E-learning is rarely implemented as stand-alone, online courses, but more often as units within existing face-to-face activities; this requires considerable integration of course production and delivery.

2. E-learning is embedded in a context where competencies and attitudes toward technology are very diverse, ranging from early adopters to a significant share of innovation-averse people (Rogers, 1995; Surry & Farquhar, 1997); thus, we cannot assume from the beginning that all people involved in a project have sufficient competencies in educational technologies, nor that they share the same vision concerning their adoption and usefulness. Communication and sharing views is thus a central issue.

3. The academic culture traditionally attributes a central role to the professor, not only in deciding the main guidelines for course content, but also in managing and fine-tuning it during the delivery. A work division between the production of contents (by experts of the subject), their technical implementation, and their delivery (possibly with tutoring) is not compatible with this culture. It is thus necessary to involve professors in all development phases, but this makes project management more difficult, since academic hierarchies interfere with it.

4. University education is far from being homogeneous in aspects like the level of standardization of contents, the type of delivery, the level of students, etc. Thus, each e-learning application has to be tuned to its specific context.

Projects in the first phase of the SVC program, launched in 1999, were seriously beset by these issues. The SVC financed the development of online courses aimed at university students and produced by large consortia of Swiss universities. The underlying logic was to gather the contributions of different professors on the same subjects to produce high-quality courses to be used throughout Switzerland, thus achieving economies of scale. An accompanying study showed that this model—largely inspired by the production of online courses in distance universities—was in most cases at odds with higher education and academic culture (Lepori & Perret, 2004). As a result, development was delayed, most projects did not complete all the units foreseen, and a lot of energy was spent in experimenting and in discussing technical issues. The average cost per project was very high (for a single university course the costs in many cases exceeded US $1 million). Also, project management proved to be difficult because of the size of the projects and academic conflicts, while project coordinators were mostly relegated to an executive role. We could say that the failure of the model proposed by the SVC led most projects to go back to more traditional academic models, well-suited for research but not for e-learning course development.

During the preparation of the second phase of the SVC (CUS, 2002), the eLab, the e-learning support centre of the Università della Svizzera italiana (USI—University of Lugano) and of the Scuola Universitaria Professionale della Svizzera Italiana (SUPSI – University of Applied Sciences of Southern Switzerland) developed a critical reflection on possible development models for e-learning courses in traditional universities. Management science has proved that the best management model for a project depends to a large extent on two elements: (a) the kind of application to be developed and (b) the specific institutional context, considering not only organizational issues and resources, but also the organizational culture and the relationship with institutional strategies (Engwall, 2003). The SVC experience thus far and an extensive body of empirical research (Lepori & Rezzonico, 2003; Lepori & Succi, 2003) showed that most classic ID models rely on assumptions which are, to a large extent, incompatible with the mainstream academic culture in traditional campus-based universities, and in many cases the success of e-learning projects was hindered by these incompatibilities.

Our effort therefore concentrated on developing a different approach: The goal was to provide simple guidelines that could fit into the existing cultural frameworks and enhance communication in our teams. This model was included in the e-learning management manual (Lepori, Cantoni, & Rezzonico, 2005), which was distributed to all new SVC projects started in summer 2004.

In order to set the context for the presentation of the model, the next section will introduce some current ID models and clarify some of their assumptions in relation to the context of SVC projects and of the introduction of e-learning in traditional higher education institutions.

ID Models and their Assumptions

The tradition of ID has collected a huge number of models that guide the design and development processes of instructional units (Andrews & Godson, 1995). Each model emphasizes a peculiar aspect of the process, striving to achieve prescriptive value without overlooking the eclectic (and often hectic) reality of practice.

Classic ID models, starting from ADDIE up to ASSURE (Heinich, Molenda & Russel, 1993) and the Dick, Carey, and Carey model (2001, see Figure 1), take a linear perspective: they describe the ID process as a structured and orderly step-by-step activity, characterized by a progressive advancement through analysis, design, development, implementation, and evaluation; the process also includes a cycle of revision for each edition or delivery of the training.

Such models, which have behaviorist roots and were mainly developed in the military context, still represent the foundations of ID as a discipline and have provided inspiration for many projects. They offer clear guidance, emphasize the intrinsic logic of design, and rely on two main assumptions:

1. **The assumption of quality information:** The designer can work on complete information (from the analysis phase), and the designer can rely

Figure 1. The Dick, Carey, and Carey model (Adapted from Dick, Carey, & Carey, 2001)

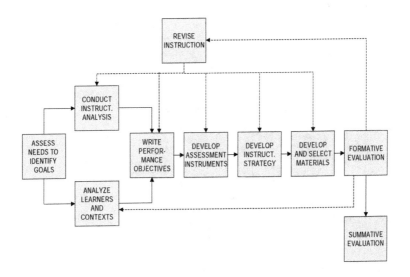

on the fact that the instructional context is stable (i.e., there are no unforeseen events).

2. **The assumption of expertise:** The designer can master the process and will not make errors, and all the team members and stakeholders will give their contributions as required, at the right moment and in a clear and unambiguous manner.

In the history of ID, a specific emphasis in the education of instructional designers was derived from the second assumption—it was more process-oriented and tool-oriented than communication-oriented.

Experience such as that presented in the analysis of SVC projects has shown that these assumptions do not always hold in the academic setting. Often stakeholders, professors, and instructors cannot express precise requirements, and it can happen that the analysis overlooks some relevant details; also the actors in the ID process may make errors. These are exactly the pitfalls that we identified for e-learning design, a setting in which technologies bring more complexity and uncertainty.

More recent works in ID have proposed a heuristic approach—less prescriptive and more practice-oriented. Morrison, Ross, and Kemp (2003, see Figure 2) proposed a model that includes all the *steps* proposed by Dick, Carey, and Carey (2001) as *elements* in a progressive discovery model: "The elements are not connected with lines or arrows. Connections could indicate a sequence, linear order. The intent is to convey flexibility, yet some order in the way the nine

Figure 2. The oval model (Taken from Morrison, Ross, & Kemp, 2003)

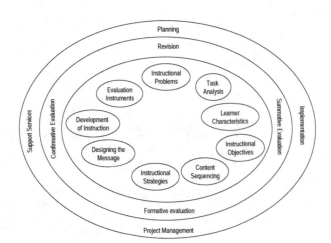

elements may be used. Also some instances may not require treating all nine elements" (p. 8). The designer will decide which ones are relevant and which do not require particular consideration. This provides play for adapting to new technological situations in the e-learning domain.

The assumption behind this model is that the designer has strong meta-cognitive skills: She or he can shape and re-shape the process according to the situation. From a relational point of view, the designer also needs strong leadership skills, as he or she has to steer the design and development process with a good deal of improvisation, without relying on the solid guidance provided by linear models.

The R2D2 model (Willis, 1995) takes a similar perspective, borrowing a strong emphasis on communication and negotiation from constructivism and placing itself at the opposite ideal end of linear models. R2D2 has four overarching principles:

1. **Recursion:** The steps/elements are revisited at different times, and decisions can be made anew, shaping a spiral-like flow.

2. **Reflection:** Is contrasted with the linear design rationality of linear models: According to Willis (Colón, Taylor, & Willis, 2000) "(r)eflective design places less faith in preset rules and instead emphasizes the need... to thoughtfully seek and consider feedback and ideas from many sources."

3. **Non-linearity:** R2D2 does not present a set of steps, but rather one of focal points, close to the idea of elements in Morrison, Ross, and Kemp (2003, see previous).

4. **Participatory design:** The whole idea behind this model is that the ID process is not only the designer's job, but rather team work, in which different people collaborate. Communication and negotiation acquire a primary role here.

The drawback of this model is that much is left to interaction, and very little guidance is provided for complex or problematic situations. Namely, when few recognized common practices exist, the discussion may expand without converging. On the other hand, R2D2 and other constructivist models are focused on the fact that instruction lives in a specific context, and its conception, design, and development should be strongly rooted in it. The community dimension is here taken as the focal point, and the model aims at providing a controlled space for discussion, maximizing sharing and mutual understanding in the design team, helping it develop a common background, and hence enabling it to become—at least to a certain extent—a community of practice (Cantoni & Piccini, 2004; Wenger, 1998; Wenger, McDermott, & Snyder, 2002).

The eLab fast prototyping model tries to merge the three perspectives (linear, heuristic, and constructivist) by providing a method organized into brief steps for the development of a "physical" focus of discussion—namely, a prototype. Its major aim is to have a development model soft enough to adapt to each project, but at the same time sufficiently structured to keep development time and costs reasonable. This was necessary also because the budget of the second series of SVC projects was significantly reduced.

Fast Prototyping: The eLab Model

The Model

The eLab chose to tackle these issues in e-learning projects in higher education with a well-shaped and sound prototype-based design and development model. The originality of the approach lies in considering fast prototyping as a communication catalyst: The main advantage of a fast prototyping model is to enhance discussion in the team in a focused way by concentrating on facts and results and not on theories or prejudices about learning technologies. Enhanced and focused communication fosters the development of mutual understanding among the different professionals involved in the project and the creation of trust—two important conditions for a successful development. The goals for which the eLab model was developed are:

1. To make the design and development process flexible with respect to ideas emerging from the progressive understanding of the project among team members, by providing moments in which new inputs can be taken into account.

2. To make the design and development process adaptable to new needs emerging from tests and results, given that the use scenario is varied (multiple institutions), partly undefined (e.g., changes in curricula because of higher education reforms), and not available in detail at the outset of the project.

3. To allow teachers, instructors, and subject matter experts to focus on the teaching and learning activities and not on the technologies themselves, fostering trialability.

4. To enhance communication with external partners.

Figure 3. eLab adapted fast prototyping model

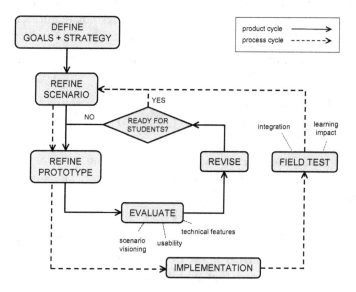

The adapted fast prototyping model for e-learning is structured in two cycles: (a) the inner or *product cycle* and (b) the outer or *process cycle* (Figure 3).

The design and development process starts with the identification of high-level learning goals and of a specific strategy (e.g., teaching level B1 English with a game-based strategy or teaching the basics about color perception with a case-based approach). This is a team effort, often accomplished in writing the project proposal.

These elements are embedded in a scenario, a narrative and semi-formal description of the instruction, which sets some parameters, namely target students, communication flow and support, organization of the schedule in terms of time allocation and as a blend of face-to-face and distance learning activities, and the use of multimedia and interactive technologies. The scenario is therefore an informal definition of the instructional and technical requirements for the project. It is paramount that the scenario is agreed upon by all team members, as it serves as leverage for the evaluation and revision of the prototype. The development of a shared scenario, guided by the instructional designer, is in itself an important activity for the project: By discussing the project in concrete terms team members are able to see the final product through students' eyes.

The product cycle. The scenario is the starting point for the product cycle, which starts with prototype development and is aimed at developing a product that fits the scenario. By *prototype* we mean structured courseware, with real content, already implemented as if it were to be used in a real setting. A prototype often includes only a part of the content, or leaves out some features, but the main point is that it is actually usable in the related scenario.

The project team then internally evaluates the prototype in two ways:

1.   The eLab staff evaluates it with standard procedures that assess its technical features and usability and produces a list of improvements that are proposed to the team.

2.   Other non-technical team members try out the prototype's fit to the scenario description in a focus group in which they envision its use in the scenario they developed.

This double revision process provides full-spectrum feedback and makes project members move one step further in the development of a shared understanding. While developing the scenario they merely described a wish-situation; now, the prototype has them evaluate single features (e.g., navigation structures, exercise feedback, etc.) and make decisions. Moreover, this discussion helps the designers gain insight into the non-technical partners' understanding of the training.

After the evaluation, the prototype is consequently revised, and a decision is made as to whether it is ready for real testing. If it is not, another product cycle is performed, starting from a refinement of the scenario according to the new possibilities explored during evaluation; if it is, the process moves onto the process cycle. When this occurs greatly depends on the single project, as discussed in the following case studies.

The process cycle. The process cycle is basically a field test. Its first step is the refinement of the scenario (a virtual description) into the description of an actual use setting: one single institution, a specific group of students, in what type of technical facilities, etc. The prototype is accordingly revised and adapted and then implemented and integrated into the course. The testing is constantly monitored, and the final evaluation of the process cycle happens in three steps: (a) with a standard questionnaire delivered to the students, which measures Kirkpatrick Levels 1-3 (satisfaction, learning, transfer; cf. Kirkpatrick, 1998); (b) through analyzing the performance of students in the course exam or assessment; and (c) with a focus group that collects feedback from the instructors.

The evaluation provides new input for the project team, which can decide to make revisions and perform another test, to conclude the implementation and produce the final courseware, or if the real situation has proved very different from the scenario, to even switch back for another product cycle.

The following case studies show the impact of this model in three SVC projects supported by the eLab. Case studies will be analyzed with respect to the type of e-learning application development, the subject matter, the institutional partners and team members, the budget, and the expected results.

EAD: Ecology in Architectural Design

The goal of this project was to develop a blended learning course on the integration of ecological issues into architectural design, both at the level of buildings and of human landscape. The project leader was the Accademia di Architettura of the USI (Academy of Architecture). The project started in July 2004 and immediately adopted a fast prototyping model. At the beginning of September 2004, the first prototype module (*Building—Climate*) had already been developed by the project leaders. Moving from the product to the process cycle, the module was then tested with more than 100 USI bachelor students in the winter semester 2004 (October 2004-February 2005). At the same time as the test phase, the module was evaluated and discussed by all other project partners.

In the case of EAD, the rapid development of the prototype module aimed to rapidly create a concrete basis for communications about the course, thus avoiding long and useless discussions focused only on abstract ideas about e-learning. By being shown an example of how the modules could be designed and could appear, all the people involved in the project, even those who were not experts in e-learning, could get a concrete idea of the course. In fact interesting discussions soon arose among project partners, in particular about the issues of information design and of graphics and layout. The emergence of these discussions also shows one of the possible drawbacks of catalyzing communications through fast prototyping: the risk of focusing on specific details and losing touch with higher-priority issues, thus creating a situation of being unable to "see the wood for the trees" (Cantoni & Piccini, 2004). In the EAD project team, for instance, the issue of graphics and layout catalyzed most of the discussion, partly because of the scientific background of the team members. This fact can be analyzed from two opposite perspectives: On one hand, it can be seen as a drawback in that, as already mentioned, focusing the discussion on details does not allow the overall picture to be seen, thus hindering discussion and decisions about more important issues; on the other, it can be turned into an advantage as well, in that the most important decisions can be made by the experts without long discussions. Of course, the responsibility for leading the discussion onto relevant issues and taking advantage also of discussions about details is up to the project manager.

However, on the basis of these discussions and of the results of the test phase, the prototype module of the EAD course was then refined and other modules developed according to a template that was approved by all partners. In June 2005, exactly halfway through the project schedule, 8 modules out of 12 had been developed and were ready to be delivered to students for a second test phase. Thus, half of the whole project time could be spent on implementing the last modules and testing and refining the whole course.

Color

The goal of this project was to develop a set of content, resources, and exercises both on the fundamentals of color (physics, perception, processes) and on color applications in different domains of the arts and visual communication. The project leader was the Dipartimento Ambiente, Costruzione e Design of SUPSI (Department of Environment, Construction and Design). The prototype of the first module (*History of color*) was developed in the first two months by the project leader and presented during a project meeting in November 2004.

The prototype immediately acted as a fuse in a powder keg. Facing a concrete object, the project partners made their thoughts clear and hidden misunderstandings emerged at once: Would the online resources be tailored to a specific partner's needs, or would they be more general-purpose? Would they foster offline activities, such as lab experience, or would the project invest in creating highly interactive online materials? The prototype triggered useful discussions, not only about the design and the graphical layout of the course modules, but also about more general issues regarding the project, such as the division of work, the assignment of tasks, the future use of the course, and so on.

Immediately after the first prototype, a second prototype module was developed (*Physiology of color*) and the general structure of the learning environment was designed. It is worth noticing here that in this case the rapid development of a prototype did not help the production of learning materials as such, but played a very important role in revealing some critical issues about the project itself, which had remained hidden during the drafting of the project proposal. Also in this case, focusing on general issues concerning the whole project might be seen as a waste of time, because they risk slowing down the project's progress; however, if these issues had not been faced immediately, a longer delay would have occurred, with very negative consequences on the development of the project. The project manager's task in this case was to have the discussion converge on key decisions, without letting it flare up into an argument.

Argumentum: E-Course of Argumentation Theory for the Human and Social Sciences

The goal of this project was to create a set of customized autonomous blended-learning courses about argumentation theory in different social contexts and for different educational purposes and targets. The Faculty of Communication Sciences of the USI led the project. In this case, the prototype module was the introductory module. This module had a rather particular status within the whole course, since it presented a general introduction to argumentation theory and was not conceived in order to be integrated into specific courses, but was instead to be freely accessible to everybody on the Internet. The introductory course was developed (both in Italian and in English) by the project leader during the first four months of the project. It was presented to all the other partners during a project meeting in February 2005 and tested with about 60 USI master's students in the first half of the summer semester 2005 (March-April 2005). In parallel with the test phase, three other courses were developed by the project leader to be used and tested in the second half of the semester in three different USI master's programs. The presentation of the prototype allowed the project team to reach a rapid agreement about the graphical appearance of the course, so that the three other modules could be developed quickly.

The main function of the prototype modules was to help the project partners understand the possibilities, the opportunities, and the limitations of the learning management system in which the course runs. In fact, while the project leader had previous experiences with e-learning projects, the partners had not. Unlike the previously presented projects, the fast development of the prototype modules did not aim primarily at getting to a shared information structure of single modules, nor at fostering discussion, but rather at leveling the knowledge of the project team members about the technologies employed by showing them their main features and possibilities for use. In this way the project partners could see, for instance, how maps could be used as tools for the metaphorical representation of contents, for accessing the content, and for orientation during the navigation into the course; what kind of learning material could be used for what purpose (e.g., PDF files for case studies, HTML pages for general contents, video files for interviews with experts, etc.); how discussion activities could be implemented in the course; and so on. Leveling the knowledge of the project team by showing them some examples led to a shared concept about the general structure of the course and of the learning materials.

Critical Discussion and Conclusions

Fast prototyping has been around quite a while, especially in human-computer interaction and computer science, as a way to foster user-centered design. Moving from the issues that have emerged in large multilingual and multi-institutional e-learning projects in the SVC program, our approach has considered the same approach as a communication catalyst. Fast prototyping can enhance e-learning development by improving both team communication and team commitment; it supports the development of a shared understanding of what is being discussed and designed and gives team members the opportunity to try out the e-learning experience in the first person and to be involved from the very beginning.

As for any development model, fast prototyping is not a panacea that ensures effectiveness and efficiency. Fast prototyping shows its advantages where (a) the project is quite big, (b) team members are not accustomed to working together, and/or (c) many of them have little experience in e-learning course development. Moreover, experience so far has highlighted a few conditions that seem to be required in order to make fast prototyping a sensible choice (or even a necessary one).

1.   Fast prototyping costs. What is developed risks being rejected and demolished, even if in critical and fruitful demolition. In order to be cost effective, a sound ratio between prototype scale and the final product is needed; when this is not feasible, examples taken from other experiences may be used.

2.   Fast prototyping is particularly helpful in order to provide a shared understanding of what the final e-learning course is likely to be; it offers the development team a common background where many misunderstandings can be avoided. Being multi-disciplinary, e-learning teams bring together people with very different backgrounds who need to share a simple, effective, and efficient way of collaborating, each of them providing her or his own contribution, while acknowledging the expertise of others. It is important to note that committing to a human-centered approach implies that also the choice of fast prototyping itself has to be negotiated and shared among team members.

3.   E-learning is a new world. It happens quite often that people working in course development do not have extensive experience. Fast prototyping provides them with a common language and an initial experience of e-learning. In fact, while point (b) above underlines the usefulness of fast prototyping to reduce team heterogeneity in general, (c) stresses its being a tool that enhances e-learning competencies inside the team.

These conditions are necessary but not enough to provide a sound fast prototyping experience. Two pitfalls in particular are to be mentioned here, both concerned with the prototyping speed. The first pitfall is the "quick and dirty" effect, (i.e., a very rapid but low quality development may negatively affect further developments, hindering understanding, collaboration, and commitment. The second one is just at the opposite pole in the speed scale: the non-fast prototyping case. Here the prototyping phase is extended so much that it only delivers a late contribution, which often has to be accepted as time resources do not allow substantial revisions. Continuous and endless prototype revisions turn into the biggest obstacle in the actual e-learning course development.

Successful e-learning projects are always team efforts (Botturi, 2006) and depend absolutely on the quality of team collaboration. The SVC experience has shown that classic ID models are often at odds with academic tradition when introducing e-learning technologies into higher education institutions, generating conflicts and misunderstandings. If properly managed and applied to a context that can benefit from it, a fast prototyping approach can provide an opportunity to enhance communication by providing a concrete focal point—the prototype—for discussion and design. This model can leverage on the human factor in order to achieve better designs and finally better e-learning applications.

References

Andrews, D. H., & Goodson, L. A. (1995). A comparative analysis of models of instructional design. In G. Anglin (Ed.), *Instructional technology. Past, present, and future* (pp. 161-182). Englewood, CO: Libraries Unlimited.

Bates T. W. (1999), *Managing technological change: Strategies for college and university leaders*. San Francisco: Jossey Bass.

Bates, T. W., & Poole, G. (2003). *Effective teaching with technologies in higher education*. San Francisco: Jossey-Bass.

Botturi, L. (2006). E2ML. A visual language for the design of instruction. *Educational Technologies Research & Development, 54(3)* (accepted for publication).

Cantoni, L., & Piccini, C. (2004). *Il sito del vicino è sempre più verde. La comunicazione fra committenti e progettisti di siti internet*. Milano, Italy: FrancoAngeli.

CEC. (2001). *The eLearning action plan: Designing tomorrow's education*, COM(2001)172, Brussels, 28.3.2001. Retrieved on June 24, 2005, from http://europa.eu.int/comm/education/policies/ntech/ntechnologies_en.html

Clark, H. H. (1996). *Using language*. Cambridge: Cambridge University Press.

Collis, B., & Van der Wende, M. (2002). *Models of technology and change in higher Education*. CHEPS report, Toegepaste Onderwijskunde.

Colón, B., Taylor, K. A., & Willis, J. (2000, May). Constructivist instructional design: Creating a multimedia package for teaching critical qualitative research. *The Qualitative Report, 5*(1-2). Retrieved June 8, 2005, from http://www.nova.edu/ssss/QR/QR5-1/colon.html

CUS. (2002), *Campus virtuel Suisse—Programme de consolidation visant à renouveler l'enseignement et l'étude (2004-2007)*, Berne. Retrieved on June 24, 2005, from http://www.cus.ch/Fr/F_Projekte/F_Projekte_Campus/S_projets_campus_2004.html)

Dick, W., Carey, W., & Carey, L. (2001). *The systematic design of instruction* (6th ed.). New York: Harper Collins College Publishers.

Engwall, M. (2003). No project is an island: Linking projects to history and context. *Research Policy, 32*(5), 789-808.

Heinich, R., Molenda, M., & Russell, J. (1993). *Instructional media and new technologies of instruction* (4th ed.). New York: Macmillan.

Kirkpatrick, D. L. (1998). *Evaluating training programs: The four levels*. San Francisco: Berrett-Koehler Publishers.

Lepori, B., Cantoni, L., & Rezzonico, S. (2005). *Edum eLearning manual*. Lugano, Switzerland: University of Lugano, Retrieved from www.edum.ch

Lepori, B., Cantoni, L., & Succi, C. (2003). The introduction of e-learning in European universities: Models and strategies. In M. Kerres & Voss B. (Eds.), *Digitaler campus. Vom Medienprojekt zum Nachhaltigen Medieneinsatz in der Hochschule*. Münster, Germany: Waxmann.

Lepori, B., & Perret, J. F. (2004), Les dynamiques institutionnelles et les choix des responsables de projets du Campus Virtuel Suisse: une conciliation difficile. *Revue Suisse de Sciences de l'Education, 2/2004*, 205-228.

Lepori, B., & Rezzonico, S. (2003). Models of eLearning. The case of the Swiss Virtual Campus. *Proceedings of the International Conference on New Learning Environments 2003*, Lucerne, Switzerland.

Lepori, B., & Succi, C. (2003). *e-Learning in higher education*. Prospects for Swiss Universities, 2nd EDUM report, Lugano. Retrieved June 24, 2005, from www.edum.ch

Lepori, B., & Succi, C. (2004). *eLearning and the governance of higher education in continental Europe. Proceedings of ELEARN 2004*, Washington, DC.

Morrison, G. R., Ross, S. M., & Kemp, J. E. (2003). *Designing effective instruction* (4th ed.). New York: Wiley & Sons.

Oliver, R., & Herrington, J. (2001). *Teaching and learning online*. Mt. Lawley: Edith Cowan University Press.

Rogers, E. M. (1995). *Diffusion of innovations* (4th ed.). New York: The Free Press.

Surry, D. W., & Farquhar, J. D. (1997). Diffusion theory and instructional technology. *Journal of Instructional Science and Technology, 2*(1), 24-36. Retrieved June 24, 2005, from http://www.usq.edu.au/electpub/e-jist/docs/old/vol2no1/article2.htm

Van der Wende, M., & van der Ven, M. (2003). *The use of ICT in higher education. A mirror of Europe*. Utrecht, Holland: LEMMA Publishers.

Wenger, E. (1998). *Communities of practice: Learning, meaning, and identity*. New York: Cambridge University Press.

Wenger, E., McDermott, R., & Snyder, W. (2002). *Cultivating communities of practice*. Boston: Harvard Business School Press.

Willis, J. (1995). A recursive, reflective instructional design model based on constructivist-interpretivist theory. *Educational Technology, 35*(6), 5-23.

Project Web Sites

Argumentum: www.argumentum.ch

Colore: www.coloreonline.ch

EAD: www.ead-project.ch

Chapter XVII

Educational Design as a Key Issue in Planning for Quality Improvement

Albert Sangrà, Open University of Catalonia, Spain

Lourdes Guàrdia, Open University of Catalonia, Spain

Mercedes González-Sanmamed, University of Coruña, Spain

Abstract

This chapter focuses on the need for redesigning courses to develop an appropriate educational or instructional model to achieve a high level of quality in e-learning. It argues that e-learning must be integrated as a process of innovation in the institution for it to become a factor of improvement in the quality of higher education. Transition from conventional education to any model of e-learning demands a well-founded planning strategy to ensure quality in education delivery. Consequently, drawing up strategic plans for the integration of e-learning in our institutions is fundamental. The authors consider there is an obvious need for a greater study into the use of instructional design models and techniques in the sphere of e-learning. The selection of the most suitable instructional design model should allow researchers and practitioners to increase the quality of the educational offerings.

Introduction

Transition from conventional education to any model of e-learning, even if it is a mixed one, demands a well-founded planning strategy to ensure quality in education delivery. Generally, faculties try to extend their face-to-face activities to a technological environment without taking into account how the educational context has changed. This chapter focuses on the need for redesigning courses to develop an appropriate educational or instructional model for this new e-context. In planning this, we could in fact develop an e-learning proposal with a high level of quality, satisfaction, and achievements.

The E-Learning Approach

Distance learning has always been allied with the popular technologies in use at the time. The evolution of this consideration, however, did not coincide with the speed of technology evolution. Distance learning has usually been seen as a "compensatory" mechanism for the general educational system: a formula to permit access to education by those people who, for various reasons, cannot attend classes in the conventional way. Consequently, distance learning has become the lesser ill or, as defined by Wedemeyer (1981), "the back door" for a certain number of people.

The birth of the large distance learning universities or "mega-universities" (Daniels, 1997) at the start of the 1960s and 1970s and, in recent years, the emergence of the social use of information and communication technologies and the conceptualization of education as a lifelong process (Delors, 1998) have revolutionized the social perception of distance learning, even turning it into a benchmark for conventional education in classrooms and an instrument of change: "Distance learning, which was once a poor and often unwelcome stepchild within the academic community, is becoming increasingly more visible as a part of the higher education family" (Phipps & Merisotis, 1999, p. 7).

Thanks to the invaluable help of today's information and communication technologies (ICT), specifically to virtual learning environments, one of the obstacles that had historically prevented distance education from being seen as a valid and efficient educational system has been overcome. It is the possibility of asynchronous interaction between students and teacher (Harasim, Hiltz, Teles, & Turoff, 1995), resulting in a new form of education—e-learning—that provides a viable alternative to or improvement on conventional classroom teaching.

The Educational Design Approach

Instructional design provides an effective means to improve quality in our learning programs. It has even been argued that instructional design is an indispensable component of quality distance education (Bates & Bourdeau, 1996). Furthermore, when ICTs are used for distance education, the use of instructional design can result in radically new teaching and learning models.

The term *instructional design* is usually used to describe the process in which:

- Learning needs and the environment in which they occur are analyzed
- Training needs are defined
- The most appropriate resources with regard to the learning processes are chosen
- Contents and activities are developed
- The learning process is evaluated

However, this concept becomes much wider when referring to distance education. Today, we are facing the challenge of making the best use of the possibilities of hypermedia technologies in order to offer much more significant learning than that provided by traditional instructional materials. As a result, we need to take into account all the elements involved in the instructional design of a course or program. Thus, when lecturers or institutions are planning quality programs and learning services, they must consider the coherence of the materials and the teaching strategy, together with the unique characteristics of the virtual learning environment (Guàrdia & Sangrà, 2005).

Planning a subject, a course, or a program for a virtual learning environment involves conceptualizing, designing, and producing learning materials and activities within a specific context and making them available to students. This is the result of a collective effort by a team of professionals (Khan, 2005): teachers, content experts, administrative staff, tutors, educational designers, graphic designers, publishers, and multimedia production staff.

Introducing E-Learning into the University: Organizational and Methodological Considerations

Issues about the Transition and Integration of ICT

Although experiments in the past have contributed to improvements in teaching and the organization of the university, the emergence of the information society and the knowledge economy has forced universities to respond to the challenge of integrating ICT into their organization and, most especially, their teaching.

Universities have reacted to this challenge in a variety of ways. Responses include strategic plans for the integration of ITC, which must play a fundamental role in the transition of universities. However, this challenge is not affecting all universities with the same intensity and at the same time (González-Sanmamed, 2005).

For e-learning to be a true instrument of transformation, we need a specific planning process to achieve it. The following questions should be considered: Why are we going to use e-learning? How widely should e-learning be used in our institution? Do we really think e-learning will help us to improve teaching and learning processes? The answers will require strategic decisions, financial investment in equipment and in learning, and a transformation of people's behavior and work methods. This is why we have to plan strategically.

When analyzing the main reasons for introducing e-learning in higher education (Sangrà, 2003a), we agree with the rationales offered by Bates (2000) and Hanna (2002):

- **To widen targets for universities:** Given that birth rates are falling, matching people to a lifelong learning approach is a strategic issue for university growth.

- **To improve university economic expectations:** From the start, some universities have seen e-learning not only as a new source of income, but also as a way to reduce costs.

- **To respond to the technological imperative:** Some universities have moved to ICT integration and e-learning when they have seen other universities doing so.

- **To improve the quality of education:** Some institutions believe they can improve the quality of education by introducing e-learning in order to gain flexibility and interactivity, to have a better educational design of courses, to facilitate wider access to information resources, and to promote collaborative learning. But what has not been proven is if quality really improves (Sangrà & Gonzalez-Sanmamed, 2004).

Pedagogical Models and E-Learning: Current Scenarios

Unfortunately, there is no accepted taxonomy of e-learning models or practices in higher education. However, there are some shared trends. In effect, the way in which e-learning is implemented in universities is directly related to institutional policies and strategies, which it is felt contribute to the development of the university.

Based on some recent research that has suggested simple yet useful typologies, we are proposing the following models:

- Courses without an Internet presence.
- Courses that are complemented with some sort of online support, such as lesson notes, e-mail, or external links.
- Courses that require active behaviour via the Internet to progress through the course (e.g., online debates, collaborative work, etc.).
- Courses that can be considered mixed because the Internet activities substitute for a good part of the physical presence activities.
- Courses that can be considered completely online or virtual.

All institutions, from traditional face-to-face universities to the most recent virtual universities, will find their model in this taxonomy. Although some say that there are just three large models—face-to-face with ICT support, mixed or blended, and virtual—this approach is too simplistic. Sangrà & Duart (2000) offer a more refined classification with three models that are defined by their focus on technology, instructor, or learner. Whatever the preferred conceptual position, we are undergoing a period of transition, of convergence, between models, with significant integration of the use of ICT and, in particular, of the Internet in face-to-face teaching, as well as the growth of online distance learning (Sangrà, 2002).

Technology, Content, Faculty...Which is the Most Important?

The intensive introduction of ICT in university education has developed through a series of phases that we could identify by the importance that different elements of the teaching strategies and methodology have assumed during this time. The first stage was of absolute concentration on the technology, limited to the implementation of an electronic platform as a basic strategy to differentiate an institution and to provide a competitive advantage. In essence this was an immediate response to the technological imperative.

A certain approach was then applied that defies common sense and ignores the results of research (Moore & Kearsley, 1996; Olcott, 1997), whereby educational pedagogy was molded to each specific technology selected, instead of ensuring that the technology adapted to well-defined teaching and learning objectives (Schmidt & Olcott, 2002) included in a strategic institutional action plan.

With the increasing adoption of electronic platforms, but with significantly fewer educational strategies than some had imagined, we then progressed to maximum concern for content as a substantial element in capitalizing on advances in university learning, to which the expectations of many multinational publishers made a decisive contribution by participating in the birth of the so-called knowledge industry. The publishers saw a great opportunity in the incipient generalization of e-learning: that of entering the education market, not only as the suppliers of resources, the role that they had played up until that point, but as learning facilitator agents with the aim of structuring around themselves the whole productive value chain of higher education.

We therefore witnessed the commitment of companies such as Bertelsmann, Havas, or Harcourt to break into the online learning market, the joint venture of Unext.com between several universities, or the now famous case of the MIT, which placed its teaching materials on the Internet. Such initiatives were based on an implicit assumption: The fundamental element of an education model is the content and whoever has the best content will be in a position to offer the best education.

However, this markedly commercial focus was abandoned when it was realized that production and content publication is one thing, and a complete educational experience that guarantees its users good learning results, is something quite different (Hanna, 2002).

The third phase reconsiders that each university's added value lies in the actions carried out by its teachers through the use of ICT in their teaching. Given their educational function, teachers must be able to adapt their strategies easily to this new role of facilitator that is required in virtual learning environments. The huge change that they must undertake, which has been stated by other researchers on previous occasions (Harasim et al., 1995; Laurillard, 1995), is to move from conveying knowledge to facilitating learning.

Institutions are starting to consider that perhaps teaching methodology and the actions teachers carry out for students, rather than the content, may be the fundamental elements of differentiation and their competitive advantage, and research tends to support this (McCormick & Scrimshaw, 2001). Providing an effective learning environment is starting to be seen as a way of distinguishing institutions and bringing them, as well as their students, prestige.

Finally, the fourth and, to date, final phase is the one which identifies the student as the nucleus of all the university's evolutionary development. Consequently, a discourse has been structured that highlights the desire to use ICT to develop a student-centered learning model.

Educational Design as a Quality Factor in E-Learning

The Quality Approach in E-Learning

The evaluation of quality in university education has, in recent years, begun to be one of the key aspects in assessing the accountability of universities and institutions that use e-learning, either partially or totally. Many international initiatives are working toward the establishment of standards that permit the quality of e-learning projects to be certified and/or accredited. These efforts are especially concerned with establishing common criteria and methodologies that enable learning via electronic media to be validated. However, there is no widespread agreement on the definition of quality or on the impact that the evaluations carried out actually have on the system of higher education. Indeed in recent years, various interpretations of quality in the field of e-learning have been used.

We suggest it is critical to consider the level at which the evaluation is taking place and we propose three levels: (a) the *institutional* level, which has to take as its benchmark the mission and the objectives that the university aims to achieve with the use of e-learning; (b) the *program or course* level, which should refer to the learning and satisfaction objectives related to the educational offer; and (c) the level of the *disaggregated elements* that comprise the programs and institutions (materials, teaching, services, library, etc.).

At each of these levels, differences can be seen according to the perspective that is taken into consideration. To complete the proposals that have already been made to this effect by Elhers (2004) and Twigg (2001), we should consider the perspectives of (a) the *students*, both because it refers to their satisfaction with regard to their educational experience and to the performance and progress that they have achieved; (b) the *teaching staff*, from the intrinsic, academic, and operational point of view; (c) the *administration and the national and regional agencies for quality assurance*, in terms of the objectives of the university itself and also of the educational system of which it is a part; and (d) the *stakeholders*, who will be the ones to facilitate the employability of the graduates of the various university courses.

Finally, it is important to place a value on the *approach* that has been given to the evaluation of quality in each case. This way, we can talk of the (a) *technological* approach, where the technical operation of the experience matters above all else; (b) *economic* approach, where it is essentially the financial results that are valued; (c) *educational* approach, where the indicators centre especially on the performance and progress of the students; and (d) *global* approach, where the focus aims at a balance between all of the previous.

The development of these parameters would allow us to construct a three-dimensional analysis outline that could be portrayed graphically as shown in Figure 1.

It is difficult to find a quality evaluation model that incorporates in full the various levels, perspectives, and focuses, since we lack a theoretical framework on quality in e-learning, which reveals to us a line of investigation that needs to be developed in future.

Is There any Significant Change in How We Teach?

Although all the models that we have previously presented are theoretical and, therefore, difficult to find in their pure form in reality, they correspond to different trends that have been used in postsecondary institutions. At present, it seems to be clear that there is a strong trend toward embracing learner-centered models. In this sense, distance learning should be a good benchmark, as historically it has given priority to the needs of the learners. Traditionally, distance education has focused on what Saba (2003) called "the centrality and independence of the student" (pp. 4-5) and on facilitating cooperation between peers who do not share the same physical space, making the transactional theory of Moore (1983) more evident.

However, despite all the options, change in educational institutions happens very slowly. Even though online education is being carried out extensively in both

Figure 1. Relationship between the sphere, the perspective, and the focus of the evaluation of quality in e-learning

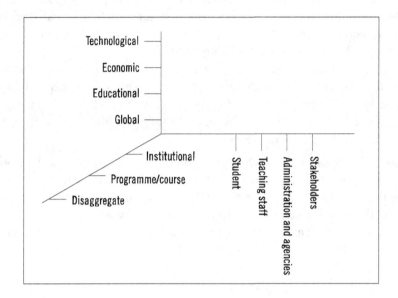

distance learning institutions and in conventional face-to-face institutions, the pedagogical methodologies that are being applied continue to be the classic ones. The result is that virtual learning environments are being used to perpetuate a teacher-centered model.

Even though the integration of ICT has grown considerably in recent years and been accompanied by calls for a paradigm change (Barr & Tagg, 1995), the use of ICT does not mean that learning models are actually changing. According to Coomey and Stephenson (2001), Laurillard (2002), Bates and Poole (2003), and Sangrà (2003b), one of the most important reasons that this is so is that the majority of teachers need more training and more support in the pedagogical and didactic aspects of e-learning and in the use of ICT in their teaching activities in order to be able to tackle a real change in teaching model.

We are faced with a new possibility of interaction between students that previously did not exist. From this perspective, the opportunity exists to create virtual learning communities, which share interests in a highly powerful methodological element. However, often the new e-learning environments are used with the same pedagogical approaches as before. Learning materials that were previously on paper have simply been digitized and uploaded to a virtual classroom.

If we change the example and take a face-to-face educational institution that has decided to incorporate a virtual campus as a supplement or alternative to conventional teaching, we find ourselves faced with a similar situation: Teachers continue to give a class in the same way as before and use the virtual learning environment without substantially modifying their way of teaching. Consequently, they use it to leave their class notes in digital format and to advise their students asynchronously. Now it is highly possible that this adds some value to the educational relationship (e.g., they may devote more time or a qualitatively better time to the students they tutor), but they could most certainly be more ambitious.

Research suggests there is no significant difference in terms of learning between face-to-face and distance education courses (Moore & Thompson, 1990; Phipps & Merisotis, 1999; Russell, 1999). However, in light of what we are suggesting, we need to question these studies. If the teaching approach remains the same, it should not be surprising that there is no significant difference between modes of delivery. What we need to study is the impact of using different modes of delivery when instructional designs are used that exploit the full potential of the technologies used in the different modes.

A radical qualitative leap is called for that allows us to take maximum advantage of the potential of virtual education; a new paradigm that focuses on who should learn, on their needs, on their pace of learning, and on their abilities, and where the teacher plays a role as guide and counselor rather than as transmitter. The nature of the new learning environments is such that there is no longer a distinction between teacher and student and a collective construction of educations (Mason, 1998). For this, instructional design is a key element.

Appropriate Use of Instructional Design Models

An instructional design model for e-learning must provide patterns and guidelines that enable us to go from the design of content to the design of environments geared toward teaching and learning (Duffy, 2004). The mere distribution of content does not imply the creation and building of knowledge. Designers must take into account the kind of learning they would like to foster and for whom the materials are intended, taking into consideration what roles the instructor, the learner, and the contents or resources play in the learning process.

The instructor's monitoring of/interaction with the learner and the latter's behavior in the various interactions are essential for determining the kind of design that should be implemented during the learning process. Given the importance of the instructor in the learning process and the importance of designing and planning the learning experience, educational institutions must provide appropriate training for their instructional staff to enable them to acquire the necessary skills for teaching in an e-learning environment. Unfortunately, often where training has been provided it has been more focused on developing skills with technology rather than on imparting good pedagogical practices and providing criteria and theoretical frameworks. Furthermore, instructors do not generally work in multidisciplinary teams, where instructors, instructional designers, programmers, editors, and experts in the discipline develop a course from its concept to its production and evaluation. This is why it becomes even more urgent to establish frameworks and tools that facilitate instructors' tasks, not only at the beginning, but also throughout the learning process until its completion.

It is clear that a series of indicators (accessibility, usability, and flexibility) that provide us with information on the impact of learning-object-based instructional design for courses in virtual teaching and learning environments should be established. These indicators, combined with examples of good practices—clear and practical frames of reference for the everyday actions that the instructional staff have to carry out, such as the coordination of subjects and courses—combined with training in strategies to strengthen instructors' teaching methodology for online learning environments would enable instructors to offer high quality teaching and learning adapted to the modern era.

Quality Indicators for E-Learning: An Experience

Improvement in the instructional design can become one of the most effective strategies to achieve better results in the teaching and learning process, in terms of academic performance as well as students' perceptions of their own satisfaction with respect to what they achieve and how they meet the objectives set.

The Universitat Oberta de Catalunya (UOC), a Spanish virtual university with more than 40,000 virtual students, designed an instrument called the balanced scorecard for methodology (BSM). This provides specific up-to-date information on the academic results obtained by students, student completion and continuation rates, and the level of satisfaction shown in terms of the activities and relations with the university. BSM also enables the analysis of possible causes for less favorable indicators. Beyond the organizational aspects linked to management, or even technology, there is also an obvious need to measure the achievement of institutional objectives in terms of the elements of the instructional design. The aim of the BSM is, therefore, to evaluate quality of the teaching and learning processes at UOC and to find ways to improve the level of quality of these processes.

The BSM research methodology was developed using a benchmarking process in the following phases:

- Determining a sample of appropriate university and higher education institutions.
- Applying a discourse analysis methodology to the documentation relating to the areas of activity at these institutions in terms of quality in its widest sense—measurement, assessment, improvement, and certification.
- Detecting the methodological elements assessed in each case.
- Elaborating an initial conceptualization and preliminary identification of the indicators for measuring methodological quality at the UOC.

The benchmarking activity and study of the documentation resulted in a document (UOC, 2002) that set out quality indicators for the different institutions analyzed, as well as certain points for reflection arising from the process. The analysis showed, amongst other aspects, the following:

- The existence of differences in terms of the definition and concept of quality.
- The difficulty in specifying focal points for continuous improvement and the assessment of quality in higher and university education at the various institutions, compared with the ways these are traditionally handled in terms of industry and the world of business.
- The methodological indicators often included assessment parameters that were not directly related to the teaching and learning process, such as assessment of university services and products.

From the rationale that quality education is that which offers good academic results, ensures a high level of continuity in studies, and promotes a high level of satisfaction amongst the students, the areas in which quality was to be measured by the BSM at UOC included students' academic performance, continuity of students at the university, and students' personal satisfaction.

The use of BSM provided researchers with information about the points that needed to be improved, so at the end of each semester BSM results can be used to design improvement plans in a number of courses, leading to general quality improvement.

Conclusion: Toward Improvement Through Innovation

E-learning must be integrated as a process of innovation in the institution for it genuinely to become a factor of improvement in the quality of higher education. It is necessary to define the university model along with the level of face-to-face and e-learning that we want in response to the needs of our students. Consequently, drawing up strategic plans for the integration of e-learning in our institutions is fundamental (Bates, 2000; Bates & Poole, 2003).

Similarly, the consideration of e-learning as a potential quality factor should afford us an improvement that can be evaluated in educational results. There are proven studies that demonstrate that similar academic results are obtained whether ICT is used or not (Moore & Thompson, 1990; Russell, 1999). If we really were to change the role of the teacher or of the contents, would we get better results? Or are we making inadequate use of the possibilities offered to us by ICT?

There is an obvious need for a greater study into the use of instructional design models and techniques in the sphere of e-learning. Although it is true to say that the application of some models has contributed to the improvement of the educational processes and to the obtaining of better results, it is also true that technology has led us to work with no clear theoretical frameworks. Educational design will be the key, providing it is in response to specific objectives and gives the guidance and mechanisms for helping to achieve good results in each of the scenarios. The importance of training teachers in the use of instructional design models suited to the improvement aims pursued is essential. The selection of the most suitable instructional design model should allow us to increase the quality of our educational offerings. To ensure success, however, it will be necessary to develop indicators that measure the relationship between the design of courses and their perceived or measured quality.

References

Barr, R., & Tagg, J. (1995, November / December). From teaching to learning: A new paradigm for undergraduate education. *Change*, 13-25.

Bates, A. W. (Tony) (2000). *Managing technological change*. San Francisco: Jossey-Bass.

Bates, A. W., & Poole, G. (2003). *Effective teaching with technology in higher education*. San Francisco: Jossey-Bass.

Bates, T., & Bourdeau, J. (1996). Instructional design for distance learning. *Journal of Science Education and Technology, 5*(4), 267-283.

Coomey, M., & Stephenson, J., (2001). Online learning: It is all about dialogue, involvement, support, and control-according to research. In J. Stephenson (Ed.), *Teaching and learning online: Pedagogies for new technologies.* London: Kogan Page.

Daniels, J. (1997). *Mega-universities in a digital world.* London: Kogan Page.

Delors, J. et al. (1998). *Learning: The treasure within.* Paris: UNESCO.

Duffy, T. M. (2004). Theory and the design of learning environments: Reflections on differences in disciplinary focus. *Educational Technology, 44*(3), 13-15.

Ehlers, U. D. (2004). Quality in e-learning from a learner's perspective. In A. Szucs et al. (Eds.), *Proceedings on the 3rd EDEN research workshop: Supporting the learner in distance education and e-learning.* Oldenburg: BIB.

González-Sanmamed, M. (2005). La integración de las tecnologías de la información y la comunicación en la Educación Superior: Experiencias en la UDC. In M. Raposo & M. C. Sarceda (Eds.), *Experiencias y prácticas educativas con nuevas tecnologías.* Orense: Servicio de Publicaciones de la Diputación de Ourense.

Guardia, L., & Sangrá, A. (2005). Diseño instruccional y objetos de aprendizaje; hacia un modelo para el diseño de actividades de evaluación del aprendizaje on-line. *RED. Revista de Educación a Distancia, número monográfico II.* Retrieved September 10, 2005, from http://www.um.es/ead/red/M4/

Hanna, D. E. (2002). *La enseñanza universitaria en la era digital.* Barcelona: Octaedro-EUB.

Harasim, L., Hiltz, S. R., Teles, L., & Turoff, M. (1995). *Learning networks.* Cambridge, MA: The MIT Press.

Khan, B. (2005). A comprehensive e-learning model. *Journal of e-Learning and Knowledge Society, 1*(1), 33-44.

Laurillard, D. (1995). *Rethinking university teaching.* London: Routledge.

Laurillard, D. (2002). Rethinking teaching for the knowledge society. *EDUCAUSE Review, 37*(1), 16-25.

Mason, R. (1998). Models of online learning, *ALN Magazine, 2(2).* Retrieved September 10, 2005, from http://www.aln.org/alnweb/magazine/vol2_issue2/Masonfinal.htm.

McCormick, R., & Scrimshaw, P. (2001). Information and communications technology, knowledge, and pedagogy. *Education, Communication, & Information, 1*(1), 37-57.

Moore, M. G. (1983). The individual adult learner. In M. Tight (Ed.), *Adult learning and education*. London: Croom Helm.

Moore, M. G., & Kearsley, G. (1996). *Distance education: A system's view*. Belmont, CA: Wadsworth.

Moore, M. G., & Thompson, M. (1990). *The effects of distance education: A summary of the literature*. University Park: American Center for Distance Education, The Pennsylvania State University.

Olcott, D. J. (1997). Transforming university outreach: Integrated technology systems design for the twenty-first century. *Journal of Public Service and Outreach, 2*(3), 55-69.

Phipps, R., & Merisotis, J. (1999). *What's the difference? A review on contemporary research on the effectiveness of distance learning in higher education*. The Institute for Higher Education Policy, Washington, DC. Also digital version, retrieved September 10, 2005, from http://www.ihep.com/Pubs/PDF/Difference.pdf.

Russell, T. (1999). *The no significant difference phenomenon*. Raleigh: North Carolina State University, Office of Instructional Telecommunications.

Saba, F. (2003). Distance education theory, methodology, and epistemology: A pragmatic paradigm. In M. G. Moore & W. G. Anderson (Eds.), *Handbook of distance education*. Mahwah, NJ: Lawrence Erlbaum Associates.

Sangrà, A. (2002). Educación a distancia, educación presencial y usos de la tecnología: una tríada para el progreso educativo. *EDUTEC, Revista Electrónica de Tecnología Educativa, 15*.

Sangrà, A. (2003a). *La integració de les TIC a la universitat: una aproximació estratègica*. Unpublished Master's Thesis (DEA), Universitat Rovira i Virgili, Tarragona.

Sangrà, A. (2003b). La EAD como factor clave de innovación en los modelos pedagógicos. *Discursos. Novos Rumos e Pedagogía em Ensino a Distância. Série Perspectivas em Educaçâo, 1*.

Sangrà, A., & Duart, J. M. (2000). Formación universitaria por medio de la web: un modelo integrador para el aprendizaje superior. In J. M. Duart & A. Sangrà (Eds.), *Aprender en la virtualidad*. Barcelona: Gedisa.

Sangrà, A., & González Sanmamed, M. (2004). *La transformación de las universidades a través de las TIC: Discursos y prácticas*. Barcelona: Ediuoc.

Schmidt, K., & Olcott Jr., D. (2002). El diseño de sistemas tecnológicos integrados: un modelo para conjugar la calidad pedagógica y la tecnología educativa. In D. E. Hanna (Ed.), *La enseñanza universitaria en la era digital*. Barcelona: Octaedro-EUB.

Twigg, C. A. (2001). *Quality assurance for whom? Providers and consumers in today's distributed learning environment.* Troy, NY: Center for Academic Transformation, Rensselaer Polytechnic Institute.

UOC. (2002). *Quadre de Comandament Metodològic.* Unpublished internal document.Wedemeyer, C. (1981). *Learning at the back-door.* Madison: University of Wisconsin.

Chapter XVIII

Cognitive Tools for Self-Regulated E-Learning

Tracey L. Leacock, Simon Fraser University, Canada

John C. Nesbit, Simon Fraser University, Canada

Abstract

Working from the premise that students need advanced self-regulated learning (SRL) skills to succeed in e-learning environments, this chapter describes the use of a software application (gStudy) designed to help students take control of their learning and become better self-regulated learners. To address the challenges educators face in developing students' metacognitive monitoring and self-regulatory skills, gStudy's cognitive tools were designed in accordance with current SRL theory. Undergraduate students who used gStudy in an educational psychology course commented that they appreciated gStudy's features, interface, and ability to positively influence their approach to learning. The authors conclude that SRL-fostering software applications such as gStudy may be key strategic elements in institutional transitions to e-learning.

Cognitive Tools for Self-Regulated E-Learning

Greater access to information and a growing need for lifelong learning have increased the importance of self-regulated learning (SRL) research for postsecondary education (Narciss & Körndle, 1998). More than ever before, students are learning outside regular classrooms, often in online learning environments that require different skills from those needed in on-campus lectures. With virtually unlimited access to information, students must take more active roles in evaluating the quality and relevance of the information available to them and in assessing their understanding of that information (Nesbit & Winne, 2003). This transition brings with it a definite shift in the roles of teachers and of students. While teachers will still be responsible for establishing clear goals and objectives and for guiding students with feedback, there will be greater onus on students to assess whether the strategies and tactics they choose really will help them to meet their educational goals. Although the need for individuals to take responsibility for their learning is growing, students often fail in monitoring whether they are meeting course requirements or advancing toward their goals (Schunk & Ertmer, 2000; Winne & Hadwin, 1998; Zimmerman, 2002).

Cognitive toolsets that help students to become better at monitoring and adapting their learning strategies offer a potential solution to this increased need for SRL in formal coursework and in lifelong learning (Brown, Hedberg, & Harper, 1994). Institutions that can seize this opportunity to produce graduates with strong SRL skills will be recognized as having successfully met the changing demands of education. Accordingly, this chapter focuses on a software application designed to help students take control of their learning and become better self-regulators. After providing a brief account of SRL theory, we introduce gStudy, a set of cognitive tools developed at Simon Fraser University to support SRL. Throughout, we look at gStudy both as a practical tool that educators can use in their courses to help students and as a research tool that researchers can use to learn more about the theories underlying SRL and their applications. We conclude by evaluating the significance of cognitive tools for SRL and applications such as gStudy in the context of institutional transitions to e-learning.

Theoretical Background

Self-regulation of learning includes analyzing learning tasks; setting goals; identifying and choosing appropriate strategies for achieving the goals; enacting tactics that fit the chosen strategies; and monitoring, evaluating, and adapting learning activities based on outcomes. Research has demonstrated that students who have strong SRL skills, evidenced by effective goal setting, strategy use, and metacognitive monitoring, are more likely to continue to pursue effortful learning strategies required to learn difficult materials (Garavalia & Gredler, 2002; Winne, 1995; Zimmerman, 2001, 2002). Further, the processes and effectiveness of SRL have been shown to be relevant in varied settings, ranging from individual learning to complex problem solving in collaborative settings (Nesbit & Winne, 2003).

Winne (2001) describes a four-stage model of SRL that can help educators understand where students may be having problems (see Figure 1). In the first stage, the learner must define the required task(s) by breaking the generic assignment down into the specific subtasks the learner will need to accomplish. Students may have difficulty identifying all of the component parts of a large and complex task, such as writing a research-based term paper. Tools that can scaffold students through this process and that can help them to track their decisions are relevant at this stage of SRL.

Next, the learner must develop a plan to complete the task. In this planning stage, the learner identifies appropriate goals and high-level strategies and begins to think about specific tactics or actions that fit those strategies. Students may not be able to recall the appropriate strategy when needed, or they may need to find new strategies for novel learning situations. Cognitive tools that can suggest strategies and tactics (e.g., changing recall to recognition) and scaffold students through their use (helping to expand the learner's learning strategy toolkit) can help with both the second phase of SRL and the third phase: enacting the plan.

In the third phase, the learner must take action on the plan. Many factors can interfere at this stage, from poor motivation to poor skills in reading or note-taking. An effective e-learning environment must include tools that help students implement their plans.

Finally, in the fourth phase, learners evaluate the success of their actions and make any necessary adaptations to stay on track toward completing the task.

Figure 1. Stages of self-regulated learning

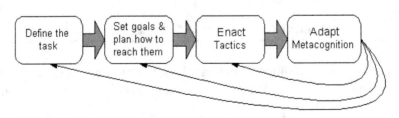

One of the significant challenges students face in this stage is how to ensure they are evaluating an accurate record of their actions and understanding. Students often overestimate both the amount of time they have spent studying and their understanding of the material they are trying to learn (Winne & Jamieson-Noel, 2002). In traditional teaching environments, students are sometimes encouraged to keep records such as study journals, but the quality of these records depends very much on the diligence of the record-keeper. Tools that reduce the cognitive load associated with record keeping will help students to base their evaluations on accurate data, rather than wishful estimates. Easy access to rich data means students can focus on interpreting the data and modifying the outcomes of the previous three phases, rather than on the act of record keeping.

The principles of SRL may seem straightforward, yet experienced educators know that the process is far from simple or intuitive for most students. Even strong students can struggle if they start off on the wrong track, and weak students can easily be overwhelmed when faced with open-ended tasks. While it may seem at first that it would be more difficult to support SRL in an online environment than in a face-to-face setting, in some circumstances the reverse may be true. The technologies available today allow the creation of tools that complement the teacher's role and help individual students to improve their strategy selection and use, while assuming some of the cognitive load.

gStudy: An E-Learning Environment Supporting SRL

gStudy is an e-learning toolset designed to help students develop and use effective SRL strategies as they learn from multimedia resources. As such, it fills a new niche among educational software applications. Whereas e-learning learning management systems (LMSs) tend to emphasize tools that the content developer can use to create effective learning environments, gStudy's design acknowledges that what the student does within that environment is at least as important as how the environment is authored. Major LMSs, such as WebCT and Blackboard, provide tools to help instructors set up predefined content, but tools to support interactions generally focus on student-student or student-instructor interactions via synchronous and asynchronous discussions; there is little explicit support for the intellectual interaction with content that is often central to learning (Moore, 1989).

gStudy is different from LMSs in two key respects. First, although instructors will generally still create pre-defined content (gStudy learning kits), the application itself contains a browser that enables students to access any Web-based content.

Thus students don't have to leave the gStudy environment to conduct online searches for additional materials for their assignments. Second, whether students are studying instructor-assigned material or materials they have found themselves, gStudy supports student efforts to organize their understanding of new content and make it personally meaningful via a unique combination of mark-up tools and information locating and viewing tools. Although there is some overlap with annotation features available in other applications, such MS Word, Adobe Acrobat, and the Wikalong browser extension (Wikalong, 2005), these applications do not provide the level of pedagogical support and customization of annotation types that gStudy does. We believe that the tools for annotating and organizing content in gStudy constitute a new approach to e-learning software.

gStudy Tools

Highlights and Labels

At the most fundamental level, gStudy provides a labeling tool for highlighting and categorizing content, including segments of text, regions of graphics, and QuickTime frames. Although the tactic of selecting and highlighting may shift the learner to a slightly more active form of engagement, this tactic is usually regarded by SRL theorists as information rehearsal, a fairly superficial form of cognitive processing (Pintrich, 1999). In gStudy, learners also categorize the highlighted text by assigning a label to it. Initially, learners are provided with a pre-stocked list of labels such as "critical detail" and "don't understand" (see Figure 2). Learners can add to this list to create personally meaningful labels such as, "useful for biology class, too." In the terminology of SRL, learners may plan to use the strategy of categorizing portions of the content in personally meaningful ways such as whether it is familiar to them, new but easy to understand, or difficult and likely to require a lot more study time. The learner can then enact this plan by choosing the highlighting and labeling of selected content as an appropriate tactic. If during review the learner decides that some segment has been misclassified, the label can be changed with a few clicks.

Notes

By itself, labeling information as fitting into a category may not entail sufficient processing to gain a deep understanding. Therefore, gStudy also scaffolds generative tactics such as note-taking (Peper & Mayer, 1986; Wittrock, 1989).

Figure 2. Labeling in gStudy: Selected text will be marked with a "critical detail" label

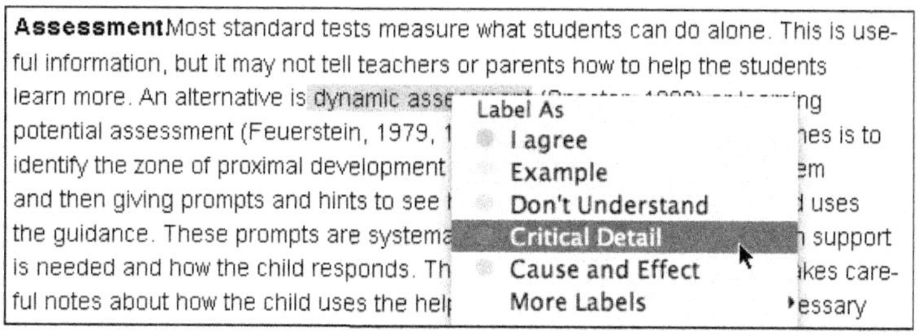

AssessmentMost standard tests measure what students can do alone. This is useful information, but it may not tell teachers or parents how to help the students learn more. An alternative is dynamic asse—————— ʌʌʌ _ ʌ _ ʌ ʌ ʌ ʌ ʌ ʌ ng potential assessment (Feuerstein, 1979, 1 es is to identify the zone of proximal development em and then giving prompts and hints to see ! d uses the guidance. These prompts are systema   n support is needed and how the child responds. Th akes careful notes about how the child uses the hel; essary

Label As
● I agree
Example
Don't Understand
Critical Detail
Cause and Effect
More Labels

gStudy provides pre-defined templates for a range of note types, and, as with labels, instructors and students can add to the default set by creating customized templates. Figure 3 shows the template for a critique note. Notice that this template is not just a blank form with the label "Critique". Rather, it is divided into three text fields (The Claim, Why the Claim is Wrong, How to Make it Right) and one slider bar (Degree of Disagreement) to help students learn what type of information they should be thinking about when critiquing a claim. Learners may choose not to complete the whole template immediately, and the separate fields make it is easy to see which parts are complete and which need to be done at a later date. The default note templates include summary, debate, comment, question, and others, each with its own set of relevant fields for students to fill in. This type of prompting with specific fields helps students assess whether a particular tactic, such as using the critique note template, is likely to be appropriate at a given point in their studying.

The design of gStudy's notes tool is informed by research on the metacognitive components of note-taking, which has shown that judging which content to annotate leads to greater learning than not making such judgments (Igo, Bruning, & McCrudden, 2005). gStudy not only encourages learners to evaluate which information to elaborate on, it also prompts them to consider what type of elaboration (i.e., what note template) is the most appropriate in each case. Providing named templates helps students to think about different types of note-taking when selecting appropriate strategies for learning assigned content, and providing specific fields within the templates helps ensure that learners will be able to act on their chosen strategies effectively. Further, when monitoring the effectiveness of a given learning plan, learners can easily survey information such as incomplete note fields, variety of note types used, and even total number of notes created to help them assess whether their study plan is working or requires modifications.

Figure 3. Critique note template in gStudy

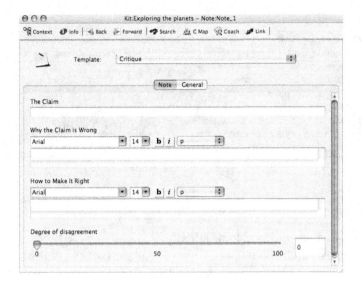

Glossary

gStudy supports both instructor and student creation of glossary items. Instructors may pre-populate a glossary with some key terms and then encourage students to elaborate on these definitions and add additional terms as they study. When students build definitions by paraphrasing provided information, they are performing a type of elaborative rehearsal (Shugarman & Hurst, 1986; Weinstein & Mayer, 1986); we have found that students almost always construct text for notes and glossary items, rather than copying provided information (Nesbit et al., 2006). Students can compare glossaries with one another, use them as flashcards, or engage in other activities to get feedback on their learning. Instructors can also use both the note and glossary templates to pre-populate some annotations, thus providing examples that students can build on in their own learning activities.

Links

Once students begin to annotate their study materials, they can create links between notes, regions of content, and glossary items to help them see the different ways that key ideas interrelate. Explicitly building up connections by linking annotations to previously understood content helps learners to see the structure in new knowledge domains, which in turn, helps them to understand the domains better (Winne, 1995). Links can also help students evaluate how their study plan is going. If the learner's annotations seem to be a collection of unrelated (unlinked) facts, this can serve as a cue to spend more time understanding how different "bits" of information relate to form a coherent whole.

Views

In addition to the annotation tools, gStudy provides multiple ways for learners to view and review the content and their annotations. When in the default contents view, students can see the original content, along with markers indicating where they have added annotations. Clicking on these markers will bring up the annotations in a new window. Alternatively, students can choose to look only at their notes, only at their labels, or only at their glossary. In each of these views, students see a table of contents listing all of the entries for that category. Selecting an entry brings up the relevant details and enables students to navigate back and forth between annotation and its sources. By allowing students to focus on only certain types of information, gStudy reduces the cognitive load associated with monitoring one's studying activity, which in turn makes it easier to identify where one's study plan may need to be adapted.

Search

If learners are unsure where to find some piece of information, or if they want to be certain to find all instances of a word or phrase, they can use gStudy's search tool, which supports both single keyword searching and more complex Boolean searching. The tool returns hits from instructor-provided course content, other Web pages students have saved into their kits, any annotations the student has made or received from collaborators in group projects, and any documents the student has created. This helps students to locate relevant information from across information sources and see connections across different areas of content. As with the different views, the search tool reduces the cognitive load associated with tracking all of the information in a kit, thus helping students to monitor their learning.

Concept Mapping

Concept maps are diagrams that provide an alternative way to represent the information that students typically see only as text. gStudy's concept mapping feature allows students to choose to view and manipulate the content of a learning kit through a node-link interface. Documents, notes, glossary items, and other gStudy objects are represented as nodes. Links between objects are represented as lines. The maps can be created in advance by an instructor, or learners may build their own concept maps as a means of working with the content and looking for gaps in their understanding. Research has shown that the use of concept maps can enhance learning (Nesbit & Adesope, 2006; O'Donnell, Dansereau, & Hall, 2002; van Boxtel, van der Linden, Roelofs, & Erkens, 2002). A concept map showing all content and annotations in a kit can help learners to get a sense of what areas they have been neglecting and what areas show rich interconnections. Maps of subsections of the kit can help students to work with relationships among concepts visually, instead of in a more traditional text-based form.

Tools in Development

Further to the already-implemented tools described above, development efforts are now focusing on two additional areas: a sophisticated help system and collaborative tools that support SRL.

The Coach

Student-initiated help systems rely on learners to identify when they need help and to act appropriately on this knowledge (Nelson-Le Gall, 1981). System-initiated help systems can be useful when students don't realize that they are engaging in maladaptive activities, but such systems often don't have sophisticated enough models of learners to be able to help in all situations (Aleven, Stahl, Schworm, Fischer, & Wallace, 2003). To address the problems associated with either approach in isolation, we are currently prototyping a mixed-initiative help system that will serve three functions:

1.   Respond to student-initiated questions (e.g., "How do I make a note?") with factual "how to" answers.

2.   Promote student understanding of tasks and tactics by providing questions to help students reflect on their studying strategies (e.g., "What types of tools do you think will help you learn this material?").

3.   Prompt the student when the system recognizes problematic behaviors (e.g., after the student has made 10 "important" label annotations, the system may prompt the student to think of ways to differentiate the items—to consider how they relate and how they differ by creating more detailed notes about some or all of the items).

We predict that this type of coaching will help students learn how to ask and answer reflective questions about their studying and will thus lead to improvements in SRL. This comprehensive coach system will make use of standard pattern-matching techniques and both general- and domain-specific ontologies that will be interpreted by an expert system (Menon, Shakya, & Kumar, 2005; Rao & Kumar, 2005; Shakya, Menon, Doherty, Jordanov, & Kumar, 2005).

Collaboration

The research team is also developing a set of tools to support cooperative and collaborative activities within the gStudy environment (Hadwin, Gress, Page, & Ross, 2005). These tools will enable sharing of annotations and new content files (e.g., team reports) among team members and support scaffolded synchronous chat. By providing a list of common chat roles and role-specific discussion prompts, gChat will help students develop the skills to participate effectively in online chat as a learning activity and build shared understandings of course concepts based on a variety of perspectives. Team members will be able to return to stored transcripts of these text-based conversations and annotate them as they would any other content in their kits.

Putting It All Together

All of the tools in gStudy are designed to work together to support self-regulated learning. Currently, gStudy is most effective in supporting phases 2-4 of Winne's model of SRL (2001). In the planning stage (phase 2), students must identify appropriate strategies and develop a plan of attack for their task. By making tool options explicit, gStudy helps translate the task of strategy and tactic identification from recall tasks to recognition tasks. Students can look at the list of available tools, templates, and views and decide which best fit their current task.

When carrying out their plans (phase 3), students are further scaffolded by the fields within note and glossary templates that help students to implement their tactics effectively. Finally, gStudy helps with the monitoring phase of SRL (phase 4) by providing multiple ways for students to look at and filter their annotations, the links they have created across different areas of content, and the content itself. Because students have access to a comprehensive, sortable record of all of the work they have done when studying with gStudy, it is easier to compare effort to outcome. For example, if a student has more difficulty than expected with definitions on an exam, he or she can easily pull up the relevant glossary items and compare the thoroughness of those definitions and the number of links to related content with the glossary items and links created for other units. This provides personally meaningful information on the effectiveness of study tactics, which the student can use in developing more effective plans for the next exam.

Because the application records student interactions with course materials and annotations, gStudy can also be useful in helping students to track their approaches to learning concepts and solving problems. Students can use this information to help identify the need to acquire broader schemas for solving classes of problems, as opposed to tunneling in on solving specific instances of problems (Winne & Stockley, 1998). With student consent, researchers can also use this log information to identify effective and ineffective approaches to studying different types of material. This knowledge, in turn, can be used to build better scaffolding for students. Many of these benefits are not easily available in traditional classrooms, but advancements in educational technologies make it possible to provide learners with exciting new tools to help them learn about and improve their approaches to studying and learning.

Challenges

Scaling Up

Scalability is a challenge that must be addressed with any widely deployed e-learning environment. In any one educational institution, there may be thousands of students and across institutions, tens of thousands. This poses potential storage and network concerns. We have demonstrated that gStudy can perform efficiently with hundreds of students in one course, but we have not yet deployed it on a larger scale. However, we have designed the application with scalability in mind. For example, students are able to download their kits onto local machines and then upload only the content they have added. This gives users local access to their study materials without overburdening the network with ongoing high data transfer demands and without requiring the huge amounts of centralized storage capacity that would be needed if users transferred entire kits for each session.

User Education

Many students and instructors are not yet familiar or comfortable with working in e-learning environments, and gStudy is a powerful application that is rich in features. This means that no matter how intuitive the gStudy interface is, there will be a need for an education component to orient new users and give them confidence in their ability to learn with the system. Currently, all gStudy users attend a one-hour face-to-face training session and then have continued access to a sample kit in which to explore and play with the available tools. As part of our plan for scaling up, we have developed a tutorial kit to guide new users through what may be their first experience with an e-learning environment. This orientation kit, coupled with the Coach, should provide a good introduction to gStudy.

Case Study: Promoting Learning Skills

This case study describes two primarily face-to-face offerings of a second year educational psychology course in fall 2004 and spring 2005. Approximately 240 students were enrolled each semester. In addition to course objectives in theories and applications of educational psychology, the instructor (Nesbit) introduced goals related to the development of learning skills. These were to raise students' awareness of their study strategies and to improve their SRL skills by supporting student efforts to refine and adapt their learning strategies and beliefs. Part way through the course students were given access to several chapters of their textbook online through gStudy (three chapters in the first offering, four in the second offering; all with the publisher's permission). One tutorial session was dedicated to introducing students to gStudy, which they then used to study the online text material as part of a course assignment.

The Strategy Reflection Assignment

Over the first few weeks of the course, students completed a series of questionnaires assessing psychological constructs that are hypothesized to relate to self-regulated learning. These included the epistemic beliefs inventory (EBI, Schraw, Bendixen, & Dunkle, 2002) and the achievement goal questionnaire (AGQ, Elliot & McGregor, 2001), among others. Near the midpoint of the course, students were required to use gStudy for at least two hours distributed over at least two sessions to study one of the online textbook chapters in preparation for an examination. They maintained a descriptive log of their gStudy sessions, including schedules, strategies, and content studied. Students then submitted a reflection assignment in which they drew connections between their studying log and their self-perceptions, as measured by the questionnaires.

Comments by Students

Written reflections from students who consented to participate in an SRL research project were kept as data. Although there were many more positive than negative comments, a representative sample of both types of comments are presented here.

Positive comments. Students frequently commented that gStudy helped them to learn and has a usable interface.

"Being able to link one idea to the next allowed me to create a web of ideas rather than single concepts. Working with the text in these ways, methods I do not typically use, enriched my comprehension and engagement."

"When there was content that needed further attention I could easily link it to a question I composed myself. I do not do this in my usual study system but it proved very useful since I returned to the questions later to test my understanding."

"I found it very useful to mark the sections of the text that I did not understand to come back to later. This differed from text book studying because I really did return to the areas of confusion."

"gStudy indicated to me that there are many ways in which I can improve my study routine to enable me to learn and retain information better."

Negative comments. Some students indicated that they preferred to study with books rather than computers, they did not need to use all the features provided by gStudy, and they had difficulty managing the interface.

"The only part of the kit I found useful was the Quick note [label] function. All of the other functions needed us to provide information to why we chose that link, and I do not study that way."

"I was not able to glance at a page I had read and interpret what I had highlighted and why. When I study with a text book I can write my own notes and colour code my own highlights."

The student feedback was used to revise some features. For example, newer versions of gStudy allow students to control the colors used for each label type. We are also planning to invest more time in training students to apply self-regulated learning strategies. We believe that these measures will alleviate the problems reported by some students. Overall, the response to gStudy has been positive. We are continuing to conduct usability studies and to evaluate specific features for their impact on learning outcomes.

gStudy as a Research Tool

The features and tools described thus far have focused on the benefits of gStudy to learners. We have described how gStudy supports the development of SRL in learners and how SRL will be a critical area of skill as students move into online learning. However, gStudy has also been designed as a research tool. In fact, the software's capacity to capture data for educational and institutional research is one of its key strengths. If learners consent, gStudy automatically logs which documents they choose to view, which buttons they click, what operations they perform, and what content they create. This provides a rich data set with which researchers can examine how learners study in an online environment.

As institutions continue to adopt e-learning technologies, educators are becoming more conscious of the need to evaluate online teaching and learning practices with the same level of scholastic rigor as other areas of research (Huber, 2002; Hutchings, 2000). The use of applications such as gStudy can facilitate this type of research. By looking at the log files and the content of students' annotations, educators can systematically study what students are doing when studying, how their study strategies and tactics evolve, and how this relates to their academic outcomes. This in turn can feed directly back into improved design of online content and learning activities.

gStudy is also useful for demonstrating accountability in e-learning at the institutional level. The data available from gStudy enable institutions to track not only system usage, but also actual changes in learner studying patterns. gStudy logs provide the information institutions need to demonstrate the basics, such as amount of time spent using the application. However, because students do their studying right in gStudy, researchers are also able to assess interaction with online content, both quantitatively (e.g., number of notes created) and qualitatively (e.g., level of understanding demonstrated in concept maps). These assessments can then be compared with student outcomes to meet institutional research needs and accountability commitments (Kelly & Nanjiani, 2005). It is this dual purpose of gStudy—to help students develop and use their SRL skills and to help further empirical research on SRL in e-learning—that makes this application so relevant to institutions moving into e-learning.

Conclusion: Transition to Cognitive Tools for SRL in E-Learning

Students are demanding greater flexibility in course delivery mode and methodology (Brandt, 2002; Lin, Young, Chan, & Chen, 2005), yet they may not be aware of the corresponding increase in personal responsibility for learning that comes with such flexibility. As educational institutions move to e-learning environments, it is important to look at the changing needs of students and to build toolsets to support these needs. By explicitly incorporating tools to foster SRL into transition plans, institutions can make a significant step toward ensuring students are prepared for the new methods of delivering education.

Further, online courses make instructor approaches to pedagogy and implementation of lessons and assignments more visible than they have been in the past. This is coupled with a growing trend toward accountability and the need to demonstrate for university administration and even outside organizations that instructors are effective teachers (Kelly & Nanjiani, 2005; Nichols & Gardner, 2002). Together these increases in student responsibility and institutional accountability have pushed the need for new ways of supporting learners to the fore.

Students who are equipped with the skills required to regulate their own learning will be better prepared to thrive in the new postsecondary environment and will also have the skills to monitor their lifelong learning needs. By supporting learners' immediate SRL needs and building up their SRL skills through scaffolded support, software applications such as gStudy will help learners succeed.

References

Aleven, V., Stahl, E., Schworm, S., Fischer, F., & Wallace, R. (2003). Help seeking and help design in interactive learning environments. *Review of Educational Research, 73*(2), 277-320.

Brandt, E. (2002). Strategies by Norwegian universities to meet diversified market demands for continuing education. *Higher Education, 44*(3-4), 393-411.

Brown, C., Hedberg, J., & Harper, B. (1994). Metacognition as a basis for learning support software. *Performance Improvement Quarterly, 7*(2), 3-26.

Elliot, A., & McGregor, H. (2001). A 2 x 2 achievement goal framework. *Journal of Personality and Social Psychology, 80*(3), 501-519.

Garavalia, L. S., & Gredler, M. E. (2002). An exploratory study of academic goal setting, achievement calibration, and self-regulated learning. *Journal of Instructional Psychology, 29*(4), 31-35.

Hadwin, A. F., Gress, C. L. Z., Page, J., & Ross, S. (2005, May). *Computer supported collaborative work: A review of the research 1999-2004.* Poster presented at the Annual Meeting of the Canadian Society for the Study of Education, London, ON, Canada.

Huber, M. T. (2002). *Disciplinary styles in the scholarship of teaching: Reflections on The Carnegie Academy for the Scholarship of Teaching and Learning.* In M. T. Huber & S. P. Morreale (Eds.), *Introduction to disciplinary styles in the scholarship of teaching and learning: Exploring common ground* (pp. 25-43). Menlo Park, CA: American Association for Higher Education.

Hutchings, P. (2000). Approaching the scholarship of teaching and learning. In P. Hutchings (Ed.), *Opening lines: Approaches to the scholarship of teaching and learning* (pp. 1-10). Menlo Park, CA: American Association for Higher Education.

Igo, L. B., Bruning, R., & McCrudden, M. T. (2005). Exploring differences in students' copy-and-paste decision making and processing: A mixed-methods study. *Journal of Educational Psychology, 97*(1), 103-116.

Kelly, T., & Nanjiani, N. (2005). *The business case for e-learning.* Indianapolis, IN: Cisco.

Lin, C. B., Young, S. S. C., Chan, T. W., & Chen, Y. H. (2005). Teacher-oriented adaptive Web-based environment for supporting practical teaching models: A case study of "school for all." *Computers & Education, 44*(2), 155-172.

Menon S., Shakya J., & Kumar V. (2005). *Rule-based mixed-initiative scaffolding*. Paper presented at the International Workshop on Applications of Semantic Web Technologies for E-Learning, Banff, Canada.

Moore, M. G. (1989). Three types of interaction. *The American Journal of Distance Education, 3*(2), 1-6.

Narciss, S., & Körndle, H. (1998). Study 2000—Problems and perspectives for the development of multimedia tools for teaching and learning in the Internet. *European Psychologist, 3*(3), 219-226.

Nelson-Le Gall, S. (1981). Help-seeking: An understudied problem-solving skill in children. *Developmental Review, 1*(3), 224-246.

Nesbit, J. C., & Adesope, O. O. (2006). Learning with concept and knowledge maps: A meta-analysis. Submitted to *Review of Educational Research*.

Nesbit, J. C., & Winne, P. H. (2003). Self-regulated inquiry with networked resources. *Canadian Journal of Learning and Technology, 29*(3), 71-91.

Nesbit, J. C., Winne, P. H., Jamieson-Noel, D., Code, J., Zhou, M., MacAllister, K., Bratt, S., Wang, W., & Hadwin, A. F. (2006). Using cognitive tools in gStudy to investigate how study activities covary with achievement goals. Submitted to *Journal of Educational Computing Research*.

Nichols, M., & Gardner, N. (2002). Evaluating flexible delivery across a tertiary institution. *Open Learning, 17*(1), 11-22.

O'Donnell, A. M., Dansereau, D. F., & Hall, R. H. (2002). Knowledge maps as scaffolds for cognitive processing. *Educational Psychology Review, 14*(1), 71-86.

Peper, R. J., & Mayer, R. E. (1986). Generative effects of note-taking during science lectures. *Journal of Educational Psychology, 78*(1) 34-38.

Pintrich, P. R. (1999). The role of motivation in promoting and sustaining self-regulated learning. *International Journal of Educational Research, 31*(6), 459-470.

Rao S., & Kumar V. (2005). *Context-aware mixed-initiative interactions for online help*. Poster presented at the 2nd Annual Scientific Conference of LORNET Research Network, Vancouver, Canada.

Schraw, G., Benedixen, L. D., & Dunkle, M. E. (2002). Development and validation of the epistemic belief inventory. In B. K. Hofer & P. R. Pintrich (Eds.), *Personal epistemology: The psychology of beliefs about knowledge and knowing* (pp. 261-275). Mahwah, NJ: Erlbaum.

Schunk, D. H., & Ertmer, P. A. (2000). Self-regulation and academic learning. In M. Boekaerts, P. R. Pintrich, & M. Zeidner (Eds.), *Handbook of self-regulation* (pp. 631-649). New York: Academic.

Shakya J., Menon S., Doherty L., Jordanov M., & Kumar V. S. (2005). *Recognizing opportunities for mixed-initiative interactions based on the principles of self-regulated learning.* Paper presented at the Workshop on Mixed-initiative Problem-solving Assistants, American Association for Artificial Intelligence Fall Symposia, Arlington, VA.

Shugarman, S. L., & Hurst, J. B. (1986). Purposeful paraphrasing: Promoting a nontrivial pursuit of meaning. *Journal of Reading, 29*(5), 396-299.

van Boxtel, C., van der Linden, J., Roelofs, E., & Erkens, G. (2002). Collaborative concept mapping: Provoking and supporting meaningful discourse. *Theory into Practice, 41*(1), 40-46.

Weinstein, C. E., & Mayer, R. E. (1986). The teaching of learning strategies. In M. C. Wittrock, (Ed.), *Handbook of research on teaching* (3rd ed., pp. 315-327). New York: Springer-Verlag.

Wikalong. (2005). *Wikalong: A wiki-margin for the Internet.* Retrieved January 3, 2006, from http://www.wikalong.org/

Winne, P. H. (1995). Inherent details in self-regulated learning. *Educational Psychologist, 30*(4), 173-87.

Winne, P. H. (2001). Self-regulated learning viewed from models of information processing. In B. J. Zimmerman & D. H. Schunk (Eds.), *Self-regulated learning and academic achievement: Theory, research, and practice* (pp. 153-189). New York: Longman.

Winne, P. H., & Hadwin, A. F. (1998). Studying as self-regulated learning. In D. J. Hacker & J. Dunlosky (Eds.), *Metacognition in educational theory and practice* (pp. 277-304). Mahwah, NJ: Erlbaum.

Winne, P. H., & Jamieson-Noel, D. L. (2002). Exploring students' calibration of self-reports about study tactics and achievement. *Contemporary Educational Psychology, 27*(4), 551-572.

Winne, P. H., & the Learning Kit Team (2005, May). *Enhancing research in educational psychology using gStudy software.* Invited address presented at the Meeting of the Canadian Association for Educational Psychology, London, ON, Canada.

Wittrock, M. C. (1989). Generative processing of comprehension. *Educational Psychologist, 24*, 345-376.

Zimmerman, B. J. (2001). Theories of self-regulated learning and academic achievement: An overview and analysis. In B. J. Zimmerman & D. H. Schunk (Eds.), *Self-regulated learning and academic achievement: Theoretical perspectives.* Mahwah, NJ: Erlbaum.

Zimmerman, B. J. (2002). Becoming a self-regulated learner: An overview. *Theory into Practice, 41*(2), 64-70.

Chapter XIX

Adopting Tools for Online Synchronous Communication:
Issues and Strategies

Elizabeth Murphy, Memorial University of Newfoundland, Canada

Thérèse Laferrière, Laval University, Canada

Abstract

This chapter considers some of the issues related to the adoption of online synchronous communication tools and proposes strategies to help deal with these issues. Two contrasting contexts of use of online synchronous tools are described. In one context, audio-conferencing using Elluminate Live™ is highlighted, in the other, video-conferencing using iVisit™. Issues related to use of these tools for synchronous communication are considered from the perspective of relative advantage, compatibility, and complexity. The advantages included the immediacy, spontaneity, intimacy, efficiency, and convenience of communication. Complexity manifested itself in relation to time management, shifting and evolving technical and pedagogical needs, and changes in instructors' roles. Compatibility issues included the demands on instructors, lack of freedom from temporal constraints, and difficulties with communication across time zones and when multi-tasking.

Introduction

For many students and teachers, the transition to e-learning or online learning has involved moving from a form of communication that is synchronous, real-time, and face-to-face, to one that is asynchronous, in delayed time, and text-based (Zemsky & Massy, 2004). This transition has resulted in flexibility related to any-time any-place learning (Oblinger & Maruyama, 1996), increased opportunities for reflection (Harasim, 1993; Heckman & Annabi, 2003; McComb, 1993), equality of participation (Ortega, 1997; Warschauer, 1997), and easy archiving of communications (Collis & Moonen, 2001; Harasim, Hiltz, Teles, & Turoff, 1995). Likewise, the transition has been accompanied by challenges such as loss of non-verbal cues (Burge, 1994; Kuehn, 1994; McIsaac & Gunawardena, 1996; Weatherley & Ellis, 2000), possible decrease in social presence (Anderson, 1996; Tu, 2002), lack of interaction (Guzdial & Carroll, 2002; Oliver & Shaw, 2003), lack of spontaneity and immediacy in communication, and feelings of isolation (Abrahamson, 1998; Badger, 2000; Besser, 1996; Brown, 1996; Tiene, 2000).

To avoid, compensate for, or overcome these challenges, institutions can complement the asynchronous aspects of e-learning with an online synchronous component. Synchronous communication occurs in real time with participants simultaneously, remotely connected to one network. In the past, this form of communication has typically privileged text-based chat. More recent synchronous learning environments combine features and tools such as audio, video, chat, whiteboards, polling features, and breakout rooms.

Text-based forms of synchronous communication have been the focus of numerous studies (see Baron, 2004; Jacobs, 2004; Murphy & Collins, 2000; Nicholson, 2002; Schwier & Balbar, 2002). There have also been a number of studies of video-conferencing (see Alexander, Higgison, & Mogey, 1999; Hearnshaw, 2000; Gage, Nickson, & Beardon, 2002) and of audio-conferencing (see Hampel & Hauck, 2004; Moore & Kearsley, 1996). However, the newer synchronous learning environments have yet to receive equal attention in the literature.

Knolle (2002) argues that investigation of contextual use of real-time technologies is necessary to provide guidance to instructors who are struggling to use these technologies. Online synchronous communication has the potential for numerous benefits including real-time interaction (Hoffman & Novak, 1996), perception of social presence (Blanchard, 2004), and sense of community (Schwier & Balbar, 2002) and immediacy (Garrison, 1990). The potential for benefits or advantages, however, does not guarantee that they will actually occur. For example, Rafaeli and Sudweeks (1997) noted that while interactivity might be possible, it was not always exercised. Even in cases where the advantages may actually be realized, there may be other disadvantages depending on the tools used for synchronous communication. These tools may be quite complex and require extensive support. In other cases, their integration into existing courses or other contexts may result in incompatibility with the teaching and learning activities or strategies already in place.

This chapter considers some of the issues related to the adoption of online synchronous communication tools. It also proposes strategies to help deal with these issues. Two contrasting contexts of use of online synchronous tools are described. In one context, audio-conferencing using Elluminate *Live*™ (EL) is highlighted, in the other, video-conferencing using iVisit™. Both technologies will be of interest to postsecondary institutions considering using synchronous communication tools either as an addition to asynchronous learning or to support remote collaboration among geographically-dispersed individuals. Both technologies operate in low-bandwidth environments, which will be of benefit in cases where the student users do not have high speed access. In addition, iVisit allows for compatibility between Mac and PC users and supports multi-party desktop conferencing. EL is also Mac and PC compatible and will be of particular interest to institutions considering replacing teleconferencing with a Web-based alternative.

The EL case, although only a small pilot, provides insights into the experiences of university instructors who are experimenting with new online technologies for the first time. The case of iVisit, although situated in an elementary and secondary context, provides an illustrative case of a large-scale implementation with 432 hours of video-conferencing activities in one year, including involvement by 13 school districts, four universities, 50 schools, and more than 11,000 iVisit connections. As with the case of EL, teachers' experiences with iVisit offer insights into the types of issues faced when transitioning from face-to-face to e-learning.

Issues related to use of these tools for synchronous communication are considered from the perspective of Rogers' (1995) framework for the adoption of innovations. Rogers highlighted five characteristics of innovations that accelerate and facilitate their adoption: relative advantage, complexity, compatibility, trialability, and observability. Relative advantage refers to the degree to which individuals perceive an innovation as advantageous. Compatibility refers to the degree to which an innovation is perceived as consistent with existing values, experiences, needs, and practices of adopters. Trialability relates to how easily an innovation might be experimented with on a limited basis by potential adopters. Observability refers to the visibility to other potential adopters of results of an innovation. The case studies reported on here did not focus on potential adopters. For this reason, the analysis is limited to consideration of relative advantage, compatibility, and complexity.

Elluminate *Live*™:
Memorial University, Newfoundland

During the 2004-2005 academic year, Memorial University decided to adopt EL in order to eliminate costs related to teleconferencing and to support a general shift in the delivery of distance courses to Web-based modes. Featured tools of EL include two-way, half duplex audio, meaning that only one person can speak at a time. There is also text-based direct messaging, application sharing, a whiteboard, polling feature, a graphing calculator, and break-out rooms. Users require a headset and microphone.

All instructors teaching distance courses in the winter semester 2005 were invited to use the technology. The 10 instructors who opted to use the technology were offered training. Support personnel were available for every session to deal with any technical problems. Following the implementation of the pilot, eight of the instructors participated in a one-on-one, face-to-face, semi-structured interview designed to gain insight into their experiences using the technology. Interview questions focused on how they used the technology, their perceptions of the advantages of EL, the challenges they faced, and their plans for future use. Each interview lasted approximately 45 minutes and was subsequently transcribed and then analyzed in relation to Rogers' framework.

Relative Advantage

An advantage of EL was its convenience compared to teleconferencing. As one instructor explained, "With teleconferencing people had to go to a site where the teleconferencing was available. This allowed them to at least stay in their own community or even in their own homes." The immediacy of communication was also cited as a benefit. Instructors referred to the value of "spontaneous discussion," "spontaneous direct talking," and "spontaneous interaction." One instructor highlighted the value of immediate, spontaneous interactions in a context of student presentations using EL, noting that it "comes very close to being able to do what I do in a face-to-face classroom [in terms of] immediate feedback, questions, and answers." One instructor described EL as a tool that contributed to a "sense of community" that captured "the closeness [and] some of the intimacy you can have in a face-to-face environment."

Instructors referred to opportunities for "making the people come alive," for "hearing the voices," and for creating a "more meaningful, purposeful experience for my students." They observed a "greater sense of intimacy," a "greater sense of knowing," and of feeling "more connected to" students. They liked the fact that the technology allowed them to communicate verbally with students. Likewise, students could "talk to each other and hear each other's voices." One instructor described how a "little more of the person was able to come through in the voice," which gave him a sense of knowing his students.

Another individual highlighted how the use of synchronous tools within an asynchronous environment offered more instructional choice and variety in teaching modes. The ability to record any class sessions and post them for later retrieval was identified as an added feature not available in a live class: "It's all there, and they can record it, they can play it again this evening." Another benefit was the efficiency of synchronous compared to asynchronous communication. One instructor commented, "It's more efficient for me. I don't have to read a hundred postings."

Complexity

Issues of complexity largely involved technical difficulties encountered. EL requires users to install software on their computers prior to use. This installation proved "to be the biggest hassle" that students faced. As a result, "some of them even avoided doing that by not having it put on their computers at all, and came to the University instead." Other students experienced challenges with the two-way audio component: "There were always some [students] who couldn't get on due to some technical problem. Their mike wasn't working." Other students experienced problems with their speakers: "[A]s we were even answering questions sometimes students were saying 'I can't hear you or I can't understand' or their machine would go dead and they wouldn't hear that answer."

Complexity was also evident in the need to become comfortable using new tools in a new context. In relation to the whiteboard, one instructor commented as follows: "I wasn't very comfortable using it...I didn't have time to figure out how to do it." In order to manage the complexity of the adoption, support was provided for every session by Distance Education Learning Technologies (DELT), the division of the university responsible for the pilot. As one instructor explained, some problems were handled by taking students "out of class": "If someone developed a problem while the session was in progress, they would take them to a breakout room and try to deal with it." In other cases, technical difficulties were handled by contacting the students directly: "We had the DELT people here all the time, and they would sometimes phone students at home and try to help them at home."

Success of the adoption depended on dedicated technical support for students who were experiencing difficulties with the technology. One instructor described this support as vital: "If he hadn't been there, I think it would have been a very bad experience because the students would have been very frustrated because they couldn't get into the system. I had no idea how to help them." Support not only ensured that technical problems could be effectively resolved, but also played an important role in terms of reassuring instructors; one individual explained, "I don't feel terribly confident with the technical aspects of it, and I'm always very appreciative of having support people in place."

Compatibility

The issue of compatibility manifested itself primarily in terms of adding synchronous communication to an otherwise asynchronous course. One instructor argued that the "anytime, anyplace asynchronous mode" was the "real advantage of distance and Web-based learning." He added: "When you introduce Elluminate Live, you're staying with the anyplace to a large extent, because anybody can download this stuff, but you're taking away the anytime."

The issue of compatibility became even more obvious in cases involving communication across time zones. One individual observed: "The three sessions were scheduled with everybody in the country having to log on at the same time, which was a bit of a problem when you are in B.C. [British Columbia]" Similarly, another person noted: "This kind of synchronous activity becomes a real burden when you've got students in Badger and Vancouver or even Calgary or anywhere across the country."

Recognition of the constraints and complications from communicating across time zones combined with the lack of freedom from temporal constraints led one instructor to caution others in their use of EL: "You have to be careful. Use it by all means, but you've got to use it for very explicit purposes and limit the sessions." Another offered similar advice: "If we're going to use EL, we need to let people know well in advance that it's going to be used." In some cases, instructors made participation strictly voluntary while, in others, they decided that "if people missed, there were no marks deducted." Some instructors got around the issue of scheduling by simply using the sessions for office hours: "I didn't want to force them to be in a place at a particular time. That takes away from the asynchronous nature of the course. So I just used it for office hours."

Compatibility also manifested itself as an issue in relation to time. One instructor described EL as something "very time-consuming" added "on top of" reading the communication and correspondence from the asynchronous component of the course. One reaction to the demands on time caused by using EL was to reduce the number of weekly sessions from two to one.

Besides issues related to time management, communication across time zones, and voluntary or mandatory participation, use of EL also raised issues of compatibility with current practices. Adopting new tools meant that instructors had to become used to communicating using multiple channels at the same time. The main channels of communication available in EL included two-way audio and direct messaging. Simultaneous management of both modes of communication was not something all instructors were necessarily comfortable with, as the following quote illustrates: "The main challenge I found was moderating two or three activities: the text messaging, the verbal thing, giving them the mike...checking to see whose hand's up... At the same time, I'm talking, responding to their verbal messages."

Compared to other forms of electronic synchronous communication, such as teleconferencing, EL placed extra demands on the moderators since "there were more things to multi-task on at the same time." One individual described how he had to divide his attention between "the student list, plus, the typed-up notes they send not only to me but to each other, plus the white board." The use of direct messaging emerged as the tool least compatible with instructors' current practices. In some instances, the unrestricted use of this tool by students resulted in "more distraction in some ways because of the side conversations that were going on."

iVisit™: Laval University, Quebec

During the 2004-2005 academic year, a research and intervention team engaged in Phase II of "Projet l'école éloignée en réseau" (The Remote Networked Schools Project). An iVisit server provided 600 access codes and passwords to teachers, students, and other university and school personnel involved in the university-school partnership. Another server was dedicated to asynchronous communication through the use of Knowledge Forum™, which is a group workspace designed to support knowledge building. These two online collaborative tools were critical features in the design of the project. The adoption of iVisit was based on two criteria: flexibility of use and low-bandwidth demand in comparison with other multi-site video-conferencing systems. Featured tools include dedicated rooms, a "push-to-talk" button, and a text-based chat window.

Users require a microphone, but headsets are not necessary unless online traffic results in poor sound quality.

In Phase I of the project (2002-2003), 18 classes in 10 sites carried out 24 different collaborative learning activities using iVisit. Of the 432 hours of video-conferencing activities, 110 were observed systematically to establish how the tool was used. Three different raters observed directly the human interaction occurring on iVisit. Using the software Camtasia, they recorded on a random basis 20 hours of conversation for the purpose of analysis. Ninety-one semi-structured interviews were conducted with students, teachers, school principals, and school district technology personnel and administrators. Interviews were conducted using the telephone or iVisit and lasted 30-40 minutes.

In Phase II (2004-2006), project participants were distributed among 13 school districts and four universities. There was participation by over 50 schools with more than 11,000 iVisit connections by the Spring of 2005. Teachers were invited to use iVisit in combination with Knowledge Forum to support collaborative learning and knowledge-building activities. School district personnel provided basic training and technical support. University-based personnel provided just-in-time technical and pedagogical support and feedback on demand. The following is an analysis of the results using Rogers' framework.

Relative Advantage

In Phase I, video-conferencing through iVisit was the tool preferred by all interveners who already had broadband access in their workplace. This tool allowed them to see each other in real time and also to communicate with several people simultaneously. Video-conferencing was used both inside and outside the classroom (e.g., by school administrators, counsellors, mentors, experts, and teachers).

As indicated in the Phase I Report (Laferrière, Breuleux, & Inchauspé, 2004), synchronous communication through iVisit helped them overcome professional isolation, team up with colleagues, and provide professional services at a distance. One school principal with two small schools 20 miles apart conducted meetings with the professional staff of the two schools joined through video-conferencing. Principals of schools hundreds of miles apart participated in school district meetings using iVisit.

In Phase II, just-in-time professional development using synchronous communication became a characteristic of the project. There was always someone present online in the iVisit Coordination Room to help teachers with the planning or conduct of online collaborative learning activities and projects. Meetings could also be scheduled ahead of time through asynchronous (e-mail) or synchronous

(Internet chat: MSN Messenger) communication and conducted in a specific virtual iVisit Room.

Ten distinct professional development activities using iVisit as a support for synchronous communication were identified in Phase I: software training, networking of participants, partnership development, planning and coordinating online educational activities with students, getting started with online learning activities, educational aid, delocalized teamwork, mentoring, emotional support, and immediate solution to or reproduction of technological problems. Onsite and online teacher-teacher interactions were observed to be of a collegial nature and provided opportunities for both informal and non-formal professional development activities.

Complexity

At the outset of the project, teachers were convinced that their tasks in a networked classroom would be more demanding. After participating in Phase I, their thinking on this matter had not changed. However, after Phase I, the demands and the support that teachers called for had been pinpointed. One of these demands related to the management of time and of learning achieved in conjunction with projects. Teachers identified a need for facilitating conditions such as technical and pedagogical support; readily available equipment; release from normal tasks to engage in certain collaborative activities; and flexible scheduling. These demands and needs were given more attention in Phase II. Technical support was offered to deal with complexity at the technical level. As capacity-building increased in classrooms, technical support was reduced and pedagogical support increased. At the same time, the need to focus on learning outcomes resulted in pressure on school principals and teachers.

Phase I teacher interviews, which focused on teachers' beliefs at the beginning and at the end of the year, revealed that some beliefs, although maintained, had broadened and become more complex. For instance, at the outset, the students' socialization was deemed necessary for their education. At the end of Phase I, teachers still believed this, but socialization was now considered integral to the learning process itself. Teachers also believed that they needed to be present in a networked classroom, but went beyond evoking a simple presence and focused on roles (including that of a leader) that must be exercised in this new situation.

Some new beliefs that implied a more complex understanding of their work also emerged. These included recognition of the importance of collaboration in the delocalized school through networking and the benefits derived from it; the discovery of the ability of students who were previously less independent and motivated to work in a network to get involved and make decisions; and the discovery or bolstering of an essential belief (i.e., that students learn actively).

In this context of use, complexity involved a change in the role of the teacher and the learner in a networked classroom.

Compatibility

Online synchronous communication for collaborative learning using iVisit also challenged existing instructional practices. For instance, secondary school teachers were more resistant to using iVisit to support student-to-student synchronous communication for learning purposes than were elementary school teachers, and they were generally less likely to engage in constructivist, student-centered, and knowledge-building pedagogies. The secondary school teachers had to reduce the time they lectured to students in order to use iVisit. The lack of time was frequently noted as a concern, and the school schedule was identified as problematic. For these teachers, using iVisit to engage students in activities such as negotiating meaning was identified as incompatible with existing practices.

Issues

As these two contexts of use illustrate, online synchronous communication can present numerous advantages, some of which actually temper or attenuate the disadvantages associated with asynchronous communication. The advantages include the following: immediacy, spontaneity, intimacy, efficiency, and convenience of communication; opportunities for more instructional choice, more tools, networking, partnership development, planning, implementing, and coordinating educational activities; and opportunities for delocalized teamwork, mentoring, and both informal and non-formal professional development activities.

These advantages offer a compelling rationale for the inclusion of synchronous forms of communication in otherwise asynchronous contexts of learning. Of particular importance and interest are the advantages relating to the capacity of synchronous tools to offer communication experiences that replicate features of face-to-face contact. For some instructors and students, these advantages may facilitate the transition to e-learning.

These advantages do not, however, obviate the issues that can arise in the use of synchronous tools. In the case of use of EL, lack of comfort with technology was the most important issue. This issue may pose a barrier to attempts to use new forms of learning. The advantage of EL and iVisit is the many features and tools offered to users. However, if students and teachers do not know how to use these tools, then the advantages may instead result in limitations. In the EL case, comments regarding the use of the whiteboard and direct messaging suggest that, in spite of initial training sessions, instructors may not make full or effective use of these tools. The experiences of instructors and students also emphasized the role of support in the adoption of new and complex tools. Without this support, the transition to the use of new e-learning tools may fail entirely.

In the case of use of iVisit, issues of complexity were numerous and varied. Some of the issues were related to time management and support in the form of a release from normal tasks or flexible scheduling to engage in collaborative planning. This issue indicates how the transition to e-learning can necessitate systemic changes that involve not only the instructors and students, but administration as well. The issue of the need for technical and pedagogical support and equipment reveals the fine balance that must be achieved in the transition. As the need declined for technical support, the need for pedagogical support increased. This situation shows how instructors' needs do not remain static but shift and evolve. These changes in need highlight the importance of monitoring the adoption of new tools to ensure timely and appropriate training and professional development. The experiences of the participants in the iVisit case also made evident how roles may need to shift when new forms of communicating and collaborating are adopted. This need to shift may give rise to confusion, if not carefully managed or understood by all.

Compatibility issues related to the use of EL and iVisit included the demands that their use placed on instructors, the lack of freedom from temporal constraints, and difficulties with communication across time zones. The issue of demands placed on instructors made evident that the transition to e-learning in this case was interpreted as an extra demand placed on top of existing workloads. Instructors and teachers perceived the use of the synchronous communication as an addition of one mode on top of another and not simply a shift from one mode to another. In the case of iVisit, the time demands even resulted in some resistance to use of the technology. While communication across time zones was not an issue in the case of iVisit, it placed some limitations and restrictions on activities in the case of EL. In general, some instructors perceived the use of synchronous technology as incompatible with the anytime advantage of online or e-learning. This issue made evident the need for institutions and instructors to make decisions about their goals for e-learning before they adopt particular tools.

The issue of multi-tasking with use of direct messaging highlights how the new e-learning environments can require instructors to adopt new behaviors and new ways of working and communicating. The issue points to the need for institutions to be aware of and put in place opportunities for instructors as well as students to develop strategies and techniques that allow them to appreciate and take advantage of new tools and new ways of interacting in e-learning environments.

The case of iVisit made evident the change that new forms of online communication may require, not only in teaching practices, but also in teachers' beliefs. The experiences of some of the teachers using iVisit highlighted the link between new tools and new practices. Their lack of comfort with constructivist, student-centered approaches, and practices can serve as a reminder that the transition to e-learning involves not only a technical leap, but a pedagogical one as well. In terms of the latter, adopting new tools may require philosophical changes in relation to instructors' beliefs about the nature of learning.

Strategies

The experiences described in these two cases suggest that the transition to new forms of e-learning using synchronous communication tools such as EL and iVisit offers many advantages. The experiences also suggest that this transition must be carefully orchestrated and managed for those benefits to be realized and for the transition to be successful and effective. The experiences reported in this chapter illustrate how the transition to e-learning with synchronous communication may involve not only the adoption of new tools, but also new beliefs, roles, practices, and new ways of behaving, communicating, collaborating, and of managing time. These changes can be individual as well as systemic and may involve students, instructors or teachers, managers, support personnel, and administrative staff. All of these changes may be more easily accepted if the appropriate strategies are identified and put in place. The strategies relate to technical as well as pedagogical and administrative issues.

Successful and effective adoption of online synchronous communication tools in contexts of teaching and learning will require extensive technical support. This support will be particularly necessary in the early stages of adoption and in cases where users are not familiar with environments supporting simultaneous multi-tool use. For both instructors and students, support should include not only assistance with downloading the software, but also support with use of the various tools and features such as chat or direct messaging, audio, and the whiteboard. Where resources do not allow for high levels of such support, students and teachers could be paired or grouped so that more technically-able users can support those who are less comfortable with the new tools. Additionally, users can be directed to the site of the software where FAQs and technical guidelines may help them solve technical problems. Without this support, instructors may not be able to address pedagogical concerns or issues that may arise in these new learning environments.

In terms of instructors, support needs to extend beyond the technical dimensions of use to encompass the pedagogical or andragogical aspects. The introduction of new tools for communication needs to be accompanied by opportunities for instructors to reflect on their practice and to consider new ways of communicating with students. Where the goal is to make use of the tools to move toward more constructivist and student-centered forms of learning, professional development opportunities could be designed to engage instructors in consideration of best practices, inquiry into beliefs about teaching and learning, and discussion of how teachers and students can maximize the affordances of the tools and provide more choice in modes of learning. Such opportunities could provide instructors with practice in multi-tasking and using a variety of tools at one time.

At the administrative level, use of synchronous communication across time zones with differing schedules and in the context of primarily asynchronous courses may require flexible or alternative scheduling. In some cases, non-mandatory or voluntary participation may be the preferred option. As well, workload demands may need to be diminished, especially at the outset in order to accommodate the addition of a synchronous component.

Conclusion

Given the issues of complexity and compatibility that can arise in the adoption of online synchronous tools in contexts of teaching and learning, the advantages and benefits of such use will need to be highlighted. This recognition may help diminish the importance of the challenges individuals face in transitioning to this his new form of learning. Once individuals witness or realize that these tools allow them to accomplish goals they could not otherwise accomplish, their tolerance of issues related to the complexity and compatibility may well increase.

As use of these new tools and others like them becomes more common, and as individuals continue to become accustomed to working in electronically mediated environments, some of the issues may diminish in importance. Such may be the case with technical concerns. Issues related to pedagogy and andragogy are likely to require more time and attention. To ensure an effective transition to this form of e-learning, instructors, students, designers, and administrators need to carefully consider the issues associated with its use and identify and implement effective strategies to ensure that its advantages are realized.

References

Abrahamson, C. E. (1998). Issues in interactive communication in distance education. *College Student Journal, 32*(1), 33-43.

Alexander, W., Higgison, C., & Mogey, N. (1999). *Case studies: Videoconferencing for teaching and learning.* Retrieved October 25, 2005, from http://www.icbl.hw.ac.uk/ltdi/vcstudies/

Anderson, M. D. (1996). Using computer-mediated conferencing to facilitate group projects in an educational psychology course. *Behavior Research Methods, Instruments, & Computers, 28*(2), 351-353.

Badger, A. (2000). Keeping it fun and relevant: Using active online learning. In K. W. White & B. H. Weight (Eds.), *The online teaching guide: A handbook of attitudes, strategies, and techniques for the virtual classroom* (pp. 124-141). Needham Heights, MA: Allyn and Bacon.

Baron, N. S. (2004). Gender issues in college student use of instant messaging. *Journal of Language and Social Psychology, 23*(4), 397-423.

Besser, H. (1996). Issues and challenges for the distance independent environment. *Journal of the American Society of Information Science, 47*(11), 817-820.

Blanchard, A. (2004). Virtual behavior settings: An application of behavior setting theories to virtual communities. *Journal of Computer Mediated Communication, 9*(2). Retrieved July 1, 2005 from http://www.ascusc.org/jcmc/vol9/issue2/blanchard.html

Brown, K. M. (1996). The role of internal and external factors in the discontinuation of off-campus students. *Distance Education, 17*(1), 44-71.

Burge, E. (1994). Learning in computer conferenced contexts: The learners' perspective. *Journal of Distance Education, 9*(1), 19-43.

Collis, B., & Moonen, J. (2001). *Flexible learning in a digital world: Experiences and expectations.* London: Kogan Page.

Gage, J., Nickson, M., & Beardon, T. (2002). Can videoconferencing contribute to teaching and learning? The experience of the motivate project. *Annual Conference of the British Educational Research Association.* Retrieved October 24, 2005, from http://www.leeds.ac.uk/educol/documents/00002264.htm

Garrison, D. R. (1990). An analysis and evaluation of audio-teleconferencing to facilitate education at a distance. *The American Journal of Distance Education, 4*(3), 13-26.

Guzdial, M., & Carroll, K. (2002). Explaining the lack of dialogue in computer-supported collaborative Learning. *CSCL 2002 Information and Conference Papers*. Retrieved June 22, 2005, from http://newmedia.colorado.edu/cscl/18.html

Hampel, R., & Hauck, M. (2004). Towards an effective use of audio conferencing in distance language courses. *Language Learning & Technology, 8*(1). Retrieved October 20, 2005, from http://llt.msu.edu/vol8num1/hampel/default.html

Harasim, L. M. (1993). *Global networks: Computers and international communication.* Cambridge, MA: MIT Press.

Harasim, L. M., Hiltz, S. R., Teles, L., & Turoff, M. (1995). *Learning networks: A field guide to teaching and learning online.* Cambridge, MA: The MIT Press.

Hearnshaw, D. (2000). Effective desktop videoconferencing with minimal network demands. *British Journal of Educational Technology, 31*(3), 221-228.

Heckman, R., & Annabi, H. (2003). A content analytic comparison of FTF and ALN case-study discussions. *Proceedings of the 36th Hawaii International Conference on System Sciences.* Retrieved June 22, 2005, from http://www.alnresearch.org/data_files/articles/full_text/heckman03.pdf

Hoffman, D. L., & Novak, T. P. (1996). Marketing in hypermedia computer-mediated environments: Conceptual foundations. *Journal of Marketing, 60*(3), 50-68.

Jacobs, G. (2004). Complicating contexts: Issues of methodology in researching the language and literacies of instant messaging. *Reading Research Quarterly, 39*(4), 394-407.

Knolle, J. W. (2002). *Identifying the best practices for using HorizonLive to teach in the synchronous online environment.* Master's thesis. California State University. Retrieved October 12, 2005, from http://www.csuchico.edu/~jknolle/research/thesis/Knolle_Thesis.pdf

Kuehn, S. A. (1994). Computer-mediated communication in instructional settings: A research agenda. *Communication Education, 43*(2), 171-183.

Laferrière, T., Breuleux, A., et Inchauspé, P. (2004). *L'école éloignée en réseau.* Rapport de recherche, CEFRIO, Québec. Retrieved July 1, 2005, from http://www.cefrio.qc.ca/rapports/école_éloignée_en_réseau_Rapport_final_2004.pdf

McComb, M. (1993). Augmenting a group discussion course with computer-mediated communication in a small college setting. *Interpersonal Computing and Technology: An Electronic Journal for the 21st Century,*

3(1). Retrieved June 22, 2005, from http://www.helsinki.fi/science/optek/1993/n3/mccomb.txt

McIsaac, M., & Gunawardena, C. (1996). Distance education. In D. Johnassen (Ed.), *Handbook of research for educational communications and technology* (pp. 403-437). New York: Macmillan.

Moore, M. G., & Kearsley, G. (1996). Distance education: A systems approach view—audioconferencing. In M. G. Moore & G. Kearsley (Eds.), *Distance education: A systems approach view* (pp. 136-39). Stamford, CT: Wadsworth Publishers.

Murphy, K. J., & Collins, M. P. (2000, March). *Communication conventions in instructional chats.* Paper presented at the Annual Convention of the American Educational Research Association, Chicago, IL. Retrieved October 11, 2005, from http://www.firstmonday.dk/issues/issue2_11/murphy

Nicholson, S. (2002). Socialization in the "virtual hallway": Instant messaging in the asynchronous Web-based distance education classroom. *The Internet and Higher Education, 5*(4), 363-372.

Oblinger, D., & Maruyama, M. (1996). *Distributed learning: CAUSE Professional Paper,* Series #14. Boulder, CO: Cause. Retrieved June 21, 2005, from http://www.educause.edu/ir/library/pdf/pub3014.pdf

Oliver, M., & Shaw, G. P. (2003). Asynchronous discussion in support of medical education. *Journal of Asynchronous Learning Networks, 7*(1), 56-67. Retrieved June 22, 2005, from http://www.aln.org/publications/jaln/v7n1/v7n1_oliver.asp

Ortega, L. (1997). Processes and outcomes in networked classroom interaction: Defining the research agenda for L2 computer-assisted classroom discussion. *Language Learning & Technology, 1*(1), 82-93.

Rafaeli, S., & Sudweeks, F. (1997). Networked interactivity. *Journal of Computer Mediated Communication, 2*(4). Retrieved June 22, 2005, from http://www.usc.edu/dept/annenberg/vol2/issue4/rafaeli.sudweeks.html.

Rogers, E. (1995). *Diffusion of innovations* (4th ed.). New York: The Free Press.

Schwier, R. A., & Balbar, S. (2002). The interplay of content and community in synchronous and asynchronous communication: Virtual communication in a graduate seminar. *Canadian Journal of Learning and Technology, 28*(2). Retrieved June 22, 2005, from http://www.cjlt.ca/content/vol28.2/schwier_balbar.html

Tiene, D. (2000). Online discussions: A survey of advantages and disadvantages compared to face-to-face discussions. *Journal of Educational Multimedia and Hypermedia, 9*(4), 371-384.

Tu, C. H. (2002). The impacts of text-based CMC on online social presence. *The Journal of Interactive Online Learning, 1*(2). Retrieved June 22, 2005, from http://www.ncolr.org/jiol/issues/2002/fall/06/

Warschauer, M. (1997). Computer-mediated collaborative learning: Theory and practice. *The Modern Language Journal, 81*(4), 470-481.

Weatherley, R., & Ellis, A. (2000). *Online learning: What do teachers need to know about communicating online?* Paper presented at the NAWEB 2000 virtual conference. Retrieved June 22, 2005, from http://naweb.unb.ca/proceedings/2000/weatherley-ellis.htm

Zemsky, R., & Massy, W. F. (2004). *Thwarted innovation: What happened to e-learning and why.* The University of Pennsylvania: The Learning Alliance. Retrieved June 22, 2005, from http://www.irhe.upenn.edu/Docs/Jun2004/ThwartedInnovation.pdf

Chapter XX

Knowledge is PowerPoint:
Slideware in E-Learning

Adnan Qayyum, Concordia University, Canada

Brad Eastman, University of British Columbia, Canada

Abstract

Slideware such as PowerPoint might be the most common software used for e-learning, yet is remarkably understudied. We begin this chapter by summarizing and analyzing literature on slideware in e-learning. We also review the debate on the cognitive style of PowerPoint, partly in the context of educational technology research on whether media influence learning. Then, we discuss the limitations of slideware and suggest strategies to consider when designing e-learning with slideware. The strategies include: accounting for differences between designing for synchronous and asynchronous delivery; avoiding software "wizards"; using graphic design principles; and advocating simplicity. Finally, we discuss the economic implications of slideware in e-learning. If slideware is immensely common in e-learning, do universities and colleges need to invest in expensive course management systems (CMS)? We advocate that administrators research slideware use in their institutions to inform decisions about which CMS, if any, is needed.

Introduction

Everyone reading this article has likely made or seen presentations using Microsoft's PowerPoint or, perhaps, Apple's entry into the slideware market, Keynote. Given that slideware will continue to be an important part of the e-learning landscape for the foreseeable future, instructors, instructional designers, and administrators need to think carefully about how to use it well.

E-learning involves a continuum of teaching, from Web-supplemented classes to fully online courses (OECD, 2005), a continuum we explore in more detail when discussing course management systems. We begin this article by reviewing literature on slideware in e-learning. This includes reviewing research on slideware use and the passionate debate on the cognitive style of PowerPoint. We analyze this debate in the context of educational technology research on media attributes and whether media influence learning. Based partly on this debate, we conclude that PowerPoint and other slideware have inherent limitations that must be taken into account when designing instruction. We then suggest instructional design considerations such as accounting for the difference between designing for synchronous and asynchronous delivery, avoiding software "wizards," using principles of graphic design, and simplicity. In the final section, we discuss the uneasy relationship between slideware and course management systems (CMS). If in many cases, e-learning is just slides posted onto a CMS, we question the need for a CMS to deliver this kind of content. We conclude by advocating that administrators initiate research on slideware use in their institutions to inform decisions about what type of CMS, if any, is needed.

Slideware in E-Learning

Slideware is ubiquitous. According to Microsoft, over 30 million PowerPoint presentations are made everyday (Flintoff, 2001). PowerPoint was developed by Bob Gaskins in Berkeley in 1984, based on the work of his Bell Northern Research colleague, Whitfield Diffie. It was first released in 1987, originally for Macintosh computers. Microsoft bought the software later that year and, once it was bundled into the MS Office Suite with the popular Word and Excel programs, PowerPoint became a juggernaut. According to conservative estimates, PowerPoint is installed on 250 million computers (Flintoff, 2001; Parker, 2001). In some countries, PowerPoint is the second most commonly taught and used software program for and by secretaries, after MS Word (Flintoff, 2001). Yet slideware is remarkably understudied in e-learning research.

Is Slideware Used for E-Learning?

Many how-to-use-PowerPoint articles exist but few exist about PowerPoint or other slideware in e-learning. We found little research that drilled deeply enough to identify which software is being used for teaching at colleges and universities. Cross-institution studies tend to be about computer access and use in general on campus (e.g., Kenneth Green's Campus Computing surveys) or about instructional methods, including computer-aided instruction (e.g., the biennial study from UCLA's Higher Education Research Institute). Software companies track, and sometimes divulge, how many colleges have purchased their products, but these numbers tend to be about sales, not use. Similarly, some colleges and institutions track data on registration numbers for software, but not use patterns, a distinction we discuss next. It is unclear how pervasive slideware is in higher education. Is it rarely used or as common as the CMS and authoring tools? We suggest it is the latter, based on research from the training sector, the growth of software for integrating PowerPoint to online learning, anecdotal evidence from other instructional designers, and our experience as instructional designers. These studies and cases intimate that slideware is a very common, if understudied, part of e-learning.

For example, in the training sector PowerPoint is the second most commonly used software for e-learning, according to one study (Bersin & Associates, 2003). Training professionals (N=3500) were asked to list their three most frequently used tools for creating computer-based learning applications. Dreamweaver was listed by 52%, PowerPoint by 48%, followed by Flash (46%), Word (22%), FrontPage (21%), and Authorware (20%).

Many companies have designed software that facilitates integrating PowerPoint presentations into online learning environments. For example, Macromedia *Breeze* and Elluminate *Live!* each allows users to use existing PowerPoint presentations in a synchronous learning environment. Presentations can also be recorded and replayed or distributed at a later date. Impatica's suite of software tools allows users to combine PowerPoint presentations with audio and/or video into a java application that can then be streamed on the Web or on CD/DVD. These software packages help instructors put their presentations onto the Web—regardless of whether those presentations were intended for Web usage or not. Brandon-Hall has even sponsored a PowerPoint to Web "bake-off" (http://cedar.forest.net/brandonhall/Power/Power.htm). Twelve companies participated in this contest where each team had 20 minutes to convert a PowerPoint presentation about the features of an atomic clock into an e-learning course. The entire development process occurred in front of an audience of 300 to 350 people, primarily classroom instructors and training managers. Certainly participating companies believed that slideware for e-learning was a viable market opportunity. The bake-off seemed to reinforce this belief.

Teaching with Slideware: PowerPoint as Chalkboard

PowerPoint is the chalkboard for teaching in the digital era, according to some (Szabo & Hastings, 2000). Professors teach with slideware because it is familiar and convenient. They make slideware presentations at meetings and confer-ences, where using PowerPoint or its look-alikes is the expected norm. For many faculty members, the practice of using slideware has spilled over into teaching because it affords many advantages. Slideware has rich graphics and video and audio capabilities. During class lectures, slides act as an outline, reminding the instructor what needs to be discussed. According to Norman (2004), many people create slideware presentations thinking about how to present to the audience, but really the slides are created for the benefit of the presenter. Slideware fosters the perception that presentations are well-organized, even if a just-in-time instructor threw notes together 10 minutes before teaching. In a study on learner perceptions of PowerPoint (Frey & Birnbaum, 2002) at the University of Pittsburgh, professors who used PowerPoint were perceived to be more organized than those who did not by 79% of students in an undergraduate course (N=160).

Slideware is sometimes used and advocated for because of the technological imperative. The rationale is that digital technologies must be used to avoid being left behind. Digital technology use is expected, and therefore it is often adopted uncritically. Students begin to ask for digital copies of lecture notes and more online communication. One of our colleagues suggested much of her work involved posting slides online that were used in face-to-face lectures. This was often done, she said, because students asked for PowerPoint slides. Posting presentations online was an easy way to distribute them. As instructional designers, we too have experienced being handed presentations and being asked to post them online. Colleagues at the University of Texas and at the University of British Columbia have also reported this practice. University of Pittsburgh research (Frey & Birnbaum, 2002) indicated that a generation of students who have grown up digital have come to expect digital technologies to be part of their learning experience. A majority of undergrads (69%) agreed or strongly agreed that PowerPoint held their attention, compared to 12% of students who preferred the blackboard or whiteboard. Most students (91%) said that the handouts from PowerPoint helped them to study, 80% said it helped them to take class notes, and 85% of students found PowerPoint presentations emphasized key points in class. Only 15% of students said that posting PowerPoint presentations before the class would make them less likely to attend class.

Employers and curriculum review committees also expect slideware. Work trends have long shaped curriculum content in many subject areas of higher education. In most business and government circles, it is seen as unprofessional to make a presentation without PowerPoint. Responding to this demand, many faculties teach their students how to make presentations via slideware. For example, MBA and public policy students often learn how to make PowerPoint presentations as part of their training, parallel to the way teacher education programs used to require future teachers to make overhead transparencies.

We suggest that slideware serves as "gateway software" for e-learning. Instructors initially use slideware as source material for e-learning, giving educational content in PowerPoint format to instructional designers, Web designers, or graduate students to post online. Instructors who get comfortable with using IT for teaching may be open to other tools like discussion boards or online quizzes.

Training sector research confirms slideware is used as source material for e-learning. Over 1000 respondents (30%) stated that 50% of their materials for e-learning programs comes in PowerPoint format (Bersin & Associates, 2003). It is also used for storyboarding and as a course authoring tool. Storyboarding on slideware is common because it allows for convenient linear and non-linear sequencing, layout, and prioritizing of information. Slideware is used for course authoring because it allows almost everyone to create rich multimedia content relatively easily.

Learning with Slideware: Power(Point) Corrupts?

There is an important, ongoing debate about learning with slideware. Critics of PowerPoint argue it fosters a specific cognitive style of communication. The software relies on auto content wizards, templates, and bullet point text. Bullet points are the defining attribute, the *point*, of Power*Point*. There are many communication problems with bullet points according to Tufte (2003), the most outspoken critic of PowerPoint.

PowerPoint easily affords organizing information hierarchically on slides as headings, bullet points, more subheading-like bullet points, and sentences or sentence-fragments. This is problematic because presenters assume there is continuity from point to point. Many audiences also accept this assumption of continuity. In fact, using bullet points creates fragmented narrative with choppy continuity where critical relationships are often left vague. Presenters using PowerPoint are able to foreshorten thought and evidence on claims by zooming from bullet point to bullet point, slide to slide. PowerPoint, Tufte argues, "weakens verbal and spatial reasoning" by encouraging hierarchical, frag-mented presentations (2003, p. 4).

However, hierarchy is not the most appropriate model for organizing all or many types of information. Interestingly, a hierarchical approach is not the model for presenting information used by many leaders of organizations, governments, and companies. They tell stories (Gray, 2005). Storytelling, that is, organizing information as a narrative structure, can be a very cogent way of communicating some types of information. Slideware discourages storytelling by fragmenting narrative and continuity.

PowerPoint fosters a sales-pitch approach to communication. We have all seen (or perhaps made) slideware presentations with lots of sizzle and little steak. In these presentations, the priority becomes persuasion through fast-paced, catchy phrases and exaggerated claims, rather than discussion through evidence, coherent explanation, reasoning, and questioning. Arizona State University researchers presented the same information to three groups in three formats: on paper, as bar graphs, and in PowerPoint with animated graphs. The group shown the PowerPoint presentation rated the information as substantially more credible than the other two presentations (Caldini et al., in Parker, 2001). Indeed, PowerPoint was originally called a persuasion technology and Adobe called their now defunct slideware *Persuasion*.

Defenders of slideware argue the software is, at best, effective for communicating information and at worst, neutral. Horn argues hierarchy is an important way to organize information and manage complexity (Horn in Atkinson, 2004). He also contends that slideware adds a visual shape to developing an argument that conventional lecturing lacks. Pinker contends, "two channels of sending information [spoken and visual] are better than one" (Pinker in Parker, 2001). Norman (2004) contends that the technology is not at fault, but rather users' lack of skills. Blaming slideware is like blaming the physical book, rather than the writer.

Learning with Media: Old Debates in New Technologies

The debate on the cognitive style of PowerPoint is not new. With each new educational technology, the learning with media debate (Clark, 1994; Kozma, 1994,) is revisited. Norman's position on PowerPoint is reinforced by 80 years of research (Clark, 1994) indicating that media do not influence learning. Instead, instructional methods are what matters. Admittedly, media and software differ. Media are technologies used for information sharing. Software is specifically encoded digital information that can, among other things, allow for creating media. Thus, software can be less restrictive than conventional media. However, in one of the few studies on learning with PowerPoint, Ahmed (1998) found little difference in test scores between students who were presented course information via PowerPoint versus traditional overheads (N=143). Tufte may be correct about PowerPoint being used poorly. However, the problem is with the "usual use" in Clark's phrase (1994, p. 23), not with any unique cognitive attributes of the software. We agree with Clark's position that instructional method matters. When using slideware for e-learning, this means design matters. So how does one design good slideware for e-learning?

Designing Slideware for E-Learning: Screwdrivers, Not Dimes

No technology is irreplaceable. However, for a given instructional strategy, some technologies are more effective, in terms of speed and cost of design and access for learners. As Chickering and Ehrmann (1996) stated, it is "[b]etter to turn a screw with a screwdriver than a hammer—a dime may also do the trick, but a screwdriver is usually better." As we reflected on writing this chapter, we realized that we often enjoy using slideware in presentations and for teaching, as many people in education do.

Despite this, in many cases, slideware is the dime, when a screwdriver is needed. Sometimes, however, instructors and instructional designers (often the same person) have to create course materials in a relatively short time. Individuals are forced to rush the design process. As a survival technique, instructors or designers resort to using familiar, if less effective, methods. They teach as they have been taught, and, in the case of slideware, use it as they have seen it used. Many academics take new technology and use it to perpetuate the "sage on the stage" model of teaching, where information is transmitted from the instructor to students. Taylor (2002) noted that in numerous examples, e-learning is equated with posting lecture notes, possibly supplemented by PowerPoint slides, online. This does not allow for more "constructivist dimensions of online education through the extensive use of mechanisms for synchronous and/or asynchronous communication available via the Internet" (p. 8). Our concern is that poorly designed slideware also creates bad e-learning courses for instructors working from behaviorist, cognitivist, or constructivist approaches.

Since there is no literature on how to use slideware for e-learning, we use instructional design (ID) principles and our anecdotal experience about how one might best use slideware as a screwdriver, not a dime. We advocate creating slideware for e-learning by being aware of the full capabilities of slideware, recognizing the important difference between using slideware for synchronous versus asynchronous learning, avoiding options like the auto content wizards, acknowledging the value of simplicity, and employing basic graphic design principles.

Instructional Design

As instructors and instructional designers, we believe learning is improved through application of a thoughtful process to creating courses. It follows that designing a slideware presentation for use on the Web should take into account instructional design principles. Instructional design has been defined as "the process for designing instruction based on sound practices" (Morrison, Ross & Kemp, 2004, p. 6). Following an ID process allows one to bring together all the elements of a presentation—audio, visual, interactivity—in the best possible manner. All instructors recognize the value of building a course in a way that optimizes the learning experience. This concern should extend to using slideware from an instructional design perspective to ensure it does not inhibit learning.

Thinking Outside the Slide: The Capabilities of Slideware

Because of its capabilities, slideware is not as appropriate as other technologies for meeting certain learning objectives. We agree with Tufte that slideware has limitations—limitations that are often ignored. Slideware cannot be used for anything and everything.

Where possible, the course author or instructional designer should start with instructional design, not with technology. Ask how to best use the technology hand that has been dealt. This means starting with learning objectives. Begin by asking what learners should come away with and whether slideware can help or hinder them. Keep in mind the purpose of a given presentation and build a presentation accordingly.

Synchronous or Asynchronous?

There is a crucial difference between using slideware for synchronous learning versus asynchronous learning. Instructors should be cautious when taking a slideware presentation prepared for face-to-face environment or for a synchronous online environment, and making it available for download or converting it to a slide show viewable on the Web. Well-designed presentations for a face-to-face or synchronous online classroom may not be suitable for an asynchronous online course. Usually, the verbal narrative (which or may not have been based on an instructor's notes) that accompanies presentations and gives context and continuity to concepts, images, or bullet points will be absent. Even if the presentation were recorded for later playback on the Web, it still might not translate well to Web-based delivery.

Despite these difficulties, many instructors do not take the time to rework presentations that will be available in an asynchronous environment. Slideware presentations in an asynchronous online learning environment lack student-instructor interactivity. Learners cannot ask for clarification about an obscure idea the same the way they can in a synchronous environment. We believe that as part of an asynchronous course, slideware needs to be used very judiciously. We would go so far as to contend that there are very few good reasons to use slideware in an asynchronous course. One might use it for slides of art or a series of images that illustrate something—a process perhaps—but there would have to be some reason to have a slide show that reveals images one at a time in a given order. For example, the order in which a presentation reveals something about war or poverty can be important and can have great emotional impact, but for a series of images of logging machinery, for example, we cannot see the advantage of posting a slideware presentation on a Web site when html pages with accompanying text could look as good and may work better.

For this reason, slideware presentations should be carefully constructed for use in an asynchronous environment. Determine what to say or show, how to say it, and rework the presentation given that learners may not be able to ask for instant clarification. Consider whether there are learning advantages to slideware over well-designed html pages with appropriate images, tables, and graphs.

Honing presentation skills are as important for e-learning, if not more so, than for face-to-face environments. A synchronous online environment makes this doubly important since it may be easier to bore people in an online environment than in a face-to-face environment. In an online environment, there is no guarantee that the learner who has logged in is actually paying attention and is not watching television news while barely noticing what is occurring in the virtual classroom.

The Wonderful Wizard?

The auto content wizard is designed to help neophyte PowerPoint users design a presentation, but it is more like a straightjacket. Ignore it. Just the name alone, "auto content," makes us cautious. It was added in the mid-nineties, when Microsoft learned that some presenters were not sure what to do with a blank PowerPoint page and found it hard to get started. Parker (2001) quoted a former Microsoft developer who recalled with laughter, "We said, 'What we need is some automatic content!'...'Punch the button and you'll have a presentation.'" The developer thought the idea was "crazy." The name was meant as a joke. But according to Parker, "Microsoft took the idea and kept the name—a rare example of a product named in outright mockery of its target customers" (p. 4).

Determine what to say, how to say it, and build the presentation without the wizard. The extra time may take will be well worth it, both for the instructor and the learner.

Simplicity

An instructor does not need to build a complex slideware presentation. In many cases, the best design is simple and short. Designers sometimes think that adding media elements (such as sounds or movies) to a presentation will make it more interesting, thus increasing retention. Unfortunately, this proposition is dubious. In an article that deals with cognitive constraints on multimedia learning, Mayer, Heiser, and Lonn (2001) suggested that adding redundant on-screen text or conceptually irrelevant video clips inhibits student understanding of a multimedia explanation. In other words, adding "bells and whistles" can get in the way of the sense-making process in learners. For example, audio narration should not be accompanied by text that reproduces the content of the narration at the same time. Text should be made available on a separate page.

Even the font and font size are important. As a rule, sans serif fonts (typefaces that do not use serifs, the small lines at the ends of characters) are easier to read on screen and when projected than are serif fonts (Bernard, 2003). Yet a number of slideware templates use a serif font as the default font. Consider using sans serif typefaces in presentations.

Graphic Design Elements

A great deal could be said about graphics use in an online course. The most important principle is that graphics have some educational purpose. "It's pretty," or "it's just very cool" are not sufficient reasons for including a graphic. Using unnecessary graphics may actually detract from learning outcomes (Mayer, Hesier, & Lonn, 2001).

If possible, employ the services of a graphic designer. If this is not possible, get a book on design basics, such as Robin Williams' *The Non-Designer's Design Book: Design and Typographic Principles for the Visual Novice* (2003). It provides advice that helps the designer to decide how to present material (including text and images) for the best possible impact and aesthetic appeal.

Instructor Education

Many instructors who use slideware may want to learn more about it. The UT TeleCampus in the University of Texas system is a good example of providing instructors with slideware training. There, faculty members are required to participate in extensive training (video-conference, online, and face-to-face) 9 to 12 months before offering their first e-learning course. According to Hardy (2005, personal e-mail) the Assistant Vice Chancellor, UT faculty are strongly discouraged from using PowerPoint "in courses, in presentations about the TeleCampus philosophies, course quality standards, instructional design, selection and use of technology, and course development processes."

The UT TeleCampus works to help instructors escape the technology straight-jacket by implementing a course development process that begins with developing course goals and objectives, identifying key and complex concepts for the course, and determining how students should demonstrate learning. From there, the faculty member determines course pacing, assignments, faculty and student roles and responsibilities, and communications and assessment strategies. Only then are appropriate technologies selected. After this groundwork has been laid, faculty review the materials used for the on-campus version of the course to determine what materials, if any, should be used in the new course. As Hardy (2005) noted, because faculty are asked to develop a new course rather than transition an on-campus course to an online format, they are much less likely to see something developed for an on- campus course (like PowerPoint) in the online version. What she has described is, in fact, the essence of good instructional design and helps ensure that slideware is used appropriately, if at all. Offering training for faculty or instructors can do a great deal to improve the quality of e-learning.

Slideware and Course Management Systems

If slideware for e-learning is pervasive, do universities and colleges need to invest in expensive course management systems? An interesting case is UBC, the ancestral home of WebCT. At UBC there are 36,626 distinct student WebCT accounts, 967 instructor accounts, and 704 accounts for teaching assistants (OECD, 2005). The numbers look substantial, but do not tell us how the CMS is used. Data from UBC's Faculty of Applied Science (see Table 1), for example, indicates that in 2003 there were 70 e-learning courses while 30 had no or trivial online presence.

The different types of e-learning are indicated in Figure 1. In *Web-supplemented* courses, e-mail is used, and course outlines and lecture notes are posted online on a site that might have external Web links (OECD, 2005). *Web-dependent* courses might have all of the above, but also include online discus-

Table 1. E-learning courses in UBC's Faculty of Applied Science

Course Type	2000*	2003*	2006**
None or trivial online presence	75	30	0
Web-supplemented	10	20	20
Web dependent	10	40	35
Mixed mode	0	0	30
Fully online	5	10	15
TOTAL COURSES	100	100	100

* Data from 2000 and 2003 are rough estimates.
** Data for 2006 is the goal for that year.

sions, assessments, and/or collaborative work. Students must participate online for key parts of the course. In *mixed mode* courses, students must participate in online activities that replace parts of face-to-face teaching, though there is still classroom-based instruction. In *fully online* courses, there is no classroom time as the course is fully on the Internet. All of these are types of e-learning, but require and use different technologies and software.

Admittedly, the UBC Faculty of Applied Science course data are estimates, and it is difficult to know in detail what type of teaching is taking place at universities or colleges. Still, discussions with people on the frontlines of e-learning paint a different picture than the numbers above. One of our colleagues suggested that 95% of WebCT use in the faculty of Applied Science was for the sole purpose of distributing PowerPoint lecture notes. Posting course outlines and notes for students online can be useful. However, is an expensive CMS needed for this? There is little accurate evidence that the CMS-based instruction is a critical success-factor for most colleges and universities[1]. We strongly recommend that colleges and universities research the type and amount of e-learning taking place before investing in an expensive CMS that may be substantially oversold and underused.

Figure 1. E-learning continuum

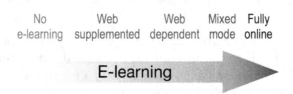

Conclusion

In the movie *Jurassic Park*, Ian Malcolm, the mathematician and critic of the theme park populated by living dinosaurs, chides the park's creator, John Hammond, for his reckless use of technology to create the park's denizens from ancient DNA. Malcolm tells Hammond, "Your scientists were so preoccupied with whether or not they could, they didn't stop to think if they should." While using slideware poorly in an online course is not nearly as disastrous as unleashing prehistoric creatures in the contemporary world, Malcolm's point about the uncritical use of technology is what we have been trying to highlight in this chapter.

Slideware may be as pervasive in e-learning as it is in other forms of communication. The use of slideware in colleges and universities remains immensely understudied, but we can safely assume that slideware is probably not going away anytime soon. Thus it is important for instructors and designers to use it only when appropriate and with an awareness of its limitations. Moreover, it is critical for administrators to research the use (or potential use) of slideware for e-learning before spending more IT dollars on a CMS that may be substantially underutilized.

References

Ahmed, C. (1998). *PowerPoint versus traditional overheads: Which is more effective for learning?* Conference presentation at the South Dakota Association for Health, Physical Education and Recreation, Sioux Falls.

Atkins-Sayre, W., Hopkins, S., Mohundro, S., & Sayre, W. (1998). *Rewards and liabilities of presentation software as an ancillary tool: Prison or paradise?* Presented at the National Communication Association Convention, New York.

Atkinson, C. (2004). *Five experts dispute Edward Tufte on PowerPoint.* Retrieved April 12, 2005, from http://www.sociablemedia.com

Bernard, M. (2003). *Criteria for optimal Web design (designing for usability).* Retrieved May 3, 2004, from http://psychology.wichita.edu/optimalweb/print.htm

Bersin & Associates (2003). *Is PowerPoint an e-learning tool. Enter rapid e-learning: Macromedia Breeze.* Whitepaper written for Macromedia. Retrieved April 11, 2005, from http://www.macromedia.com/resources/elearning/

Chickering, A. W., & Ehrmann, S. C. (1996). *Implementing the seven principles: Technology as lever.* Retrieved October 11, 2000, from http://www.tltgroup.org/programs/seven.html

Clark, R. (1994). Media will never influence learning. *Educational Technology Research and Development, 42*(2), 21-30.

Flintoff, J. P. (2001). *Too much of a good thing.* Retrieved April 14, 2005, from http://www.flintoff.org

Frey, B., & Birnbaum, D. (2002). *Learners' perceptions on the value of PowerPoint in lectures.* (ERIC Document Reproduction Service: ED467192)

Gray, J. (2005). Lessons from great orators of the past: Too many speakers lean on PowerPoint. *The Globe and Mail,* (May 6), C1.

Hardy, D. (2005). (Personal communication, July 14, 2005).

Kozma, R. (1994). Will medial influence learning? Reframing the debate. *Educational Technology Research and Development, 42*(2), 7-20.

Mayer, R., Heiser, J., & Lonn, S. (2001). Cognitive constraints on multimedia learning: When presenting more material results in less understanding. *Journal of Educational Psychology, 93*(1), 187-198.

Morrison, G., Ross, S., & Kemp, J. (2004). *Designing effective instruction* (4th ed.). Hoboken, NJ: Wiley.

Norman, D. (2004). In defense of PowerPoint. Retrieved May 17, 2005, from http://www.jnd.org/dn.mss/in_defense_of_powerp.html

OECD. (2005). *E-learning in tertiary education: Where do we stand?* Paris: Centre for Education Research & Innovation.

Parker, I. (2001). Absolute PowerPoint. Can a software package edit your thoughts? *The New Yorker* (May 28). Retrieved March 24, 2005, from http://www.physics.ohio-state.edu/~wilkins/group/powerpt.html

Szabo, A., & Hastings, N. (2000). Using IT in the undergraduate classroom: Should we replace the blackboard with PowerPoint? *Computers & Education, 35*(3), 175-87.

Taylor, J. C. (2002). Automating e-learning: The higher education revolution. In: S. Schubert, B. Reusch, & N. Jesse (Eds.), *Informatik bewegt. Informatik 2002. Jahrestagung der Gesellschaft für Informatik.* Annual convention of the society für computer science. Bonn, Germany.

Tufte, E. (2003). *The cognitive style of PowerPoint.* Retrieved February 12, 2004, from http://www.edwardtufte.com/tufte/books_pp

Williams, R. (2003). *The non-designer's design book: Design and typographic principles for the visual novice.* Berkeley, CA: Peachpit Press.

Endnote

[1]   If a CMS is critical to the operations of universities and colleges, it is probably because computer-based administration is critical to universities. Recognizing this, Blackboard and WebCT have integrated some administrative functions in newer lines and versions of their software. This will likely continue after the merger of these two CMS giants.

About the Editors

Mark Bullen is the associate dean of the Learning & Teaching Centre (LTC) at the British Columbia Institute of Technology (BCIT) in Vancouver, Canada. His main areas of responsibility are curriculum and instructor development and educational research and innovation. The Learning & Teaching Centre has a staff of over 60 instructional designers, technical writers, graphic designers, desktop and web publishers, media producers and technical support personnel. Before joining BCIT in 2005, Bullen spent 23 years at the University of British Columbia (UBC) where he was involved in distance education course development and e-learning research as director of the Centre for Managing & Planning E-Learning (MAPLE) and assistant, associate, and acting director of the Distance Education & Technology Department. Mark has extensive international consulting experience related to online course development and the planning and management of e-learning. He has taught workshops on developing and delivering online instruction and the planning and management of e-learning in Mexico, Malaysia, Taiwan, Bhutan, Croatia, and Canada and has been a consultant on distance education projects in Mongolia, Indonesia, and Bhutan. Bullen is an adjunct professor in the Master of Distance Education at Athabasca University and in the Master of Educational Technology at the University of British Columbia. He has been involved in distance education since 1982 when he began working at the University of British Columbia as a producer of educational television programs. Before that, he spent four years at the Canadian Broadcasting Corporation as a television news journalist. He has a PhD in adult education (1997), a master's degree in educational psychology (1989) and a BEd

(1982) from the University of British Columbia. He is also a graduate of the BCIT Diploma of Technology in broadcast journalism (1977).

Diane P. Janes is an assistant professor, Extension, with the University of Saskatchewan, Canada, and is an instructional designer and member of the Centre for Distributed Learning (CDL), a research think tank on technology and learning. Janes joined the USask Extension team in July 2003. Originally from Newfoundland and Labrador, from 1996-2003 she was a project manager/instructional designer with the Distance Education and Technology unit, under the leadership of Dr. A.W. (Tony) Bates, Director, at the University of British Columbia (UBC). She was a member of the core design team for the Post-Graduate Certificate in technology-based distributed learning, a series of five Web-based, graduate-level distance education courses launched internationally at UBC in the fall of 1997. This Post-Graduate Certificate was revised in 2002 and has become the Master of Educational Technology (MET) offered by the Faculty of Education at UBC. In 2002, she was appointed adjunct faculty with the University College of Cape Breton (now Cape Breton University) and Memorial University of Newfoundland's Masters in Education – Instructional Technology (where she continues to teach online) and was also made an associate member in the School of Nursing, UBC. In 2006, she began teaching as a visiting assistant professor in the MET, with the UBC's Faculty of Education. While much of her work is in online, Web-based course development in the areas of nursing, dentistry, pharmacy, education, economics, law, political studies, and physical therapy, she's also consulted on distance education, instructional development, and program evaluation in Canada, Mexico, and New Zealand. Janes has a master's degree in educational technology and completed a PhD at the University of British Columbia (2005). Her research interests include faculty development, collaborative online learning, online teaching pedagogy, e-research, program evaluation, and instructional design. She was a book review editor for the *Canadian Journal of Learning and Technology* (formerly the *Canadian Journal of Educational Communications*) from 1993 to 2005 (http://www.cjlt.ca). She has served as prairie representative on the national board of the Canadian Association of Distance Education from 2004-2006 (http://www.cade-aced.ca/), is a reviewer and editorial board member for several international journals, and has had a number of publications and conference presentations to her credit.

About the Authors

Marco Adria, PhD, is an associate professor of communications and director of the Master of Arts in Communications and Technology program at the University of Alberta, Canada. Dr. Adria teaches communications theory and the management of communications technologies. He is the author or co-author of many publications in the areas of organizational communication, popular culture, and nationalism, including three books and several journal articles. He has had a longstanding interest in online and distance learning, having taught university courses online since 1993.

Tony Bates is president and CEO of Tony Bates Associates, Ltd., Canada, a consultancy company specializing in planning and managing e-learning, and distance education. He was director of distance education and technology at the University of Columbia, Vancouver, Canada, between 1995-2003. He has designed, researched, and managed distance education for over 30 years. He is the author of nine books, including *Technology, e-Learning, and Distance Education* (Routledge, 2005) and *Managing Technological Change* (Jossey Bass, 2000). He has worked as a consultant in over 30 different countries, for the World Bank, UNESCO, other NGOs, government ministries, and universities. He has five honorary degrees, from open universities in Canada, Portugal, Catalonia, and Hong Kong, and from Laurentian University in Canada.

Maggie Beers is an instructional development consultant and the academic lead for the technology enabled knowledge (TEK) initiative at the British Columbia Institute of Technology, Canada. Her project portfolio includes educational research and faculty development. Beers completed her PhD in the faculty of education at the University of British Columbia, where she investigated tools and approaches to prepare second language teachers to use educational technology to teach culture. She received her undergraduate and Master of Arts degree in Spanish and Latin American literature from the University of California Santa Barbara, and has taught extensively in the U.S., Canada, Spain, and France.

Karen Belfer is an instructional development consultant with the Learning and Teaching Centre (LTC) at the British Columbia Institute of Technology (BCIT), Canada. As a consultant, she has managed projects internationally and in various Canadian institutions. Her focus is the implementation of educational technologies to enhance the learning process (e.g., eportfolios, social software, Web-based). Belfer did her undergraduate and her master's at the Anahuac University in Mexico, where she taught for over 10 years. She is now working on her PhD. Belfer has extensive experience in faculty training, research, development, design, implementation, and evaluation of the use of technology in higher education. Her research interests are in the assessment of online psychosocial learning environments, instructional design, and teamwork.

Luca Botturi holds a Master in Communication Sciences and Communication Technologies and a PhD in communication sciences with a thesis in instructional design from the University of Lugano, Switzerland. He currently is instructional designer at the eLab and researcher at the New Media in Education Lab, both at the University of Lugano, where he also coordinates the master in communication, major in education and training in the School of Communication Sciences. He is also contract professor at the Università della Valle d'Aosta (Italy) in communication theory and Web design. His research interests include effective e-learning design and design team communication.

Katy Campbell is associate dean, Faculty of Extension at the University of Alberta, Canada. Dr. Campbell's research program and publications focus on three areas: the sociocultural process of learning design, the lifeworld of the designer, and the faculty experience of design as transformative practice. These main threads are framed by a feminist epistemology of ethical, relational knowing, and from a critical theory perspective. From within these frameworks Dr. Campbell explores, in her research, teaching, and instructional design practice, issues of inclusivity in learning design and practice (especially related to gender issues). She has authored the text "E-ffective Writing for E-Learning Environments" (2004, Idea Group Publishing) and serves on several editorial boards.

Lorenzo Cantoni graduated in philosophy and holds a PhD in education and linguistics. He is a professor at the University of Lugano (Switzerland), Faculty of Communication Sciences, where he is also deputy-director of the Institute of Institutional and Educational Communication. Cantoni is director of the laboratories webatelier.net: production and promotion over the Internet, NewMinE Lab: New Media in Education Lab; is executive director of TEC-Lab: Technology Enhanced Communication Lab and co-director of eLab: eLearning Lab. His research interests are where communication, education and new media overlap, ranging from computer mediated communication to usability, from e-learning to e-government.

Dianne Conrad has been a practicing adult educator for over 25 years and has experience in distance, professional, continuing, and online education. Building on her doctoral research, Conrad's recent publications have focused on the development of community among online learners and the positioning of e-learning as a societal phenomenon. Conrad is currently the director of the Centre for Learning Accreditation at Athabasca University, Canada.

Mary E. Dykes is an instructional designer at the University of Saskatchewan Extension Division. She received an MEd in educational technology from the UofS in May 2003 and was a member of Dr. Richard A. Schwier's research team studying virtual learning communities between 2002-04. Dykes joined the Extension Division's Instructional Design Group in November 2005 for a one-year term. For many years prior to this, she worked at the Main Library of the UofS providing reference assistance and library instruction to students and faculty. For more information, visit http://www.extension.usask.ca/idg/profiles-mary.html.

Brad Eastman is a project manager and instructional designer for the University of British Columbia, Canada. Eastman has worked with instructors in the School of Nursing, Dentistry, Medicine, the Center for Advanced Wood Processing, and the Forest Sciences department. He is responsible for the instructional design of online courses, and, as a project manager, and oversees the work of course authors, graphic designers, and Web programmers. Eastman has done presentations on best practices for new online instructors, knowledge management, building online communities of practice and effective use of PowerPoint. He also teaches for Vancouver Community College, has done development work for the National Research Council of Canada and has assisted in developing courseware for Cisco Systems.

Martha A. Gabriel is an associate professor in the Faculty of Education, University of Prince Edward Island, Canada. She researches and writes on appropriate pedagogies for teaching and learning in online environments. There is a strong knowledge mobilization component in her work as she conducts workshops and a summer institute on better practices in online teaching and learning. She recently completed a three-year research investigation on effective pedagogy in e-learning environments, and is developing further research studies in the area.

Mercedes González-Sanmamed is a professor and researcher at the Universidade da Coruña, Spain, in the Department of Education. She received her PhD (Hon.) in education (Universidade de Santiago, 1993). Her research interests are mainly related to teacher training, ICT integration, and the European dimension of education. She participated in several European research projects. She is an expert evaluator for the European Commission and for *ANECA*, the Spanish Universities Evaluation Agency.

She was director of the CUFIE (University Centre for Educational Innovation and Faculty Training) from its creation until 2004. She is currently in charge of faculty development and European higher education at the Agencia para la Calidad del Sistema Universitario de Galicia. She has written a number of specialized articles, chapters, and books such as "Former et se Former Dans un Cadre Multilateral (2001)," "Présence et Distance Dans la Formation à L'échange (2002)," and "La Transformación de las Universidades a Través de las TIC (co-ed., 2004)."

Lourdes Guàrdia is a professor and researcher at the Universitat Oberta de Catalunya (UOC), Spain, in the Department of Education and Psychology. She received the diploma of advanced studies from educational sciences doctoral programme at the Universidad del País Vasco, and she has a degree in linguistics. She was the head of instructional design department at the UOC for 6 years and the director of innovation and educational projects for 2 years. She published several articles and chapters on instructional design and ICT, which is her main research interest and now is coordinating several courses of the international master's degree in e-learning at UOC.

Cathy Gunn works in academic development specializing in technology-facilitated learning. She has contributed to, and managed change at all levels within a large research university since the early 1990s. Research and teaching interests span a range of topics including organizational change, evaluating innovations, information technology in education, and the psychology of learning.

Gunn has many publications reflecting this breadth of experience, and is currently serving as president of The Australasian Society for Computers in Learning in Tertiary Education (ascilite). She has a PhD in computer-based learning research and an MSc in human computer interaction from Heriot-Watt University, Scotland.

Mandy Harper is an experienced education practitioner in biological sciences at secondary and tertiary level. She has a master's degree in zoology from the University of Auckland, New Zealand, and a diploma of teaching. She has expertise in using education research to inform the design and development of teaching programs. Harper is committed to teaching practice that is reflective and innovative, and addresses the learning needs of students. She is passionate about building positive learning environments that facilitate student success as learners and the confidence to continue learning in the biological sciences. Recently, Harper has managed the introduction of new teaching practices based on e-learning and student centered philosophies in large first year courses across the faculty.

Margaret Haughey specializes in distance and online learning in the field of educational administration and policy. Experienced in both K-12 and postsecondary sectors, her current research interests range from faculty use of pedagogical models involving blended learning in universities to the transformation of learning models for compulsory schooling through the integration of digital technologies.

Oriel Kelly has been a staff developer in the tertiary sector for 12 years. Before becoming the manager of the Centre for Educational Development, she was the manager of e-learning at Manukau Institute of Technology, New Zealand, though still working within the staff development section. She has a deep interest in the evolving technology supported learning and teaching environment and in assisting faculty to add e-learning to their repertoire of teaching strategies.

Richard F. Kenny is an associate professor with the Center for Distance Education at Athabasca University, where he teaches learning theory and instructional design. He has a PhD in instructional design from Syracuse University and over 30 years of experience in education, having taught at both the K-12 and university levels. He has also worked as an instructional designer at the school system level and in university distance education. Kenny's current research interests encompass instructional design and change agency; the design and development of online learning to foster problem-solving and critical thinking; and mobile learning applications and strategies.

Thérèse Laferrière is a full professor of pedagogy at Laval University, Canada. Her research activities focus on networked learning environments and especially teacher-student(s) interactions and peer interactions as electronically linked classrooms become reality in elementary and secondary schools as well as in faculties of education and post-secondary education in general. She is the first coordinator of technology and teacher education (TATE), a special interest group of the Canadian Society for the Study of Education (CSSE), and an associate researcher at the Institute for Knowledge Innovation and Technology (IKIT) at the University of Toronto.

Tracey L. Leacock is a research associate and adjunct professor in the Faculty of Education, Simon Fraser University, Canada. Her research is in the areas of educational psychology and educational technology. Her work focuses primarily on the use of technology to enhance self-regulated learning and writing skills, with a related interest in the evaluation of multimedia learning resource quality. She has been developing and delivering online and hybrid courses at the post-secondary level for close to 10 years and has served as a mentor for other faculty new to these methods.

Benedetto Lepori obtained his master's degree in mathematical physics at the University of Rome and a PhD in communication sciences at the University of Lugano, Switzerland. Since 1988, he has worked as management and administration consultant for research matters in Switzerland. He was national expert at the European Commission for the FAST program in 1994. Since 1997 he is responsible of the Research Office of the University of Lugano. He participates to the European Network of Excellence PRIME, as co-coordinator of the European Network of Indicators Producers and coordinator of the funding activity. His research interests cover the Swiss higher education and research policy, the production of S&T indicators and the introduction of ICT in higher education.

Tannis Morgan is a project manager/course developer with the office of learning technologies distance education unit at the University of British Columbia (UBC), Canada. She has been working in educational technology since 1993, where she was involved in conceptualizing software for self-directed language learning programs. Morgan has an undergraduate degree in linguistics from Université Laval in Québec, and a master's degree in language education with a focus on Internet-based language learning. She is currently working on a PhD at UBC, where her research centers the development of learning community in online and mixed mode environments.

Dirk Morrison is an associate professor with the Department of Curriculum Studies, and a member of the educational communications and technology group, in the College of Education, University of Saskatchewan, Canada. Morrison's research interests broadly include the application of learning theory to the design practice of distance and distributed learning. More specifically, his current research is focused on the use of ICT in higher education and how the appropriate pedagogical use of such technologies can influence the facilitation of higher order thinking skills in online learning environments.

Bill Muirhead is the associate provost of teaching and learning at the University of Ontario Institute of Technology, Canada. Muirhead has extensive expertise in teacher training, online education, course development, and international education at both K-12 and postsecondary levels. His current research interests are in the areas of online education, distance education, and the design of hybrid teaching-learning environments. A past president of the Canadian Association for Distance Education, Muirhead is the recipient of numerous national awards for his work pertaining to transformational practice. In 2005, he was appointed editor-in-chief of the collaborative learning object exchange.

Elizabeth Murphy is an associate professor of educational technology and second-language learning in the faculty of education at Memorial University of Newfoundland, Canada. Past research projects include evaluation of the Telesat Multimedia Satellite Trials for schools in Newfoundland and the evaluation of MusicGrid, which pioneered broadband e-learning using music as a vehicle. She was also funded by the Social Sciences and Humanities Research Council of Canada (SSHRC) with Thérèse Laferrière to study collaborative learning in online discussions. Her current research is also funded by SSHRC and involves investigating the practice of the high school distance education teachers in Newfoundland.

John C. Nesbit is an associate professor in the Faculty of Education, Simon Fraser University, Canada, where he specializes in the fields of educational psychology and educational technology. His primary research interests are self-regulated learning from multimedia, evaluation of multimedia learning resources, and methods for analyzing learner interactions with multimedia. He is an avid Wikipedian, has published 20 journal articles, four book chapters, and over 20 peer-reviewed conference papers. Nesbit is co-investigator in the Learning Kit project funded by the Canada Social Sciences and Humanities Research Council. Among other projects, he is currently using eye-movement data to study how learners read concept maps.

Adnan Qayyum is a PhD student in educational technology at Concordia

University, Montreal, Canada. He has worked as a researcher and instructional designer at distance education & technology at the University of British Columbia. He has published on the economics of e-learning, the response of adult learners to using learning technologies, learning environments for non-formal adult education, and cultural issues relating to using learning technologies. He is an adult educator by training and has taught university and college classes. His interests include educational technology, distance education, evaluation, theories of learning, and planning issues in education.

Albert Sangrà is a professor and researcher at the Universitat Oberta de Catalunya (UOC), Spain, and academic director of the International Master's Degree in e-Learning at this university. He received his degree in education, with a major in organisation and educational technology (University of Barcelona, 1986). He received a postgraduate degree in applications of IT in open and distance education (Open University, UK, 1999) and a diploma in strategic use of IT in education (Harvard University, USA, 2000). He is currently finishing his PhD in educational technology. His research interests are related to the integration of ICT in higher education and to quality in e-learning, in particular. He has also worked as a consultant in several e-learning projects in Europe, America, and Asia. He is a member of the executive board of *EDEN* (European Distance and E-Learning Network) and expert evaluator for the European Commission and for *ANECA*, the Spanish Universities Evaluation Agency. He has written a number of specialized articles, chapters and books such as "Aprender en la Virtualidad" (2000), "La Transformación de las Universidades a Través de las TIC" (co-ed., 2004), "e-Learning Europe—Learning Europe" (2005), and "Los Materials de Aprendizaje en Contextos Educativos Virtuales" (2005).

Richard A. Schwier, EdD, is a professor of educational communications and technology at the University of Saskatchewan, Canada, where he coordinates the graduate program in educational technology. He is the principal investigator in the virtual learning communities research laboratory, and is currently studying the characteristics of formal online learning communities. Schwier's other research interests include instructional design and social change agency.

Stefano Tardini earned a PhD in language sciences from the Catholic University of Milan (2002), with a thesis on linguistic and semiotic aspects of virtual communities. He is currently the executive director of the eLearning Lab of the University of Lugano, Switzerland. He is also collaborating with the Politecnico of Milan and the Università Europea of Rome. He is engaged in e-learning projects for the creation of online courses in different fields, such as healthcare communication, intercultural communication and argumentation theory. His research interests include e-learning, computer mediated communication, virtual communities, cultural semiotics, and argumentation theory.

Ellen Vogel is an assistant professor in the Faculty of Health Sciences, University of Ontario, Institute of Technology, Canada. Dr. Vogel is a registered dietitian with a track record in the implementation and evaluation of comprehensive, multi-faceted community-based health promotion programs. Since 2003, she has applied her qualitative research expertise to a groundbreaking study examining the capacities of nursing faculty in the adoption of new and emerging technologies for teaching and learning. In 2002, Dr. Vogel became a Fellow of Dietitians of Canada. In 2003, Dr. Vogel was awarded a postdoctoral fellowship from the Office of the Chief Scientist at Health Canada.

Gail Wilson is an educational developer at the University of Western Sydney, Australia. Her career encompasses over 30 years as an adult educator, human resource developer, and senior manager in the public and corporate sectors. Her current doctoral research focuses specifically on the role of faculty in blended learning environments and professional development of faculty for e-learning. Other research interests include the scholarship of online pedagogy, and the use of electronic portfolios as a form of electronic scholarship to document faculty achievements in teaching and course development. She is a current member of the executive committee of the Higher Education Research and Development Society of Australasia (HERDSA).

Helen Wozniak is currently responsible for the management of e-learning projects within the College of Health Sciences at the University of Sydney, Australia. She has had a keen interest in the development of innovative teaching and learning practices many of which were developed during her 20 years as a clinical supervisor and lecturer in orthoptics. The research and ideas described in this chapter were formulated during this time. Her teaching and learning innovations were recognized with the awarding of the University of Sydney 2004 Vice-Chancellor's Award for Outstanding Teaching.

Index

learning paradigm 189
learning styles 149
level of student performance 150
LMS 337
low-socioeconomic backgrounds 143

M

maps 3
Martha Cook Piper 2
mastery learning 142
Mastery Learning Supported by
    Formative Assessment 147
McGill 21
McGill University 21
media 345
mentor 39
MERLOT 10
Microsoft 337
model for faculty support 22
monitoring 302
MSN 94
museums 3

N

nation 1
national culture 5
national identity 6
national life 10
nationalism 1
networks 7
new source of income 288
no formal teaching development
    strategy 140
Norman 339
note-taking 304
notes 306
nurturing perspective 181

O

OLFC 38
online 196
online community 201

online discussions 11, 158
Online Filing Cabinet 38
online instruction 195
online instructors 185
online learning 194, 247
online learning environment 158
online teaching 195
Open University 128
organizational units 20
orientation 221

P

parallel 22
participate in the formative learning
    activities 148
participation 217
participatory design 66
pedagogy 105
Peer Learning 129
performance required for
    postsecondary science 147
personal learning styles and goals 142
perspectives on teaching 176
plan strategically 288
Polytechnic 47
polytechnic 66
portals 5
practices 6
principles of good teaching 176
problem solving 248
problem-based learning 245
process cycle 275
product cycle 275
professional development 36
project team communication 267
Project-based Faculty Development
    130
project-based faculty development for
    e-learning 130
projects 133
promising results were recorded 150
prototype 276

Q

quality 291
quality information 272
Queen's University 19

R

reflective of the diversity 143
relative advantage 321
renewed perspective 267
repositories 7
resource-based learning activities 187
Rogers 123

S

Salmon 128, 217
scaffold 303
Seeds of Change 143
self-directed learning 248
self-knowledge 204
self-regulated learning (SRL) 302
simplicity 337
Skills Acquisition 126
smart podiums 86
social 2
social capital 9, 160
social change 1
social constructivist pedagogy 158
social dimensions 11
social interaction 5
social learning community 201
social life 2
social networks 9
social obligations 8
social presence 198
social reform 181
social reform perspective 184
social software 9
socialization 5
socially 2
society 2
sociocultural 2

SRL 303
Strategic Planning 47
strategic plans 288
structure 231
structures to provide faculty support
    31
student interactions 42
Student-Centered 249
student-centered model 151
students 189
successful transition 47
support 34
supporting 43
Supporting Learners 215
symbols 4
synchronous 337
synchronous communication 158, 320
synchronous learning environments
    320

T

teacher authenticity 201
teacher-centered 237
teacher-centered paradigms 202
teacher-lead 235
teaching perspectives 233
teaching-learning exchange 198
team-building 187
technical solution 55
technology enabled knowledge (TEK)
    initiative 67
technology-enhanced learning 105
TEK initiative 67
teleconferencing 322
theoretical basis 142
time-delay 200
time-independence 200
tools 3
traditional classroom learning 196
traditional teaching 197
training 338